PELICAN BOOKS

An Outline of
European Architecture

NIKOLAUS PEVSNER

Sir Nikolaus Pevsner was born in 1902 and educated at Leipzig. He took a Ph.D in the History of Art and Architecture in 1924 and was successively connected with the Universities of Leipzig, Munich, Berlin and Frankfurt. For five years he was on the staff of the Dresden Gallery, and whilst a lecturer at Göttingen University from 1929 to 1933 he specialized in the history of art in Great Britain. From 1949 to 1955 he was Slade Professor of Fine Art and a Fellow of St John's College, Cambridge. In 1959 he became Professor of the History of Art at Birkbeck College, University of London, and he remained there until his retirement in 1969 when he became Emeritus Professor.

Since its inception he edited the *Pelican History of Art and Architecture* and wrote most of *The Buildings of England* by counties, as well as editing the whole series. He was a Royal Gold Medalist of the R.I.B.A., and honorary doctor of Leicester, York, Leeds, Oxford, Cambridge, East Anglia, Zagreb, Keele, Heriot-Watt, Edinburgh and Pennsylvania Universities, an honorary fellow of St John's College, Cambridge, F.S.A. and F.B.A. He was appointed C.B.E. in 1953 and received a knighthood in 1969.

His book on *Italian Painting from the end of the Renaissance to the end of the Rococo* is considered a standard work, and among his other publications are: *An Inquiry into Industrial Art in England, German Baroque Sculpture, High Victorian Design, Sources of Modern Art, The Englishness of English Art* (Reith Lectures, 1955) and *Pioneers of Modern Design*. The last two have been published in Penguins. He also wrote *Studies in Art, Architecture and Design, The Anti-Rationalists, Some Architectural Writers of the Nineteenth Century* and *A History of Building Types*, which won the Wolfson Literary Award; and he is co-author of the *Penguin Dictionary of Architecture*.

Sir Nikolaus died on 18 August 1983. In his obituary *The Times* wrote: 'He won the admiration of scholars all over the world and of all shades of opinion through the breadth of his knowledge ... and the quality of his writing ... He had a great capacity for getting down to essentials in any phase of art and for distinguishing between what was inevitable in the circumstances and what was likely to blow over as a passing fashion. His judgements were often refreshingly unconventional for the simple reason that they were consistent.'

NIKOLAUS PEVSNER

An Outline of
European Architecture

PENGUIN BOOKS

PENGUIN BOOKS

Published by the Penguin Group
27 Wrights Lane, London W8 5TZ, England
Viking Penguin Inc., 40 West 23rd Street, New York, New York 10010, USA
Penguin Books Australia Ltd, Ringwood, Victoria, Australia
Penguin Books Canada Ltd, 2801 John Street, Markham, Ontario, Canada L3R 1B4
Penguin Books (NZ) Ltd, 182–190 Wairau Road, Auckland 10, New Zealand

Penguin Books Ltd, Registered Offices: Harmondsworth, Middlesex, England

First published in Pelican Books 1943; second edition 1945; third edition 1951;
fourth edition 1953; reprinted 1954; fifth edition 1957; reprinted 1958, 1959, 1961;
sixth Jubilee edition 1960; reprinted 1961; seventh edition, in this new format, 1963;
reprinted 1964; 1966; reprinted (with revised Bibliography) 1968, 1970, 1972;
reprinted 1974, 1975, 1977, 1978, 1979, 1981, 1982, 1983, 1985, 1988

Made and printed in Great Britain by
Butler & Tanner Ltd, Frome and London

Set in Monotype Times

The first edition of this book was dedicated to my three children. Dedications, like books, should be kept up to date, and I therefore dedicate this edition to my three children, three children-in-law, and nine grandchildren

Contents

Foreword

A history of European architecture in one volume can achieve its goal only if the reader is prepared to concede three things.

He must not expect to find a mention of every work and every architect of importance. If this had been attempted, all the space available would have been filled with nothing but names of architects, names of buildings, and dates. One building must often be accepted as sufficient to illustrate one particular style or one particular point. This means that in the picture which the reader is going to see gradations are eliminated, and colour is set against colour. He may regard that as a disadvantage, but he will, it may be hoped, admit that the introduction of subtler differences would have doubled or trebled the already considerable bulk of the book. Thus the nave of Lincoln will be discussed but not the nave of Wells, and S. Spirito in Florence but not S. Lorenzo. Whether St Michael's, Coventry, is really a more complete or suitable example of a Perpendicular parish church than Holy Trinity, Hull, the Palazzo Rucellai of the Italian Renaissance than the Palazzo Strozzi, is of course debatable. Unanimity cannot be achieved on matters of that kind. Yet, as architectural values can be appreciated only by describing and analysing buildings at some length, it was imperative to cut down their number, and devote as much space as possible to those finally retained.

Besides this limitation, two more have proved necessary. It was out of the question to treat European architecture of all ages from Stonehenge to the twentieth century, or the architecture of all the nations which make up Europe today. Neither would, however, be expected of a volume called European Architecture. The Greek temple, most readers probably agree, and the Roman forum, belong to the civilization of Antiquity, not to what we usually mean when we speak of European civilization. But it will also be agreed that Greece and Rome are the most indispensable of all premisses for an understanding of European civilization. Hence they appear in the first chapter of this book, but appear only very briefly. The same is true of the Mediterranean civilization of the first Christian decades and its expression in the Early Christian churches of Rome, Ravenna, and the Near East and the Byzantine churches. They belong to a civilization different from ours but one of its sources. That again accounts for the way in which they are treated here. A different case is that of say Bulgaria. If it is never mentioned at all in the following pages the reason is that Bulgaria in the past belonged to the Byzantine and then to the Russian orbit, and that her importance now is so marginal as to make her omission pardonable. So everything will be left out of this book that is only of marginal interest in the development of European architecture, and everything that is not European or – as I thus propose using the term European – Western in character. For Western civilization is a distinct unit, a biological unit, one is tempted to say. Not for racial reasons certainly – it is shallow materialism to assume that – but for cultural reasons. Which nations make up Western civilization at any given moment, at what juncture a nation enters it, at what juncture a nation ceases to be of it – such questions are for the individual historian to decide. Nor can he expect his decision to be universally accepted. The cause of this uncertainty regarding historical categories is obvious enough. Though a civilization may appear entirely clear in its essential characteristics when we think of its highest achievements, it seems blurred and hazy when we try to focus its exact outlines in time and space.

Taking Western civilization, it is certain that prehistory is not part of it, as the prehistory of every civilization – the word expresses it – is a stage *prae*, i.e. before that civilization itself is born. The birth of a civilization coincides with the moment when a leading idea, a *leitmotiv*, emerges for the first time, the idea which will in the course of centuries to follow gather strength, spread, mature, mellow, and ultimately – this is fate, and must be faced – abandon the civilization whose soul it had been. When this happens, the civilization dies, and another somewhere else, or from the same soil, grows up, starting out of its own prehistory into its own primitive dark age, and then developing its own essentially new ideology. Thus it was, to recall only the most familiar example, when the Roman Empire died, and Western civilization was born out of prehistoric darkness, passed through its Merovingian infancy, and then began to take shape under Charlemagne.

So much of omissions in time. As for limitations in space, a few words will suffice. Whoever makes up his mind to write a short history of European architecture, or art, or philosophy, or drama, or agriculture, must decide in which part of Europe at any time those things happened which seem to him to express most intensely the vital will and vital feelings of Europe. It is for this reason that, for example, Germany is not mentioned for her sixteenth-century but for her eighteenth-century buildings, that Italian Gothic is hardly touched upon, and Scandinavian architecture not at all. Spain also could not be granted the space which the exciting qualities of so many of her buildings deserve, for at no time has Spanish architecture decisively influenced the development of European architecture as a whole. The only bias towards the work of one nation that has been permitted (and needs no special apology) is towards British examples when they could be introduced, without obscuring the issue, instead of examples from abroad. The issue, to say it once more, is Western architecture as an expression of Western civilization, described historically in its growth from the ninth to the twentieth century.

London, January 1942 and Easter 1960

Foreword to this Edition

It is now twenty years since the first edition of this book came out, 160 pages long, with 60 illustrations on 32 plates, on brownish paper and with a photograph of the author looking a good deal younger than he does now. As book and author grew older, they both grew in bulk. The second edition (1945) offered 240 pages and 48 plates and gave Spain her due, which she had not received before. The third edition in 1951 added a certain amount on French Gothic, the French seventeenth century, and on Italian Mannerism, and came to 300 pages with 64 plates. The fourth edition of 1953 was changed only in minor ways, but the fifth of 1957 put more in on Early Christian and Byzantine and on the French late eighteenth century and reached 72 plates. Then, in the same year, at the hands of Prestel Verlag in Munich, the book received the accolade of a splendid bound edition with about six hundred superb illustrations, and this Penguin Books took over and provided with more English material than had been necessary for Germany. This Jubilee edition, as it was called, because it came out in the year of Penguin's twenty-fifth birthday, had as additions much on the German Baroque and a whole chapter on the years between 1914 and the mid twentieth century. Meanwhile for a Dutch (1949), a Japanese (no date), a Spanish (1957), and an Italian (1960) edition much material had had to be added on these countries.

For this seventh edition a change of format has been made and a style and technique of illustrating adopted which has proved satisfactory in some other recent Pelicans (including my own *Pioneers of Modern Design*). So the number of illustrations could once again be raised. It now stands at 295, and the number of pages at 496. My chief additions this time are on matters French, and especially the sixteenth to eighteenth centuries. But there are also plenty of other, smaller, changes, something like sixty of them.

The fitting in of such changes is always troublesome, and there is the danger that, as they go on from edition to edition, they could gradually encrust the original thoughts and render them unrecognizable. Overweighting with provisos and footnotes must be avoided. If ballast is not kept evenly distributed, there is disaster. However, it is not for me but for readers and reviewers to diagnose the present state of health of the book.

London, Summer 1962

Introduction

A bicycle shed is a building; Lincoln Cathedral is a piece of architecture. Nearly everything that encloses space on a scale sufficient for a human being to move in is a building; the term architecture applies only to buildings designed with a view to aesthetic appeal. Now aesthetic sensations may be caused by a building in three different ways. First, they may be produced by the treatment of walls, proportions of windows, the relation of wall-space to window-space, of one storey to another, of ornamentation such as the tracery of a fourteenth-century window, or the leaf and fruit garlands of a Wren porch. Secondly, the treatment of the exterior of a building as a whole is aesthetically significant, its contrasts of block against block, the effect of a pitched or flat roof or a dome, the rhythm of projections and recessions. Thirdly, there is the effect on our senses of the treatment of the interior, the sequence of rooms, the widening out of a nave at the crossing, the stately movement of a Baroque staircase. The first of these three ways is two-dimensional; it is the painter's way. The second is three-dimensional, and as it treats the building as volume, as a plastic unit, it is the sculptor's way. The third is three-dimensional too, but it concerns space; it is the architect's own way more than the others. What distinguishes architecture from painting and sculpture is its spatial quality. In this, and only in this, no other artist can emulate the architect. Thus the history of architecture is primarily a history of man shaping space, and the historian must keep spatial problems always in the foreground. This is why no book on architecture, however popular its presentation may be, can be successful without ground plans.

But architecture, though primarily spatial, is not exclusively spatial. In every building, besides enclosing space, the architect models volume and plans surface, i.e. designs an exterior and sets out individual walls. That means that the good architect requires the sculptor's and the painter's modes of vision in addition to his own spatial imagination. Thus architecture is the most comprehensive of all visual arts and has a right to claim superiority over the others.

This aesthetic superiority is, moreover, supplemented by a social superiority. Neither sculpture nor painting, although both are rooted in elementary creative and imitative instincts, surrounds us to the same extent as architecture, acts upon us so incessantly and so ubiquitously. We can avoid intercourse with what people call the Fine Arts, but we cannot escape buildings and the subtle but penetrating effects of their character, noble or mean, restrained or ostentatious, genuine or meretricious. An age without painting is conceivable, though no believer in the life-enhancing function of art would want it. An age without easel-pictures can be conceived without any difficulty, and, thinking of the predominance of easel-pictures in the nineteenth century, might be regarded as a consummation devoutly to be wished. An age without architecture is impossible as long as human beings populate this world.

The very fact that in the nineteenth century easel-painting flourished at the expense of wall-painting, and ultimately of architecture, proves into what a diseased state the arts (and Western civilization) had fallen. The very fact that the Fine Arts today seem to be recovering their architectural character makes one look into the future with some hope. For architecture did rule when Greek art and when medieval art grew and were at their best; Raphael still and Michelangelo conceived in terms of balance between architecture and painting. Titian did not, Rembrandt did not, nor did Velazquez. Very high aesthetic achievements are possible in easel-painting, but they are achievements torn out of the common ground of life. The nineteenth century and, even more forcibly, some of the most recent tendencies in the fine arts have shown up the dangers of the take-it-or-leave-it attitude of the independent, self-sufficient painter. Salvation can only come from architecture as the art most closely bound up with the necessities of life, with immediate use, and functional and structural fundamentals.

That does not, however, mean that architectural evolution is caused by function and construction. A style in art belongs to the world of mind, not the world of matter. New purposes may result in new types of building, but the architect's job is to make such new types both aesthetically and functionally satisfactory – and not all ages have considered, as ours does, functional soundness indispensable for aesthetic enjoyment. The position is similar with regard to materials. New materials may make new forms possible, and even call for new forms. Hence it is quite justifiable if so many works on architecture (especially in England) have emphasized their importance. If in this book they have deliberately been kept in the background, the reason is that materials can become architecturally effective only when the architect instils into them an aesthetic meaning. Architecture is not the product of materials and purposes – nor by the way of social conditions – but of the changing spirits of changing ages. It is the spirit of an age that pervades its social life, its religion, its scholarship, and its arts. The Gothic style was not created because somebody invented rib-vaulting; the Modern Movement did not come into being because steel frame and reinforced concrete construction had been worked out – they were worked out because a new spirit required them.

Thus the following chapters will treat the history of European architecture as a history of expression, and primarily of spatial expression.

1 Athens, the Parthenon, begun 447 B.C.

1 Twilight and Dawn

The Greek temple is the most perfect example ever achieved of architecture finding its fulfilment in bodily beauty. Its interior mattered infinitely less than its exterior. The colonnade all round conceals where the entrance lies. The faithful did not enter it and spend hours of communication with the Divine in it, as they do in a church. Our Western conception of space would have been just as unintelligible to a man of Pericles's age as our religion. It is the plastic shape of the temple that tells, placed before us with a physical presence more intense, more alive than that of any later building. The isolation of the Parthenon or the temples of Paestum, clearly disconnected from the ground on which they stand, the columns with their resilient curves, strong enough to carry without too much visible effort the weight of the architraves, the sculptured friezes and sculptured pediments – there is something consummately human in all this, life in the brightest lights of nature and mind: nothing harrowing, nothing problematic and obscure, nothing blurred.

Roman architecture also thinks of the building primarily as of a sculptured body, but not as one so superbly independent. There is a more conscious grouping of buildings, and parts are less isolated too. Hence the all-round, free-standing columns with their architrave lying on them are so often replaced by heavy square piers carrying arches. Hence also walls are emphasized in their thickness, for instance, by hollowing niches into them; and if columns are asked for, they are half-columns, attached to, and that is part of, the wall. Hence, finally, instead of flat ceilings – stressing a perfectly clear horizontal as against a perfectly clear vertical – the Romans used vast tunnel-vaults or cross-vaults to cover spaces. The arch and the vault on a large scale are engineering achievements, greater than any of the Greeks, and it is of them as they appear in the aqueducts, baths, basilicas (that is, public assembly halls), theatres, and palaces, and not of temples, that we think when we remember Roman architecture.

However, with very few exceptions, the grandest creations of the Roman sense of power, mass, and plastic body belong to a period later than the Republic, and even the Early Empire. The Colosseum is of the late first century A.D., the Pantheon of the early second, the Baths of Caracalla of the early third, the Porta Nigra at Trier of the early fourth.

By then a fundamental change of spirit and no longer only of forms was taking place. The relative stability of the Roman Empire was overthrown after the death of Marcus Aurelius (180); rulers followed one another at a rate such as had been known only during short periods of civil war. Between Marcus Aurelius and Constantine, in 125 years, there were forty-seven emperors; less than four years was the average duration of a reign. They were no longer elected by the Roman Senate, that enlightened body of politically experienced citizens, but proclaimed by some provincial army of barbarian troops, often barbarians themselves, rude soldiers of peasant stock, ignorant of and unsympathetic to the achievements of Roman civilization. There was constant internecine warfare, and constant attacks of barbarians from outside had to be repulsed. Cities declined and were in the end deserted, their market-halls and baths and blocks of flats collapsed. Soldiers of the Roman army sacked Roman towns. Goths, Alemans, Franks, Persians sacked whole provinces. Trade, seaborne and landborne, came to an end, estates and farms and villages became self-supporting once again, payments in money were replaced by payments in kind; taxes were often paid in kind. The educated *bourgeoisie*, decimated by wars, executions, murder, and a lower and lower birthrate, had no longer a share in public affairs. Men from Syria, Asia Minor, Egypt, from Spain, Gaul, and Germany, held all the important positions. The subtle political balance of the Early Empire could no longer be appreciated and no longer maintained.

When a new stability was brought about by Diocletian and Constantine about 300, it was stability of an oriental autocracy, with a rigid oriental court ceremonial, a merciless army, and far-reaching State control. Soon Rome was no longer the capital of the Empire; Constantinople took her place. Then the Empire fell into two: that of the East to prove mighty, that of the West to become the prey of Teutonic invaders, the Visigoths, the Vandals, the Ostrogoths, the Lombards, and then for a while to be part of the Eastern – the Byzantine – Empire.

Now during these centuries the massive walls, arches, vaults, niches, and apses of Roman palaces and public buildings with their grossly inflated decorations rose all over the vast Empire. But while this new style left its mark on Trier as much as on Milan, its centre was the Eastern Mediterranean: Egypt, Syria, Asia Minor, Palmyra – that is, the country in which the Hellenistic style had flourished in the last century B.C. And the Late Roman style is indeed the successor to the Late Greek or Hellenistic. The Eastern Mediterranean led in matters of the spirit too. From the East came the new attitude towards religion. Men were tired of what human intellect could provide. The invisible, the mysterious, the irrational were the need of that orientalized, barbarized population. The various creeds of the Gnostics, Mithraism from Persia, Judaism, Manichaeism, found their followers. Christianity proved strongest, found lasting forms of organization, and survived the danger under Constantine of an alliance with the Empire. But it remained Eastern in essence. Tertullian's: 'I believe in it because it is absurd' would have been an impossible tenet for an enlightened Roman. Augustine's: 'Beauty cannot be beheld in any bodily matter' is equally anti-antique. Of the greatest of the late Pagan philosophers, Plotinus, his pupil and biographer said that he walked like one ashamed of being in the body. Plotinus came from Egypt, St Augustine from Libya. St Athanasius and Origen were Egyptians; Basil was born and lived in Asia Minor, Diocletian was a native of Dalmatia, Constantine and St Jerome came from the Hungarian plains. Judged by the standards of the age of Augustus, none of them was a Roman.

Their architecture represents them, their fanaticism and despotism on the one hand, their passionate search for the invisible, the immaterial, the magic on the other. It is impossible to divide neatly

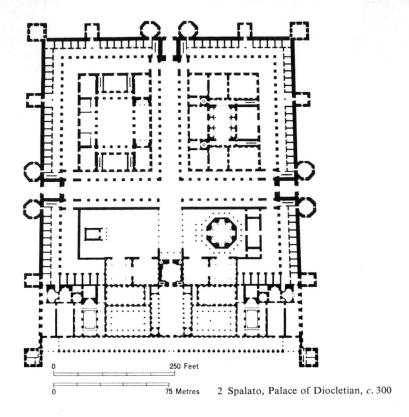

0   250 Feet

0   75 Metres   2 Spalato, Palace of Diocletian, c. 300

the one from the other, the Late Roman from the Early Christian.

For the Late Roman aspect of the time about 300 it is sufficient to look at two buildings, Diocletian's palace at Spalato in Dalmatia and the Basilica of Maxentius (better known as the Basilica of Constantine) in Rome.

The palace of Spalato is an oblong about 700 by 570 feet in size. It is surrounded by a wall with square and polygonal towers like a military camp. But towards the sea the whole front between two square towers is opened in a long gallery on columns. The columns carry arches, the earliest arcade on columns known. This creates a lightness quite un-Roman. Inside the palace there is a cross of colonnaded main streets, and here also the colonnades are arcades. The principal entrance is on the north, the sea on the south. The

3 Spalato, Palace of Diocletian, *c.* 300

north–south street first runs between the quarters for the garrison, the workshops, etc. Past the crossing there are two monumental courts, that on the west with a small temple, that on the east with the imperial mausoleum, a domed octagon with niches inside and surrounded by an outer colonnade. Between the two courtyards was the approach to the entrance hall of the palace proper, a domed circular hall with four niches in the diagonals. Some of the minor rooms were apsed or even of trefoil shapes – a great variety of spatial forms disposed so as to express most forcefully by means of ruthless axiality the power of the emperor.

The Basilica of Maxentius is even more overpowering, because it is more compact – an oblong hall, 265 feet long and 120 feet high, vaulted by three bold groin-vaults and buttressed by six tunnel-vaulted side bays, three on each side. Each of the bays spans 76 feet. The whole was heavily decorated, as the deep coffering of the surviving side bays still shows. Groin-vaults had appeared in Rome already in the first century before Christ, tunnel-vaulting in the Parthian palace of Hatra in Persia about the time of the birth of Christ. In the Colosseum both were used competently, though not yet on so daring a scale.

Constantine completed the basilica several years after he had defeated Maxentius at the Milvian Bridge and recognized Christianity as the official religion of the Empire (Edict of Milan 313).

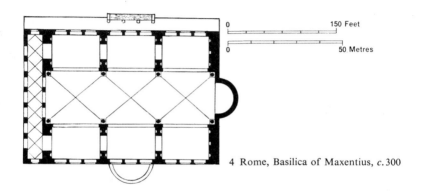

0   150 Feet

0   50 Metres

4 Rome, Basilica of Maxentius, c. 300

Constantine built many large churches, but none of them survive in their original form, although we know a good deal about them. The church of the Holy Sepulchre in Jerusalem was amongst them and the church of the Nativity at Bethlehem, the original St Irene, St Sophia, and Holy Apostles in the newly created capital of Byzantium or Constantinople, and St Peter's, St Paul's (S. Paolo fuori le Mura), and St John Lateran in Rome. Not one of these churches was vaulted. That is significant. It means that Early Christianity looked at the mighty vaults of the Romans as something too earthly. A religion of the spirit did not want anything so physically overwhelming. There was, as far as we can see, much variety in Constantine's churches, but their basic type was that known as the basilica. Once created – we shall have to see when – it remained the standard Early Christian church building in the Occident as well as in large parts of the Orient.

A mature and exceptionally perfect basilica is S. Apollinare Nuovo at Ravenna, built in the early sixth century by Theodoric, King of the Ostrogoths in Italy. However obscure the origin of the Goths, however savage their early invasions, Theodoric was a man of high culture, brought up at the court of Constantinople, and given the title Consul thirteen years after he had become King. A basilican church consists of a nave and aisles separated by a colonnade. At the west end may be an anteroom, known as the narthex, or an open courtyard with cloisters, known as the atrium, or both. There may also very occasionally be two tower-like erections to the left and right of the narthex. At the east end is an apse. No more is necessary; a room for the faithful to gather, and then the holy way to the altar. In some of Constantine's churches, for instance Old St Peter's and S. Paolo fuori le Mura, the aisles were doubled. In the same churches and several others a transept was inserted as a halt

6 Ravenna, S. Apollinare Nuovo, early sixth century

0   150 Feet

0   50 Metres

Rome, Basilica of Maxentius, *c.* 300. Engraving by Piranesi

7 Ravenna, S. Apollinare Nuovo, early sixth century

between nave and apse.[1] Other churches had a women's gallery
above the aisles, for instance St Demetrius at Saloniki (*c.* 410).
Occasionally, in North Africa, a second apse was added at the west
end (Orleansville 325 and 475). Apses could be round or polygonal,
the latter an Eastern preference. In many churches, on the pattern
of Syria, it seems, the east apse was flanked by two separate rooms,
the diaconicon or vestry and the prothesis in which gifts were
received. Instead of the two rooms the aisles could be given apses
(Kalat Seman, Syria, *c.* 480–90). Very rarely, and only in one part
of Asia Minor, whole churches were tunnel-vaulted (Binbirkilisse,
South-east Asia Minor, fifth century). That must have changed the
character of the building more than any of the other variations on
the basilican theme. Even so, it is true to say that the main theme

remained the same everywhere, the monotonous mesmerizing rhythm of the progress between the arcades towards the altar. There is no articulation in that long colonnade to arrest our eyes,[2] nor in the long row of window after window up in the clerestory, and at Ravenna the solemn and silent figures of martyrs and holy virgins, with their motionless faces and stiff garments, march with us. They are not painted but made of mosaic, innumerable small squares of glass.[3] Their aesthetic function is patent. Fresco painting as well as Roman stone mosaic of the tessellated pavements creates an opaque surface and thereby confirms the closedness and solidity of the walls, glass mosaic with its ever-changing reflections seems immaterial. It denies the wall though it faces it. It was thus ideally suited to cover the surfaces of buildings which were meant to serve the spirit and not the body.

And Roman, not Early Christian, is also the basilica as a type in use for sacred buildings. The name basilica is telling; it is a Roman name and it was used for public halls. The word is Greek and means royal. So it may have come to Rome with Hellenistic regal pomp. But Roman basilicas are in no surviving form the immediate predecessors of the Early Christian church building. They usually have colonnades not only between 'nave' and 'aisles', but also on the narrow sides, that is, a complete ambulatory, like a Greek temple turned inside out – or rather outside in. Apses were not uncommon; even two apses are found; but they are as a rule cut off from the main body by the colonnades. Thus as a general term for a large-

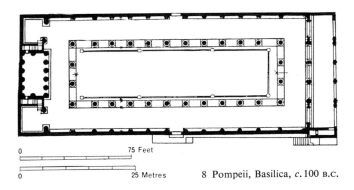

0   75 Feet

0   25 Metres   8 Pompeii, Basilica, c. 100 B.C.

aisled hall the word basilica may have been transferred from Pagan to Christian, but hardly the building type as such. Other guesses have been made: the *scholae*, or the private halls in large houses and palaces (for instance, that of the Flavian emperors on the Palatine), smaller apsed rooms, which may indeed have been used for private worship by Christians.

However, without any doubt the connexion between Early Christian basilicas and buildings erected for pagan religious sects of the first Christian centuries is much more direct and pertinent.

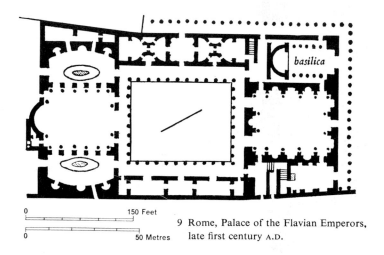

0   150 Feet

0   50 Metres

9 Rome, Palace of the Flavian Emperors, late first century A.D.

The so-called Basilica of Porta Maggiore is a little subterranean building of only about 40 feet length. With its nave and aisles, its piers and apse, it looks exactly like a Christian chapel. Stucco reliefs reveal that it was the meeting-place of one of the many mystical sects which had come to Rome from the East, before and after the advent of the sect of the Christians. It is datable to the first century A.D. Of the mid second century seems to be the somewhat larger Temple of Mithras (*c*. 60 by *c*. 25 feet) found recently in the City of London. This also had nave and aisles and an apse. Mithraism, with its faith in a saviour, in sacrifice and rebirth, was the most formidable competitor of Christianity for the spiritual dominance of the Late

10 Rome, 'Basilica' of Porta Maggiore, first century A.D.

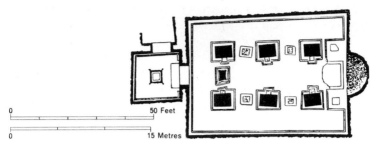

11 Rome, 'Basilica' of Porta Maggiore, first century A.D.

Empire. No wonder then that the earliest form of the Christian church was identical with that used in the cult of Mithras.

Once Constantine had recognized Christianity, churches were built everywhere. 'Who', exclaimed Eusebius, 'can number the churches in every town.' Most of them were basilican. But there was also a considerable number of centrally planned churches. The form was a development of a type of Roman mausoleum and therefore often served the purpose of commemorating a saintly martyr. It was for obvious functional reasons also used for baptisteries. Baptism, it must be remembered, was by immersion, not by aspersion. Types again vary widely, from the simplest circles with heavy walls and hollowed-out niches on the Roman pattern (Theodosian Mausolea on the side of Old St Peter's, St George Saloniki) and circles with an ambulatory (S. Costanza Rome *c*. 320, etc.) or a double ambulatory (S. Stefano Rotondo Rome *c*. 475) to octagons with an ambulatory (Baptistery of St John Lateran, *c*. 325, *c*. 435, and much

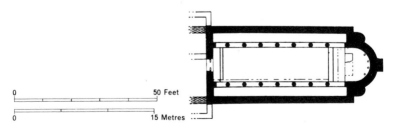

12 London, Temple of Mithras, probably mid second century A.D.

reconstructed *c.* 465) to quatrefoils (Tigzirt, North Africa).[4] Another type of central plan is the Greek cross, inscribed and detached. A Greek cross is a cross with arms of equal length. An inscribed Greek cross is one inscribed in a square. The crossing of the Greek cross has usually a vault, and the corner pieces smaller and lower vaults. So there is a quincunx of vaults. This arrangement, already known to the Romans (Tychaeum of Mismieh), seems to have become more popular in the fifth century (Gerash 464, with closed corner chambers),[5] and was to be the standard church type of the later Byzantine Empire, right down to the fourteenth century. Its resumption in the Renaissance and after will be referred to later. The much simpler and more directly effective form of the detached Greek cross is found, for example, in the so-called Mausoleum of Galla Placidia at Ravenna about 450.

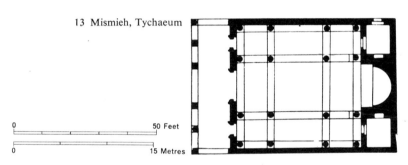

13 Mismieh, Tychaeum

0   50 Feet

0   15 Metres

The culmination of all these experiments was reached in the age of Justinian (527–65). The grandest of his churches were Holy Apostles and Hagia Sophia at Constantinople and S. Vitale at Ravenna, the town which was the Byzantine capital in Italy. Holy Apostles, of which not a stone remains, was apparently a detached Greek cross vaulted with five domes. To erect domes on square walls (the Pantheon in Rome had had a circular wall) was an Eastern innovation. The circular base of the dome could be reached by squinches, that is, small arches across the corners, erected on top of each other, each with a larger diameter than the one below and each slightly projecting in front of the one below until a vaguely octagonal shape is reached to start the dome from, or more elegantly

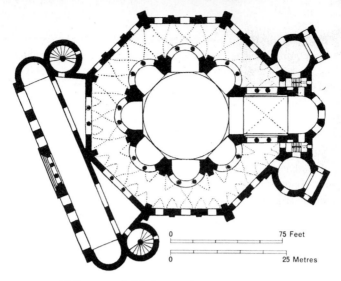

0   75 Feet

0   25 Metres

14 Ravenna, S. Vitale, completed 547

by pendentives, that is, spheric triangles. The latter was the Byzantine method.

S. Vitale in Ravenna is also centrally planned, but it offers a far more sophisticated solution. Basically it is an octagon with an octagonal ambulatory and a gallery. The centre is covered by a dome on squinches. There are in addition a narthex with apses at both ends and a projecting altar space flanked by the circular prothesis and diaconicon. The designer clearly believed in the expressive possibilities of curves, and so he separated the central octagon from the ambulatory not by plain arches but by seven apsed shapes (the eighth is the chancel), open in three arches each towards the ambulatory. This motif, a motif of purely aesthetic, not functional, purpose, determines the spatial character of the interior. It replaces a clear spatial distinction by a floating and welling of space from the centre into the surrounding outer layer, the extent of which remains in semi-darkness. This sense of uncertainty is reinforced by the lining of the walls with marble slabs and mosaics. The austere, gaunt figures of the mosaics seem just as immaterial, as magical and weightless as the surging and drooping arches of the

15 Ravenna, S. Vitale, completed 547

33

octagon. The masterly carving of the capitals is a final confirmation of the spatial and spiritual intention of the architect. The lush acanthus foliage of Rome is replaced by flat intricate patterns carved in lacy open-work on the plain sloping surfaces of the capital so that an indeterminate back layer everywhere darkly transpires. It is the exact counterpart in architectural decoration to the spatial effect of the arcaded niches opening into the back layer of the ambulatory. Capitals of the same type are to be found in Justinian's principal churches at Byzantium. S. Vitale was consecrated in 547. Justinian's SS. Sergius and Bacchus at Byzantium is very similar. The sources of the subtle spatial configurations of these two churches are not certain. They seem to lie in Italy rather than the Orient. A comparable effect had already been obtained at a remarkably early date, about A.D.125, in the Villa of the Emperor Hadrian near Tivoli; and the church of S. Lorenzo at Milan, built about 450–75 and internally wholly remodelled in the sixteenth century, is the direct forerunner of S. Vitale. Hagia Sophia is even more complex and achieves by its concealed complexity a magic scarcely ever surpassed. The principle underlying its plan is a combination of the basilican with the central plan. This principle had already been established under Constantine. But at his church of the Holy Sepulchre in Jerusalem, of which very little original work remains, the combination was not much more than a juxtaposition: a basilica, followed by a courtyard and a large rotunda. At the church of the Nativity at Bethlehem, the plan, Constantinian or of c. 530, consists of a basilica with a trefoiled east end. Among the first known examples of the integration of longitudinal and central is a church at Koja Kalessi (South Asia Minor) of the late fifth century. Here a short nave of two bays with aisles is followed by a raised dome flanked by transepts which do not project beyond the aisle walls. To the east of the dome are a chancel bay and an apse with side chambers. The whole is inscribed in one parallelogram.[6] The same is true of Hagia Sophia. The size here is about 320 by 220 feet, and the building was erected in the unbelievably short time of five years: from 532 to 537. The dome was heightened by 20 feet after 558, and much reconstruction was done after 989. The original architects came from Asia Minor, Anthemius of Thralles and Isidore of Miletus. If at Koja Kalessi it looks to the

16 Ravenna, S. Vitale, capital

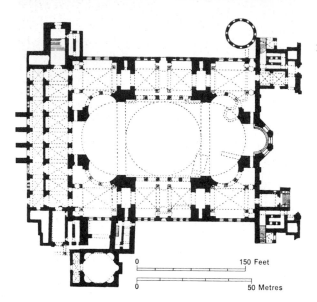

17 Constantinople,
Hagia Sophia, 532–7

0 ⊢——————⊢ 150 Feet

0 ⊢——————⊢ 50 Metres

18 Constantinople, Hagia Sophia, 532–7. The Turkish minarets have been
removed from the photograph

19 Constantinople, Hagia Sophia, 532-7

eye as if a dome were inserted in a basilica, Hagia Sophia is not a
basilica at all, though it is, as we shall see, not without longitudinal
emphasis. But the central dome reigns supreme, not raised on a drum
but floating gently, though majestically, over the square central
space. The dome has a diameter of 107 feet and is abutted to the
east and west most ingeniously and beautifully by lower half-domes.
The great open space thus created is longitudinal, 220 by 107 feet,
and stresses the west–east direction as much as the sense of church
services demanded. Each of the half-domes is in its turn abutted by

two niches or apses or exedrae, with curved open arcading as at S. Vitale. All this is a structurally perfect support for the dome, and it has been the ambition of the architects to conceal the mechanics of their method from the eye. This is, it might be said, what by means of flying buttresses Gothic architects did in their interiors, but nothing could be further from Gothic aspiration than the calm, flowing-down curves of the domes and apses of Hagia Sophia. The space they comprise seems vast, yet not overbearing. To the north and south of the dome the architects might have repeated the same arrangement. They did not; for perfect centrality would have been less complex and mysterious than they wished their church to appear. So they added aisles accompanying the whole domed composition, aisles with galleries, screened from the great dome by five arches on the ground floor, and seven on the upper floor. What lies behind these screens is, again as at S. Vitale, a distant mysterious foil to the light, many-windowed central space.

The exteriors of Byzantine churches received little enrichment – occasionally marble facings, but hardly anything else. Towers did not exist either. It is doubtful when towers were first introduced. The low erections to the left and right of narthexes or porches on the west fronts of certain Syrian churches (Turmanin, also S. Apollinare in Classe near Ravenna), to which attention has already been drawn, can hardly be called towers, and no campanile is with certainty datable before the ninth century. Hagia Sophia has its domes now guarded by the four verticals of its minarets, but they are Turkish. Justinian's church and equally the adjoining St Irene, another large church which combines longitudinal and central elements, and also the a little more distant Holy Apostles dominated the rounded hills of Byzantium with the related shallow curves of their domes. The skyline of Justinian's capital must have been utterly different from any we know now – its undulating rhythm the most convincing counterpart of the mysteries of the interiors.

Twenty-one years after the consecration of S. Vitale the Langobards conquered Italy. Churches of the type of S. Apollinare were still built in Rome, but the great age of Early Christian architecture was over, and what happened in the Eastern Empire from the seventh century onwards does not concern us here. The Mohammedans

20 Turmanin, Basilica (mostly destroyed), sixth century

overran Syria about 635, Egypt in 639, and Spain in 711. They might have settled even in France, if it had not been for the resistance of the Franks under their leader Charles Martel. The battle of 732 was as far north as the Loire. Charles Martel was the effective ruler of the Frankish kingdom, but the Kings were of the Merovingian house. Their ancestor Clovis had accepted Christianity in 496, or what he understood as Christianity. The spirit of this oriental religion remained alien to the barbarians of the north, although there is plenty of evidence of communication between the Frankish kingdom and the Orient, chiefly by means of the flourishing colonies of Syrian traders as far north as Tours, Trier, and even Paris, where a Syrian was made Bishop in 591. But among natives of Gaul no understanding of the mentality and the degree of civilization demonstrated in this oriental architecture can be presumed. The Gaul of the sixth century was a savage country. The pages of Gregory of Tours are crowded with assassination, rape, and perjury.

It is difficult to form a picture of the state of architecture in Gaul before the late eighth century. Baptisteries and other small structures remain in the south (Fréjus, Marseilles, Venasque) of the same central types as those in Italy. Some basilican churches and chapels also can be described on the strength of excavations with more or less certainty; the earliest seem to have favoured the Eastern custom of polygonal apses (Lyons St Irénée *c.* 200, Metz St Peter *c.* 400, St Bertrand-de-Comminges, Vienne, etc.). No larger churches survive, but early descriptions prove their existence. The church of

Tours about the year 475 was 160 feet long and had 120 columns, that of about the same time at Clermont Ferrand was 150 feet long and had aisles and transepts. What carved details we know from other places indicate a Late Roman style declining and soon falling into utter barbarity.

In Britain that was not so. Some of the high crosses erected to commemorate those who had died or mark a sacred spot or a boundary have carving of leaf scrolls, birds and beasts, and also human figures of great tenderness and skill (Ruthwell Cross, Bewcastle Cross, Reculver Cross). They date from about 700. At that time Anglo-Saxon Britain was without doubt the most civilized country of the north. Its development had indeed been very different from that of other countries. The Anglian and Saxon invaders were no less cruel and barbaric than the hordes who had battered their way into the Late Roman provinces from the later fourth century onwards. But Christianity had come from another source. Monasticism originated in Egypt. The earliest monks were hermits living in solitude in their huts or caves. Soon hermits moved together, without however abandoning their individual huts. Only churches or chapels and some additional halls were communal. Monks in such monasteries are called coenobites. Two such Egyptian monasteries, the White and Red Monasteries near Sohag, both of the early fifth century, have been mentioned. In this form monasticism had found a first European home early in the fifth century on the island of Lérins not far from Marseilles, and from there it had reached Ireland (St Patrick, 461). Irish monasteries flourished in the sixth and seventh centuries. Their missions went to Scotland (St Columba to Iona, 563), to France (St Columbanus 615, Luxeuil), to Italy (St Columbanus, Bobbio), to Germany (St Kilian c. 690, Würzburg), to Switzerland (St Gall 613). Traces and fragments of monasteries with monks' stone huts and communal buildings exist at Skellig Michael on the west coast of Ireland, and have been excavated at Nendrum in County Down (the church is Romanesque) and in other places (Tintagel, Cornwall).

England began to be converted by Aidan and Cuthbert from Lindisfarne and Durham in the seventh century. But by then a mission from Rome was also active, spreading Christianity and a

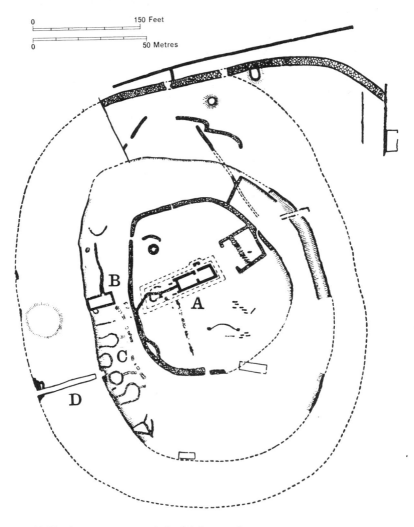

21 Nendrum, monastery, sixth–eighth centuries

monasticism different from that of Egypt and Ireland. St Benedict had founded Monte Cassino about 530. Monasticism as we know it is Benedictine monasticism. The conflict between Irish and Benedictine, between Oriento–Celtic and Roman ideals came to an end with the Synod of Whitby in 664. But the ideals and personalities were not as nearly opposed to one another as at first it might seem. The great protagonist on the Roman side was Theodore, Archbishop of Canterbury, who came from Tarsus in Syria, and Hadrian, who accompanied him, was a native of North Africa.

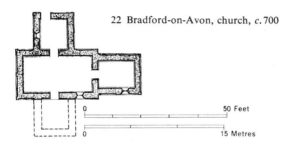

22 Bradford-on-Avon, church, c. 700

0   50 Feet

0   15 Metres

Of early Anglo-Saxon as of Merovingian architecture we know little. More churches of about 700 survive than in France, but they are mostly small. At Canterbury and elsewhere in Kent apses were, it seems, usual; in Northumberland and the neighbouring counties there are long, narrow, straight-ended buildings, such as for instance at Monkwearmouth and Jarrow, founded in 674 and 685. Chancels are separate, and the effect of the interiors is of a tall, tight gangway leading towards a small chamber. Aisles do not exist; instead there were additional side chambers, called *porticus*, accessible by narrow doorways rather than wide arcaded openings.[7] Externally masonry was rude and primeval. Geographically between the two regions lies Brixworth in Northamptonshire, the only partly preserved aisled basilica, built with the use of Roman bricks, probably in the seventh century. Yet, just as in France, literary sources tell us of buildings clearly far more ambitious than even Brixworth. Thus, for instance, Alcuin tells us of York as he knew it, that it had thirty altars and many columns and arches, and of Hexham about 700 we hear that

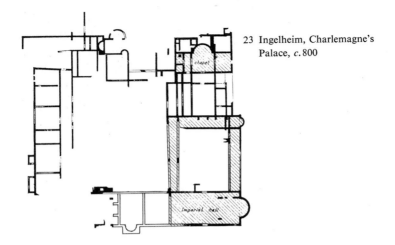

23 Ingelheim, Charlemagne's Palace, *c.* 800

it was *mirabili longitudine et altitudine* and had many columns. At Hexham the crypt of this church survives, composed of narrow vaulted gangways and chambers comparable to Roman catacombs and the first crypt of St Peter's in Rome, which was built as a narrow semicircular gangway at the end of the sixth century.

Alcuin left Northumberland in 781 to become head of Charlemagne's palace schools and then abbot of St Martin's at Tours and the reorganizer of the schools there. Charlemagne, who had become King in 771 and was crowned Emperor of a new Holy Roman Empire on Christmas Day 800 by the Pope in Rome, called other men of high intellectual achievements to his court too: Peter of Pisa and Paul the Deacon from Italy, Theodulf from Spain, and Einhard the German, his later biographer. These appointments were part of a completely conscious programme of a Roman Renaissance, doubly remarkable in one who had to work hard late in life to learn to read and write, whose private life was hardly less profligate than those of his Merovingian predecessors, and who was by natural inclination a warrior and an administrator rather than a patron of learning and the arts. The style and character of the architecture built for him and his successors is a perfect visual demonstration of his programme. His palaces – he had no fixed capital – with hall, chapel, and large range of rooms are clearly organized in their relative positions like the palaces of the Roman emperors on the Palatine,

and connected by vast colonnades of evidently Roman Eastern derivation. To visualize these palaces we have to rely on excavations and description. Only in one case a substantial piece of one of Charlemagne's palaces still stands: the Chapel Palatine of Aachen (Aix-la-Chapelle), the principal residence of the emperor's old age. It was originally connected with the Great Hall (of which now only parts of the bare, high walls remain) by colonnades nearly 400 feet long. An equestrian statue of Theodoric, looted from Ravenna, was significantly placed in this colonnaded forecourt, and columns of the chapel also came from Italy. So undoubtedly did its ground plan. There can be little doubt that the architect took his inspiration from S. Vitale. But he could see no sense in the curved-out niches, so he flattened them out, thus re-establishing the straightforward division between central octagon and ambulatory. He also eliminated the columns on the ground floor. Simple wide openings alternate with short, sturdy piers. The plainness and massiveness of this ground floor (and also of the giant niche of the façade) strike a note utterly different from the subtle spatial harmonies of S. Vitale. Yet the upper floors with their polished antique columns, superimposed in two orders, re-echo something of the transparency, and the floating of space from one unit into another, which make the beauty of Justinian's churches.

Aachen sums up the historic position of Carolingian architecture at the extreme end of Early Christian and at the beginning of Western developments. Roman-Christian intentions are everywhere traceable, but appear marred or in other cases rejuvenated by the naïve vigour of an unskilled, but very determined, somewhat barbarous youth. Of the major churches of which we know some are in plan surprisingly pure Early Christian. Thus for instance Fulda, begun in 802, derives directly from St Peter's and the other Roman basilicas with transepts.[8]

What the decoration of such neo-Early Christian churches was like we cannot say. But the surviving external decoration of a charming gatehouse or guest-hall of one of Charlemagne's favourite monasteries, Lorsch in the Rhineland, shows that considerable elegance could be attained. The front is faced with red and white stone slabs and in addition there is a system of attached columns

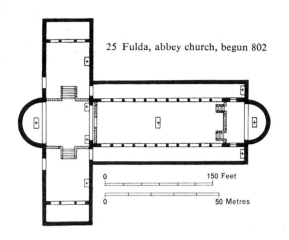

25 Fulda, abbey church, begun 802

0   150 Feet

0   50 Metres

26 Lorsch Abbey, gatehouse, late eighth century

below with arches between, that is, the system of for instance the Colosseum in Rome, and of small fluted pilasters above. Their capitals are unorthodox, and so are the triangles taking the place of arches, a motif derived from Roman sarcophagi and much welcomed in Anglo-Saxon England. Yet the whole façade is a remarkably civilized paraphrase of Roman and Early Christian motifs.

Centula (or St Riquier, near Abbeville), on the other hand, was in most of its features northern, original, and unprecedented. The church, which was built by Charlemagne's son-in-law, Abbot Angilbert, in 790–9 no longer stands, and is known to us only by

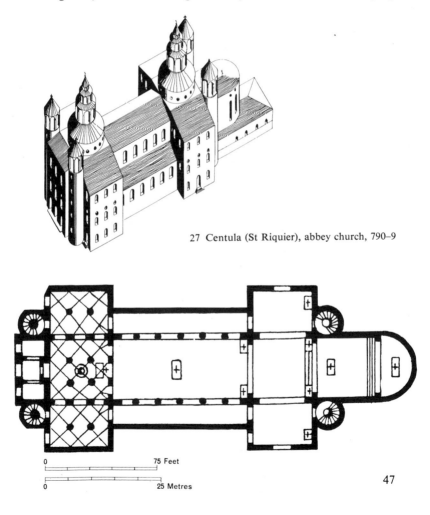

27 Centula (St Riquier), abbey church, 790–9

0   75 Feet

0   25 Metres

an engraving reproduced from a twelfth-century drawing and by a still older description. First of all it had in its exterior just as much accent on the west as on the east parts. Both were strongly emphasized by towers over the crossings rising in several stages and by additional lower staircase towers – a group varied and interesting, and very different from the detached campanile or clocktower which is familiar from contemporary Italian churches. Then there were two transepts, one in the east and one in the west. Also the east apse was separated from the transepts by a proper chancel. This became almost a matter of course in the coming centuries. The western part has a complicated spatial organization, with a low, probably vaulted entrance hall and a chapel above, open towards the nave. Such a westwork, as it is called in Germany, survives relatively well preserved at Corvey on the Weser, and Corvey, founded from Corbie in France, was built in 873–85. Ancient descriptions prove westworks also for the cathedral of Rheims and other important ninth- and tenth-century churches.

Some of the ideas of Centula appear again in the Abdinghof church at Paderborn in Westphalia recently excavated. This church was built as a cathedral by Charlemagne himself, and an altar in it was consecrated in 799 by the same pope who crowned Charlemagne. It had a west apse flanked by similar staircase towers, a west transept like Fulda, and an east chancel with apse again as at Centula, the whole no doubt forming a lively group. The same would have been true of St Gall in Switzerland, if the church had been rebuilt in accordance with an immensely interesting original plan on vellum which, about the year 820, had been sent by some bishop or abbot close to the emperor's court to the Abbot of St Gall as an ideal scheme ('exemplar') for rebuilding the whole monastery. The church has again a west apse and in addition two detached round west campanili, a curious semicircular atrium round the west apse, and at the east end a short chancel with an apse. The plan is strikingly similar to that of Cologne Cathedral, as recent excavations have revealed it. The building was begun in the early ninth century with just such a semicircular west atrium but then, in 870, completed differently. It also had a chancel preceding the east apse.

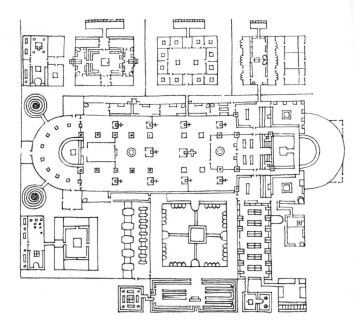

28 St Gall, ideal plan for a rebuilding, c. 820

On the plan for St Gall the monastic quarters are arranged round the church according to the orderly and human principles of St Benedict, so different from the haphazard plans of Egypt and Ireland – a characteristic contrast of Eastern and Western layout. The position of dormitory, refectory, and storerooms remained standard for centuries to come.

Yet another Carolingian church plan is again completely different: Germigny-des-Prés near Orléans, consecrated in 806. This has the Byzantine plan of the quincunx or inscribed Greek cross with a tall raised central dome, tunnel-vaulted arms, and four lower corner vaults. It has in addition to the east apse also north and south apses, and these apses are of horseshoe plan as are also the arches inside. The church is badly restored, but the motifs mentioned are original and point to sources neither Roman nor Germanic. If it is remembered that Germigny was built for Theodulf of Orleans who, as has been said, came from Spain, these surprising motifs fall into place.

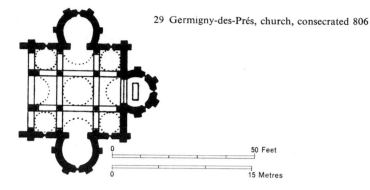

29 Germigny-des-Prés, church, consecrated 806

In Spain the Visigoths had ruled from the early fifth to the early eighth century, when their domination was ended by the advance of Islam. We know little of architecture under the Visigoths, but one precious survival is parts of a group of three small churches at Tarrasa in Catalonia. Such grouping of churches, two longitudinal and a central one between, was a tradition of the early church soon to be discontinued. Only very rarely do they survive. The best example apart from Tarrasa is Grado on the north coast of the Adriatic.[9] At Trier the same arrangement, on a much larger scale and dating back to the fourth century, has been excavated. The middle one of the three churches at Tarrasa may date from anything between the mid fifth and the late seventh century. Its plan is that of Germigny except that it has only one horseshoe apse. It also has horseshoe arches in elevation. So the Spanish source of Charlemagne's Germigny is beyond doubt. Other early Spanish churches, however, are very different and closer in character to Anglo-Saxon work. S. Juan de Baños, for example, dedicated in 661, consisted originally of a short nave separated from the aisles by arcades with horsehoe arches, exaggeratedly projecting transepts, a square apse, two rectangular eastern chapels or vestries inorganically detached from the apse and, as another inorganic appendix, a rectangular west porch. There is no spatial flow nor even a unity of plan in this minute building. The exterior colonnades originally running along the north, south, and west walls are of Late Antique-Oriental origin, as incidentally is the horseshoe arch.

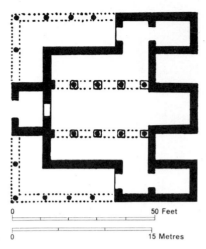

0   50 Feet

0   15 Metres

30 S. Juan de Baños, consecrated 661 (the east parts have later been altered)

This motif, however, the Arabs, when they conquered the South of Spain in the eighth century, made so much their own that for several centuries to come it remained the hall-mark of Mohammedan and Mozarabic, i.e. Christian Spanish, architecture under Arab influence. The Arabs, as against the Vikings and Hungarians, were far from uncivilized. On the contrary, their religion, their science, and their cities, especially Cordova with her half-million inhabitants, were far ahead of those of eighth-century Franks in France or Asturians in Northern Spain. The Mosque at Cordova (786–990), a building of eleven aisles, or rather eleven parallel naves, each twelve bays long, with interlaced arches and complicated star-ribbed vaults, has a filigree elegance more in keeping with the spatial transparency of S. Vitale than with the sturdy uncouthness of the North.

Owing to their proximity to Mohammedan sophistication, the Asturias show a certain airiness here and there which is absent in any other contemporary Christian buildings. At S. Maria de Naranco near Oviedo, for example, the fluted buttresses outside – as a structural device and a decorative motif still remotely evocative of Rome – and the slender arcade inside which now separates nave

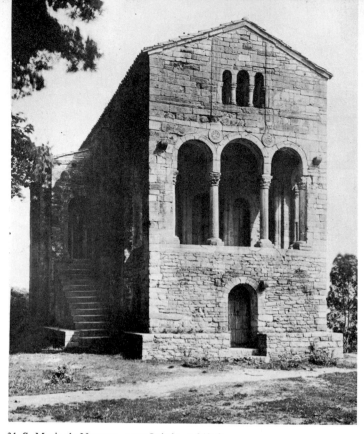

31 S. Maria de Naranco, near Oviedo, *c*. 842–8

from choir are in strange contrast to the heavy tunnel-vault, the odd shield-like or seal-like medallions from which spring the transverse arches of the vault, and the clumsy spiral shafts with their crude block capitals along the walls.

The building incidentally is of very special interest, in so far as in all probability it was designed between 842 and 848 as a Royal Hall for Ramiro I of Asturias – the only surviving early medieval example of such a building. It has a low vaulted cellar or crypt, and above this the hall proper, now the nave of the church. This is reached by flights of outside steps leading to porches in the centres of both the

32 S. Maria de Naranco, near Oviedo, *c*. 842–8

long sides of the building. On the east and the west' there were originally open loggias, communicating with the main room by arcades, of which one, as has been said before, survives. The present choir is in fact one of the loggias blocked up towards the outside.

In British ninth- and tenth-century architecture one would look in vain for such subtleties. Where buildings are preserved complete or nearly complete, we can see that their ground plans were still much of the same oddly bitty kind as those of about 700 had been. Aisles proper, it is true, occur more often now, and also cruciform plans with transepts and a kind of crossing. West towers appear too, as against the earlier west porches. The earliest of them are apparently of the tenth century. But decoration has, if anything, deteriorated compared with the accomplished skill of the Ruthwell and Reculver crosses. Typical examples are Bradford-on-Avon and the tower of Earl's Barton. At Bradford the band of blind arcading has short pilasters without any tapering or swelling and raw oblong blocks instead of capitals. At Earl's Barton the only structural part of the decoration is the emphasizing of the three storeys by plain string courses. All the rest, the wooden-looking strips arranged in rows vertically like beanstalks, or higher up in crude lozenge patterns, is structurally senseless. Yet they are in a similar relation to Carolingian architecture as Asturian decoration was to the Muslim style. But while the day-to-day proximity of Arab to Spanish civilization created the mixed idiom of Naranco and the Mozarabic style of the tenth century, the British builders reduced the Romanizing motifs of Carolingian decoration to ungainly rusticity. The so-called long-and-short work up the edges of Earl's Barton tower, and so many other contemporary English towers, is another indication of the rawness of the minds and the heaviness of the hands of these late Anglo-Saxon architects, if architects they can be called.

33 Earl's Barton, Northamptonshire, tower, tenth or early eleventh century

2 The Romanesque Style

c. 1000–*c*. 1200

Less than thirty years after Charlemagne had died, the Empire was divided. France and Germany henceforth took separate courses. Internal struggles, earl against earl, duke against duke, shook both. And from outside, the Vikings ravaged the North-West – Normans they called them in France, Danes in England – the Hungarians menaced the East, the Saracens, i.e. Mohammedan Arabs, the South. No progress was possible in art and architecture. What we know is almost as primitive as Merovingian work, although forms taken up under Charlemagne and his immediate successors were still used. But the spirit in which they were used was blunt and crude. And since during the pre-Carolingian centuries intercourse with Roman architecture had not entirely ceased, the period between about 850 and 950 seems even more barbaric.

Yet during these dark and troubled years the foundations of medieval civilization were laid. The feudal system grew, one does not know from what roots, until it had become the framework round which all the social life of the Middle Ages was built, a system as characteristic and unique as medieval religion and medieval art, strictly binding lord and vassal, and yet so vague, so dependent on symbolical gestures that we today can hardly recognize it as a system at all. By the end of the tenth century it had received its final form. By then political stability too had been re-established in the Empire. Otto the Great was crowned in Rome in 962. At the same time the first of the reform movements of monasticism set out from Cluny in Burgundy. The great abbot Majeul was enthroned in 965. And again at the same time the Romanesque style was created.

To describe an architectural style it is necessary to describe its individual features. But the features alone do not make the style. There must be one central idea active in all of them. Thus several essential Early Romanesque motifs can be traced singly in Carolingian architecture. Their combination, however, is new and determines their meaning.

The most significant innovations of the late tenth century are those in the ground plan – three above all, and all three caused by a new will to articulate and clarify space. This is most characteristic. Western civilization was only just beginning to take shape, but already at that early stage its architectural expression was spatial, as against the sculptural spirit of Greek and Roman art – and spatial in an organizing, grouping, planning way, as against the magic floating of space in Early Christian and Byzantine art. The two chief plans for the east ends of Romanesque churches were conceived in France: the radiating plan and the staggered plan. The earliest surviving examples of the radiating plan are at Tournus and at Notre Dame de la Couture, Le Mans, both of the first years of the eleventh century. The type can perhaps be traced back to the church of St Martin at Tours, one of the most famous of Christianity, in the form in which it was rebuilt after a fire in 997 (consecrations 1014 and 1020).[10] The staggered plan appears for the first time at Cluny, apparently in Abbot Majeul's rebuilding dedicated in 981. The functional reasons were the growing worship of saints on the one

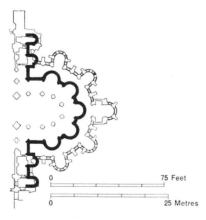

34 Tours, St Martin, the black parts begun 997

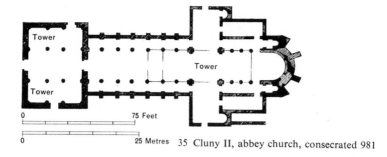

35 Cluny II, abbey church, consecrated 981

hand, and on the other the growing custom of every priest saying Mass every day. So more altars were needed, and to accommodate them more chapels in the eastern parts, i.e. the parts reserved for the clergy, were the obvious solution. One can imagine how crudely Anglo-Saxon or Asturian architects would have added them. The architect of the new age groups them into one coherent unified entity, either by laying an ambulatory round the apse and adding radiating chapels, or by running the aisles on past the transepts, finishing them in small apses parallel or nearly parallel with the main apse and, in addition, placing one, two, or even three apses along the east wall of each transept.

Almost exactly at the time when the French began to evolve these new schemes, in Saxony, the centre province of Otto's empire, just north of the Harz mountains, another system was found to articulate the whole of a church, the system followed by Central European architects for the next two centuries. St Michael's at Hildesheim was begun immediately after the year 1000. It has two transepts, two chancels, and two apses, a logical development of ideas first tried out at Centula.[11] Thus the monotony of the Early Christian arrangement was replaced by a grouping less single-minded and rhythmically more interesting. And St Michael's went decisively beyond Centula in dividing the nave into three squares (they are not exact but were no doubt meant to be so), with aisles separated from the nave by arcades that have an alternation of supports, pillars to stress the corners of the squares, columns in between. The crossings between nave and transepts were clearly singled out by means of chancel arches not only to the east and west, but also to the north and south.

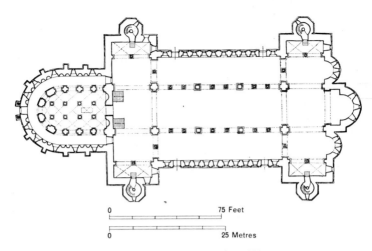

36 Hildesheim, St Michael, *c.*1000

In later buildings each transept was to be square too, and the aisles consisted of sequences of squares. On the east side of Hildesheim a square chancel was inserted between crossing and apse. Chapels branched off the transepts parallel to the main apses – a complex ground plan, yet fully ordered by an active conquering power of reason.

Who conceived this system we do not know. What we do know, however, and have no reason to question, is the fact, recorded by his biographer, that St Bernward, the bishop who was responsible for the building of St Michael's, was 'foremost in writing, experienced in painting, excellent in the science and art of bronze founding and in all architectural work'. Similarly we know, for example, of Aethelwold, the great English bishop, that he was a 'theoreticus architectus', well versed in the building and repairing of monasteries, of Benno, Bishop of Osnabrück in the eleventh century, that he was 'an outstanding architect, a skilful planner ("dispositor") of masonry work'. We also possess the plan of about 820 for St Gall, which has been mentioned before, and was obviously the sender's – that is, a bishop's or abbot's – conception. Such and many similar contemporary references justify the view that, while actual building operations were of course at all times the job of the craftsman, the designing of churches and monasteries in the early Middle Age may often have been due to clerics – at least to the same extent to which Lord Burlington was responsible for the design of his Chiswick villa. After all, in those times nearly all the literati, the educated, the sensitive were clerics.

The same tendency towards an elementary articulation which the new ground plans reveal can be found in the elevations of the eleventh-century churches. At St Michael's, Hildesheim, the system of alternating supports, the rhythm of *a b b a b b a* (*a* representing square piers and *b* columns), serves to divide up the long stretch of wall, and ultimately the space enclosed by the walls, into separate units. This system became the customary one in Central European Romanesque architecture. In the West, and especially in England, another equally effective method was developed for achieving the same aim. It had been created in Normandy early in the eleventh century. The Normans by then had lived in the north-west of France for a hundred years and from being Viking adventurers had become clear-minded, determined, and progressive rulers of a large territory, adopting French achievements where they saw possibilities in them – this applies to the French language, suppler than their own, to feudalism, and to the reform of Cluny – and imbuing them with the energy of their native spirit. They conquered Sicily and parts of Southern Italy in the eleventh and twelfth centuries, and created an eminently interesting civilization there, a blend of what was most advanced in the administration of Normandy and in the thought and habits of the Saracens. In the meantime they had also conquered England, to replace there by their own superior mode of life that of the Northern invaders who had come before them. The Norman style in architecture, the most consistent variety of the Early Romanesque style in the West, strongly influenced France in the eleventh century: in England it did more than that: it made English medieval architecture. One cannot discuss the Romanesque style without taking into consideration English Norman cathedrals and abbey churches. French writers too often forget that the fulfilment of what had been initiated at Jumièges about 1040 and Caen about 1056 lies at Winchester, at Ely, at Durham, to mention only a few.

The new principle was the separation of bay from bay by tall

37 Ely Cathedral, nave, twelfth century

shafts running through from the floor to the ceiling – a flat ceiling
everywhere; for the art of vaulting the width of a nave was all but
lost. Thus again an articulation was achieved that conveys to us at
once a feeling of certainty and stability. There is no wavering here –
as there was none in the ruthless policy of William the Conqueror
in subduing and normanizing England. Blunt, massive, and over-
whelmingly strong are the individual forms which architects used in
these early buildings, sacred as well as secular. For the Norman
keep, the other architectural type which the Normans brought
from France, has got the same compactness, the same disdain of

38 Castle Hedingham, Essex, c. 1140

embellishment as the Norman church. The earliest datable keep is
that of Langeais on the Loire. It was built in 992. The largest of all
keeps are English, the White Tower in London (118 by 107 feet) and
the keep of Colchester in Essex (152 by 111 feet). Both are of the
last third of the eleventh century. There were, of course, reasons of
defence for the bareness of the keep, but it was a matter of expression,
i.e. of aesthetics, too, as a comparison with such a piece of building
as the transept of Winchester Cathedral (c. 1080–90) proves. At
Winchester the solid wall, though opened up in arcades on the
ground floor and the gallery floor and again in a passage-way in
front of the clerestory window, remains the primary fact. We feel
its mighty presence everywhere. The tall shafts are bound to it and
are themselves massive, like enormous tree-trunks. The columns of
the gallery openings are short and sturdy, their capitals rude blocks,
the simplest statement of the fact that here something of round
section was to be linked up with something of square section. If the

39 Winchester Cathedral, north transept, *c.* 1080–90

63

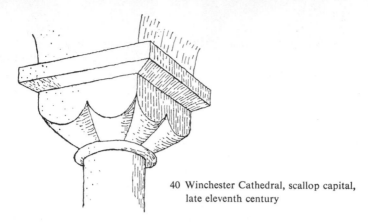

40 Winchester Cathedral, scallop capital,
late eleventh century

elementary block form of the capital is given up, it is replaced by
fluting, the future favourite motif of the Anglo-Norman capital, in
its most primitive form. This plainness is typical of the eleventh
century, a plainness of statement expressed in terms of the plainest
of forms.

By the end of the century changes began to appear, all pointing
towards a new differentiation. More complex, more varied, more
lively forms can be found everywhere. There is perhaps less force in
them, but more individual expression. Now comes the àge of St
Bernard of Clairvaux (died 1153), who called it his aim as a preacher
(and he was one of the greatest of medieval preachers) to move
hearts, not to expound scripture, the age of Abelard (died 1142), the
first to write an autobiographical account of his personal problems
of love and scholarship, and in England the age of Henry II and
Thomas Becket (died 1170). They stand before us as human beings;
William the Conqueror as a natural phenomenon, irresistible and
relentless. Just before 1100 – when Western Christianity rallied
round the banners of the first Crusade – the pioneer work was done
in architecture; Early Romanesque was transformed into High
Romanesque. Durham is the crucial monument in England, begun
in 1093, the east parts vaulted in 1104, the nave *c*. 1130. The nave
appears higher than it is because, instead of the flat ceiling usual
until then and usual in England for some time to come, it is covered
by a rib-vault. As our eyes follow the lines of the shafts upwards,
this movement does not come to a standstill where the walls end,

but is carried farther up with the ribs. The vaults of Durham choir (now renewed) are probably the earliest rib-vaults of Europe. In this lies Durham's eminence in the history of building construction.

Engineering skill had developed considerably during the century between the earliest examples of the Romanesque style and 1100. To vault in stone naves of basilican churches was the ambition of the craftsmen, for reasons of safety against fires in church roofs as well as for reasons of appearance. The Romans had known how to vault on a large scale; but in the West there were before the mid eleventh century only vaulted apses, tunnel- or groin-vaulted aisles, or narrow tunnel-vaulted naves without aisles (for instance Naranco), and even smaller tunnel-vaulted naves with aisles.[12] Now at last the

41 Durham Cathedral, 1093–c. 1130, nave

vaulting of the wider naves of major churches was mastered, and – as always happens when an innovation is the full expression of the spirit of an age – mastered independently by several ingenious architects in several centres of building activity at about the same time. Burgundy remained faithful to massive tunnel-vaults. The earliest in France that can be dated seem to belong to the early eleventh century (upper storey of the ante-church at Tournus); those at Cluny, when this mightiest monastery of Europe was rebuilt, about 1100, had a span of about 40 feet and a height of 98. Speier, the imperial cathedral on the Rhine, received her first groin-vaults in the eighties, yet wider (45 feet) and yet higher (107 feet). The vaults of Speier, moreover, seem to be the earliest large-scale groin-vaults in medieval Europe. And then there is Durham. A good deal of controversy still remains about dates of early vaults (especially concerning S. Ambrogio in Milan, whose rib-vaults some count amongst the pioneer works, while others date them about the second and third quarters of the twelfth century). The powerful initiative of the second half of the eleventh century, however, is beyond doubt.

Now the most remarkable fact about the vaults of Durham is that rib-vaults as against ribless groin-vaults are accepted as one of the *leitmotivs* of the Gothic style. Their structural advantages, chiefly the possibility of erecting the ribs and other arches first and independently on a separate centering and then filling in the cells between the ribs in a lighter material, will be discussed later (p. 91). These advantages, as John Bilson has proved, were already fully realized at Durham,[13] yet the style of Durham is not therefore Gothic. Technical innovations never make a new style, though they can be welcomed and made use of by one. The chief reason of the designer of Durham for introducing so telling a feature as the rib-vault must have been the very fact that it is so telling, that it represents the ultimate fulfilment of that tendency towards articulation which had driven Romanesque architects forward for over a hundred years. Now the bay has become a unity not only by the two-dimensional means of lines of demarcation along the walls, but by the three-dimensional means of those diagonal arches set across. Where the two arches meet, where later architects inserted their bosses, there each unified bay has its centre. We move along through the cathedral, not driven towards the altar without halt as in Early Christian churches but stepping from spatial compartment to spatial compartment in a new measured rhythm.

The rib-vault imparts indeed at Durham to the whole structure an alertness opposed to the weight of inert wall so oppressive in eleventh-century interiors. This alertness is taken up in the more animated expression of the arcades and their mouldings, and the introduction of a few sharp ornamental forms, the zigzag above all. Still, in spite of this quickening of rhythm Durham is far from playful or busy. The circular pillars of the arcades are still of overpowering strength, their sheer bulk being emphasized by the elementary decoration, lozenges, zigzags, flutes, exquisitely carved into their surfaces. The fact, incidentally, that all ornament at Durham is abstract is typical only of Norman architecture in England and Normandy, not of Romanesque architecture in general. Germany, it is true, created at the end of the tenth century an even more severely abstract type of capital, the one which we call block capital and which is also known, even less tellingly, as cushion capital. But in France, in Spain, in Italy there are many examples of capitals with foliage and also with figures and scenes, beginning already in the tenth century and reaching remarkable achievements in the middle of the eleventh (San Pedro de Nave, Jaca, St Isidore Leon, St Benoît-sur-Loire). The best-known instance in England is characteristically enough in the crypt of Canterbury, dating from

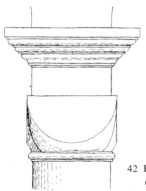

42 Hildesheim, St Michael, block capital,
   early eleventh century

43 Canterbury Cathedral, crypt, decorated block capital, *c*.1120

c. 1120. Canterbury had been the gateway through which a Continental style had passed once before, about 600, and another one was going to pass in 1175. The capitals here have foliated decoration, and some even beasts. But nature had no immediate influence on these. They derive from sample-books kept in the lodges of the masons and based on illuminated manuscripts, ivories, previous work of the lodge, etc. Originality was a conception unknown; so was observation of nature. Style as a restrictive force of discipline ruled as unchallenged as authority in religion. Still, Durham seems more humane than Winchester, and twelfth-century capitals seem more humane than the block shapes of the eleventh, just as the sermons of St Bernard seem more humane and more personal than those of the theologians before him.

The exterior of Durham Cathedral is one of the most magnificent sights of England. There it stands, flanked on one side by the Bishop's Castle, on the top of its steep wooded hill with its mighty tower over the crossing and the two slenderer western towers to balance its weight. They are not Norman in their present form, the western towers dating from the thirteenth, the central tower (originally with a spire) from the fifteenth century. But towers were planned from the beginning, and where they were carried out, they ended in spires of moderate pitch such as those at Southwell. The outside appearance of Romanesque churches thus differed just as widely from that of Early Christian churches as their interiors. While at S. Apollinare Nuovo the exterior hardly mattered – even church towers, when they were introduced, stood separate from their churches – a few Carolingian and then most larger Romanesque churches were designed to display variety and magnificence outside as well as inside. St Michael's at Hildesheim, with its two choirs,

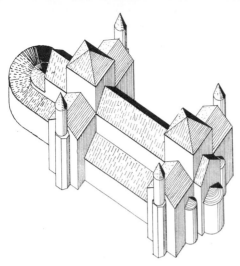

44 Hildesheim, St Michael, *c.* 1000, reconstruction

tower over both crossings, and staircase turrets on both ends of both transepts, is the earliest surviving example of a truly Romanesque exterior.

Altogether Germany was eminently important for the development of art and architecture in the early eleventh century. These were the years of Ottonian and Salian power, the years before the Emperor Henry IV had to humiliate himself before a Cluniac pope. There is nothing in the arts of Italy or France to emulate the bronze doors of Hildesheim Cathedral. Similarly, in architecture, Speier, as has already been said, probably possessed one of the earliest vaulted naves in Europe. These vaults were an addition to a cathedral built, still with flat timber ceiling, about 1030–60. The principal beams of the ceiling rested on immensely tall shafts which ran right up, completely uniform in every bay. Between the shafts, against the walls, were blank arches forming an arcade which embraced both the openings into the aisles below and the clerestory windows above – a grand and austere motif derived no doubt from the Late Roman architecture of Trier. Equally bold and unornamental was the chief contemporary enterprise at Cologne, the church of St Mary-in-Capitol (begun about 1030), where the east apse with ambulatory is repeated as the end motif of the transept at its north and south end so that a trefoil shape results, with big tunnel-vaulted arms and a minimum of carved decoration to deflect attention from the majestic ensemble, an ensemble that points as vigorously back to Byzantium as it points forward to the Renaissance.

Even more important for the future of European architecture was another element, also, it seems, created in Germany in the eleventh century: the two-tower façade. Its first appearance has been traced to the cathedral of Strassburg in its form of 1015. Then, however, the motif was at once taken up by the most active province of France: by Normandy; and from Jumièges (1040–67), and the two abbeys of William the Conqueror at Caen (La Trinité, begun *c*. 1062, and St Étienne, begun *c*. 1067), it reached Britain.

Perhaps we should not speak at all of France concerning the eleventh and twelfth centuries. The country was still divided into separate territories fighting each other, and consequently there was no one universally valid school of architecture, as, thanks to the Norman kings, there already was in England. The most important schools in France are those of Normandy, Burgundy, Provence, Aquitaine (or rather, broadly speaking, the whole South-West), Auvergne, and Poitou. Their comparatively static customs were crossed by a strong current from the north and west of France right down to the far north-west of Spain, the current of the principal pilgrimage routes. Pilgrimages were one of the chief media of cultural communication in the Middle Ages, and their effects on church planning are evident. They can be seen from Chartres via Orléans, Tours, Poitiers, Saintes to Spain; from Vézelay via Le Puy, Conques, or via Périgueux to Moissac and on to Spain; and from Arles to St Gilles and then to Spain. The goal was Santiago de Compostela, a sanctuary as celebrated as Jerusalem and Rome. The Cluniac Order had much to do with the development of the pilgrimage routes, yet, oddly enough, the principal pilgrimage churches, St Martial in Limoges (near completion in 1095 and now destroyed), St Sernin in Toulouse (begun *c*. 1080, and the grandest of all in its exterior), and Santiago itself (begun in 1077) have certain features in common which differ from those of Cluny itself. They are tall and dark, with galleries above the arcades and tunnel-vaults above the galleries, that is, without clerestory windows. Their east ends are developed on the system of Tours, with ambulatory and radiating chapels, and Tours has indeed been claimed as their pattern.

70

47 Toulouse, St Sernin, choir, consecrated 1096

48 Santiago de Compostela, begun 1077

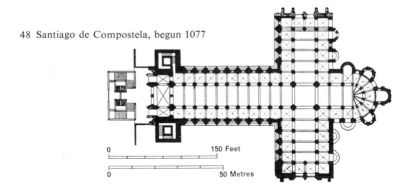

0   150 Feet

0   50 Metres

Toulouse, St Sernin, begun *c.* 1080

49 Cluny III, abbey church, late eleventh–early twelfth centuries.
Reconstruction by Kenneth John Conant

Be that as it may, Cluny, to say it once again, certainly was not
the pattern. Cluny, as it was rebuilt at the end of the eleventh century
(High Altar consecrated in 1095) and early in the twelfth and destroyed by the French themselves in 1810, had two transepts (as
later became the rule in English cathedrals), each with an octagonal
tower over the crossing.[14] The more important of these, the one
farther west, had octagonal towers to the right and left of the
crossing as well (one of these survives), and two eastern apses to
each arm. The eastern transept had four apses too. Moreover, the
chancel apse had an ambulatory with five radiating chapels. Thus

one saw looking at the church from the east a graded development in many carefully proportioned steps from the low radiating chapels over the ambulatory, the main apse, the chancel roof, the tower over the eastern crossing, to the tallest tower farther west – a structure so complex, so polyphonous, as earlier centuries in the West could not have conceived, and the Greeks would have detested, but the ideal expression no doubt of that proudest moment in medieval Christianity, when the Reform had conquered the throne of the popes, asserted the superiority of the papal tiara over the imperial crown, and called up the knights of Europe to defend the Holy Land in the first Crusade (1095).

One motif at Cluny which also distinguished the church from those of the pilgrimage routes is regionally Burgundian, the elevation with pointed arcades, a blank triforium (that is, no gallery), and clerestory windows. The transverse arches of the tunnel-vault also were pointed, perhaps for the first time in Europe. The detail, especially in the triforium, is curiously aware of Roman precedent, and Roman fragments could indeed easily be studied in Burgundy. Such Roman motifs as fluted pilasters, pointed arches, tunnel-vault, and a triforium instead of a gallery also characterize Autun Cathedral of the early twelfth century, and the splendid church of the Magdalen at Vézelay of about the same date has not even a triforium but simply an arcade and a large clerestory. The vaults here are groined on the pattern of Speier. The church was supposed to possess the relics of the Magdalen; they made it a favourite goal of pilgrimages. It stretches out at the top of a small town climbing up the hill towards it. The main entrance is through an aisled narthex or galilee of three bays (a Cluniac motif), and on through one of the wildest of Romanesque figure portals. The nave has nothing of that violence. With its later and lighter choir in the far distance, its length of about 200 feet between narthex and crossing, its unusually high nave vaults, its arches of alternating grey and pink courses, and its inexhaustible profusion of capitals with sacred stories, it possesses a noble proportion and a proud magnificence without being less robust than Durham.

After Burgundy, an important but not very unified school, the other regional schools of France are clearer and more consistent in

50 Autun Cathedral, early twelfth century

51 Vézelay, La Madeleine, early twelfth century

52 Jumièges, abbey church, begun *c.* 1040, consecrated 1067

their characteristics. Auvergne churches are much like the pilgrimage churches, though the dark lava makes them more sombre still. Their regionally distinguishing features – four radiating chapels instead of three or five, and a curious raising of the inner bays of the transepts so as to afford north and south abutment for the crossing towers – are not of great significance. The other schools are more individual. Provence built churches of tall and narrow proportions, with pointed tunnel-vaults over the naves and either no aisles or narrow aisles vaulted by tunnels or half-tunnels. There are no galleries, but clerestory windows. The decorative detail is evidence,

53 St Savin-sur-Gartempe, early twelfth century

as in Burgundy and even more so, of a conscious classical revival. No wonder in a province so rich in Roman remains.

In Normandy right to the end of the eleventh century, that is, the time of the rib-vaults of Durham, main spaces seem to have been left timber-covered. There are at Jumièges and St Étienne at Caen spacious galleries and large clerestories. The principal beams, as has been said before, were, just as at Speier, carried on mast-like shafts running through from the floor to the ceiling.

The earliest vault seems to be the groin-vault over the chancel of the Trinité at Caen of the last years of the eleventh century. Soon

54 Angoulême Cathedral, early twelfth century

after that the rib-vaulting of Durham was taken over, but, when it replaced the flat ceilings of both the Trinité and St Étienne at Caen, the form used was sexpartite, not quadripartite, a system which allowed the bays to be square as they automatically were in groin-vaults, but at the same time to give them six instead of four supports. These sexpartite vaults date from *c.* 1115–20.

A completely different system is that developed in Poitou. Here aisles are narrow and as tall as the naves, that is, there are no galleries and no clerestories. This system, called with a German term that of the hall church, makes buildings dark and gaunt, but impressively single-minded-looking. The most impressive of all is St Savin, where nave and aisles are covered by parallel tunnel-vaults and separated by an arcade of very tall, very plain circular piers – a somewhat menacing array. The date is as late as the twelfth century, that is, later than those west English churches which also favoured arcades with tall, massive circular piers (Tewkesbury 1087, Gloucester, etc.). It is a most impressive motif, and one would like to be able to determine its origin.

Finally there is one more important French regional school, again quite different from all others, that of Aquitaine with Angoulême and Périgueux as its centres. They preferred aisleless churches – only occasionally are there aisles of nave height – consisting of several domed bays, with or without transept, with or without apse, with or without radiating chapels (but never with an ambulatory). The grave majesty of their domes is unparalleled. The centralizing tendency which is apparent wherever domes are used culminates at St Front in Périgueux, where during the second quarter of the twelfth century the decision was taken to create a purely central building – a great rarity in the High Middle Ages – by leaving without the western bay of its nave an Aquitanian aisleless church which had already its transepts. Thus a Greek cross resulted, with a square for the centre and four squares for the arms. Each square has in its turn short arms again and is covered by a vast dome. The

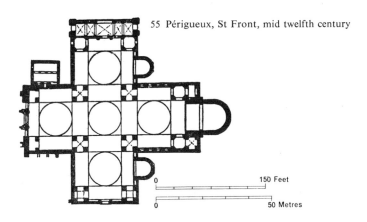

55 Périgueux, St Front, mid twelfth century

0   150 Feet

0   50 Metres

56 Périgueux, St Front, second quarter of the twelfth century

interior (for the exterior is badly restored) is the classic expression of Romanesque clarity and determination.[15] There is no sculptural decoration anywhere except for some arcading along the walls. The system goes back to Justinian. It was created for his mausoleum, the church of the Holy Apostles, of which nothing remains. From there it was taken over by the Venetians when they began to rebuild St Mark's in 1063. Whether the inspiration for Périgueux came from Byzantium or Venice cannot be said. The impression inside St Mark's is certainly utterly different from that of Périgueux. Venice, the most oriental and most romantic of European cities, and the most powerful centre of trade with the East, had endowed her grandest church with all the magic of the Orient, mosaics, luxuriant capitals, arcades to separate centre from arms, and concealed spatial relations in the sense which we have seen at Ravenna. At Périgueux it is stripped of all that suspicious glamour and appears pure and sheer, great for its architectural nobility and none other. St Mark's belongs to Eastern, Périgueux to Western architecture. There is even something strikingly Roman in the bareness of Périgueux. No wonder that the ground plan was reinvented in almost identical form by the Italians of the Renaissance.

If a direct line seems to run here from the Romanesque to the Renaissance, there are more immediate connexions between Romanesque and Gothic. They are the use of the pointed arch in Burgundy, Provence, and also the domed churches of the south-west and the nave of Durham, the use of flying buttresses concealed below the roof of aisles but still fulfilling the function of supporting the vault (e.g. St Sernin Toulouse, Auvergne, Durham nave), and of course the use of ribs.

And there is one more immediate connexion: the figure portal. This was a development of the twelfth century. In the eleventh century and still about 1100 Spain led Europe not only in the art of the figure capital but also in major figure sculpture. The cloister of Santo Domingo de Silos is the most impressive example. This style of long, highly stylized figures with small heads, highly expressive gestures, and feet placed as if they were engaged in a ritual dance was taken over in the south of France, especially at Moissac about 1115–25. Here the two portals are divided by a post or *trumeau*

with wildly interlaced animals, and to the right and left stand one
saintly image on each side, carved in relief in the same intensely
emotional style out of the strip of wall right and left of the portals.
At the same time the figure portal began to develop in Burgundy.
Autun and Vézelay of *c.* 1130–5 are the foremost examples. At
Vézelay, which has already been referred to, there are to the left and
right of the double portal pairs of prophets arguing with one
another. They are also in relief, but, as they are carved on parts of
the wall which stand at right angles to each other, they seem to have
left the wall entirely to form a group.

At St Denis about 1135–40 they have indeed left the wall. They
stood like shafts or columns detached from the wall.[16] But St Denis,
as we shall see presently, is a Gothic, no longer a Romanesque
building. Yet these figures were still entirely Romanesque, as are
those of the Portail Royal of Chartres of about 1145 – long, strictly
frontally placed with stylized parallel folds and small heads. Still in
an entirely Romanesque setting, the same kind of columnar figures,
but now much sturdier and more substantial, stand round the

57 St Gilles du Gard, abbey church, *c.* 1135 etc.

grandiose Portico de la Gloria of Santiago de Compostela, the work of Maestre Mateo of 1188.

Santiago is the leading Romanesque building of Spain. It belongs, as we have seen, to the group of the French pilgrimage churches and is in its silvery-grey granite more impressive than any of those on French soil.

So much, or so little, for Spain. And so much also for France. Germany could not do better than develop the theme set at Hildesheim, and the cathedrals and monastery churches of the central Rhineland, notably Speier, Mainz, Worms, and Laach, make a splendid display of towers over their crossings and staircase towers, of double transepts and double chancels in an unending variety of proportion and detail. The second main school of German Romanesque architecture is that of Cologne. Of the Saxon school something has already been said – the others are more provincial. Cologne, before 1940, possessed an unrivalled number of churches dating back to the tenth, eleventh, twelfth, and early thirteenth centuries. Their loss is one of the most grievous casualties of the

58 Worms Cathedral, c. 1170–c. 1230

59 Milan, S. Ambrogio, second quarter of the twelfth century

war. Their hall-mark (after St Mary-in-Capitol) is a resolutely
centralizing scheme for the east ends, a scheme in which both
transepts and the chancel end in identical apses. The exteriors were
as glorious and varied as any higher up the Rhine.

North Italy has one church of the same type: S. Fedele at Como.
Some have tried to construct a dependence of Cologne on Como,
but it is now certain that if there is any relation it must have operated
the other way. In other respects the connexions between Lombardy
and the Rhine are still controversial. Nobody can deny them; but
priority in types and motifs can never be established beyond doubt.
The most likely answer to the question is that along the routes of the
Imperial campaigns into Italy there was a continuous give and take
of ideas and workmen. Probably Saxony and the Rhine were leading
to the end of the eleventh century, and North Italy in the twelfth.

At the time gangs of Lombard masons must have travelled far and wide, just as they did again in the Baroque. We find their traces in Alsace as well as in Sweden, and one man from Como appears in Bavaria in 1133. The *leitmotiv* of this Lombardo-Rhenish style is the dwarf-gallery, that is, the decoration of walls, and especially those of apses, high up under the eaves with little arched colonnades.

In her ground plans North Italy was less enterprising. Some of the most famous churches have not even a projecting transept, that is, keep close to Early Christian traditions. This applies, for instance, to the cathedral of Modena and S. Ambrogio in Milan. S. Ambrogio is the most impressive of them all, with its atrium and its austere front, its low squat nave, its massive piers, its wide domed cross-vaults, and its broad primitive ribs (on these see page 66). Generally speaking the interior characteristics of these Lombard cathedrals are cross-vaults or rib-vaults, galleries in the aisles,

60 Florence, S. Miniato al Monte, eleventh to twelfth century

polygonal domes over the crossings, their outside characteristics isolated towers round or square in plan, and those miniature arcadings already referred to. The extreme case of such decorative arcading is the front and the leaning tower of the cathedral of Pisa in Tuscany, both of the thirteenth century.

Pisa strikes one altogether as of rather an alien character – Oriental more than Tuscan. Similarly alien is the style of Venice with its Byzantine and of Sicily with its Arab connexions. To see the Italian Romanesque at its most Italian, that is, at its most purely Tuscan, one has to look to such buildings as S. Miniato al Monte in Florence, which, in spite of its early date (its ground floor may even be contemporary with the transept of Winchester), possesses a delicacy of treatment, a civilized restraint in sculptural decoration, and a susceptibility to the spirit of Antiquity unparalleled anywhere in the North – a first synthesis of Tuscan intellect and grace with Roman simplicity and poise.

3 The Early and Classic Gothic Style

c. 1150–*c.* 1250

In 1140 the foundation stone was laid for the new choir of St Denis Abbey near Paris. It was consecrated in 1144. Abbot Suger, the mighty counsellor of two kings of France, was the soul of the enterprise. There are few buildings in Europe so revolutionary in their conception and so rapid and unhesitating in their execution. Four years was an exceptionally short time in the twelfth century for rebuilding the choir of a large abbey church. Whoever designed the choir of St Denis, one can safely say, invented the Gothic style, although Gothic features had existed before, scattered here and there, and, in the centre of France, the provinces around St Denis even developed with a certain consistency.

The features which make up the Gothic style are well enough known, too well in fact, because most people forget that a style is not an aggregate of features, but an integral whole. Still, it may be just as well to recapitulate them and re-examine their meaning. They are the pointed arch, the flying buttress, and the rib-vault. Not one

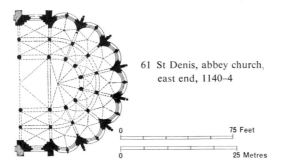

61 St Denis, abbey church, east end, 1140–4

0   75 Feet

0   25 Metres

of them, as we have already seen, is a Gothic invention. What was decisively new, however, was the combination of these motifs for a new aesthetic purpose. This purpose was to enliven inert masses of masonry, to quicken spatial motion, to reduce a building to a seeming system of innervated lines of action. These aesthetic advantages are infinitely more significant for an understanding of the Gothic style than whatever technical advantages the use of ribs, flying buttresses, and pointed arches may have meant. Such technical advantages were not absent, although they have been vastly over-estimated by Viollet-le-Duc and his innumerable followers.

The technical advantages are threefold. First of all a tunnel-vault presses down on the whole of the walls on which it rests. The groin-vaults of Romanesque Germany or Vézelay pressed down on only four points. But Romanesque groin-vaults require square bays to be constructed satisfactorily. If you try to build a Romanesque, that is, an essentially round-arched, groin-vault over an oblong bay, you will have to use arches of three distinct diameters, over the long and short side of the rectangle and across the diagonal. Only one of the three can be semicircular; the others may be stilted or depressed. If the transverse arch, that is, the most visible one, is made semi-circular, then the diagonal becomes depressed, and depressed arches are structurally dangerous, because obviously the safety of an arch increases the closer its thrust approaches the vertical, and decreases the nearer the horizontal its thrust. Complete verticality would result in complete safety, complete horizontality would burst the two walls apart at once.

The pointed arch enables the designer to get nearer the desired verticality than the semicircular, and in addition to construct vaults over bays other than square. Instead of stilting and depression there will now simply be three different degrees of pointing. The rectangular bay is useful for another reason as well. In a square bay the four points of support are far from each other, and as they are the points on to which the whole weight of the vault is conducted, they carry a disproportionately great responsibility in securing the stability of the building. With oblong bays you can double the number of the supports and thus halve the share of each in holding the building.

Moreover, the oblong Gothic vault was constructed with ribs to strengthen the groins, and that also was technically advantageous. For a tunnel-vault or a Romanesque groin-vault needs a wooden centering underneath its whole length and width to build it up. In the case of rib-vaults a centering is erected only strong enough to support the transverse arches and diagonal ribs until their mortar has set. The cells between the transverse arches and ribs can then be filled in with the help of a light, moving, easily and speedily dissembled and re-erected centering. The saving in timber is evident. Whether the ribs also kept the cells independent of one another, even after the vault had been completed, and actually reduced the cells to the nature of membranes, remains doubtful. There are cases where after shelling or bombing ribs have remained intact while cells have come down, but there are others also where quite clearly vaults have stood although parts of their ribs have fallen out. So it can be regarded as certain that the primary object of the Gothic vault was its appearance of immaterial lightness rather than any actual lightness, that is, once again an aesthetic rather than a material consideration.

The various technical and visual innovations appeared for the first time combined into a Gothic system at St Denis. Rib-vaults cover the varying shapes of bays, buttresses replace the massive walls between the radiating chapels which now form a continuous wavy fringe to the ambulatory. Their side walls have disappeared entirely. If it were not for the five-ribbed vaults, one would feel as if walking through a second, outer ambulatory, with exceedingly shallow chapels. The effect inside the church is one of lightness, of air circulating freely, of supple curves and energetic concentration. No longer is part demonstratively separated from part. The transept, recent excavations have shown, was not intended to project beyond the nave and chancel walls as it had always done until then. Articulation remains; but it is a far more sophisticated articulation. Who was the great genius to conceive this? Was it Abbot Suger himself, who so proudly wrote a little book about the building and consecration of his church? Hardly; for the Gothic, as against the Romanesque style, is so essentially based on a co-operation between artist and engineer, and a synthesis of aesthetic and technical

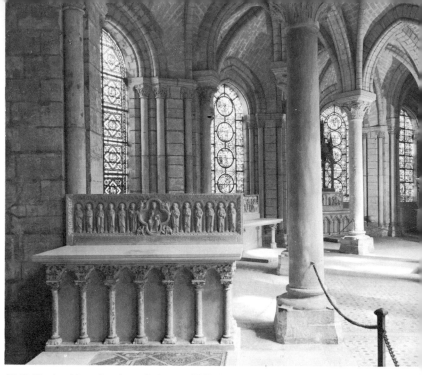

62 St Denis, abbey church, ambulatory, 1140–4

qualities, that only a man of profound structural knowledge can
have invented such a system. We are here at the beginning of a
specialization that has gone on splitting up our activities into
smaller and smaller competencies, until today the patron is not
an architect, the architect not a builder, the builder not a mason, let
alone such distinctions as those between the quantity surveyor, the
heating engineer, the air-conditioning engineer, the electrical
installation expert, and the sanitation expert.

The new type of architect to whom St Denis and the later French
and English cathedrals must be ascribed is the master craftsman as
a recognized artist. Creative master craftsmen had of course existed
before, and probably always designed most of what was built. But
their status now began to change. It was a very gradual development. Suger in his book does not say one word about the architect
of St Denis, nor in fact about the designer of the church as such. It

seems curious; surely he must have known very well what a daring work he had put up. To explain his silence one must remember the often-quoted and often-misunderstood anonymity of the Middle Ages. It does not mean of course that cathedrals grew like trees. They were all designed by someone. But in the earlier medieval centuries the names of these men, immortal as their work seemed, did not count. They were content to be workmen working for a cause greater than their own fame. However, during the twelfth and, above all, the thirteenth centuries the self-confidence of the individual grew, and personality came to be appreciated. The names of the architects of Rheims and Amiens cathedrals were recorded in a curious way on the pavement of the naves. Nicolas de Briart, a preacher, complained that master-masons got higher wages than others by simply going about with their staffs in their hands and giving orders, and – he adds – *'nihil laborant'*. A century after this the King of France was godfather to the son of one of these men and made him a considerable present in gold to enable him to study at a university. But two hundred years had to elapse after the time of Suger to make such intimacy possible.

One of the earliest cases in which we can form a live impression of the personality of one of the great master-masons of the early Gothic style is that of William of Sens, architect of the choir of Canterbury Cathedral – a work as revolutionary in England as St Denis was in France. A fire had destroyed the old choir in 1174, as we are told by Gervase, the chronicler of the cathedral, who had himself lived through the events he relates. There was great despair among the brethren, until after a while they began to consult 'by what method the ruined church might be repaired. Architects, both French and English, were assembled; but they disagreed. Some suggested repair, while others insisted that the whole church must be taken down, if the monks wished to dwell in safety. This overwhelmed them with grief. Among the architects there was one, William of Sens, a man of great abilities and a most ingenious workman in wood and stone. Dismissing the rest, they chose him for the undertaking. And he, residing many days with the monks and carefully surveying the burnt walls . . . did yet for some time conceal what he found necessary to do, lest the truth should kill us in our hopelessness. But he went on preparing all things that were necessary, either himself or by the agency of others. And when he found that the monks began to be somewhat comforted, he confessed that the damaged pillars and all that they supported, must be destroyed, if the monks wished to have a safe and excellent building. At length they agreed . . . to take down the ruined choir. Attention was given to procure stones from abroad. He made the most ingenious machines for loading and unloading ships, and for drawing the mortar and stones. He delivered also to the masons models (cut-out wooden templates) for cutting the stones. . . .' Then the chronicler tells us exactly what during each of the following four years was done. At the beginning of the fifth year, however, William, while on the scaffolding, fell down to the ground from a height of fifty feet. He was badly hurt and had to 'entrust the completion of the work to a certain ingenious monk who was overseer of the rough masons. . . .' But though lying in bed, he gave orders 'what was first and what last to be done. . . . At length, finding no benefit from the skill of his surgeons, he went to France to die at home', and an English successor was appointed.[17]

So here we have the craftsman, equally skilled in masonry and engineering work, diplomatic with his patrons and appreciated by them, but never while conducting work abroad forgetting the land of his youth. At Sens, wherefrom he came, a new cathedral had been begun about thirty years before he went over to Canterbury, a cathedral with certain features evidently imitated at Canterbury.

We are fortunate in possessing at least one even more complete record of the personality and work of a Gothic architect, a notebook, or rather textbook, prepared about 1235 by Villard de Honnecourt, an architect from the Cambrai region of Northern France. This textbook, preserved at the National Library in Paris, is an eminently personal document. Villard addresses his pupils. He promises them tuition in masonry and carpentry, drawing of architecture and figures, and geometry. Of all this the book contains examples, drawn and briefly described. It is invaluable as a source of information on the methods and attitude of the thirteenth century. Villard, although an architect, draws a Crucifixion, a Madonna, and figures of the sleeping disciples as they were represented in the

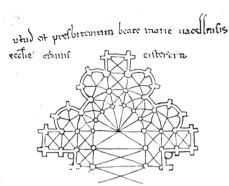

utud ot prefbitcummm beate marie uacellmfis
cccfic' obumf ciftercrn.

63 A Cistercian plan and a disciple
on the Mount of Olives.
From Villard de Honnecourt's
textbook, c. 1235

Cc cft un maue tem fi cumr il eft cheus.

scene on the Mount of Olives, all these evidently for stone carvers to
work from. He also drew figures of Pride and Humility, the Church
Triumphant and the Wheel of Fortune. But there are worldly scenes
too, wrestlers, men on horseback, a king with his retinue. Then
there are many animals, some surprisingly realistic, others quite
fantastic. There are simple geometrical schemes for drawing human
heads and animals. He records parts of buildings, the ground plans
of church choirs, a tower of Laon Cathedral (he says: 'I have been
in many countries, as you can see from this book, but I have never
seen such another tower'), windows from the cathedral of Rheims
(he says: 'I was on my way to Hungary when I drew this because
I liked it best'), and a rose window at Lausanne. He traces a laby-
rinth, and draws foliage. He designs a foliated end for a choir stall
and a lectern with three evangelists. He has diagrams of mouldings
and of timber construction. He adds proudly a good many pieces of

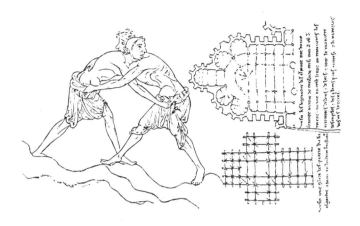

64 Pair of wrestlers, a Cistercian plan, and the plan of Cambrai Cathedral. From Villard de Honnecourt's textbook, *c.*1235

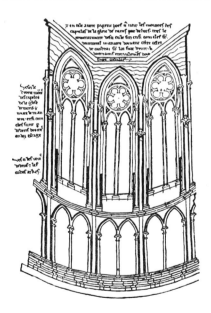

65 One of the radiating east chapels of Rheims Cathedral. From Villard de Honnecourt's textbook, *c.*1235

machinery, a sawmill, a device for lifting heavy weights, and also such automata as a lectern eagle that turns its head, or a heatable metal orb for a bishop to hold in his hand. He even notes a recipe for getting rid of superfluous hair.

Such was the range of knowledge and experience of the men who built the great Gothic cathedrals. They were invited abroad as the bringers of the new Gothic style, and we have a record of 1258 from Germany (Wimpfen) telling us of a prior who 'called in a mason most experienced in the art of architecture and who had come recently from Paris (*noviter de villa Parisiensi venerat*)'. He was told by the prior to build the church 'more Francigeno' of ashlar stone. We can be sure that such travelling masons kept their eyes open, and noted buildings, sculptures, and paintings with the same eagerness. They knew as much of the carving of figures and ornaments as of building construction, although their drawing technique was still elementary.

St Denis must owe its novelty to a master-mason of this calibre. And many a bishop and architect burned with ambition to emulate Suger and St Denis. Between 1140 and 1220 new cathedrals were begun on an ever-growing scale at Sens, Noyon, Senlis, and then Paris (Notre Dame, *c.* 1163 seqq.), Laon (*c.* 1170 seqq.), Chartres (*c.* 1195 seqq.), Rheims (1211 seqq.), Amiens (1220 seqq.), and Beauvais (1247 seqq.). These are by no means all; there are many more all over France. We must, however, here confine ourselves to a brief analysis of the main development in the Île de France and the surrounding regions, which just then became the centre of a national French kingdom. It is a development as consistent and as concise as that of the Greek temple.

Of St Denis we possess only the choir and, very restored, the west front. This is of the two-tower type of Caen which now became *de rigueur* for North French cathedrals, but, against Caen, enriched by a still round-headed triple portal. It is this that we have already referred to because of the columnar figures which once adorned it. Chartres followed St Denis at once. Of the cathedral of about 1145 only the west portals remain, the Portail Royal, whose figures have also been mentioned in the preceding chapter, gloriously vigorous, tense, and alert. We can guess what the naves of St Denis and

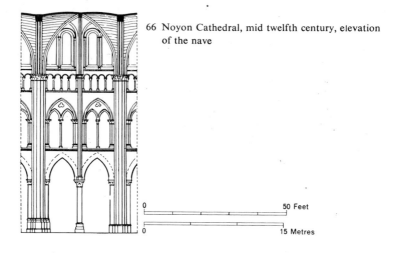

66 Noyon Cathedral, mid twelfth century, elevation of the nave

0   50 Feet

0   15 Metres

Chartres were like from remaining indications at St Denis and from the exactly contemporary cathedral of Sens. They had galleries just like the Romanesque churches of Normandy which must have been more inspiring to the earliest Gothic masons of France than any others. The earliest Gothic elevation then was three-storeyed, of arcade, gallery, and clerestory; and no doubt there were rib-vaults. At Noyon about fifteen years later, an important innovation appeared. The walls are enriched by a triforium, i.e. a low wall-passage, between gallery and clerestory. This division of the wall into four zones instead of three does away with much that had remained inert before. The arcades have alternating supports, composite piers as major and round ones as minor divisions. In accordance with this the vaults are sexpartite, as they had been about 1115–20 in the Romanesque abbey churches of Caen. That means that between two transverse arches ribs run across diagonally from composite to composite pier, while the shafts on the round piers are followed up by subsidiary ribs parallel with the transverse arches and meeting the diagonal ribs in the centre of the whole bay. The effect is more lively than we know in the Romanesque style.

However, the architects of the two cathedrals immediately following must have felt that in the walls, piers, and vaults of Noyon there was still too much left of Romanesque weight and stability. The

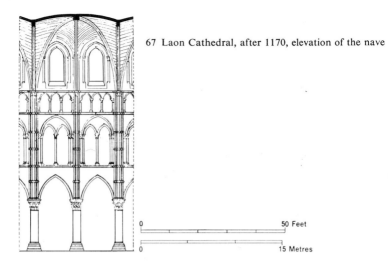

67 Laon Cathedral, after 1170, elevation of the nave

68 Laon Cathedral, nave, after 1170

alternating supports and sexpartite vaults especially produced square, that is, static, bays. So at Laon, after some experimenting with alternating supports, all the piers are circular, although on the upper floor an alternation between groups of five and of three thin shafts rising from the circular piers is still preserved, and there are still sexpartite vaults. The many thin shaft-rings, or annulets, round the shafts also still emphasize the horizontal. All the same, in walking along the nave the halting at every major support is avoided. That was a decisive step to take. Notre Dame in Paris goes yet one step further. The shafts on the circular piers are no longer differentiated, and the shaft-rings are left out. But the wall was still, it seems, originally in four stages, with gallery and then, instead of the triforium, a row of circular windows below those of the clerestory. However, the proportions have now changed sufficiently to show what tendency lay behind these gradual modifications. The gallery arcades have coupled openings in the choir – as was the Norman

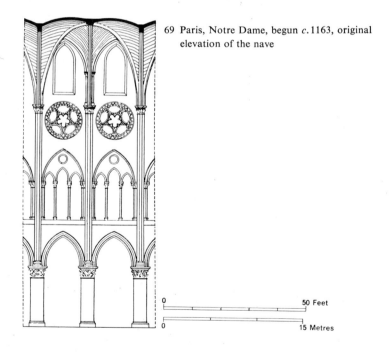

69 Paris, Notre Dame, begun *c.*1163, original elevation of the nave

0   50 Feet

0   15 Metres

70 Paris, Notre Dame, nave, late twelfth century

tradition – but trebled, that is, much slimmer, openings in the slightly later nave, and the separating colonnettes are exceedingly slender.

Still more daring than the elevation of Notre Dame is its ground plan. Already at Sens and Noyon a slightly centralizing tendency can be noted: at Sens by a lengthening of the chancel between transept and ambulatory, at Noyon by semicircular endings of the transepts to the north and south. Now in Paris the architect has placed his transept almost exactly half-way between the two west towers and the east end. He has adopted the most ambitious plan for nave and chancel, the one with double aisles, familiar from Old St Peter's in Rome as well as from Cluny. His transepts project very little beyond the outer aisles, and there were originally no radiating chapels at all. The present ones, as well as the present chapels between the buttresses of nave and chancel, are a later addition. The resulting spatial rhythm is much smoother than that of Romanesque cathedrals or of Noyon. It is no longer split into numerous units which one has to add up mentally, as it were, to summarize the spatial totality, but concentrated in a few, in fact three, sections: west, centre, east. The transept acts as the centre of the balance. The façade and the double ambulatory round the apse are the two scales. Within the rhythm the evenness of the narrowly spaced arcade columns is most important. It leads you on towards the altar as forcibly as did the columns of Early Christian basilicas.

71 Paris, Notre Dame, begun c. 1163, ground level (*top*), upper level (*bottom*)

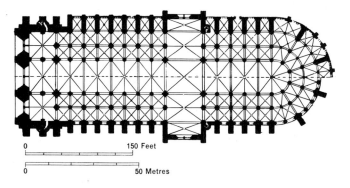

0   150 Feet

0   50 Metres

The movement which had grown from St Denis to Noyon and from Noyon to Paris reached maturity in the cathedrals designed from the end of the twelfth century onwards. Early Gothic changed into High Gothic. Chartres was rebuilt after a fire in 1194. The new choir and nave at last do away with the sexpartite vault and return to vaults with only diagonal ribs. But whereas the Romanesque rib-vaults were placed over square or squarish bays, the bays now are roughly half that depth. The speed of the eastward drive is thereby at once doubled. The piers remain circular, but they have on each side a circular attached shaft. Toward the nave this shaft reaches right up to where the vault starts (as the shafts of Jumièges and Winchester had already done). So the isolation of the circular column is overcome. Nothing at arcade level stops the vertical push. And the wide and tall gallery has disappeared. There is now only a low triforium, dividing the tall arcades from the tall clerestory windows. These innovations constitute the High Gothic style. The plan is less radical than that of Paris, but has the transept also midway between the west front and the choir end.

A few words must be said about Bourges here, which is one of the most impressive of the French Gothic cathedrals, but one which remains curiously separate from the main stream of development. The cathedral was begun in 1195. Its plan, with double aisles, no

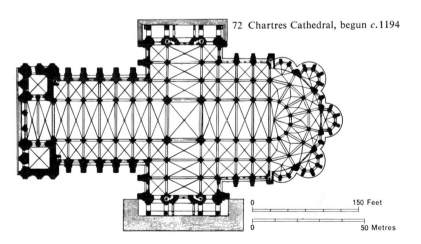

72 Chartres Cathedral, begun c. 1194

0   150 Feet

0   50 Metres

74 Chartres Cathedral, begun c. 1194,
elevation of the nave

0 ⊢————————⊣ 50 Feet

0 ⊢————————⊣ 15 Metre

75 Nave vaults of Chartres Cathedral, begun c. 1194, and Lincoln Cathedral,
begun 1192

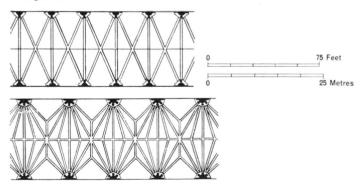

0 ⊢————————⊣ 75 Feet

0 ⊢————————⊣ 25 Metres

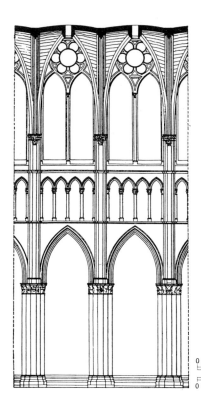

76 Rheims Cathedral, begun 1211, elevation of the nave

0   50 Feet

0   15 Metres

transepts at all, and a double ambulatory, derives from Paris. Its exceedingly tall arcades – the piers are 56 feet high – its pier shape with the circular core and the attached shafts, and its use of the triforium instead of a gallery are High Gothic in the new Chartres sense, a parallel to Chartres rather than a derivation, but the sexpartite vaults are Early Gothic and so is the peculiar stress on horizontals to counteract the verticalism of the arcade. The outer aisles are lower than the inner, and that allows a triforium above the inner aisles apart from the main triforium. Thus, looking at the elevation one sees five horizontal divisions, not three: outer arcade, outer triforium, main arcade, main triforium, clerestory – a strange, rich effect very different from the single-mindedness of Chartres.

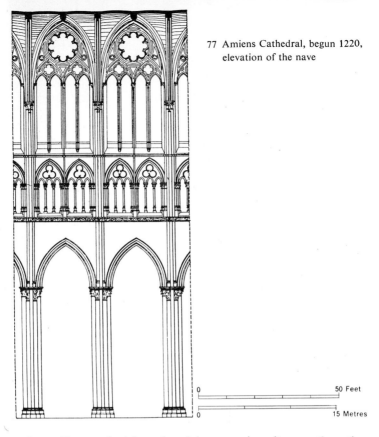

77 Amiens Cathedral, begun 1220, elevation of the nave

	50 Feet
0	
0	15 Metres

Once Chartres had introduced its new piers, its new three-tier elevation, and its quadripartite vaults, Rheims, Amiens, and Beauvais did nothing more than perfect it and carry it to the boldest and most thrilling extremes. Rheims was begun in 1211, Amiens in 1220, Beauvais in 1247. As in the plans so in the interiors a balance is achieved no doubt – but not the happy, seemingly effortless and indestructible balance of the Greeks. High Gothic balance is a balance of two equally vehement drives towards two opposite directions. One's first impression is of breathtaking height. At Sens the relation between width and height of nave had been only 1:1·4, at Noyon 1:2, at Chartres 1:2·6, in Paris 1:2·75. In Amiens it has become 1:3, and in Beauvais 1:3·4. And even Beauvais is

78 Cologne Cathedral, begun 1248, nave

outstripped by Cologne, begun in 1248. Here the proportion is 1:3·8.[18]
The absolute height at Noyon had been approximately 85 feet. In
Paris it is 115 feet, in Rheims 125, in Amiens 140, and in Beauvais
157. The drive upward is just as forcible as, or, owing to the slenderness of all members, even more forcible than, was the drive eastward
in Early Christian churches. And the eastward drive has not by any
means slackened either. The narrowness of the arcades and the
uniform shape of the piers do not seem to call for even a momentary
change of direction. They accompany one on one's way, as closely set

79 Amiens Cathedral, begun 1220, nave

and as rapidly appearing and disappearing as telegraph poles along a
railway line. There is not time at first to stop and admire them. Yet in
pressing forward, the transept halts us and diverts our eyes to the right
and left. Here we stop, here we endeavour for the first time to take in
the whole. In an Early Christian church nothing of this kind was provided, in a Romanesque church so much of it that movement went
slowly from bay to bay, from compartment to compartment. At
Amiens there is only one such halt, and it cannot be long. Again
nave and aisles, now of the chancel, close round us, and we do not

come to an ultimate rest until we have reached the apse and the ambulatory, gathering with splendid energy the parallel streams of east-bound energy and concentrating them in a final soaring movement along the narrowly spaced piers of the apse and the narrow east windows up to the giddy heights of the vault ribs and vaulting bosses.

This description is an attempt at analysing a spatial experience, ignoring of course the fact that a normal thirteenth-century churchgoer would never have been admitted to the chancel. What will have become evident from it is how spectacularly Rheims, Amiens, and Beauvais are the final achievement of an evolution which had begun back in the eleventh century in Normandy and at Durham and had worked, one after another, seemingly small but very significant changes at St Denis, Noyon, Laon, Paris, and Chartres. This final achievement is, to say it once more, far from reposeful. It possesses the tension of two dominant directions or dimensions, a tension transformed by a supreme feat of creative energy into a precarious balance. Once one has felt this, one will recognize it in every detail. The piers are slender and erect, part of the upward drive. The tempo of the drive is indeed accelerated. At Rheims the piers end in a broad band of leaf capital, and the five vaulting-shafts stand on it. At Amiens the middle one of the three vaulting-shafts is the continuation of one of the shafts round the circular pier, separated from it only by a narrow abacus band. For piers and shafts do remain all the same, round, firm, and shapely, with their exquisite realistic foliage. The mouldings of the arcades are sharp and manifold with rolls and deep hollows, highlights and black but precise shadows. The clerestory is all opened up into vast sheets of glass. Yet they are subdivided by vigorously moulded shafts and by geometrical tracery. The introduction of tracery, an invention of the Gothic style, is especially telling. Its development can be traced from Chartres to Rheims and from Rheims to Amiens. Before Rheims tracery is just a punching of pattern into the wall, the wall itself remaining intact as a surface. At Rheims, for the first time, we find what is called bar tracery as against plate tracery. The stress now rests on the lines of the pattern, not on the surface of the wall. Each two-light window is crowned by a circle with a sexfoil ornament – repose at the end of forceful action. Amiens is an enrichment of Rheims, with four-light windows and three circles instead of one. The same energetic vitality appears in the vaults. Each boss signifies Gothic balance – the firm knotting of four lines of energy, conducted by shafts and then by ribs.

The exteriors of the Gothic cathedrals of the later twelfth and the early thirteenth century were in perfect harmony with the interiors – at least in the form in which they were planned; for hardly any were executed completely. Few visitors and even few students realize that. Laon is the only one (except for Tournai in Southern Belgium) that can give a true idea of what a French cathedral was intended to look like. It has five tall towers and was designed to have seven: two on

80 Laon Cathedral, west front, completed *c*. 1225

the west front, one sturdier one over the crossing, and two on each of the transept fronts. Chartres was to have eight, Rheims six. This vehement verticalism of the exteriors, a Gothic innovation in France, more in keeping with the Rhineland than with the French Romanesque, began to be questioned only, it seems, after about 1220 at Notre Dame in Paris. The famous façade of Notre Dame moreover has the towers straight-topped, but in the other cathedrals just mentioned there is every reason to believe that the towers were designed to carry spires. The spire is the supreme expression of the heavenward urge. It is a creation of the Gothic mind. Romanesque spires are no more than pyramid or conical roofs. The spire over the south tower of Chartres Cathedral is the first in France, that of Oxford Cathedral the first in England. How well one can understand Villard de Honnecourt's admiration of the tower design at Laon, already referred to. For Rheims Cathedral one must look at illustrations of the façade of the long demolished parish church of St Nicaise to realize what a difference spires would have made to its appearance. One of the preserved original drawings for the front of Strassburg Cathedral (the so-called Design B) is a confirmation. If one tries to add in one's mind the two missing towers at Laon and spires to all seven, one will get near to an ideal of external Gothic splendour on a par with that of the interiors.

It has often been said that the elements of which the exteriors are composed, chiefly the flying buttresses as they had first appeared, it seems, at Notre Dame and Canterbury, i.e. in the 1160s and 1170s, are no more than the structural necessities to make the mystical excelsior of the interiors possible. That is not so; they possess a fascination of intricate pattern, not fantastic and irresponsible but conducted by logic, which is indeed an expression of the same high tension as governs the interiors.

This balance of high tensions is the classic expression of the Western spirit – as final as the temple of the fifth century B.C. was of that of the Greek spirit. Then it was rest and blissful harmony, now it is activity, only just for one moment held in suspense. And it requires concentrated effort to master the contrasts and partake of the balance. Like a Bach fugue, a Gothic cathedral demands all our emotional and intellectual powers. Now we find ourselves lost

81 Rheims Cathedral, west front, c. 1235 and second half of the thirteenth century, upper gallery and towers fifteenth century

in the mystical ruby and azure glow of translucent stained glass, and now called back to alert attention by the precise course of thin yet adequately strong lines. What is the secret of these vast temples? Is it in their miraculous interiors with vast stone vaults at an immense height, walls all of glass, and arcades much too slim and tall to carry them? The Greek architect achieved a harmony of load and support convincing at once and for ever; the Gothic architect, far bolder constructionally, with his Western soul of the eternal explorer and inventor, always lured by the untried, aims at a contrast between an interior all spirit and an exterior all intellect. For inside the cathedral we cannot and are not meant to understand the law governing the whole. Outside we are faced with a frank exposition of the complicated structural mechanism. The flying buttresses and buttresses, though by no means without the fascination of intricate pattern, will chiefly appeal to reason, conveying a sensation similar to that of the theatre-goer looking at the stage apparatus behind the scenes.

One need hardly point out in so many words how exactly the Gothic cathedral re-echoes in all this the achievements of Western thought in the thirteenth century, the achievements, that is, of classic scholasticism. Scholasticism is the name for the characteristically medieval blend of divinity and philosophy. It grew up with the Romanesque style, the centuries before the eleventh having in the main not done more than simplify, regroup, and, here and there, modify the doctrines of the Fathers of the Church and the philosophers and poets of Rome. During the twelfth century, when the Gothic style was created and spread, scholasticism developed into something just as lofty and at the same time just as intricate as the new cathedrals. The first half of the thirteenth century saw the appearance of the compendia of all worldly and sacred knowledge, St Thomas Aquinas's *Summa*, and the works of Albert the Great and St Bonaventura, the *Specula* of Vincent of Beauvais, and in poetry Wolfram von Eschenbach's *Parsifal*. One of these encyclopedic tomes, the *De Proprietatibus Rerum* by the English Dominican Bartholomaeus Anglicus, written about 1240, begins with a chapter on the essence, unity, and the three persons of God. The next chapter deals with the angels, the third with Man, his soul and senses.

114

There follow chapters on the elements and temperaments, on anatomy and physiology, on the Ages of Man, on food, sleep, and similar physical needs, on diseases, on sun, moon, stars, and zodiac, on time and its divisions, on matter, fire, air, water, on the birds of the air, the fishes of the water, the beasts of the land, on geography, on minerals, trees, colours, tools. Vincent of Beauvais, who writes about 1250, divides his work into the Mirrors of Nature, of Doctrine, and of History. And just as the Mirror of Nature starts from God and Creation, so the Mirror of History starts from the Fall of Man, and leads up to the Last Judgement. The cathedral was – besides being a strictly architectural monument of the spirit of its age – another *Summa*, another *Speculum*, an encyclopedia carved in stone. The Virgin stood at the centre post of the centre portals of Rheims Cathedral. Figures were placed into the jambs of this portal representing such scenes as the Annunciation, the Visitation, the Presentation. High up in the gables of the three portals appear the Crucifixion, the Coronation of the Virgin, and the Last Judgement. But there are also in the Gothic cathedrals the lives of Christ, the Virgin, and saints told in the stained glass of the windows, and, spread over the plinths, the jambs, the voussoirs, and up against the buttresses, saints with the attributes by which they are recognized – St Peter with the key, St Nicholas with the three golden balls, St Barbara with the tower, St Margaret with the dragon – and scenes and figures from the Old Testament, the Creation of Man, Jonah with the Whale, or Abraham and Melchisedek, and the Roman Sibyls who had foretold, it was believed, the coming of Christ, and the Wise and the Foolish Virgins, and the Seven Liberal Arts, and the months of the year with their occupations – the grafting of trees, sheep-shearing, harvesting, pig-slaughtering – and the signs of the zodiac, and the elements. The profane and the sacred – a compendium of knowledge; but everything, as St Thomas puts it, 'ordered towards God'. For Jonah is represented, not because he comes into the Old Testament, but because his three days inside the whale represent the resurrection of Christ, as Melchisedek offering bread and wine to Abraham represented the Last Supper. To the medieval mind everything was a symbol. The meaning that mattered lay behind the outward appearance. The simile of the two swords, the emperor's and the pope's, was a symbolic expression of political theories. To Guilielmus Durandus the cruciform church represented the Cross, and the weathercock on the spire the preacher who rouses the sleeping from the night of sin. The mortar, he says, consists of lime, i.e. love, sand, i.e. earthly toil which love has taken upon itself, and water, uniting heavenly love and our earthly world.

All this one must keep in mind to realize how alien this world is to ours, despite all our enthusiasm for the cathedrals and their sculptures. We are liable to a reaction in these vast halls which is far too romantic, nebulous, sentimental, whereas to the cleric of the thirteenth century everything was probably lucid. Lucid, but transcendental. That is the antagonism which defeats us in our age of agnosticism. In the thirteenth century the bishop and the monk, the knight and the craftsman believed firmly – though each to the measure of his capacity – that nothing exists in the world which does not come from God, and derive its sense and sole interest from its divine meaning. The medieval conception of truth was fundamentally different from ours. Truth was not what can be proved, but what conformed to an accepted revelation. Research was not conducted to find truth, but to penetrate more deeply into a pre-established truth. Hence authorities meant more to the medieval scholar than to anyone now, and hence also the faith of the medieval artist in the 'exemplar', the example to be copied. Neither originality nor the study of Nature counted for much. Even Villard de Honnecourt copied in nine out of ten of his pages. Innovations came by degrees and much less deliberately than we can imagine.

Yet the Gothic style surely was a deliberate innovation and the work of strong and self-confident personalities. Its forms allow us to assume that, and we find in fact within scholasticism, as the chief innovation of the thirteenth century, a marked departure from the purely transcendental attitude of the Romanesque and earlier centuries. St Peter Damiani, in the first half of the eleventh century, had said: 'The world is so filthy with vices that any holy mind is befouled by even thinking of it.' Now Vincent of Beauvais exclaims: 'How great is even the humblest beauty of this world! I am moved with spiritual sweetness towards the Creator and Ruler of this world, when I behold the magnitude and beauty and permanence of His creation.' And beauty according to St Thomas Aquinas (or a close follower of his philosophy) 'consists of a certain consonance of diverging elements'.

But it is never – not yet – the beauty of the world as such that is praised. It is the beauty of God's creation. We can enjoy it wholeheartedly; for God Himself 'rejoices in all things, because everyone is in actual agreement with His Being' (St Thomas). Thus stone-carvers could now portray the loveliest leaves, the thorn, the oak, the maple, the vine. When St Peter Damiani wrote, ornament was abstract or severely stylized. Now youthful life pulses in it, as it pulses in shafts and ribs. But the ornament of the thirteenth century is, even at its most naturalistic, neither petty nor pedantic. It is still subordinate, never forward, always ministering to a greater cause, that of religious architecture.

Yet it would not have been possible at an earlier age than that of St Francis's song to Brother Sun and Sister Earth and Brother Wind, than that of the '*dolce stil nuovo*', and the French epics of chivalry. The earliest monastic orders had lived in the seclusion of their cloisters; the new orders of the thirteenth century, the Dominicans and Franciscans, had their monasteries in towns and preached to the burghers. The first Crusades had been called up to liberate the Holy Land, the fourth, the one of 1203, was deflected by the Venetians to Constantinople, which they needed for the benefit of their commerce. But still in the fifth there was in the person of the French King Louis IX, St Louis, a true Christian knight, a hero in whom the ideals of religion and chivalry burned with equal ardour. Wolfram's *Parsifal* is the greatest epic of the thirteenth century. Here at the moment when Rheims Cathedral was begun, the young knight is taught to 'keep his soul pledged to God, without losing his hold on the world'. And he is taught that 'in joy and in grief right measure' should always be his guide. That sounds like the Greek 'Nothing in excess', but it is not. It is just as in architecture, a balance gained as the ultimate prize by him who indefatigably strives for his redemption, a noble and upright ideal worthy of the great cathedrals and the superb sculptures of their portals. At Chartres, under the name of St Theodore, one can see him, the knight of the Parsifal virtues, standing in the porch of the south transept, and at Rheims, as an unknown king, under a canopy of one of the buttresses, and on horseback at Bamberg, and again with the most beautiful young women that Western sculptors ever carved, women both vigorous and maidenly, around the choir of Naumburg Cathedral.

In England the emissaries of Henry VIII and of Cromwell have destroyed the majority of what there was of cathedral sculpture. A few pieces that are left, such as a headless figure at Winchester, are of the same character and quality as thirteenth-century sculpture in France. But neither the façade of Wells nor the surviving statues at Lincoln and Westminster are up to the standards at Chartres and Rheims. The English are not a sculptural race. Their architecture, however, the style which they evolved, is just as exquisite as that of the French cathedrals, and at the same time typically English, known under the name of Early English.

Originally it came from France, as did the Gothic style in all countries, and as did so much else of culture and manners. John of Salisbury, the urbane English philosopher, who was as much at home in France as in England, calls France *omnium nitidissima et civilissima nationum*'; and the new architectural style must have been included in people's minds with the other accomplishments of Paris. But the first to favour and spread Gothic architecture were the Cistercians, the new reformed order of the twelfth century, to which St Bernard belonged, and they favoured it for reasons of soundness rather than of beauty. Cistercian houses in England were among the first to use pointed arches. Into cathedral architecture it was introduced by William of Sens at Canterbury. Details there are French in character. What is, however, unusual in France is the duplicating of the transepts as we find it at Canterbury and then at Lincoln, Wells, Salisbury, and many more cathedrals. It is not a feature invented in England. Cluny, the centre of the most influential order before the foundation of the Cistercians, had it – not, however, in the shape of the church in the tenth century, but as it was rebuilt in the late eleventh century. The fact that this duplication remained solitary in France but became so popular in England is eminently characteristic of the different approach to architecture in the two

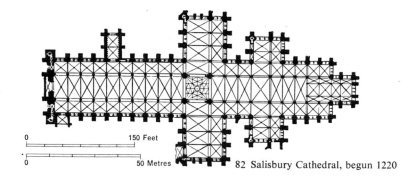

0   150 Feet

0   50 Metres   82 Salisbury Cathedral, begun 1220

countries. The Gothic style in France, as we have seen, tends all to spatial concentration. The Early English style lacks that quality. A cathedral such as Salisbury, with its square east end and its square double transepts, is still the sum, as it were, of added units, compartment joined to compartment. Looking at, say, Lincoln and then at Rheims, this difference comes out most eloquently. Rheims seems vigorously pulled together, Lincoln comfortably spread out. The same contrast can be found in the west façades. The English ones are comparatively insignificant. Porches, added to the naves and developed sometimes into superb pieces of independent decorative

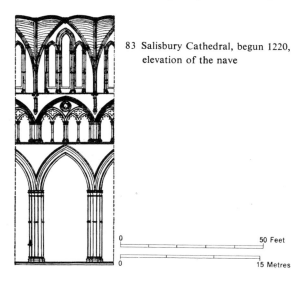

83 Salisbury Cathedral, begun 1220, elevation of the nave

0   50 Feet

0   15 Metres

119

84 Rheims Cathedral, begun 1211, from the north

85 Lincoln Cathedral, begun 1192, from the south. Engraving by Wenzel Hollar

architecture, serve as main entrances instead. And where there are fully developed façades, as at Wells and Lincoln, they have an existence unrelated to the interiors behind, are screens, as it were, placed in front of the church proper, and not the logically designed outward projection of the inside system, as are French façades. It has been said that this seemingly conservative attitude of English architects was due to the survival of so many big Norman cathedrals, the foundations and walls of which were used in the rebuilding. But this materialistic explanation, like so many of the same kind, does not hold good. Salisbury was a new foundation. There was nothing on the site when the first stone was laid in 1220 (the same year in which Amiens Cathedral was begun), yet the ground plan is of the same type as Lincoln. The preference for the 'additive' plan must therefore be accepted as a national peculiarity; and once one has realized that, one will recognize its essential similarity to the Anglo-Saxon ground plans of churches such as Bradford-on-Avon, and also its harmony with the specifically national qualities in Early English elevations.

Canterbury cannot unreservedly be called English; Wells and Lincoln are. Wells was begun just before 1191, Lincoln in 1192. If one compares the nave of Lincoln vaulted about 1233 or a little later with that of Amiens, the national contrast is obvious. Yet both cathedrals are of the aristocratic, youthful yet disciplined, vigorous yet graceful spirit of the thirteenth century. The bays in Lincoln are wide, while they are narrow in Amiens, the piers are of comfortable proportions; no shafts run right through from bottom to top. Those supporting the ribs of the vaults rest on corbels just above capitals of the piers – an illogical arrangement from the French point of view. The triforium gallery has broad, low openings and pointed arches, so low that they seem round[19] – another inconsistency, a French critic would say. And most curious of all to anybody thinking in terms of Amiens or Beauvais is the vault. For while the French vault is the logical termination of the bay system, the vault of Lincoln has, besides the transverse ribs separating bay from bay, and the four cross ribs, a ridge-rib running all along the centre of the vault parallel to the arcades, and so-called tiercerons, i.e. ribs springing from the same capitals as the cross ribs, but leading up to other points along the ridge or at right angles to the ridge (see plan on p. 105). Thus the vault in Lincoln assumes the shape of a sequence of stars – more decorative but less logical than the French system. There is in addition another aspect to such vaults, an aspect even less logical. For while, when one looks at the Lincoln vaults on paper, the definition as a sequence of stars is correct, the eye in looking up at the vaults inside the church does not interpret them like that. Owing partly to the fact that the transverse arches are not more substantial than the ribs and have exactly the same profile, one does not take in the pattern as one of bays following each other, but rather as a pattern of spreading palm branches issuing from the capitals of the vaulting shafts left and right and meeting at the ridge. Thus the rhythm of one's progress along the church is no longer determined by the bays but by the springing points, and what is bay below, at arcade level is syncopated by the width of half a bay all the way through at vault level.

In all this, the Early English style appears the true representative of a national character that seems scarcely changed to this day. There is still the same distrust of the consistent and logical and the extreme and uncompromising. Now it has not been possible to discover these peculiarly English qualities in Norman architecture, and it is worth mentioning in this context that just about the middle of the thirteenth century there are other indications as well of an awakening of national consciousness. The Provisions of Oxford of 1258 are the first official document with a text not only in French (or Latin) but also in English. And they declare that no royal fiefs shall in future go to foreigners, and that the commanders of royal castles and ports must in future all be English. It is known that Simon de Montfort's revolt was a national movement, and that Edward I was influenced by Simon's ideas to a considerable extent. The same tendency towards national differentiation can incidentally be noticed during the same period in other European countries. It may be connected with the experiences of the Crusades. Here the knights of the West, though united in a common enterprise, must for the first time have become aware of the contrasts of behaviour, feelings, and customs of the nations.

As far as architecture is concerned, the Crusades have had,

86 Lincoln Cathedral, nave, c. 1215–35

beyond this, one more immediate effect. They caused a complete reform in the planning and building of castles. Instead of the Norman reliance for defence on the keep, a system of concentric curtain walls with towers at intervals was now adopted. It came from the mighty walls of Constantinople built as early as about 400 and with a height for the inner and higher wall of over 40 feet. It had then been adopted by the Infidels and from them taken over by the Crusaders in Syria and the Holy Land. One of the earliest examples in France is Château Gaillard built in 1196–7 by Richard Cœur de Lion, King of England. The Tower of London, as it was enlarged by Richard Cœur de Lion and then by Henry III and his successors, is a particularly spectacular instance. What is, however, more especially important here is the fact that the new functional standard was accompanied at least in a number of cases by a new aesthetic standard. Symmetry as a planning principle of castles was rediscovered, rediscovered from the Romans who had used it for towns and castra. The act of rediscovery belongs to the French. Philip Augustus's castles of the Louvre in Paris and of Doudran not far from Paris are square or nearly square with four round angle towers and a gatehouse with round towers in the middle of one side. The engineers of the Emperor Frederick II built similar castles in South Italy (Lucera, Castel Maniaco Syracuse, Castel Ursino Catania) about 1240, independent of, or dependent on, France. At the same time the new towns of the thirteenth century, built for military and commercial reasons by the French and the English, aimed at regular patterns too. The best-preserved English example is New Winchelsea, but the grandest of all the 'new towns' is Aigues-Mortes of about 1270, etc., a chequerboard with straight walls, angle towers, and gatehouses with towers. The English came somewhat later, but Harlech in Wales of 1286–90 is the most majestic of the type remaining in northern Europe. The most accomplished in all Europe is Frederick II's Castel del Monte, an octagon, with elements derived from ancient Rome as well as the French Gothic.

In religious architecture in England, what lends itself most readily to a comparison with the all-round symmetry of Winchelsea or Harlech is the thirteenth-century chapter-house, again something specifically English, again something hardly known abroad and –

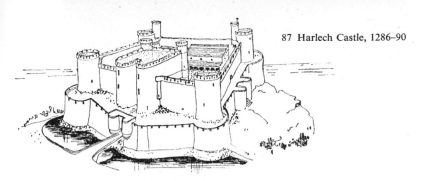

87 Harlech Castle, 1286–90

owing to the British inferiority complex in matters of art – insufficiently appreciated over here. Salisbury chapter-house of about 1275 is centrally planned, an octagon with a central pillar and spacious windows filling the walls entirely except for the arcade strip just above the stone benches for the members of the Chapter. But while in France such glass walls give a sensation of a rapturous union with a mysterious world beyond ours, the proportions of the windows at Salisbury, with their generously sized tracery circles, keep the interior in safe and happy contact with the ground. A sunny breadth is achieved which makes Amiens feel both over-pointed and over-excited.

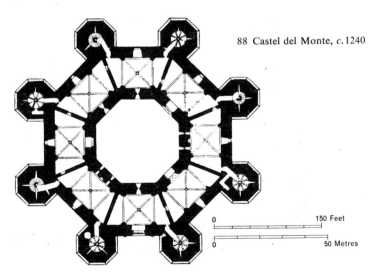

88 Castel del Monte, c. 1240

0   150 Feet

0   50 Metres

89 Salisbury Cathedral, chapter-house, c. 1275

At the same time the Early English style has just as much refine-
ment, crispness, and *noblesse* in every individual motif as the French
style of the great cathedrals. It is in fact this essential similarity of
detail that reminds one all the time of the ultimate identity of spirit
behind French and English thirteenth-century architecture. To feel
this, it is only necessary to look at the central pier at Salisbury or
the piers of the nave arcade in Lincoln with their slender detached
shafts and their resilient crocket capitals (of a type equally charac-

teristic of *c*. 1200 in England and France), or at the clarity and erectness of the English lancet window (English in that it presupposes a solid wall into which it is placed as against the French elimination of the whole wall), or at the masterly carving of the leaves around the capitals of Southwell chapter-house, throbbing with life, yet kept under the strict discipline of architecture, economic in treatment, nowhere fussy or ostentatious, and of a precision of surface to be compared only with the classic Greek art of the Parthenon.

90 Southwell Minster, capital, late thirteenth century

But the Classic is only a moment in the history of a civilization. The most progressive had reached it in France and England at the end of the twelfth century. The most progressive were tired of it and embarked on new adventures shortly after the middle of the thirteenth. In France, however, the magnificent creative impulse soon flagged – after the Sainte Chapelle in Paris, the chapel of the Kings of France (1243–8), had been designed as one tall room with – except for a low dado-zone – walls entirely of glass.

Earlier still, in the building of the nave, the transept, and the whole upper parts of St Denis from 1231 onwards and then at Beauvais the vaulting-shafts run up without any break at the level of the arcade piers and the triforium is glazed. No horizontal stress, no solid, dark zone of masonry remained, and the elevation had become two-storeyed instead of three-storeyed. The end of this development in France is the amazing church of St Urbain of Troyes, where, from 1261 to *c*. 1277, the structural members had been given an unprecedented brittleness and slenderness, and the system of the Sainte Chapelle had been transferred to a major church. Then, about 1275, France relaxed. Several cathedrals were, it is true, built afresh, in those parts of the country only recently conquered by the Kings, but they contributed nothing new and merely followed the established system of St Denis and Beauvais.[20] England on the other hand kept up her creative energy for another century. In fact, the architecture of England between 1250 and 1350 was, although the English do not know it, the most forward, the most important, and the most inspired in Europe.

91 Beauvais Cathedral, begun 124

4 The Late Gothic Style

c. 1250–*c.* 1500

Late Gothic, though by the predominant use of the pointed arch still part of the Gothic style, is essentially different from the High Gothic of the great French cathedrals of Paris, Rheims, and Amiens, and the English cathedrals of Salisbury and Lincoln. It is a complex phenomenon – so complex, indeed, that it might be wise to approach it from the point of view of changes in decoration first, before trying to recognize in what way spatial changes were involved. As for decoration, the difference between early and late thirteenth century can clearly be seen within Lincoln Cathedral. The retrochoir, or Angel Choir, was begun in 1256. It is of supreme beauty, but it no longer possesses the freshness of spring or early summer; this abundance of rich and mellow decoration has the warmth and sweetness of August and September, of harvest and vintage. But what generous fulfilment in the luxuriant foliage of the corbels and the gallery shafts and capitals, the full mouldings of the arcades and tracery of the gallery, and, above all, the two gorgeous layers of tracery up in the clerestory : one in the windows and one separating the wall-passage from the interior.

While here there is still breadth and fullness, in other equally advanced work of the same date a tendency becomes noticeable towards the more sophisticated and at the same time the more complicated. This tendency runs parallel with the dominant tendency in contemporary philosophy – the abstruse intricacies of Duns Scotus (born *c.* 1270) and his pupil Occam (died *c.* 1347) – and also with that in French architecture. But whereas the result in France is on the whole lean and retrospective, England went on inventing wholly original forms, refusing to listen to any authority of the past.

Lincoln Cathedral, Angel Choir, begun 1256

93 Exeter Cathedral, nave vault, early fourteenth century

After all, it had also been Occam who wrote: 'Whatsoever Aristotle may have thought on this, I do not care.' The most perfect expression of this new profuseness, this delight in the decorative rather than the strictly architectural, is in the kind of tracery which is called flowing as against the geometrical tracery of 1230 to about 1300. The economy of the Early English – a feature of all classic phases – is in strong contrast to the infinite variety of the Decorated. Where there had been exclusively circles with inscribed trefoils, quatrefoils, etc., there are now pointed trefoils, and ogee or double curved arches, shapes like daggers and shapes like the *vesica piŝcis*, and whole systems of reticulations.

94 Exeter Cathedral, nave, early fourteenth century

95 Lincoln Cathedral, the Bishop's Eye, c. 1325

133

96 Selby Abbey, east window, *c.*1325

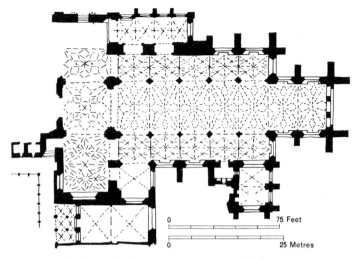

97 Bristol Cathedral, chancel, begun 1298

To study this new English flow in terms of space, one must go to one west country and one east country church: the cathedral (then abbey church) of Bristol, and the cathedral of Ely. The chancel of Bristol was begun in 1298 and built chiefly during the first quarter of the fourteenth century. It differs in four significant things from all English cathedrals of the preceding period. It is an aisled hall, not a basilica – that means that its aisles are as high as its nave, so that no clerestory exists. This type of church elevation had existed in Romanesque South-western France (see p. 80), but it had then nowhere attempted what it now does: the creation of a unified room with piers inserted, instead of the classic Gothic principle of a staggered elevation from aisle to nave. This tendency towards the unified room has its origin in the refectories and dormitories of monastic architecture and such retrochoirs as that of Salisbury.

Its introduction into the body proper of the church made the Bristol architects change, with a self-assurance remarkable at such an early date, the shapes of both piers and vaults. The composite piers – an innovation which also occurs in France, Germany, and Holland – have capitals for only a few of the minor shafts, while the

135

others run through into the vault without any caesura. As for the vaults, they have no special emphasis on the transverse arches, and appear entirely as star-shaped patterns made up of primary, secondary, and tertiary ribs, or ribs, tiercerons, and liernes, as they are called. The liernes, which – that is their definition – start from neither a springer along the wall nor from one of the main bosses, are a significant innovation, too. Moreover, to support the weight of the nave vault, which in a basilican Gothic church is conducted down by flying buttresses to the roof of the aisles and then by buttresses to ground level, the aisles are crossed at the level of the springing of their vaults by curiously ingenious and yet naïve struts

98 Bristol Cathedral, choir aisle, begun 1298

or bridges thrown across below the transverse arches. From their centres ribs sprout up to help in forming transverse pointed tunnel-vaults to abut the nave vault. The device may thus have been thought out for technical reasons: it is aesthetically most effective all the same. A classic Gothic interior is meant to affect us in two directions only: the façade-altar direction and the other, at right angles to it, which makes us see the sheets of stained glass and the tracery on the right and the left. At Bristol our eyes are lured all the time into glimpses diagonally up and across.

The same effect can be studied on a larger scale in Wells Cathedral, where in 1338 an enormous arch or strut of similar design and

99 Wells Cathedral, strainer arches of the crossing, 1338

function was placed between nave and crossing to support the crossing tower. It is grossly baffling, but undeniably impressive. At Bristol itself the cathedral architect has given a more playful version of the same spatial motifs in the small antechapel to the Berkeley Chapel. Here a flat stone ceiling is supported by arches and ribs between which all cells are left out so that one looks up towards the ceiling through a fascinating grille of lines in space. There was no structural reason for this. The master invented it entirely for the sake of pleasing confusion. Classic Gothic ribs, just like classic Gothic arches, keep strictly to the strata of space assigned to them; they never stray into others.

At Ely more than anywhere else the new attitude towards space has found an adequate form. Between 1323 and c. 1330 the crossing of the cathedral was rebuilt in the form of an octagon. The choice of this shape by the designer, who probably was Alan of Walsingham, one of the principal officials of the cathedral, can have been nothing but a deliberate attempt at breaking the thirteenth century's discipline of right angles. The diagonal axes, with their large windows and flowing tracery, destroy the precise dividing lines between nave, aisles, transepts, and choir which had been the groundwork in the

100 Ely Cathedral, Lady Chapel, 1321–49

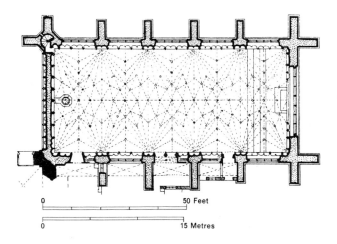

plan and elevation of a classic Gothic church. It has been argued that the glass of Amiens or the Sainte Chapelle also breaks this logicality of the earlier Middle Ages by opening the room towards a mysterious transcendental world. That is not so; the sheets of glass may give a diaphanous character to the enclosure, but it is an enclosure all the same. It does not really allow the eye to wander into dim, incomprehensible distances. The octagon of Ely has this very effect, an effect of surprise and ambiguity. The stone octagon, moreover, is crowned by one of timber taking the place of the usual square crossing tower, and this, designed by the King's Carpenter, William Herle, who was called in as a consultant, is set at an angle to the lower stone octagon, as if turned through $22\frac{1}{2}$ degrees. This, as soon as it is noticed, adds yet further to the surprises of Ely. Ely in its polygonal crossing had been preceded by Siena, where the cathedral was all but completed in 1264 and has a hexagonal crossing. The effect is as surprising as at Ely, even if it appears a little accidental, owing to the irregular placing of the crossing and the haphazard shapes of the bays and vaults surrounding it.

The Lady Chapel at Ely (1321–49) achieved the same aim by subtler and more delicate means. The rectangular chapel, isolated from the main building, as only chapter-houses usually are, has all the way round an exquisite arcading with crocketed ogee arches gathered together by larger three-dimensional or nodding ogee arches. Ogee-curved quatrefoils with seated figures fill the spandrels. The arches are covered with a luxuriant growth of vegetation, no longer as crisp as that of the thirteenth century, but, with its undulations of knobbly leaves and its intricacy of minute detail, at once more sophisticated and, strangely enough, more uniform in its general appearance. This delight in the convolutions of vegetable growth and the concealment of structure by botanical disguises went so far in one exceptional case as to convert the mullions and tracery of a whole window into a tree trunk and branches. The case is that of the Jesse Window at Dorchester, Oxfordshire, which is about contemporary with the work at Ely and Bristol. The figures of the ancestors of Christ are partly carved against the stone-carved tree, partly represented in stained glass on the panels between trunk and branch or branch and branch.

101 Ely Cathedral, Lady Chapel, 1321–49, detail

For these were decades in England which liked to mix their media and play from one into the other just as they liked in their carved foliage to glide from one form into the other instead of isolating part from part, as had been the rule in the carving of the leaves of Southwell. Now all one sees is an incessant ripple and flow, lights and shadows whisking over bossy surfaces, fascinating but far removed from the clarity of a hundred years before.

The three-dimensional ogee arch is in this connexion a motif of great significance. It does what the octagon does in Ely Cathedral, and the piers without capitals, the vaults without transverse arches, and the bridges in the aisles did in Bristol – it sets space into a motion quicker, more complicated, and less single-minded than any to be experienced in Early English churches. Its immediate forerunner in the three-dimensional treatment of a wall is the chapter-house of York Cathedral, *c.* 1290, where the seats around the walls have not blind arcades behind, as at Salisbury about fifteen years before, but are placed into tiny polygonal niches. Their forty-four times repeated projection causes a spatial ripple too slight still to be felt as breaking the continuity of the wall, but quite noticeable, once one is aware of the coming of this new tendency.

But whereas in England the new experience of space in motion expresses itself in so intricate a way, the Continent, with one or two rare exceptions, tried to achieve a similar result with opposite means. The most important exception is a church already mentioned in passing: St Urbain at Troyes. In this building, erected at the personal expense of a pope, the earliest (wholly solitary and quite insignificant) ogee arch appears, here slender circular piers carrying vaults without any interposed capitals, and here an intricate lacework of window tracery in two layers of different designs. The master of Bristol must have known Troyes. But in terms of France, Troyes is an end rather than a beginning. The choir of the Cathedral of St Nazaire at Carcassonne begun about 1270 and that of St Thibault (Côte d'Or) of the early fourteenth century are the only comparable buildings. The leading tendencies in all Continental countries were not towards space in terms of three-dimensional intricacy, but of uninterrupted breadth and plainness.

These tendencies in Spain, Germany, Italy, and France were connected chiefly with the rise of the orders of friars, the Franciscans and Dominicans (or Grey Friars and Black Friars), founded in 1209 and 1215, and spreading from 1225 onwards at a rate comparable only to those of the Cluniac and Cistercian spreads in their respective centuries. Even before 1236 El Tudense, Bishop of Tuy, could write in his *Historia:* 'At this time the Grey Friars and the Black Friars built their houses all over Spain, and in all of them, without ever ceasing, the Word of the Lord was preached.' For what characterized all friars' churches more than anything else is that they were churches for rousing sermons to be preached. Otherwise the churches of the friars were not designed to plans as standardized as those of the Cistercians. On the contrary, as early as 1252 a Dutch friar, Humbertus de Romanis, complained: 'Nos autem quot domus tot varias formas et dispositiones officinarum et ecclesiorum habemus.' But they were all large, simple, and useful, with little to suggest a specifically ecclesiastical atmosphere. They did not need much in the way of eastern chapels, as many of the friars were not priests, but they needed spacious naves to house the large congregations which came to listen to their sermons, or, to put it in the words of Pecock's *Repressor*, 'large and wyde chirchis that therebi the more multitude of persoones mowe be recevyed togitere for to have theryn prechingis'.

The friars, it is known, were the orders of the people. They scorned the secluded and leisurely existence of the other orders on their country estates, chose busy towns to settle in and there developed their sensational preaching technique as a medium of religious propaganda to a degree never attempted since the days of the Crusades. Thus all they needed was a large auditorium, a pulpit, and an altar.

Italy built the earliest of all Franciscan churches, S. Francesco in Assisi, begun in 1228, as a vaulted aisleless room with a vaulted transept and a polygonal chancel, very much on the pattern of contemporary church work in Anjou. Later the Italian Franciscans and Dominicans have aisleless halls with timber roofs and Cistercian chancels (especially in Siena), or aisled flat-roofed (S. Croce, Florence, 1294), or aisled vaulted buildings (S. Maria Novella, Florence, 1278; SS. Giovanni e Paolo, Venice, late thirteenth century; Frari, Venice, 1340). But, whether aisled or unaisled, vaulted or unvaulted, each church is always one spatial unity, with piers (often round or polygonal) merely subdividing it. In this is shown a very important new principle. In an Early or High Gothic church the nave and aisles were separate channels of parallel movement through space. Now the whole width and length of the room, thanks to the wide bays and thin supports, appears all one. The same intention led in France to the two-aisled (or two-naved, if that description is preferred) church of the Jacobins at Toulouse (*c.* 1260–

1304), and in Spain to friars' churches with a wide nave and no aisles, but chapels between the buttresses. This type appears, it seems, for the first time at St Catherine at Barcelona, begun *c.* 1243. It then became the accepted Catalan church type, even for non-monastic churches, and even where slim supports divide off aisles (Barcelona Cathedral, begun 1298), and it also influenced France, where the most impressive late-thirteenth-century church, the cathedral of Albi, can be explained only in Catalan terms.[21] It was begun in 1282 and appears from outside as a mighty compact block without any of the elaborate articulation which buttresses and flying buttresses give to classic Gothic exteriors. Inside it originally had the internal buttresses carried up to full height without the gallery or balcony put in later. The bays are narrow and the vaults quadripartite, which results in a very quick tempo from the west to the polygonal east end with its radiating chapels.

Outer plainness, whatever happened inside, is also typical of friars' churches in Germany (e.g. Erfurt) and England too. In England it was often a little relieved by a tower or spire over the bay between nave and chancel. Internally this bay was marked by solid walls to the nave and aisles as well as the chancel and chancel aisles. But in plan the whole church often formed a completely unrelieved

102 London, former church of the Greyfriars (Franciscans), begun 1306

rectangle. However, we have sadly few friars' churches to look at. Hardly any survive in their entirety, and that is probably the reason why the influence of their style on the development of the fourteenth century is generally underestimated. As to Germany, the interiors were at first aisleless as in Italy, and then, chiefly after 1300, halls, that is, churches of the same type as Bristol, with aisles of the same height as the nave. There was a long history of the hall church in Germany, going back to the Romanesque style, and in one case even to the year 1015. It may thus not be necessary to suppose connexions with the aisled halls of South-west France. Gothic halls were built directly the style had been taken over (Lilienfeld), inspired probably (as in England) by refectories and suchlike monastic rooms. The type spread during the second half of the thirteenth and the early fourteenth century. After 1350 the *Hallenkirche* became almost a matter of course. Its Golden Age was initiated by the church of the Holy Cross at Schwäbisch Gmünd, where the choir was begun in 1351. The architect was Heinrich Parler 'de Gemunden in Suebia' whose son became master mason of Prague Cathedral, the cathedral of the then capital of the Holy Roman Empire, and one of the chief centres of the new style. In Bavaria the principal master was one Hans of Landshut, usually (though erroneously) known as Hans Stethaimer. Of all the Franconian churches St Lawrence in Nuremberg makes the finest display of the possibilities of the hall church. In the form it assumed at Gmünd, at Landshut, at Nuremberg, and also in the many examples in Westphalia and the Hanseatic coast towns, it invites the eye, by means of its extremely slender round or polygonal piers, to wander off the main Gothic lines of vision, the strict west–east view and the view to the south or north into the lower aisles. Just as at Bristol diagonal vistas spread in all dimensions. Space seems to flow directionlessly around us while we walk in the church. Proof of the master builders' conscious development are the cases in which a choir in the new Late Gothic style was added without any aesthetic mediation to an earlier nave. These cases are the extreme opposite to those of Beverley Minster and Westminster Abbey in England, where fourteenth-century architects continued thirteenth-century work without any essential changes. Their architects had a style of their own which was also the style of their age, but they preferred to put it aside in these particular cases, in order to keep in conformity with a predetermined style. That is eminently English, and nothing could be more alien to the German approach as exhibited most dramatically at St Lawrence at Nuremberg in the choir, begun in 1439 to the design of Konrad Heinzelmann. Having walked along the nave in the rigidly prescribed way of the Romanesque or earlier Gothic basilica, one is startled and at once delighted by the sudden entrance into the wider and airier

103 Nuremberg, St Lawrence, choir, begun 1439 by Konrad Heinzelmann, completed by Konrad Roritzer

world of the choir where supports are slender and nave and aisles with ambulatory of equal width. The bays also are wide, and the vaults have a rich star-like configuration (as created by the English 150 years before), weighing down the vertical push of the piers. These have no capitals (again a motif of English priority), and so the streams of energy conducted upwards flow away undammed into ribs extending in all directions. Some of the latest and best German churches of this period – for instance Annaberg in Upper Saxony, the centre of a district suddenly grown very rich by finds of silver – have octagonal piers with concave sides – a particularly clear indication of the tendency to make the space of nave and aisles surge up from all directions against the stone divisions. The same type of piers occurs in Cotswold churches (Chipping Campden). Flying ribs as in the antechapel to the Berkeley Chapel at Bristol, incidentally, are also a speciality of the boldest of these Late Gothic German churches. Their first appearance is in the work of Peter Parler in the cathedral of Prague (1352, etc.).

Prague also may be the place of origin of the double-curved or three-dimensional ribs of Annaberg, another motif first to be found in England, in such early fourteenth-century work as the south aisle of St Mary Redcliffe at Bristol. The case in point at Prague is the Vladislav Hall of the Castle (cf. p. 291), built by Benedict Ried in 1487–1502, and one of the largest secular halls of the Middle Ages. The way in which the ribs grow out of the wall shafts has a decided vegetable character. No wonder that in some of these Bohemian and Upper Saxon churches shafts and ribs are replaced by the naturalistic representation of the trunks and branches of trees, yet one more motif which, as we have seen, was anticipated in England by more than 150 years.[22] Trunks and branches blend to perfection with the splintering and twirling draperies of the carved images appearing in profusion on exteriors and interiors of the Late Gothic churches of Germany. Again St Lawrence in Nuremberg is a pattern of how sculpture and architectural detail and also the wandering of the eye through space all act in concert. The magnificent stone spire of the tabernacle rises in an asymmetrical position into the vault, and the huge locket of Veit Stoss's wood-carved Annunciation hangs down, joyful and transparent, into the space in front of the altar, so that one sees it against the light of the central upper window. There are two rows of windows all the way round, and this, like the close pattern of the star-vault, adds weight to the horizontals. The contrast between plain outer walls with undecorated windows and the *Waldweben* inside is eminently characteristic of Late Gothic mentality, especially in Germany, a combination of mystical piety and sound practical sense, faith in a godly life within this world, the gathering of the ideas out of which Luther's Reformation was to grow. Luther was born before the tabernacle and the Annunciation were commissioned. The discrepancy between interiors of undulating flow, in which the individual may lose himself as between the trees of a forest, and exteriors of powerful solidity with unbroken walls and two rows of windows, heralds the mood of the German Reformation, torn between mystical introspection and a hearty new thrust into this world. Moreover, the new rooms of German Late Gothic had a practical advantage – the same as the aisleless halls of the Italian friars: they were much better suited for listening to long sermons than the old interiors with separated avenues.

However, practical considerations alone did not create the new style, nor can it be said that the spirit of the coming Reformation alone created it. For it is just as noticeable in Spain as in Germany. In Spanish architecture of the fifteenth century there was a good deal of German influence. Masters from Cologne and Nuremberg were called to Burgos and established such German motifs as star-vaults and net-vaults. But these masons and stone-carvers from the North would hardly have been so successful if there had not been an indigenous Spanish trend towards the new Late Gothic expression. The star-vaults seemed no more than a variation of the theme of the Mohammedan dome with its flying ribs forming stars of many kinds. The conciseness of the classic French cross-vaults, and indeed classic French ideals altogether, had not appealed to Spaniards. As in Germany, imitation of French Gothic is rare, and as in Germany there are wide aisles, although they are lower than the nave (that is, basilican), and side chapels between the buttresses, the feature introduced by the friars. How strong the Spanish desire for unified space was is perhaps best seen at Gerona, where the cathedral had been started in the French way with a choir, ambulatory, and radiating

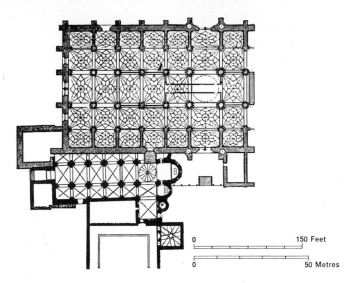

104 Salamanca Cathedral, by Juan Gil de Hontañon, begun 1512

chapels in 1312. When these eastern parts were complete, work for
some reason stopped, and it was not until 1416 that the then master-
mason, Guillermo Boffiy, suggested the adding of a new nave. His
daring suggestion was a nave, without aisles, the width of apse and
ambulatory put together. There was opposition among the cathedral
authorities, and so – a curiously modern idea – a commission was

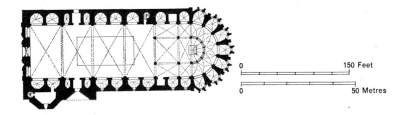

105 Gerona Cathedral, choir, begun 1312, and nave, by Guillermo Boffiy,
begun 1417

106 Gerona Cathedral, choir, begun 1312, and nave, by Guillermo Boffiy, begun 141

appointed to decide. Its members were twelve leading architects. Their answers have been preserved. Seven members were in favour of continuing the basilican scheme westward, but five were taken with Boffiy's idea. In 1417, in fact, Boffiy was commissioned to start, on his scheme. It is a masterpiece of building technique, with a clear span of 73 feet, one of the widest vaulted rooms of medieval Europe. The room is somewhat bare but it has great power, and it certainly is, with its sharp contrast of one room in the west and a system of three spatial units of staggered height and width in the east, the most convincing proof of the change of style from High to Late Gothic.

But when did the one phase end and the other begin? Our Spanish and German examples extended right through the fifteenth century, our examples from England were confined to the early years of the fourteenth. And there is indeed a notable difference between Gerona and St Lawrence in Nuremberg on the one hand and Bristol and Ely on the other. Bristol and Ely do not possess the contrast of square exterior volume and floating interior space. Nor did Britain, even at the late date of the Nuremberg choir of St Lawrence, go to such extremes. Nevertheless British architectural style shortly after Bristol and Ely changed once more and changed most signally. The change is so obvious that, while for the Continent the terms High and Late Gothic are sufficient to indicate the chief stages, in England tradition has for more than a hundred years preferred a division into three Gothic phases: Early English, Decorated, and Perpendicular. Early English was at an end when the Angel Choir was growing. Decorated is the style of Bristol and Ely. Perpendicular corresponds to what we have seen of Late Gothic in Germany and Spain, and it is a contribution of equal national vigour. Once it had been created by a few strong-minded, clear-headed architects, it brushed aside all the vagaries of Decorated and settled down to a long, none too adventurous development of plain-spoken idiom, sober and wide-awake. People have tried to connect the coming of this new style with the Black Death of 1349. This is wrong; for it is there in all its perfection as early as 1331–7 in the south transept and as early as 1337–77 in the choir of Gloucester Cathedral. The thick circular piers of the Norman choir were left standing, but with their galleries hidden behind a screen of lean uprights and

107 Gloucester Cathedral, chancel, 1337–c.

horizontals divided up into rows of panels. The east wall was opened into one huge window with, except for the few main partitions, nothing but a system of glazed panels. The number of horizontal divisions invalidates all that might have been left of the upward soar of earlier Gothic architecture. In this the same new tendency is visible as in the double row of windows in German churches. But while on the Continent the walls were made solid too, English Perpendicular walls remained glass screens. And just as thus the wall structure was less drastically changed than in Germany or Spain, so the spatial character of Perpendicular rooms returned – under renewed influence, it seems, of French buildings of about 1240 to 1330 – to the clarity of the High Gothic style. Basilican plans were only very rarely given up in favour of the spatially more promising aisled-hall plan of Bristol and Germany. The only fanciful feature in Gloucester, and indeed in many other Perpendicular parts of cathedral and abbey churches, is the decoration of the vaults. There is as much imagination displayed in them as in the German and Spanish vaults. In fact neither of these two countries, let alone France, produced anything so complicated as the schemes of Bristol and Gloucester at so early a date. On the other hand, Perpendicular vault decoration is harsher than that of Continental Late Gothic, just as Perpendicular tracery is harsher than German, Spanish, or French tracery of about 1500 (or than English tracery of 1320). The ribs of Gloucester form patterns as abstract and as angular as the matchsticks on the walls of Earl's Barton tower three hundred years before, patterns equally remote from the luxuriance of Ely, the resilience of Lincoln, and the structural logicality of classic French rib-vaults.

Of structural logicality especially there is none in Perpendicular vaults. These close-knit patterns of ribs have no longer anything to do with vault construction. The main transverse ribs and cross ribs are no longer distinguishable from the innumerable tiercerons (i.e. ribs connecting the caps of the vault shafts with points on the ridge-rib) and liernes (i.e. ribs neither springing from the vault shafts nor leading to any of the main crossings). The whole is in fact a solidly built tunnel-vault with plenty of decoration applied to it. The use of the term tunnel-vault implies that the effect of Perpendicular

108 Gloucester Cathedral, chancel vault, *c.* 1355

vaults is as much an emphasis on the horizontal, as it were, lid character as the star-vaults of Germany and Spain. This interpretation is confirmed by the general substitution in English Perpendicular exteriors of low-pitched, often parapeted roofs for the higher pitch of the twelfth and thirteenth centuries.

Gloucester is the most consistent example of the Perpendicular in English cathedrals. The naves of Winchester and Canterbury (chiefly of the later fourteenth century) are less uncompromising. In other cathedrals the late Middle Ages did little major work. To find English architecture of 1350 to 1525 at its best, one should visit not cathedrals and abbey churches, but manor-houses and parish churches for the happiest ensembles, and the royal chapels for the highest architectural standard. This change in the relative importance of buildings is due to social and historical reasons.

Taking domestic architecture first, what had happened between the age of Harlech and that of, for instance, Penshurst in Kent begun, it seems, in 1341, is that half a century of internal peace had made owners of large houses in the country give up thoughts of military defence and allow themselves more domestic comforts. The extremely compact arrangement of rooms in the earlier castles was no longer necessary. Its essentials were kept – the hall as the centre of household life, with the high-table for the lord and his family at one end, the entrance and a screened-off gangway at the other, a parlour or chamber with perhaps a solar above beyond the high-table end of the hall, and kitchen, pantry, larders, buttery, etc., on the other side of the screens – but more rooms were added and the hall itself was provided with larger windows of several lights and a bay-window at the high-table end. The grandest of surviving fourteenth-century halls is John of Gaunt's at Kenilworth, 90 by 45 feet in size. In some houses at that time a separate dining-room must already have existed. That appears from a passage in *Piers Plowman*. It means a first step towards the desertion of the hall as the living-room and dining-room of everybody, master and men. But nearly three centuries had to pass by after Penshurst had been

109 Penshurst Place, Kent, probably begun 1341

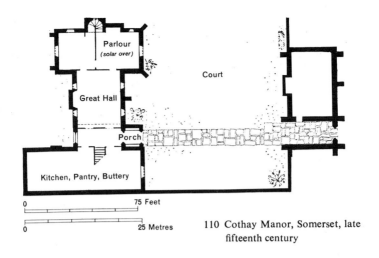

110 Cothay Manor, Somerset, late fifteenth century

designed before the hall had finally become a vestibule and nothing else.

It took nearly as long to recover the principle of symmetry for the English house which had governed the plans of Harlech and Beaumaris with such splendid success. In the fourteenth and fifteenth centuries a manor-house, or, for that matter, a *Burg* in Germany, were picturesque agglomerations of rooms. Symmetry did not go farther than that sometimes in the fifteenth and early sixteenth centuries one straight axis ran from the gatehouse to the entrance of the hall. But the hall was not the exact centre of the main block, and its entrance was eccentric anyway. The gatehouse, even when it was in the middle of the outer front, did not separate identical halves. The results of this undisturbed growth are in Britain, as well as in Germany, extremely charming. But if one enquires about strictly aesthetic qualities, they are certainly not as high as those of Harlech.

A comparison between the English cathedral of the thirteenth century and the English parish church of the fifteenth shows the same changes. They are due largely to social developments. A new class had come into its own, the class responsible for the erection of the scores of splendid parish churches in Germany and in the Netherlands, and the class to which in France the business-minded royal administrators of the William of Nogaret type, in Italy the Medici and their friends and competitors, and in Northern Germany the leaders of the Hanseatic League, belonged. In England Richard Cœur de Lion had been on the throne when Lincoln and Wells were designed, and Henry III, the Saintly King as Rome called him, ruled when Salisbury and the new Westminster Abbey were designed. Simon de Montfort, a hero of the national English cause against too papal a policy, stood up against Henry III, when the Angel Choir was added to Lincoln Cathedral. Less than a hundred years later Edward III, who was crowned in 1327 and died in 1377, accepted with pleasure the honour of membership in the London Guild of the Merchant Taylors, i.e. the cloth merchants of the City. This is an eminently revealing fact, especially if it is viewed in conjunction with commercial and industrial developments in the Netherlands, Germany, Tuscany, and Catalonia. In England the age of Edward III saw a rapid development of business enterprise. Flemish weavers were

111 Windsor Castle, St George's Chapel, begun 1481

called into the country, trade interests played a considerable part in the vicissitudes of the Hundred Years War. Vast capital was accumulated by men such as Dick Whittington and John Poulteney, whose country seat was Penshurst. In fact more of the manor-houses of the late Middle Ages were owned by merchants or their descendants than is usually realized. After the decimation of the old aristocracy caused by the Wars of the Roses, the proportion of *nouveaux riches* amongst the peers of the realm grew ever more rapidly, until in the council of sixteen whom Henry VIII named to reign for his little son not one was a peer of twelve years' standing.

Thus by 1500 the most active patrons of art were the king and the towns. The Crown had, between 1291 and about 1350, built St Stephen's Chapel in the Palace of Westminster which was burnt in 1834. Judging from surviving drawings it was a building of great importance. Then in the fifteenth century Henry VI and VII built Eton College Chapel (begun in 1441) and King's College Chapel, Cambridge (1446–1515), Henry VII and VIII St George's Chapel, Windsor Castle (begun in 1481), and Henry VIII the Chapel of Henry VII at the east end of Westminster Abbey (1503–19). They are buildings of extremely simple exteriors and plans, but with plenty of masterfully executed decoration. The contrast is especially poignant at Cambridge. To design this long, tall, narrow box of a college chapel, no spatial genius was needed. There is no differentiation at all between the nave and choir. The decoration too is repetitive, the same window tracery is used twenty-four times, and so is the panel motif for the fan-vaulting. They were rationalists, the men who designed and enjoyed these buildings, proud constructors, of a boldness not inferior to that of the Catalans. Yet they succeeded – and here we are faced with the same problem as in the contemporary German churches – in combining this practical, matter-of-fact spirit with a sense of mystery and an almost oriental effusion of ornament. Standing at the west end of the nave one can hardly think of the supreme economy with which this effect of exuberance has been attained. The fan-vault in particular helps, wherever it is used, to create an atmosphere of heavy luxuriance. Yet it is an eminently rational vault, a technician's invention, one is inclined to surmise. It originated from the vault designs of chapter-houses and their

112 Cambridge, King's College Chapel, 1446–1515

113 Cambridge, King's College Chapel, 1446–1515

development into the palm-like spread of bunches of ribs towards a heavily bossed ridge-rib in the choir (early fourteenth century) and then the nave of Exeter. That had been the spatial imagination of the Decorated at its boldest moment. Then the Perpendicular came in and systematized and solidified it all, again first at Gloucester, in the east walk of the cloisters (after 1357). By giving all ribs the same length, the same distance from each other, and the same curvature, and by applying the ubiquitous panelling to the spandrels, the palm-vault of Exeter is converted into the fan-vault of Gloucester.

To translate the fan-vault from the small scale of a cloister into the terms of the height and width of a nave was, it seems, not risked before the later fifteenth century. A little later, during the first years of the sixteenth, John Wastell, mason of Bury St Edmunds, adopted the fan-vault for King's College Chapel. The fact that he was not a King's Mason and was yet entrusted with this royal job shows how the status and the fame of the outstanding mason had risen. Yet the training of the masons still remained the same as that of, say, Villard de Honnecourt. If we take a distinguished late-fourteenth-century mason such as Henry Yevele (died 1400), Master of the King's Works of Masonry, he yet appears unquestionably still more as the successful London mason and contractor and distinguished member of his city guild than as a royal architect in the modern sense. We find his name coupled in one document with Chaucer's, in another with Dick Whittington's. So we imagine him in his stately fur-lined robes (which incidentally were part of his salary from the king), in his house by St Magnus, London Bridge, or one of his two manor-houses in Kent. Of work by him, the nave of Westminster Abbey, already mentioned because of its strange imitation of a style nearly 150 years older, and the masonry of Westminster Hall (1394–1402) survive. Such men, dignitaries of their guilds and the fraternities to which they belonged, built the town-halls and guild-halls of the cities of England, the Netherlands, the cities of the Hanseatic League, and of Italy. One has to wander through such towns as Louvain, Ypres, Malines to realize to the full the might of late medieval commerce. The most impressive of Flemish halls was the Cloth Hall at Ypres, begun in the late thirteenth century, four-square and of overwhelming dignity, but alas all but destroyed

114 Ypres, Cloth Hall, *c*. 1260–1380

during the First World War. But the later town-halls of Bruges, Ghent, Brussels, Louvain, Oudenaarde, Middelburg, and so on are less severe but equally proud. In Italy the Palazzo della Ragione at Padua (1306, etc.) is unparalleled in sheer size, the town-hall at Siena (1288–1309) in the regularity of its composition and the height of its tower, the Doge's Palace at Venice (*c*. 1345–*c*. 1365; continued along the Piazzetta between 1423 and 1438) in splendour.

As regards church building, the power of the towns appears in the

115 Venice, Doge's Palace, *c*. 1345–1438

predominance and the scale of the parish churches already referred to. Their towers are among the outstanding features of Late Gothic architecture, no longer groups of them, as befitted the balanced views of the High Gothic phase, but single towers shooting up to unprecedented heights. The tallest of all medieval spires – 630 feet – is that of Ulm Münster, a parish church. Antwerp Cathedral, with its 306 feet, was a parish church too.[23] In England Louth is 300 feet high, Boston 295. The variety of tower types in the English counties is infinite and surprising in contrast to the comparative standardization of plans and elevations – at least in churches built all at one go. Some of these cover an area larger than many a cathedral. St Mary Redcliffe at Bristol is the most spectacular of all. Prosperous small towns such as Long Melford and Lavenham and Blythburgh and Aldeburgh in Suffolk and dozens of others had parish churches in which the whole local population could assemble, and the villagers from the neighbourhood still find accommodation. York has (or had before the Second World War) twenty-one surviving medieval churches besides the Minster; Norwich still possesses thirty-two medieval parish churches.

Where existing churches were not entirely pulled down, they were enlarged, aisles were widened, naves heightened, new aisles or chapels added to the old, and the result is the picturesque, happy-go-lucky irregularity of plan and elevation of most English parish churches. However, while such churches may reflect most truly the history of their towns from the Anglo-Saxon to the Tudor age, they do not really reflect the aesthetic vision of any one period. What the fifteenth century in England desired the chief parish church of a prosperous town to look like appears in such a building as St Nicholas, King's Lynn. The church was erected as a chapel of ease from 1414 to 1419. One plan is responsible for the whole building, and that plan is as uncomplicated as those of the contemporary royal chapels. It consists of a rectangle of 162 by 70 feet, within which are comprised nave and aisles as well as aisled chancel. There is no structural articulation between west and east parts. All that interferes with the uniformity of the outline is the tower taken over from a previous building, the porch, and the slightly projecting apse. This sturdy plainness is no doubt a reflection of a change of taste

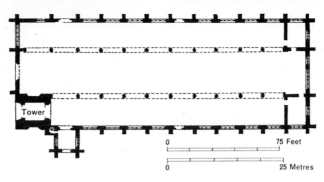

116 King's Lynn, St Nicholas, 1414–19

which the friars' architecture had brought about. It is evidently in accordance with the style of the exteriors of German churches. But inside, such churches as St Nicholas, King's Lynn, or the two parish churches of Coventry, or Holy Trinity, Hull, have nothing of the romanticism of Nuremberg. They stick to the traditional basilican elevation, piers are thin, mouldings wiry, and tracery is of the straightforward Perpendicular type. There are no corners left in mysterious semi-darkness, nor any surprising vistas. Where the fantasy of the Late Gothic designer shows itself in the English parish church is in wooden screens and wooden roofs. An almost inconceivable profusion of screens originally divided naves from choirs, aisle chapels from nave chapels, and the many guild chapels from the public spaces. The most lavishly decorated are in Devon on the one hand, in East Anglia on the other. But the greatest glory of the English parish churches is their timber roofs, roofs constructed as boldly by the carpenter as any Gothic stone vaults by masons, and looking as intricate and technically thrilling as any configuration of flying buttresses around the east end of a cathedral. There is a variety of types: the tie-beam roof, the arch-braced roof, the hammerbeam roof (used for Westminster Hall by Yevele's colleague, the King's master carpenter, Hugh Herland, in 1380), the double hammerbeam roof, and others. The most ingenious of them all is the one of the unaisled church of Needham Market, looking like a whole three-aisled building hovering over our heads without any visible support from below. The Continent has nothing to emulate these

163

118 Swaffham, Norfolk, timber roof, 1454 or later

achievements of a ship-building nation. They are, in fact, strongly reminiscent of ships' keels upside down.

Such roofs add a quality of structural richness to English churches which they would otherwise lack. However, even they, looked at in detail, appear with their hard lines of rafters, purlins, and braces sinewy, sharp, and angular – as English in fact as the ribs of Gloucester choir and the decoration of Earl's Barton tower – directly one compares them with contemporary work in France, Germany, or Spain and Portugal.

For even in France the fifteenth century had brought a belated acceptance of the principles which in England had been incorporated in the Decorated style. The power of conviction of the classic Gothic cathedrals of the thirteenth century had been such that their characteristics of proportion, of quadripartite rib-vaults, of glazed triforia, were still universally acceptable in the fourteenth and even the fifteenth century. Decoration also remained subdued and tracery essentially geometrical. The double curve and the free flow of intertwined lines which it allowed found favour late. The French term for the resulting style is Flamboyant. Early cases are an overmantel in the palace of the dukes of Burgundy at Dijon and the glorious openwork screen at the dais end of the Duke of Berry's great hall at Poitiers, both of the late fourteenth century, i.e. two to three generations later than the time when similar forms were the rage in England. Whether France received inspiration from England remains a moot point. The largest number of major displays of the Flamboyant style are to be found in Normandy and the adjoining regions, but there are outstanding Flamboyant façades also in other parts of France (Vendôme), and screens and suchlike decorative pieces have their proud, exuberant Flamboyant ornament everywhere. Spatially the French contribution is negligible. La Chaise Dieu is a hall-church begun c. 1342. The east end of St Séverin in Paris of 1489–94 is also of hall type. In it one finds a concave-sided

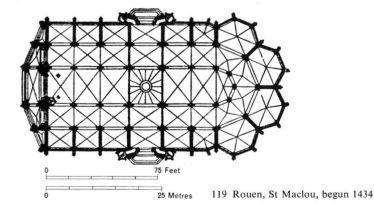

0   75 Feet

0   25 Metres   119 Rouen, St Maclou, begun 1434

pier, and even a twisted pier just as in some Late Gothic German hall-churches. The façade of St Maclou at Rouen added in 1500–14 to a church begun in 1434 has a truly Late Gothic canted shape introducing diagonals into the classic parallelism of the three portals. But even here the east end still has its ambulatory and its radiating chapels, as has indeed St Séverin.

As for Spain, the briefest comparison between an English parish church or even King's College Chapel and, say, the decoration of the front of the church of St Paul's at Valladolid (begun shortly after 1486, probably by Simon of Cologne) is enough to realize the contrast between English restraint and Spanish extremism. Substitute the St Lawrence portal of Strassburg Cathedral for Valladolid,

120 Valladolid, St Paul, west front, begun by Simon of Cologne (?) after 1486

121 Strassburg Cathedral, Portal of St Lawrence, *c.* 1495

and you will see Anglo-German contrasts as glaringly. It might be said that German Late Gothic decoration is as extreme as Spanish, which would not be surprising, since Germany and Spain, as against France, England, Italy, are the countries of the extremes in European civilization. However, there are obvious differences between the Spanish and the German ways of decorating. Ever since Mohammedan days Spain has had a passion for filling large surfaces with close-knit two-dimensional ornament. The Germans share this *horror vacui*, but there is always a marked spatial curiosity in their ornament. That connects German Late Gothic with German Rococo, just as the flatness and the frantic movement of the Charter-house vestry at Granada, which dates from the middle of the eighteenth century (see p. 258), seems heralded in the details of the Valladolid façade. Valladolid has no dominant motifs. The figure sculpture is petty in scale. Ogee arches and 'Tudor' arches (i.e. depressed pointed arches) follow each other. The background is patterned from top to bottom, and the patterns change with every string course. There is something of a thistly undergrowth about this ensemble which makes English Perpendicular appear strong and pure. There can be no question which of the two countries would open itself to Puritanism and which would become the stronghold of Baroque Catholicism.

The high-water mark, however, of Late Gothic frenzy was reached in Portugal during the spectacularly prosperous age of King Manuel I (1495–1521). Manueline decoration in such places as Batalha and Tomar is outrageously rich, a rank growth of forms, sometimes taken, it seems, from crustacean organisms, sometimes from tropical vegetation. Much Portuguese decoration was inspired by Spain and France, but here the architecture of India, Portuguese India, is the only parallel that comes to mind. If this connexion is real it is the first instance in Western history of non-European influence on European architecture.

However, no influence can ever act unless the one party is ready to receive the message of the other. If the countries of the Pyrenean Peninsula had not already been possessed by a passion for overdone decoration, the art of the colonies would have remained mute to them. When the Indies became Dutch, their style did indeed after a time begin to influence the furniture of Holland and helped to give it its peculiar Baroque opulence, but architects wisely kept away from it. The Dutchmen of the seventeenth century could never have made of it what the Portuguese could, at that particular moment, the moment just before the ornamental imagination of the late Middle Ages was harnessed into the Renaissance yoke.

The Renaissance on the other hand could never have been conceived in a country which had as recklessly indulged in ornamental vagaries as Spain and Portugal, or as daringly explored spatial mysteries as Germany. In Italy there thus exists no Late Gothic style at all except for the special case of Milan Cathedral, begun in 1387, which is in the north of the country and was visited and

considered by numerous, even if unsuccessful, French and German experts. This absence of the Late Gothic from the central – architecturally central – regions of Italy is the most striking illustration of the fact that by the fifteenth century the present natural divisions of Europe were more or less established. The Romanesque style had been international, though regionally subdivided, just as the Holy Roman Empire and the Church of the eleventh and twelfth centuries had been international forces. Then, in the thirteenth century, France became a nation and created the Gothic style.

Germany went through the crisis of the Interregnum and decided on a national, as against the previous international, policy. The same decision was taken at the same time in England, while in Italy, a wholly different development of many small town-states set in. Gothic came into Germany, Spain, England, and Italy as a French fashion. Cistercian monasteries first, and then Cologne, Burgos and León, Canterbury, and Frederick II's Castel del Monte (see p. 124) followed it closely. But already in Frederick II's Italian buildings there appear purely antique pediments side by side with the novel rib-vaults of France. The appreciative treatment of Roman motifs in Frederick II's Capua Gate is unparalleled anywhere in the North, and in the South only by Nicolò Pisano's pulpits. Nicolò Pisano was the first of the great Italian sculptors, the first in whose work the Italian character dominates over international conventions. His transformation of the current style in sculpture into something more static and more harmonious was paralleled by similar transformations of Gothic architecture. The role of the friars in this transformation has been mentioned. There is no *excelsior* in their wide, airy, aisleless halls. The large ones with aisles, such as S. Maria Novella and S. Croce in Florence, have such wide arcades and such shallow aisles that the static nature of the rooms is hardly disturbed. The cathedral of Florence – a cathedral, but built under the supervision of the guild of the wool merchants 'in honour of the Commune and people of Florence' – belongs to the same family. Its piers with their substantial bases and heavy capitals do not point upward. The uninterrupted cornice provides a strong horizontal division. The cross-vaults are dome-shaped, and clearly isolate bay from bay. Clarity is also the expression of the dark structural members against the whitewashed surfaces of walls and vaults.

Clarity is helped moreover by the composition of the east parts, a central composition with a crossing the width of nave and aisles (as at Ely) and with transepts and chancel of identical shape (five sides of an octagon) and no ambulatories or chapels. This monumental, spacious and unmysterious effect was planned by the first architect, Arnolfo di Cambio, who began the building in 1296, and taken up on a yet more monumental scale by a group of artists including the painters Taddeo Gaddi and Andrea da Firenze, called in as consultants, and finally modified and executed by Francesco Talenti after 1367.

To a traveller coming from the north such Italian interiors of the fourteenth century must have appeared wonderfully calm and serene. It was only here – this will now be appreciated – that the style of the Renaissance could be conceived, here, in the land of Roman traditions, of sun, blue sea, and noble hills, of vineyards and olive plantations, of pine groves, cedars, and cypress trees.

123 Florence Cathedral, nave begun by Arnolfo di Cambio, 1296, consecrated 1436

5 Renaissance and Mannerism

c. 1420–*c*. 1600

The Gothic style was created for Suger, Abbot of St Denis, counsellor of two kings of France, the Renaissance for the merchants of Florence, bankers to the kings of Europe. It is in the atmosphere of the most prosperous of Southern trading republics that about 1420 the new style emerged. A firm such as that of the Medici had its representatives in London, in Bruges and Ghent, in Lyons and Avignon, in Milan and Venice. A Medici had been Mayor of Florence in 1296, another in 1376, yet another in 1421. In 1429 Cosimo Medici became senior partner of the firm. Just over one hundred years later another Medici was created the first Duke of Tuscany. But Cosimo, whom they called in Florence the Father of the Fatherland, and his grandson Lorenzo the Magnificent, were only citizens, not even, by any official title, the first of their city. To these and the other princely merchants, the Pitti, the Rucellai, the Strozzi, it is due that the Renaissance was at once wholeheartedly accepted in Florence and developed with a wonderful unanimity of purpose for thirty or forty years, before other cities of Italy, let alone foreign countries, had grown to understand its meaning. This pre-disposition of Tuscany cannot be explained by social conditions alone. The cities of Flanders in the fifteenth century were socially of quite a comparable structure; so up to a point was the City of London. Yet the style in the Netherlands was a flamboyant Late Gothic; in England it was Perpendicular. In Florence what happened was that a particular social situation coincided with a particular nature of country and people, and a particular historical tradition. The geographical and national character of the Tuscans had found its earliest expression in Etruscan art. It was again clearly noticeable in the eleventh and twelfth centuries in the crisp and graceful façade of S. Miniato, and in the fourteenth in the spacious, happily airy Gothic churches of S. Croce, S. Maria Novella, and the cathedral of S. Maria del Fiore. Now a flourishing trading republic will tend to worldly ideals, not to the transcendental; to the active, not to meditation; to clarity, not to the obscure. And since the climate was clear, keen, and salutary, and the people's minds were clear, keen, and proud, it was here that the clear, proud, and worldly spirit of Roman Antiquity could be rediscovered, that its contrast with Christian faith did not bar its way, that its attitude to physical beauty in the fine arts and beauty of proportion in architecture found an echo, that its grandeur and its humanity were understood. The fragments of the Roman past in art and literature had been there all the time, and had never been entirely forgotten. But only the fourteenth century reached a point that made a cult of the Antique possible. Petrarch – the first Poet Laureate of modern times, crowned on the Capitol in 1341 – was a Tuscan; so was Boccaccio, so was Leonardo Bruni who translated Plato. And as the Medici honoured the philosophers and called them into their innermost circle, as they honoured the poets and wrote poetry themselves, so they regarded the artists in a spirit quite different from that of the Middle Ages. The modern conception of the artist and the respect due to his genius is again of Tuscan origin.

Seven years before Petrarch was crowned in Rome, the civic authorities responsible for the appointment of a new master-mason to the cathedral and city of Florence decided to elect Giotto, the painter, because they were convinced that the city architect should be a 'famous man' above all. So for the sole reason that they believed that 'in the whole world no one better could be found in this and many other things' than Giotto, they chose him, although he was not a mason at all. About sixty years later, as we have seen, two painters were among the experts called in to decide on the plans for the completion of Florence Cathedral. These events mark the beginning of a new period in the professional history of architecture, just as Petrarch's crowning marks a new period in the history of the social status of authors. Henceforth – this is especially characteristic of the Renaissance – great architects were not usually architects by training. And henceforth great artists were honoured and admitted into positions outside their craft simply because they were great artists. Cosimo Medici is probably the first who called a painter, in recognition of his genius, divine. Later this became the attribute universally given to Michelangelo. And he, sculptor, painter, and architect, a fanatical worker and a man who never spared himself, was deeply convinced that it was his due. When he felt slighted by some of the pope's servants in an anteroom of the Vatican, he fled from Rome, deserting his post without hesitation and leaving a message that the pope could look for him elsewhere, if he wanted him. Leonardo da Vinci at the time when this happened evolved the theory of the ideal nature of art. He endeavoured to prove that painting and architecture were of the liberal arts, not arts in the trade sense of the Middle Ages. There are two sides to this theory. It demands from the patron a new attitude towards the artist, but also from the artist a new attitude towards his work. Only the artist who approached his art in an academic spirit, that is, as a seeker

124 Florence, Foundling Hospital, begun by Brunelleschi, 1421, completed in 1445

after law, had a right to be regarded as their equal by the scholars and authors of humanism.

Leonardo has not much to say about Antiquity. But the universal fascination of Antiquity was evidently both aesthetic and social, aesthetic in so far as the forms of Roman architecture and decoration appealed to artists and patrons of the fifteenth century, social in so far as the study of the Roman past was accessible to the educated only. So the artist and architect who until then had been satisfied with learning their craft from their masters and developing it according to tradition and their powers of imagination, now devoted their attention to the art of Antiquity, not only because it enchanted them but also because it conferred social distinction on them. So strongly had this revival impressed the scholars from the sixteenth to the nineteenth century that they called the whole period that of rebirth, *rinascita* or Renaissance. Early writers by using this term meant the rebirth of art and letters in quite a general sense. But in the nineteenth century – a century of unlimited period revival – the emphasis was laid on the imitation of Roman forms and motifs. In re-examining the works of the Renaissance today, one must, however, ask oneself whether the new attitude towards Antiquity is really their essential innovation.

The very first building in Renaissance forms is Filippo Brunelleschi's Foundling Hospital, begun in 1421. Brunelleschi (1377–1446) was a goldsmith by training. Yet he had been chosen to complete the cathedral of Florence by adding the dome over the crossing, a masterpiece of construction and of a shape distinctly Gothic in character. At the same time, however, he designed the Foundling façade, a work of a completely different kind, consisting of a colonnade on the ground floor with delicate Corinthian columns and wide semicircular arches letting enough sun and warmth penetrate into the loggia, and a first floor with generously spaced moderately sized rectangular windows under shallow pediments corresponding exactly to the arches beneath. Medallions in coloured terracotta by Andrea della Robbia – the famous babes in swaddling clothes sold in cheap copies of all sizes by the souvenir-dealers of Florence – are placed into the spandrels of the arcade. A subtly scaled architrave divides ground floor from first floor. Now the pediments over the windows are certainly a Roman motif. So seem to be the Corinthian columns. But arches on such slender columns are really in their expression just as different from those of, say, the Colosseum, as they are from any Gothic arcades. Their source and that of several other motifs of the façade is the Tuscan Proto-Renaissance of S. Miniato, SS. Apostoli, and the Baptistery, i.e. the architecture of Florence in the eleventh and twelfth centuries, and nothing else. This is an eminently significant fact. The Tuscans, unconsciously of course, prepared themselves for the reception of the Roman style by first going back to their own Romanesque Proto-Renaissance.

The relation of Brunelleschi's churches to the past is very similar. S. Spirito, which he designed in 1436, is a basilica with round-headed arcades and a flat roof; Romanesque, one can say, in these general characteristics. The bases and capitals of the Corinthian columns, on the other hand, and the fragments of an entablature above are Roman, rendered with a correctness and understanding of their vigorous beauty that were beyond the power of the architects of the Proto-Renaissance. The curious niches of the aisles are also

125 Florence, S. Spirito, by Brunelleschi, designed 1436

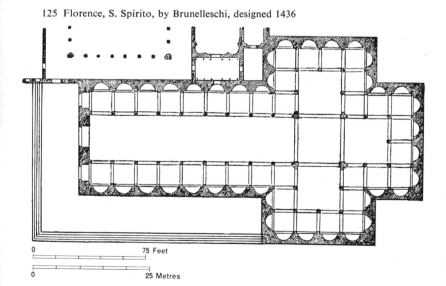

126 Florence, S. Spirito, by Brunelleschi, designed 143

Roman, though treated in a very original way. But while the motifs mentioned so far can be traced back to the Middle Ages or Antiquity, the spatial expression created with their aid is wholly new and has all the serenity of the Early Renaissance. The nave is just twice as high as it is wide. Ground floor and clerestory are of equal height. The aisles have square bays, again half as wide as they are high. The nave consists of exactly four and a half squares, and the odd half was intended to be disposed of in a special way to be mentioned presently. Walking through the church, one may not at once consciously register all these proportions, but they contribute all the same decisively to the effect of serene order which the interior produces. It is difficult today to imagine the enthusiasm of the Early Renaissance for such simple mathematical relations in space. One must remember in order to appreciate it that at that very moment – about 1425 – painters in Florence discovered the laws of perspective. Just as they had no longer been satisfied with an arbitrary presentation of the space inside their pictures, so architects were now anxious to find rational proportions for their buildings. The effort of the fifteenth century to master space is comparable only with that of our own age, although that of the Renaissance concerned an ideal world and ours a material. The invention of printing towards the middle of the century proved a most powerful conquest of space. The discovery of America towards its end produced results nearly as important. Both must be named with the discovery of perspective as aspects of Western space enthusiasm, an attitude utterly alien to Antiquity, and one to which attention has already been drawn more than once in this book.

The feature of S. Spirito most important in this connexion is the ground plan of its eastern parts. For here Brunelleschi, following in the footsteps of Arnolfo di Cambio and Francesco Talenti, has departed decisively from the normal composition of Romanesque or Gothic churches. The way in which he made the transepts exactly identical with the choir, ran an aisle round all three, and placed a dome over the crossing makes us feel, looking eastward, as if we were in a centrally planned building, a type usual in Roman architecture, both religious and secular, but, in spite of Florence Cathedral and a few others, very rare in medieval Christian churches.

Even the west end was intended to be finished in a way stressing this centralizing tendency at the expense of practical advantages. Brunelleschi had originally meant to continue the aisle round the west as round the east, north, and south ends. He would then have had to put in four instead of the customary three entrances, to comply with the four bays of aisle along the inner side of the façade. It would all have been exceedingly unusual – a sacrifice to aesthetic consistency and the desire for centralization. Indeed, during the very year in which S. Spirito was begun, Brunelleschi had designed a completely central church, the first of the Renaissance. It is S. Maria degli Angeli. After three years, in 1437, the building was discontinued and only ground-floor walls now remain. But we can read

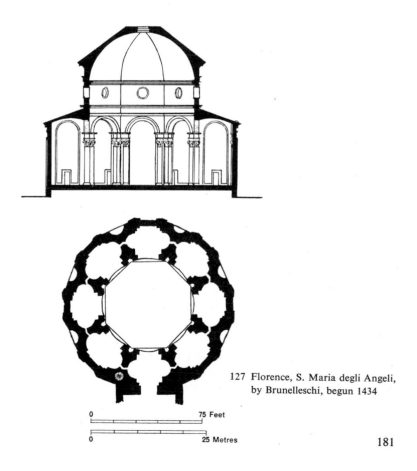

127 Florence, S. Maria degli Angeli, by Brunelleschi, begun 1434

0   75 Feet

0   25 Metres

181

the plan, and compare it with reliable engravings taken, it seems, from lost original drawings. S. Maria degli Angeli was to be wholly Roman in character and very massive, the outcome no doubt of a long stay of Brunelleschi in Rome to which we can with a good deal of certainty assign the date 1433. The light, slim columns of the other buildings are here replaced by pilasters attached to solid piers at the eight corners of the octagon. Eight chapels surround it, each with niches hollowed out into the thickness of the walls. The dome also was to be of one piece inside and out like a Roman dome and not on the Gothic principle of an outer and a separate inner shell, still applied by Brunelleschi to Florence Cathedral. Of Romanesque or Proto-Renaissance connexions there are here none left. What Roman building in particular inspired Brunelleschi we can no longer say. There were plenty of remains still in existence in the fifteenth century and drawn by architects, which have now disappeared.

However, one more central building, or rather part of a building, was begun shortly after S. Maria degli Angeli and completed, and this is a direct copy of an existing Roman monument. Michelozzo di Bartolommeo (1396–1472) began in 1444 to add to the medieval church of the SS. Annunziata a round east end with eight chapels or niches exactly as he had seen it done in the so-called temple of Minerva Medica in Rome. So while in the early works of Brunelleschi we cannot emphasize too much the independence of the new forms from those of Roman Antiquity, the discovery of how much could be learned from Rome to satisfy topical aesthetic needs came as early as the thirties and forties. That it appears most clearly in centrally planned buildings is eminently characteristic. For a central plan is not an other-worldly, but a this-worldly conception. The prime function of the medieval church had been to lead the faithful to the altar. In a completely centralized building no such movement is possible. The building has its full effect only when it is looked at from the one focal point. There the spectator must stand and, by standing there, he becomes himself 'the measure of all things'. Thus the religious meaning of the church is replaced by a human one. Man is in the church no longer pressing forward to reach a transcendental goal, but enjoying the beauty that surrounds him and the glorious sensation of being the centre of this beauty.

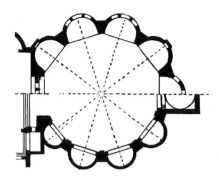

128 Rome, Temple of Minerva Medica, *c.* 250 (*top*), Florence, SS. Annunziata, east end, by Michelozzo, 1444 (*bottom*)

No more telling symbol could have been conceived for the new attitude of the humanists and their patrons to Man and religion. Pico della Mirandola, one of the most interesting of the philosophers round Lorenzo the Magnificent, delivered an address in 1486 on *The Dignity of Man*. Machiavelli, a little later, wrote his book *The Prince* to glorify the power of Man's will, and set it as the prime moving force against the powers of religion that had up to his time interfered with practical thought. And again a little later Count Castiglione composed his *Courtier* to show his contemporaries their ideal of universal man. The courtier, he says, should be agreeable in his manners, graceful, a good *causeur*, and a good dancer, yet strong and fit, well versed in the pursuits of chivalry, riding, fencing, and jousting. At the same time he should read poetry and history, be acquainted with Plato and Aristotle, understand all the arts, and practise music and drawing. Leonardo da Vinci was the first amongst artists to live up to this ideal: painter, architect, engineer, and musician, one of the most ingenious scientists of his time, and enchanting in his personal ways. Only Christianity apparently did not occupy his mind at all. Lorenzo Valla, a Roman humanist, somewhat earlier had published his dialogue *De voluptate*, in which he openly praised the pleasures of the senses. The same Valla proved with a philological sagacity unknown before the rise of Humanism that the so-called Donation of Constantine, the document on which all papal claims to worldly domination rested, was faked. Yet he died a canon of the Lateran Cathedral in Rome. The philosophers of Florence founded an academy on Plato's model, kept Plato's supposed birthday as a holiday, and preached a semi-Greek, semi-Christian religion in which Christ's love is mixed up with Plato's principle of divine love that makes us pine for beauty of soul and body in human beings. On one of the frescoes in the choir of S. Maria Novella an inscription can be read stating that the frescoes were completed in 1490, 'when this loveliest of lands distinguished in riches, victories, arts and buildings enjoyed plenty, health, and peace'. About the same time Lorenzo the Magnificent wrote his most famous poem, which begins as follows:

> Quant'è bella giovinezza,
> Che si fugge tuttavia.
> Chi vuol esser lieto sia;
> Di doman' non c'è certezza.

The lines are well known, and rightly so. They are here quoted in Italian, because they should be remembered in all their original melodiousness. Literally translated they mean:

> How lovely is youth,
> But it flies from us.
> If you want to be happy, be happy now;
> There is no certainty of tomorrow.

Now these men, if they built a church, did not want to be reminded by its appearance of that uncertain tomorrow and of what might come after this life had ended. They wanted architecture to eternalize the present. So they commissioned churches as temples to their own glory. The eastern rotunda of the Annunziata was intended to be a memorial in Florence to the Gonzaga, rulers of Mantua. At the same time Francesco Sforza of Milan seems to have thought of such a temple. A record of what was intended survives in a medal of about 1460 by the sculptor Sperandio. It seems to represent a building of perfectly symmetrical plan: a Greek cross (for the term see p. 81) to be covered with five domes, just as Périgueux and St Mark's in Venice had been three or four hundred years before. The

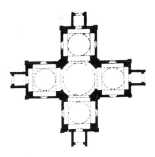

129 Reconstruction of the plan of the Sforza Chapel, Milan, from Sperandio's medal of *c*.1460

design may be due to that mysterious Florentine sculptor and architect Antonio Filarete (died about 1470) who worked for Francesco Sforza from 1451 to 1465. His fame now rests mainly on the Milan hospital, the Ospedale Maggiore, which was begun in 1457, a vast enterprise not carried on in elevation to his designs, though in plan. The plan is remarkable in that it appears the first of those large symmetrical piles with many inner courtyards – nine at Milan – taken up in the sixteenth and seventeenth centuries for such royal schemes as the Escorial, the Tuileries, and Whitehall.

But Filarete's ambitions were for planning on a yet grander scale. He wrote a treatise on architecture, dedicated in different copies to Francesco Sforza and to one of the Medici of Florence, where the architect returned when he left Milan. Perhaps the most interesting part of the treatise is the description of an ideal town, Sforzinda; for this is the first wholly symmetrical town plan in Western history, a regular octagon with radial streets and with palace and cathedral on the square in the centre – again the central obsession of this first century liberated from the ties of medieval authority. Thus it is not surprising to find that the churches of Sforzinda, of Zagalia (another town drawn up in the treatise), and of the hospital – this church was never built either – were meant to be of central plan. They introduce us to yet more varieties. Sforzinda and the Hospital are square with a central dome and subsidiary little domed chapels in the four corners – a plan whose Early Christian antecedents and later Byzantine popularity have been discussed earlier on. At Milan it had

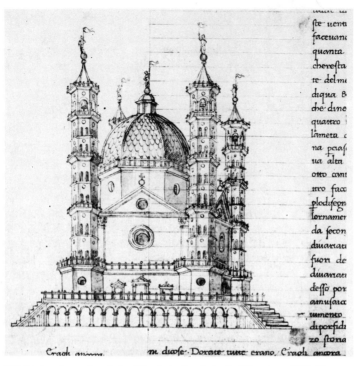

ste ueni
faceuani
quanta
chere fta
te del mi
diqua B
che dine
quattro
lameta c
na paaʃ
ua alta
otto coni
uro facc
plodifegn
tornamer
da fecon
diuariati
fuon de
diuariari
deʃʃo por
anuʃaa
umento
diporfidi
zo ftona

Craoh anima.   m. diuoʃe · Dorme uune erano, Craoh ancora.

130 Design for a church for Sforzinda, by Antonio Filarete, c. 1455–60

131 Projected chapel for the Ospedale Maggiore, Milan, by Filarete, c. 1455

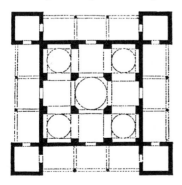

186

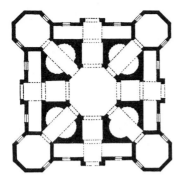

appeared in the Chapel of the Holy Sepulchre at S. Satiro in 876. In Tuscany also it must have been known; for Michelozzo used it in 1452 at S. Maria delle Grazie at Pistoia. So Filarete may have been inspired by Tuscany as well as Milan. Zagalia has an octagonal central dome and octagonal chapels in the corners. All three churches were to be provided with four fantastically tall minarets over the four corner chapels, or somewhere between them and the centre (for the drawings are ambiguous in this).[24] A chapel actually built at S. Eustorgio in Milan in 1462 to Michelozzo's designs is square and domed and has little turrets on the four corners, but no chapels below. Michelozzo also designed a palace for the Medici Bank at Milan. It was begun in the forms of the Florentine Renaissance, but continued with the more irresponsible detail of the North Italian Gothic. The same happened to the hospital.

Evidently the Lombards were not yet capable of an understanding of the Renaissance. The cathedral of Milan was carried on in a flamboyant Late Gothic right through the fifteenth century. Similarly in Venice the Porta della Carta of the Doge's Palace and the Cà d'Oro belong to the 1430s and 1440s, and the first serious Renaissance structures were begun only after 1455 (Arsenal Gate, 1457, etc., Cà del Duca). In style they are Tuscan, just as Michelozzo and Filarete designed in the Tuscan style in Milan, and as the greatest of all Quattrocento architects and the one to spread the style among the art-loving and self-glorifying minor rulers of Northern Italy was Tuscan.

Leone Battista Alberti (1404–72) came from a patrician Florentine family. In our context he represents yet a new type of architect. Brunelleschi and Michelangelo are sculptor-architects, Giotto and Leonardo da Vinci painter-architects. Alberti is the first of the great dilettante-architects, a man in whose life and thoughts art and architecture played just that part which it should play according to Count Castiglione's (much later) treatise. Alberti was a brilliant horseman and athlete – it is recorded that he could jump over a man's head with his two feet close together – his witty conversation was famous, he wrote plays and composed music, he painted and studied physics and mathematics, he was an expert on law, and his books deal with domestic economy as well as with painting and architecture. Alberti's *Della Pittura* is the first book to look at the art of painting with a Renaissance spirit. The whole of the first part deals with geometry and perspective exclusively. The *Ten Books of Architecture* are written in Latin and modelled on Vitruvius, the newly rediscovered Roman writer on architecture. They prove that, while he was working in Rome as a member of the Papal civil service, he had plenty of time to study the ruins of Antiquity. It is also evident that his job allowed him to travel freely and stay away from Rome for long periods.

Before the coming of the Renaissance such a man could hardly have taken an active, constructive interest in building. But as soon as the essence of architecture was considered to be philosophy and mathematics (the divine laws of order and proportion) and archaeology (the monuments of Antiquity), the theoretician and dilettante was bound to assume a new significance. Roman architecture, both system and details, must be studied and drawn to be learnt; and the system behind the styles of Antiquity was soon – with the help of Vitruvius – found to lie in the orders, i.e. the proportions belonging to the Doric, Ionic, Corinthian, Composite, and Tuscan columns and entablatures. By means of books on the orders foreign countries were taught the rules of classical building.

But Alberti was not a dry theorist. In him the spirit of the scholar lived in a rare and happy union with genuine imaginative and creative powers. The front of S. Francesco in Rimini, begun in 1446 but never completed, is the first in Europe to adapt the composition of the Roman triumphal arch to church architecture. So Alberti was much more serious than Brunelleschi in reviving the Antique. And he did not confine himself to motifs. The side of the church, opened in seven round-headed niches with heavy piers dividing them, has perhaps more of the gravity of Flavian Rome than any other building of the fifteenth century. Now these niches hold sarçophagi, the monuments of the humanists of Sigismondo Malatesta's court. For the east end apparently a large dome was projected, as dominating as that of the Annunziata in Florence, and again as a monument to the glory of Sigismondo and his Isotta. Sigismondo was a typical Renaissance tyrant, unscrupulous and cruel but sincerely fascinated by the new learning and the new art. The church of S. Francesco is in fact known under the name of the Temple of the Malatesta; and on its façade an inscription runs in large letters with Sigismondo's name and the date – nothing else. Compare this inscription with that above the medieval church of St Hubert at Troyes: 'Non nobis,

133 Rimini, S. Francesco (Tempio Malatestiano), façade, begun by Alberti, 1446

134 Rimini, S. Francesco, south side

135 Florence, Palazzo Medici, by Michelozzo, begun 1444

Domine, non nobis, sed nomini tuo da gloriam' – and you have the quintessence of the change from the one age to the other.

The same pride as that of Sigismondo Malatesta is exhibited by Giovanni Rucellai, a merchant of Florence for whom Alberti designed the second of his church fronts. Again his name appears over-conspicuously on the façade of S. Maria Novella, and when in his old age he wrote an account of his life he said of the architectural and decorative work he had commissioned for the churches of his beloved native town: 'All these things have given me, and are giving me, the greatest satisfaction and the sweetest feelings. For they do honour to the Lord, to Florence, and to my own memory.' It is this attitude that made it possible for the donors of the frescoes inside the choir of the same church to appear life-size in the costumes of the day as if they were actors in the sacred stories. It is this attitude also that made the patricians of Florence – and the cardinals of Rome – build their Renaissance palaces. That of the Medici begun by Michelozzo in 1444 was the first. The most famous are that of the Pitti, designed, some say by Brunelleschi shortly before he died in 1446, some by Alberti about 1458, and considerably enlarged a century later, and that of the Strozzi. Concerning the latter, the

Ricordo di Lorenzo Strozzi says of Filippo Strozzi, his father, who built the palace, that: 'Having richly provided for his heirs and being eager for fame more than wealth and having no safer means of his person being remembered, (he) decided to build a building that should bring renown to himself and his family.' These Tuscan Quattrocento palaces are massive yet orderly, faced with heavily rusticated blocks and crowned by bold cornices. Their windows, symmetrically placed, are divided into two by graceful columns (a Romanesque motif again). What one expects of Renaissance delicacy and articulation is to be found chiefly in their inner courtyards. There the ground floors are opened as cloisters with the graceful arcades of the Foundling Hospital and S. Spirito, and the upper floors are also enlivened by an open gallery of pilasters dividing the walls into separate bays, or some such feature.

Only in Rome was a severer treatment of courtyards evolved. It appears first in the Palazzo Venezia and there dates from *c*. 1465–70. It is derived from the classic Roman motif of columns attached to solid piers, the motif of the Colosseum and also of the front of Alberti's S. Francesco in Rimini. Maybe it was he who suggested its resuscitation in Rome, though his name cannot be documentarily connected with the Palazzo Venezia. A most attractive compromise between the Florentine and the Roman systems appears in the Ducal Palace at Urbino, another of the architecturally and altogether aesthetically most enterprising smaller courts of Italy. Here Piero della Francesca worked, the painter in whose architectural settings Alberti's spirit is so clearly reflected, and here Alberti must have appeared on his journeys. Here, moreover, we find in the 1460s Francesco di Giorgio, one of the most interesting later Quattrocento architects and one whose name will have to be mentioned in other connexions again later. But the design of the courtyard and the delightful decoration inside the palace is probably due not to him, but to Luciano Laurana, who worked at Urbino between 1466 and his death in 1479. The courtyard preserves the airy lightness of the Florentine arcades, but strengthens the corners by pilasters. Once the effect of this motif has been noticed, it makes Michelozzo's and his followers' uninterrupted sequence of columns and arches look unstable and uncomfortable. The courtyard of the Palazzo Venezia

136 Urbino, Palazzo Ducale, courtyard, by Luciano Laurana (?), *c.* 1470–5

in Rome, on the other hand, appears heavy-handed in comparison with Laurana's happy balance of motifs.

Alberti himself designed one palace in Florence, the Palazzo Rucellai, begun in 1446 for the same patron as the façade of S. Maria Novella. The courtyard here has no emphasis, but Alberti used pilasters in the façade and thereby introduced a splendid new means for articulating a wall.[25] There are three superimposed orders of pilasters with a free Doric treatment on the ground floor, a free Ionic on the first floor, and Corinthian on the top.

While these pilasters divide the front vertically, sensitively designed cornices emphasize the horizontal divisions. The top cornice is probably the earliest in Florence, earlier even than that of Michelozzo's Palazzo Medici. Before then projecting eaves in the medieval way had been used. The windows of the Palazzo Rucellai are bipartite as in the other palaces, but an architrave separates the

137 Florence, Palazzo Rucellai, by Alberti, built in 1446–5!

main rectangle from the two round heads. The relation of height to width in the rectangular parts of the windows is equal to the relation of height to width in the bays. Thus the position of every detail seems to be determined. No shifting is possible. In this lies, according to Alberti's theoretical writings, the very essence of beauty, which he defines as 'the harmony and concord of all the parts achieved in such a manner that nothing could be added or taken away or altered except for the worse'.

Such definitions make one feel the contrast of Renaissance and Gothic most sharply. In Gothic architecture the sensation of growth is predominant everywhere. The height of piers is not ruled by the width of bays, nor the depth of a capital, or rather a cap, by the height of the pier. The addition of chapels or even aisles to parish churches is much less likely to spoil the whole than in a Renaissance building. For in the Gothic style motif follows motif, as branch follows branch up a tree.

One could not imagine a donor in the fourteenth century decreeing, as Pope Pius II did when rebuilding the cathedral of his native town (renamed Pienza to perpetuate his name), that no one should ever erect sepulchral monuments in the church or found new altars, or have wall-paintings executed, or add chapels, or alter the colour of walls or piers. For a Gothic building is never complete in that sense. It remains a live being influenced in its destiny by the piety of generation after generation. And as its beginning and end are not fixed in time, so they are not in space. In the Renaissance style the building is an aesthetic whole consisting of self-sufficient parts. A composition in the flat or in space is arrived at by grouping such parts according to a static system.

Now the Romanesque style is – as has been shown – also a static style. It is also a style in which the adding of clearly defined spatial units is essential. How then can the difference in principle be formulated between a Norman and a Renaissance church? Walls are equally important in both, whereas the Gothic style always endeavours to invalidate them. But a Romanesque wall is primarily inert. If it is ornamented, the exact place where decoration is applied seems arbitrary. One hardly ever feels that a little more or a little less ornament, or ornament shifted to a slightly higher or slightly lower position, would make a decisive difference. In the Renaissance building this is not so. The walls appear active, enlivened by the decorative elements which in their sizes and arrangement follow laws of human reasoning. It is ultimately this humanizing that makes a Renaissance building what it is. Arcades are airier and more open than they had been. The graceful columns have the beauty of animate beings. They keep to a human scale too, and as they lead from part to part, even when a building is very large, one is never overwhelmed by its sheer size. This, on the other hand, is just what the Norman architect wishes to achieve. He conceives a wall as a whole and then keeps the expression of might and mass to the smallest detail. Hence, one need scarcely add, Romanesque sculptors could not yet rediscover the beauty of the human body. This rediscovery, and the discovery of linear perspective, had to come with the Renaissance. S. Spirito, or the Palazzo Rucellai, prove this to anyone susceptible to their specific character.

To illustrate the principle of an all-pervading order which Alberti postulates in an interior as well, the plan of S. Andrea in Mantua, Alberti's last work, may be analysed. As in S. Spirito, the east parts are a central composition. Alberti had in fact also made a contribution to the architects' burning problem of the completely central plan. His S. Sebastiano in Mantua is a Greek cross. It was designed in 1460, that is, just before or just after the Sforza Temple of Sperandio's medal. But Alberti's solution is original, whatever its date,

138 Mantua, S. Andrea, by Alberti, begun 1470

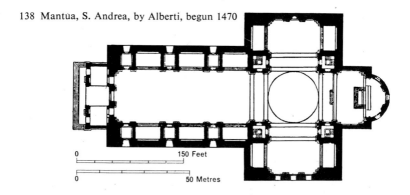

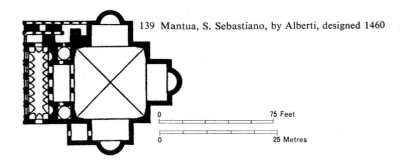

139 Mantua, S. Sebastiano, by Alberti, designed 1460

0   75 Feet

0   25 Metres

austere and aloof, with its curiously pagan façade. No wonder that a cardinal could write of it in 1473: 'I can't see if this is going to turn out a church or a mosque or a synagogue.' From the point of view of practical church functions such central buildings are conspicuously useless. So we find from the beginning attempts at combining the traditional longitudinal plan with aesthetically more welcome central features. S. Spirito was one example. The most influential one, however, is S. Andrea in Mantua. Here the architect replaces the traditional nave and aisles arrangement by a series of side chapels taking the place of the aisles and connected with the nave alternately by tall and wide and low and narrow openings. The aisles thus cease to be part of the eastward movement and become a series of minor centres accompanying the spacious tunnel-vaulted nave. As to the walls enclosing the nave, the same intention is evident in the replacement of the simple basilican sequence of columns following each other without caesura by the rhythmical alternation on the *a b a* principle of the closed and the open bays. Columns are given up entirely and replaced by giant pilasters. To what extent the keeping of the same proportions throughout is responsible for the deeply restful harmony of S. Andrea will be appreciated, if one realizes that the same *a b a* rhythm, identical even in details, and the same giant pilasters – the first, side by side with S. Sebastiano, in western architecture – are used as the chief motif of the façade of the church, and that the proportion of the arches of the crossing repeats that of the side chapels.

Alberti was not the only architect to experiment with such rhythmical combinations in the longitudinal church building. The

197

North of Italy proved especially interested in the application of the principle to the church with nave and aisles, after a Florentine architect had given the first hints at Faenza Cathedral (1474). Ferrara, Parma, and other centres picked them up, and soon we see this trend of thought unite forces with that interested in central plans on the Byzantino-Milanese scheme of a central dome with four smaller and lower domes in the corners. Venice and the Veneto had begun to build central churches of this type shortly before 1500 (S. Giovanni Grisostomo), and in 1506 an otherwise little-known architect, Spavento, found the classic solution for its application to the basilica. S. Salvatore in Venice consists of a nave of two of the Milano–Venetian units plus an exactly identical crossing. Only the transepts and apses are tacked on a little incongruously.

S. Salvatore stands historically in a similar relation to Alberti's S. Andrea in Mantua as, in the field of domestic architecture, the Cancelleria in Rome stands to Alberti's Palazzo Rucellai. The Cancelleria was built in 1486–98 as the private residence of Cardinal Riario, nephew of Sixtus IV, one of the most formidable of the Renaissance popes. These popes considered themselves worldly rulers almost more than priests. Julius II, another nephew of Sixtus IV, under whom the new St Peter's was begun, and for whom Michelangelo painted the Sistine Chapel and Raphael the *Stanze* of the Vatican, asked Michelangelo to portray him in a statue for Bologna with a sword instead of a book; for, he said: 'I am a soldier, not a scholar.' Of Alexander VI, and his son Cesare Borgia, it is enough to mention the names in this connexion. The Palazzo

140 Venice, S. Salvatore, by Spavento, 1506

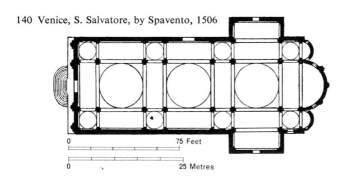

The inscription on the building reads:

RAPHAEL   RIARIVS   SAVONENSIS   SANC

141 Rome, Cancelleria, 1486–98

Riario has a ground floor without pilasters, because it seemed more reasonable to preserve the integrity of the rustication, where only small windows were required. On the first and second floors there are pilasters, but not in the simple sequence of the Palazzo Rucellai. Again the *a b a* rhythm is used to give life and rule to the façade. It will also be noticed that, whereas Alberti's horizontal divisions had to serve as cornices and at the same time window sills, the unknown architect of the Cancelleria gives each function its clearly visible architectural expression. Moreover, the corner bays of the building are slightly projected, so that to the right and the left there is no vagueness about the composition either.

The Cancelleria is the first Renaissance building of more than local importance in Rome. About the time, however, when it was completed, Rome took the leadership in architecture and art out of the hands of Florence. This moment marks the beginning of the High Renaissance. The Early Renaissance was essentially Tuscan. The High Renaissance is Roman, because Rome was at that time the only international centre of civilization, and the High Renaissance has an ideal classicity which made it internationally acceptable and in fact internationally canonic for centuries. Rome's place in the history of the Renaissance style corresponds exactly to that of Paris and the cathedrals around Paris in the history of the Gothic style. We do not know to what part of France the architects of Notre Dame, Chartres, Rheims, and Amiens belonged by birth and up-bringing, but we do know that Donato Bramante came from Umbria and Lombardy, Raphael from Umbria and Florence, and Michelangelo from Florence. These are the three greatest architects of the High Renaissance, and none of them – again the case we have met before – was an architect by training. Bramante was originally a painter, so was Raphael, and Michelangelo was a sculptor.

Bramante was the oldest of them. He was born in 1444 near Urbino. There he grew up while Piero della Francesca painted, Laurana worked at the Ducal Palace, and Francesco di Giorgio was busy writing a treatise on architecture – the third of the Renaissance, after Alberti's and Filarete's – in which incidentally he took a close interest in central planning. Some time between 1477 and 1480 Bramante went to Milan. His first building there, the church of

S. Maria presso S. Satiro, presupposes a knowledge of Alberti's S. Andrea in Mantua, a building started only a few years before. It looks as if Bramante had studied the plans carefully. His own church had no space for a chancel, and so – delighted to make a daring show of his knowledge of linear perspective – he feigned one in flat relief. If you stand in the right position, the trick comes off to perfection.

The same church, S. Maria, has a sacristy, centrally planned; and S. Maria delle Grazie, Bramante's next architectural work in Milan, has an east end also on a central plan, very similar incidentally to Alberti's S. Sebastiano in Mantua. But when S. Maria delle Grazie was begun in 1492, another artist, the most universal that ever lived, and one who was to influence considerably the slightly older Bramante, had already lived at Milan for nine years. Leonardo had gone to Milan in 1482 as an engineer, a painter, a sculptor, a musician – as anything and everything, but not as an architect. Yet in his fertile mind architectural problems moved all the time. In Florence he had already sketched the plans of Brunelleschi's S. Spirito and S. Maria degli Angeli, and in Milan he looked carefully at the specifically Milanese solutions proposed by Filarete. The outcome was drawings in his sketch-books showing several kinds of complex central structure, for instance one with a central octagon and eight chapels, each of the Milanese plan with centre dome and little square corner bays. So here we find as against the central schemes worked out by Renaissance architects before Leonardo not a major contrasted with a number of radiating minor members, but a system of these grades each subordinate to the one above. Another project is for historical reasons even more interesting. It appears as a rapid sketch in Leonardo's Paris Manuscript B and consists of a Greek cross with four apses, entirely surrounded by an ambulatory and with small square bays to fill the corners and angle towers or turrets projecting diagonally beyond these corner pieces. Bramante must have seen this, and remembered it years after he had left Milan and moved to Rome.

Apart from what Bramante had learnt from Leonardo, the change from the Milanese to the Roman atmosphere, which took place in 1499, altered his style decisively. His architecture assumed at once

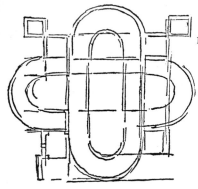

142 Sketch for a church on the Greek cross plan with angle towers, by Leonardo da Vinci, MS B fol. 57 v

143 Design for a centrally planned church with octagon and eight chapels, by Leonardo da Vinci, MS 2037 fol. 5v

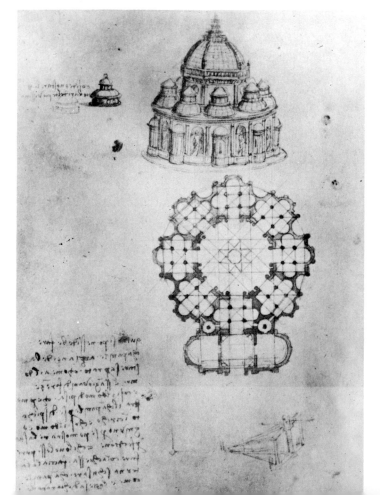

an austerity far beyond anything in Milan. This appears already in his first Roman designs, the cloister for S. Maria della Pace and the Tempietto of S. Pietro in Montorio. At S. Maria della Pace the courtyard had piers and attached columns in the Roman way on the ground floor, and an open gallery on the first whose slim columns support a straight architrave instead of arches. At S. Pietro in Montorio Bramante appears even graver. The Tempietto of 1502 is the first monument of the High as against the Early Renaissance – truly a monument, i.e. more a sculptural than a strictly architectural achievement. It was built to mark the spot on which St Peter was supposed to have been crucified. One can thus call it an enlarged

144 Rome, Tempietto of S. Pietro in Montorio, by Bramante, 1502

reliquary. In fact the intention had been to alter the courtyard in which it stood into a circular cloister to house the little temple. The first impression of the Tempietto after the churches and palaces of the fifteenth century is almost forbidding. The order of the colonnade is Tuscan Doric, the earliest modern use of this severe, unadorned order. It supports a correct classical entablature, again a feature that adds weight and strictness. There is, moreover, except for the metopes and the shells in the niches, not a square inch of decoration on the whole of the exterior. This in conjunction with the less novel but equally telling simplicity of the proportions – the ratio between width and height of the ground floor is repeated in the upper floor – gives the Tempietto a dignity far beyond its size. Here for once the classic Renaissance has achieved its conscious aim to emulate classic Antiquity. For here is – beyond motifs and even beyond formal expression – a building that appears as nearly pure volume as a Greek temple. Space – that all-important ingredient of Western architecture – seems here defeated.

But Bramante did not stop there. Only four years after he had accomplished the ideal Renaissance expression of architectural volume, he set out to reconcile it with the ideal Renaissance expression of space, as it had been evolved by the fifteenth-century architects from Brunelleschi to Leonardo da Vinci. In 1506 Julius II commissioned him to rebuild St Peter's, the holiest of Western churches. St Peter's still survived then essentially in its Constantinian form (see p. 26). Nicholas V, the first pope in sympathy with Humanism and the Renaissance, had begun rebuilding it outside the old east end in a way so similar in character to Alberti's S. Andrea in Mantua that Alberti can perhaps be assumed to be the originator of the design. But nothing more than the foundations had been laid when Nicholas V died in 1455, and nothing further happened. Julius II's St Peter's was to be a building on a strictly central plan, an amazing decision, considering the strength of the tradition in favour of longitudinal churches on the one hand and the immense religious significance of St Peter's on the other. With the pope adopting this symbol of worldliness for his own church, the spirit of Humanism had indeed penetrated into the innermost fortress of Christian resistance.

204

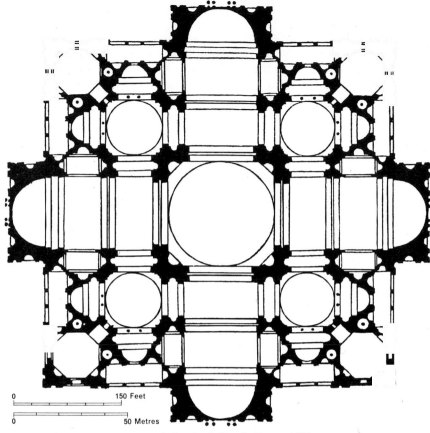

145 Bramante's original plan for St Peter's, Rome, 1506

Bramante was over sixty when the foundation stone was laid of the new St Peter's. It is a Greek cross, with four apses, so extremely symmetrical that on the plan nothing indicates which of the apses was to hold the high altar. The main dome was to be accompanied by minor domes over corner chapels and by towers in the corners further out still. All this was clearly in the Milanese and Leonardo traditions. But Bramante amplified his rhythm by enlarging the corner chapels into Greek crosses so that each of them has two apses of its own, the other two being cut off by the arms of the major Greek cross. Thus a square ambulatory is created framing a huge central dome, designed to be hemispherical like the dome over the Tempietto. Four corner turrets complete the exterior into a square with projections for only the main apses. So far Bramante's scheme was not more than a magnificent development of fifteenth-century ideas. What is new and entirely of the sixteenth century is the modelling of the walls and above all the piers supporting the central dome, the only parts of Bramante's plan that were executed and are still partially visible. In them nothing is left of the human scale and gentle modelling of Early Renaissance members. They are massive pieces of masonry, boldly hollowed out as if by the sculptor's moulding hand. This conception of the plastic potentialities of a wall, in its origin Late Roman, and first rediscovered (though less massively used) by the late Brunelleschi of S. Maria degli Angeli, was to be of the greatest importance for the future development of Italian architecture.

The immediate future, however, belonged to Bramante the master of classic harmony and greatness, not to Bramante the herald of the Baroque. Raphael (1483–1520) was the architect to follow most closely the Bramante of the Tempietto and the Damasus and Belvedere Courts of the Vatican (1503 seqq.), Bramante's other Roman masterpiece. Of Raphael's architectural works few are documented. Amongst the buildings attributed to him on good evidence is the Palazzo Vidoni Caffarelli in Rome, a very near descendant of the Palazzo Caprini, which Bramante had designed just before he died in 1514 and which Raphael had bought in 1517. It is now altered out of recognition. The Palazzo Caffarelli is also no longer as Raphael intended it to be. It was at a later date considerably enlarged in width and height. Here again the change of scale which marks the High Renaissance is noticeable. Balance and harmony are still the aims, but they are now combined with a solemnity and greatness unknown to the fifteenth century. Tuscan Doric columns replace the pilasters of the Palazzo Rucellai and the Cancelleria, and the happy *a b a* rhythm is contracted into a weightier *a b* with a new accent on the *a* by the duplication of the columns, and on the *b* by the straight architraves over the windows. The design of the rustication on the ground floor also emphasizes the horizontality, i.e. the gravity, of the composition.

The development from the Early to the High Renaissance, from delicacy to greatness, and from a subtle planning of surfaces to a bold high relief in the modelling of walls encouraged an intensified study of the remains of Imperial Rome. Only now was their drama fully understood. Only now did humanists and artists endeavour to visualize and perhaps re-create the Rome of the ruins as a whole. Raphael's Villa Madama as originally planned, with a circular courtyard and manifold apsed and niched rooms, is the boldest attempt at emulating the grandeur of Roman baths. Its delicious decoration is derived immediately from such remains of Imperial Rome as Nero's Golden House. These remains had been found below ground – hence the name Grottesche given to this kind of ornament favoured by Raphael and his studio. It is thus, considering the plan and decoration of the Villa Madama, evidently more than coincidence that Raphael was appointed in 1515 by Leo X, the Medici pope, to be Superintendent of Roman Antiquities, that he had Vitruvius translated by a humanist friend for his private use,

146 Rome, Palazzo Vidoni Caffarelli, by Raphael, *c*. 1515–20 (altered later)

and that he (or in all probability he) drew up a memorandum to the pope advocating the exact measuring of Roman remains, with ground plans, elevations, and sections separate, and the restoration of such buildings as could be '*infallibilmente*' restored.

Here precisely archaeology in the academic sense begins, representative of an attitude quite different from that of the fifteenth-century admirers of Roman architecture. It produced scholars of ever wider knowledge and ever deeper appreciation of Antiquity, but artists of weakened self-confidence, classicists where Bramante and Raphael had been classics.

At this point a warning must be sounded against confusion between the three terms classic, classical, and classicist. The difference between classic and classical is pointed out on p. 453, n. 15. If classic is the term denoting that rare balance of conflicting forces which marks the summit of any movement in art, and if classical is the term for anything belonging to or derived from Antiquity, what then is classicist? A definition is far from easy. In our context it can be arrived at only in a somewhat roundabout way.

Neither classic nor classicist are terms which signify historic styles such as Romanesque, Gothic, and Renaissance. They coincide rather with aesthetic attitudes. However, in so far as aesthetic attitudes as a rule change with historic styles, the two sets of terms can often be co-ordinated. In England the position until a relatively short time ago was that the term Renaissance was used to cover the art from the fifteenth right up to the early nineteenth century. But there had been so many fundamental changes of style during these more than three hundred years that the term covering such a long period could not stand for any distinct aesthetic characteristics. Thus, on the example of the Continent, it was gradually divided up into Renaissance and Baroque, the Baroque to cover the work of such artists as Bernini, Rembrandt, Velazquez. However, since our knowledge of, and susceptibility to, distinctions in aesthetic expression have grown considerably within the last fifty years or so, it is becoming more and more patent that Renaissance and Baroque do not really define the qualities of all art of importance in the fifteenth, sixteenth, and seventeenth centuries. The contrast between Raphael and Bernini or Rembrandt is evident, but art of the period between roughly 1520 or 1530 and 1600 or 1620 does not fit into the categories of the Renaissance or the Baroque. So a new name was introduced about thirty or thirty-five years ago: Mannerism, a name which was not specially coined, but which in a derogatory sense had already been used to characterize certain schools of sixteenth-century painting. The name in its new sense is only now becoming known in this country. It has much to recommend it. It certainly helps to make one see the important differences between art of the High Renaissance and art of the later sixteenth century.

If balance and harmony are the chief characteristics of the High Renaissance, Mannerism is its very reverse; for it is an unbalanced, discordant art – now emotional to distortion (Tintoretto, El Greco), now disciplined to self-effacement (Bronzino).

The High Renaissance is full, Mannerism is meagre. There is luxuriant beauty in Titian, stately gravity in Raphael, and gigantic strength in Michelangelo, but Mannerist types are slim, elegant, and of a stiff and highly self-conscious deportment. Self-consciousness to this extent was a new experience to the West. The Middle Ages, and the Renaissance too, had been much more naïve. Reformation and counter-Reformation broke up that state of innocence, and this is why Mannerism is indeed full of mannerisms. For the artist now for the first time was aware of the virtues of eclecticism. Raphael and Michelangelo were recognized as the masters of a Golden Age, the equals of the Ancients. Imitations became a necessity in quite a new sense. The medieval artist had imitated his masters as a matter of course, but he had not doubted his own (or his time's) ability to surpass them. This confidence had now gone. The first academies were founded, and a literature on the history and theory of art sprang up. Vasari is its most famous representative. Deviation from the canons of Michelangelo and Raphael was not ostracized, but it assumed a new air of the capricious, the demonstrative, or the daring: forbidden pleasures. No wonder that the sixteenth century saw the sternest ascetics and the first writers and draughtsmen to indulge in the hidden sins of pornography (Aretino and Giulio Romano).

So far only names of painters have been mentioned because the qualities of sixteenth-century painting are at least a little more

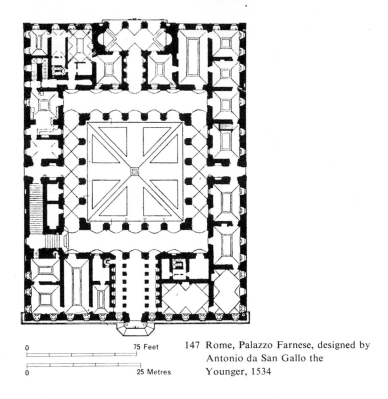

147 Rome, Palazzo Farnese, designed by
Antonio da San Gallo the
Younger, 1534

familiar than those of architecture. The application of the principles
of Mannerism to architecture is relatively recent and still controversial. Yet if we now turn to buildings and compare the Palazzo
Farnese with the Palazzo Massimi alle Colonne as the most perfect
examples of High Renaissance and Mannerist palace architecture in
Rome, the contrast between their emotional qualities will at once
reveal itself as a contrast between the two styles as we have found
them in painting. The Palazzo Farnese was first designed in 1517
and then redesigned on a much larger scale in 1534 by Antonio da
San Gallo the Younger (1485–1546). It is the most monumental of
Roman Renaissance palaces, an isolated rectangle of about 150-feet
frontage, facing a square. The façade has strongly emphasized
quoins, but no rustication. The ground-floor windows are provided

with straight cornices, those on the first floor with alternating triangular and segmental pediments, supported by columns (i.e. so-called aedicules), a Roman motif revived during the High Renaissance. The top floor and the overpowering top cornice were added later and in a different spirit (see p. 229). The symmetry and spaciousness of the interior are worth noting, especially the magnificent central entrance with the tunnel-vaulted passage leading into the courtyard. This possesses the cloistered ground floor of all Renaissance palaces, now, in accordance with the Bramante tradition, with Tuscan Doric columns and a correct frieze of metopes and triglyphs instead of the light columns of the Tuscan fifteenth century. The first floor has no gallery, but noble, pedimented windows set into blank arcades, and an Ionic order. This is correct according to Roman usage (Theatre of Marcellus): the sturdier Tuscan Doric must be on the ground floor, the elegant Ionic on the first, and rich Corinthian on the second. In this (but only in this) the later second floor of the Palazzo Farnese follows the archaeological example.

148 Rome, Palazzo Farnese, courtyard, by Antonio da San Gallo the Younger, 1534, top storey by Michelangelo, 1548

The Palazzo Massimi by Baldassare Peruzzi of Siena (1481–1536), a member of the Bramante-Raphael circle in Rome, begun in 1535, disregards all the canons of the Ancients. Nor does it really show much regard for the achievements of Bramante and Raphael. Both the Palazzi Vidoni and Farnese were logical structures in which the knowledge of any one part gives a clue to the whole. The entrance loggia of the Palazzo Massimi, with its coupled Tuscan Doric columns and its heavy cornice, is in no way a preparation for the upper floors. Both the Palazzi Vidoni and Farnese are modelled into a generous though not overcharged relief. In the Palazzo Massimi there is a poignant contrast between the deep darkness of the ground-floor loggia and the papery thinness and flatness of the upper parts. The first-floor windows are shallow in relief compared with what the High Renaissance regarded as appropriate, the second- and third-floor windows are small and have curious leathery surrounds. They are in no way differentiated in size or importance as they would have been in the Renaissance. Moreover, a slight curve of the whole façade gives it a swaying delicacy, whereas the

149 Rome, Palazzo Massimi alle Colonne, by Peruzzi, begun 1535

squareness of the Renaissance front seemed to express powerful solidity. The Palazzo Massimi is no doubt inferior to the Palazzi Vidoni and Farnese in dignity and grandeur; but it has a sophisticated elegance instead which appeals to the over-civilized and intellectual connoisseur.

Now this brings us back to the fact that classicism is an aesthetic attitude first appreciated during this phase of Mannerism. The Early Renaissance had rediscovered Antiquity and enjoyed a mixture of detail copying and a naïve licence in the reconstruction of more than details. The High Renaissance was in its use of Roman forms hardly more accurate, but the Antique spirit was for a brief moment truly revived in the gravity of mature Bramante and Raphael. After their death imitation began to freeze up initiative. Classicism is imitation of Antiquity and even more of the classic moment of the Renaissance, at the expense of direct expression. The attitude culminated, needless to say, during the late eighteenth and early nineteenth centuries, in that phase of classicism *par excellence* which is on the Continent often called Classicism pure and simple, but which in England goes under the name of Classical Revival. The idea of copying a whole Antique temple exterior (or a whole temple front) for Western use is the quintessence of classicism. The sixteenth century did not go quite so far. But it did conceive that blend of academic rigidity with distrust of emotional freedom which made the latter-day all-out revival possible.

A pupil of Raphael, Giulio Romano (1499–1546), artist-in-chief to the Duke of Mantua, designed a house for himself about 1544. It is a striking example of Mannerist classicism – apart from being one of the earliest architect's houses on such an ambitious scale. The façade is again flatter than would have pleased the High Renaissance. Detail, e.g. in the window surrounds and the top frieze, is hard and crisp. There is a proud aloofness, an almost arrogant taciturnity and a stiff formality about the building that reminds one at once of the Spanish etiquette accepted everywhere in the later sixteenth century. Yet the apparent general correctness is broken by an occasional, as it were, surreptitious licence here and there (one such licence in Giulio Romano's work as a draughtsman has been mentioned before). The smooth band above the windows of the

150 Mantua, Giulio Romano's house, built for himself *c.* 1544

rusticated ground floor seems to disappear behind the keystones of the windows. The entrance has a most illicit depressed arch, and the pediment on top with no base to it is nothing but the main string course at sill height of the first-floor windows lifted up by the effort of the arch. These windows themselves are recessed in blank arcades like those of the Palazzo Farnese, but as against the logical and structurally satisfying surrounds and pediments there, one flat ornamental motif runs without hiatus along sides, top, and pediments. It is exquisite, but very self-conscious, just like the contemporary sculpture of Benvenuto Cellini.

This style, first conceived in Rome and Florence, appealed almost at once to North Italy and the transalpine countries. Giulio Romano was the first to show it north of the Apennines; Sammicheli, though fifteen years older, followed, partly under direct Roman influence, partly under the influence of Giulio's early Mantuan masterpiece, the Palazzo del Tè of 1525–35, and reshaped the appearance of Verona in this spirit of Mannerist classicism. At Bologna Sebastiano

Serlio, a pupil of Peruzzi, though six years his senior, and twenty-four years older than Giulio, preached it. In 1537 he began to publish a first part of a treatise on architecture which proved a source of lasting inspiration to classicist minds on the other side of the Alps. Serlio himself went to France in 1540 and was almost at once made *peintre et architecteur du roi.* The school of Fontainebleau, where Serlio and the Italians Rosso Fiorentino and Primaticcio worked, is the transalpine centre of Mannerism. We shall revert to it in more detail later. Spain accepted the new style even earlier – a violent reaction against the violence of her Late Gothic. Charles V's new and never finished palace on the Alhambra at Granada (begun in 1526 by Pedro Machuca) looks, with its vast circular colonnaded inner court and the motifs of its 207-foot-long façade, as though it were based on the Raphael of the Villa Madama and Giulio Romano, somewhat provincially interpreted. England and Germany were slower in succumbing to the dictatorship of classicism. The style was not in all its implications appreciated before the second decade of the seventeenth century (Inigo Jones and Elias Holl, see pp. 307 and 311), and then not so much in its problematical Giulio Romano-Serlio form as in that created by the happiest and most serene of all later sixteenth-century architects, Andrea Palladio (1508–80).

Palladio's style, though it first followed Giulio, Sammicheli, and Serlio, and as far as possible Vitruvius, the obscure and freely misinterpreted Roman authority on architecture, is highly personal. His work must be seen at and around Vicenza. He designed no churches there (though his S. Giorgio Maggiore and Il Redentore in Venice are amongst the few really relevant churches in the Mannerist style, as will be shown later). What he was called upon to do was almost exclusively the designing of town and country houses, *palazzi* and *ville*, and it is significant that the far-reaching effect of his style can quite adequately be demonstrated without any analyses of his churches. For from the Renaissance onwards secular architecture became as important for visual self-expression as religious architecture, until during the eighteenth century the ascendancy of domestic and public buildings over churches was established. For the Middle Ages, in a book such as the present, little had to be said

151 Granada, Palace of Charles V, by Pedro Machuca, begun 1526, courtyard

on castles, houses, and public buildings. Of Renaissance examples here discussed, half were secular. This will remain the proportion for the next two hundred years in the Roman Catholic countries. In those converted to Protestantism secular architecture was dominant at an even earlier date.

Palladio's buildings, despite their elegant serenity, would hardly have had such a universal success if it had not been for the book in which he published them and his theory of architecture. Palladio's *Architettura* took its place by the side of Serlio's, and later superseded it, especially after its revival in England early in the eighteenth century. His style appealed to the civilized taste and the polite learning of the Georgian gentry more than that of any other architect. Palladio is never dry or demonstratively scholarly. He combines the gravity of Rome with the sunny breadth of Northern Italy and an entirely personal ease not achieved by any of his contemporaries. In his Palazzo Chiericati, begun in 1550, the Tuscan Doric and correct Ionic order of the Bramante tradition, with their straight entablatures, are unmistakable. But the freedom in placing what had been confined to the courtyards of Roman palaces into the façade, thus opening up most of the façade and retaining only one solid

152 Vicenza, Palazzo Chiericati, by Palladio, begun 1550

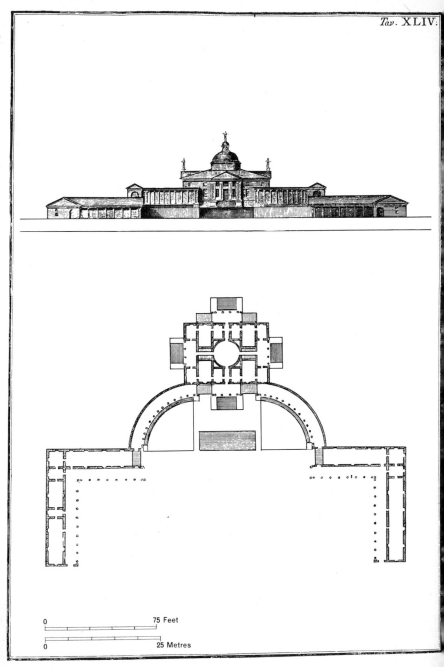

0   75 Feet

0   25 Metres

153 Meledo, Villa Trissino, by Palladio, *c*.1552

piece in the centre of the first floor surrounded on all sides by air, is all Palladio's. He was especially fond of colonnades in his country houses, where he used them to connect a square main block with far out-reaching wings.

The contrast between solid and diffused had a great fascination for him. In one of his most complete schemes, the Villa Trissino at Meledo on the Venetian mainland, the house is almost completely symmetrical. The extreme case, still existent and well preserved, of such complete symmetry is the Villa Capra, or Rotonda, just outside Vicenza (c. 1550–4), an academic achievement of high perfection and one specially admired by Pope's England. As a house to live in it has nothing of the informal snugness of the Northern manor-house, but it has nobility and, with its slender Ionic porticoes, its pediments, its carefully placed few pedimented windows, and its central dome, it appears stately without being pompous. Now to get the totality of a Palladian countryside composition one has to add to such a nucleus the curved colonnades and low outbuildings by which the villa takes in the land around. This embracing attitude proved of the greatest historical consequence. For here for the first time in Western architecture landscape and building were conceived as belonging to each other, as dependent on each other. Here

154 Vicenza, Villa Capra (Rotonda), by Palladio, c. 1550–4

for the first time the chief axes of a house are continued into nature; or, alternatively, the spectator standing outside sees the house spread out like a picture closing his vista. It is worth mentioning that in Rome at about the same time Michelangelo planned a comparable vista for the Palazzo Farnese which he had been commissioned to finish. He suggested that the palace should be connected with the Farnese gardens on the other side of the Tiber.

It may seem odd to us that the Farnese family should have gone to Michelangelo the sculptor to complete their palace after San Gallo's death. But it must be remembered that Giotto, Bramante, and Raphael were painters, and that Brunelleschi was a goldsmith. All the same, the story of how Michelangelo became an architect is worth telling, because it is equally characteristic of him and his age. He had as a boy been apprenticed to a painter, until, when Lorenzo the Magnificent had discovered him, given him lodgings in his palace, and drawn him into his private circle, he was sent to learn in a freer, less medieval way the art of sculpture from Lorenzo's favourite sculptor, Bertoldo. His fame rested on sculpture. His huge David, the symbol of the civic pride of Renaissance Florence, he began at the age of twenty-six. A few years later Julius II commissioned him to prepare plans for an enormous tomb which the pope wanted to erect for himself during his lifetime. Michelangelo regarded it as his *magnum opus*. The first scheme provided for more than forty life-size or over life-size figures. The famous Moses is one of them. Architecture of course was also involved, though only as an accompaniment. However, when Julius had decided to rebuild St Peter's to Bramante's design, he lost interest in the tomb and forced upon Michelangelo the task of painting the ceiling of the Sistine Chapel instead. Michelangelo never forgave Bramante for having, as he suspected, caused this change of mind. So for nearly five years – as he worked without an assistant – he had to stick to painting.

Then he returned to the tomb of Pope Julius, and perhaps in connexion with conceptions that had passed through his mind when thinking of how architecturally to relate large figures with the wall against which they were going to stand, he began to take an interest in the plans of the Medici family to complete their church of S.

Lorenzo in Florence by at last adding a façade. The church was Brunelleschi's work. Michelangelo in 1516 designed a façade two storeys high, with two orders and ample accommodation for sculpture. The commission was given to him, and for several years he worked in the quarries – a work he loved. Then, however, in 1520, the Medici found too many difficulties in the transport of the marble and cancelled the contract. But they at once made another one with Michelangelo for the erection of a family chapel or mausoleum by S. Lorenzo. This was in fact begun in 1521 and completed, though less ambitiously than originally planned, in 1534. The Medici Chapel is thus Michelangelo's first architectural work, and the work, it must be added, of one never initiated into the secrets of building technique and architectural drawing. It has already – though again chiefly conceived as background for sculpture – all the characteristics of his personal style. Architecture without any support from sculpture is to be found in his work for the first time in another job for the Medici at S. Lorenzo, the library and the anteroom to the library. The library was designed in 1524, the anteroom (with the exception of the staircase for which the model was supplied as late as 1557) in 1526.

The anteroom is high and narrow. This alone gives an uncomfortable feeling. Michelangelo wanted to emphasize the contrast to the long, comparatively low and more restful library itself. The walls are divided into panels by coupled columns. At the ground-floor height of the library itself the panels have blank windows and framed blank niches above. The colour scheme of the room is austere, a dead white against the sombre dark grey of columns, window niches, architraves, and other structural or decorative members. As for the chief structural members, the columns, one would expect them to project and carry the architraves, as had always been the function of columns. Michelangelo reversed the relations. He recessed his columns and projected his panels so that they painfully encase the columns. Even the architraves go forward over the panels and backward over the columns. This seems arbitrary, just like the relations between ground-floor loggia and flat façade above, or between second- and third-floor windows, in the Palazzo Massimi. It is certainly illogical, because it makes the

155 Florence, Biblioteca Laurenziana, anteroom, by Michelangelo, designed 1526

carrying strength of the columns appear wasted. Moreover, they have slender corbels at their feet which do not look substantial enough to support them and in fact do not support them at all. The thinness of the Massimi front characterizes the blank windows with their tapering pilasters, fluted without any intelligible reason in one part only. The pediment over the entrance to the library is held only by the thin line around the door, raised into two square ears. The staircase tells of the same wilful originality; but the sharpness of detail which Michelangelo developed in the twenties is now replaced by a heavy, weary flow as of lava.

It has often been said that the motifs of the walls show Michelangelo as the father of the Baroque, because they express the superhuman struggle of active forces against overpowering matter. I do not think that anybody who examines without prejudice his sensations in the room itself would subscribe to this statement. There seems to me no expression of struggle anywhere, though there is conscious discordance all the way through. This austere animosity against the happy and harmonious we have seen already, although hidden under a polished formalism, in Giulio Romano. What Michelangelo's Laurenziana reveals is indeed Mannerism in its most sublime architectural form and not Baroque – a world of frustration much more tragic than the Baroque world of struggles between mind and matter. In Michelangelo's architecture every force seems paralysed. The load does not weigh, the support does not carry, natural reactions play no part – a highly artificial system upheld by the severest discipline.[26]

In its spatial treatment the Laurenziana is just as novel and characteristic. Michelangelo had exchanged the balanced proportions of Renaissance rooms for an anteroom as tall and narrow as the shaft of a pit, and a library proper, reached by a staircase, as long and narrow as a corridor. They both force us, even against our wills, to follow their pull, upward first and then forward. This tendency to enforce movement through space within rigid boundaries is the chief spatial quality of Mannerism. It is well enough known in painting, for instance in Correggio's late Madonnas, or in Tintoretto's Last Supper with the figure of Christ at the far, far end. The most moving of all examples is Tintoretto's painting of the Finding of the Body of St Mark (Brera, Milan, c. 1565). Nowhere else is Mannerist space so irresistible. In architecture this magic suction effect is introduced into Giulio Romano's extremely severe cathedral at Mantua with its double aisles, the inner one with tunnel-vaults, the outer one and the nave flat. The uninterrupted rhythm of its monotonous columns is as irresistible as that of an Early Christian basilica. In secular architecture its most familiar and easily accessible example is no doubt Vasari's Uffizi Palace in Florence. It was begun in 1560 to house Grand Ducal offices. It consists of two tall wings along a long narrow courtyard. The formal elements are familiar to us: lack of a clear gradation of storeys, uniformity coupled with heretical detail, long, elegant, and fragile brackets below double pilasters which are no pilasters at all, and so on. What must be emphasized is the finishing accent of the

156 Florence, Uffizi, by Vasari, begun 1560

composition towards the River Arno. Here a loggia, open in a spacious Venetian window on the ground floor and originally also in a colonnade on the upper floor, replaces the solid wall. This is a favourite Mannerist way of linking room with room, a way in which both a clear Renaissance separation of units and a free Baroque flow through the whole and beyond are avoided. Thus, Palladio's two Venetian churches terminate in the east, not in closed apses, but in arcades – straight in S. Giorgio Maggiore (1565), semicircular in the Redentore (1577) – behind which back rooms of indistinguishable dimensions appear. And thus Vasari, together with Vignola (1507–73), designed the Villa Giulia, the country *casino* of Pope Julius III (1550–5), as a sequence of buildings with loggias towards semicircular courts and with vistas across the entrance through the first loggia towards the second, through it towards the third, and through that into a walled back garden.

For the garden of the sixteenth century is still walled in. It may have long and varied vistas, as you also find them at the Villa Este in Tivoli or at Caprarola, but they do not stretch out into infinity as in the Baroque at Versailles. Neither do the low colonnades on the ground floors of Mannerist buildings, such as the Palazzo Massimi and the Uffizi, indicate infinity – that is, a dark, unsurveyable background of space, like a Rembrandt background. Back walls are too near. The continuity of the façade is broken by such colonnades –

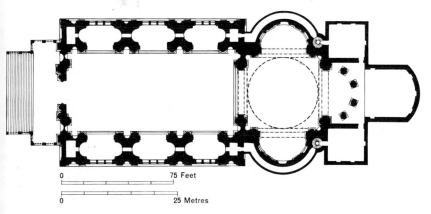

0   75 Feet

0   25 Metres

157 Venice, Il Redentore, by Palladio, begun 1577

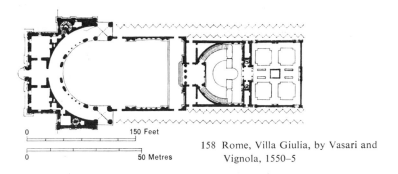

158 Rome, Villa Giulia, by Vasari and Vignola, 1550–5

that is what the Renaissance would have disliked – but the layer of opened-up space is shallow and clearly confined in depth. Palladio's Palazzo Chiericati is the most perfect example of this screen technique in palace architecture, although, in its serenity, different from Florentine and Roman Mannerism and particularly from Michelangelo. Palladio's palace may have a certain coolness too, but it is not icy like the Laurenziana.

This frozen self-discipline is not usually connected with the genius of Michelangelo and therefore needs special emphasis, emphasis above all because textbooks sometimes still treat Michelangelo as a master of the Renaissance. The truth is that he belonged to the Renaissance for only a very few years of his early career. His Pietà of 1499 may be a work of the High Renaissance. His David may be in the spirit of the Renaissance too. Of his Sistine Ceiling this can be said only to a limited extent; and of his work after 1515 hardly at all. His character made it impossible for him to accept the ideals of the Renaissance for long. He was the very opposite of Castiglione's *Courtier* and Leonardo da Vinci: unsociable, distrustful, a fanatical worker, negligent in his personal appearance, deeply religious, and uncompromisingly proud. Hence his dislike for Leonardo, and for Bramante and Raphael, a dislike made up of contempt and envy. We know more of his character and his life than of those of any artist before. The unprecedented adoration for him caused the publication of two biographies while he was alive. Both are based on a systematic collecting of material. It is good that it should be so; for we feel we must know much about him to understand his art. In the

Middle Ages the personality of an architect could never to that degree have influenced his style. Brunelleschi, though clearer to us as a character than the architects of the Gothic cathedrals, is still surprisingly objective in his forms. Michelangelo was the first to turn architecture into an instrument of individual expression. The *terribilità* that frightened those who met him fills us with awe, immediately we are faced with any work of his, a room, a drawing, a piece of sculpture, or a sonnet.

For Michelangelo was a consummate poet too, one of the profoundest of his age; and in his poems he gives to posterity a reckoning of his struggles. The fiercest of them was that between a platonic ideal of beauty and a fervent faith in Christ. It is in the most concentrated form the struggle between the age of the Renaissance in which he lived when he was young, and that of the Counter-Reformation and Mannerism that began when he was about fifty years old, just before the sack of Rome in 1527. Now new stricter religious orders were founded, the Capuchins, the Oratorians, and above all the Jesuits (1534). Now new saints arose, St Ignatius Loyola, St Teresa, St Philip Neri, St Charles Borromeo. In 1542 the Inquisition was reintroduced, in 1543 literary censorship. In 1555 the Emperor Charles V abdicated and retired to the silence of a Spanish monastery. A few years later his son, Philip II, began his bleak and enormous palace of the Escorial, more a monastery than a palace. Spanish etiquette stood for a discipline as rigid as that of the early Jesuits and the papal court of the same decades. In Rome nothing seemed left of the Renaissance gaiety. The Venetian ambassadors wrote home that even the carnivals were cold and lean. Pius V, the strictest of the popes, had meat on his table only twice a week.

Michelangelo too had always been exemplarily sober and self-denying. He trained himself to need little sleep, and used to sleep with his boots on. While at work he sometimes fed on dry bread, eaten without putting his tools aside. He felt his duties to his genius more heavily than the light-hearted architects of the Renaissance – and he could therefore venture to reply to a critic who objected to his having represented Giuliano de'Medici on his tomb beardless, though he wore a beard in life: 'Who in a thousand years will care for what he looked like?', a saying utterly impossible before the Renaissance had freed artists. For while the Middle Ages did not demand portrait likeness, because it is part of what is merely accidental in human nature, and while the early Renaissance had enjoyed portrait likeness, because it had only just discovered the artistic means for attaining it, Michelangelo refused to comply with it, because it would have hemmed in his aesthetic freedom. Yet his religious experience was of the most exacting, and it grew more so as he grew older and the century grew older, until he, the greatest sculptor of the West, and the most admired artist of his age, gave up painting and sculpture almost entirely. Architecture alone he still carried on, and he refused to accept a salary for his work at St Peter's.

The final break seems to have come after he had passed his seventieth year. Between the Medici buildings of the mid twenties and 1547 he seems to have designed and built only the fortifications of Florence in 1529 – an engineering job, we would say, but a type of job in which Leonardo da Vinci and San Gallo, his predecessor in most of his Roman works, also excelled. In 1534 he had left Florence for good and gone to Rome. In 1535 Paul III appointed him Superintendent of the Vatican Buildings, an all but nominal appointment at first. In 1539 he was consulted about the placing of the equestrian statue of Marcus Aurelius on the Capitol, and a general plan for the new buildings surrounding the statue must have been made then. Their style makes a date in the early forties probable (though construction only began in the sixties). Then in 1546 San Gallo died, and now Michelangelo was called upon almost at once to complete the Palazzo Farnese, redesign St Peter's, and replan the Capitol. The Capitol is an early example of town-planning in the sense that a group of buildings is conceived together with the square between them and the approach to them. Bernardo Rossellino (Alberti's executant at the Palazzo Rucellai and the resident architect of Nicholas V's new St Peter's) had preceded Michelangelo in this, when he designed for Pope Pius II the square, cathedral, and palace of Pienza (*c*. 1460), and Venice was busy throughout the first half of the sixteenth century in making of her Piazza and Piazzetta the most inspired (and the freest) piece of Renaissance town-planning. In Michelangelo's *œuvre* town-planning could not play so important a part. To him architecture was too direct an emotional experience and too much an expression in terms of the structural shaping of stone. There is thus more to grip our sympathy in the Palazzo Farnese and St Peter's than in the Capitol. At the Palazzo Farnese we shall now easily discover his Mannerism in the second-floor details. The triplicating of the pilasters and especially the odd discordant framing of the windows with corbels on the sides not supporting anything and special corbels immediately above, on which the segmental pediments rest, are Michelangelo's personal expression, individual to an unprecedented extent and impossible before the breaking up first of the transcendentally ordered world of the Middle Ages and then of the aesthetically ordered world of the Renaissance.

Michelangelo's architectural masterpiece, the back and the dome of St Peter's, are also an expression of revolt against Bramante and the spirit of the Renaissance, although they are not to the same extent Mannerist. When Michelangelo was appointed by Paul III, the Farnese Pope, to be architect of St Peter's, he found the church essentially left as it had been at Bramante's death. Raphael and San Gallo had designed naves to comply with the religious demands of the first post-Renaissance generation. But they were not begun. Michelangelo returned to the central plan, but he deprived it of its all-governing balance. He kept the arms of the Greek cross, but where Bramante had intended sub-centres repeating on a smaller scale the motif of the main centre, Michelangelo cut off the arms of the sub-centres, thus condensing the composition into one central dome resting on piers of a dimension that Bramante would have refused as colossal, i.e. inhuman, and a square ambulatory round. As for the exterior, he altered Bramante's plans in exactly the same spirit, replacing a happily balanced variety of noble and serene motifs by a huge order of Corinthian pilasters supporting a massive attic and by strangely incongruous windows and niches surrounded by aedicules and smaller niches of several sizes – a mighty yet some-what discordant ensemble. In front of the principal entrance of St Peter's Michelangelo wanted to add a portico of ten columns with four columns in front of the middle ones. This – it was never built,

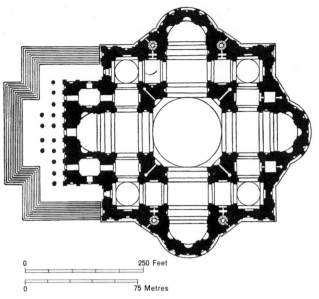

0   250 Feet

0   75 Metres

159 Plan for the completion of St Peter's, Rome, by Michelangelo, 1546

because Maderna after 1600 added a nave – would have destroyed
Bramante's ideal symmetry, and in fact the classic ideal of symmetry
altogether; for the duplication of the centre columns is of course an
utterly un-antique conception. Bramante's dome was to be a perfect
hemisphere, Michelangelo raised his on a higher drum and at first
wanted to give it a steeper outline, a very personal, dynamic version
of Brunelleschi's Gothic dome of Florence Cathedral. Then, however, towards the end of his life, he seems to have changed his mind
and preferred a lower, more heavily weighing-down shape, a
Mannerist shape, whereas his first idea, with its upward thrust,
heralded the Baroque. It is indeed this that Giacomo della Porta, in
actually building the dome, reverted to and further developed. So
Michelangelo – just as the other greatest masters of his generation,
Raphael and Titian – in growing out of the Renaissance conceived
Mannerism as well as Baroque. The sixteenth century was inspired

160 Rome, St Peter's, dome, designed by Michelangelo,
1558–60, and della Porta, 1588–90

by Michelangelo's Mannerism, the seventeenth appreciated his *terribilità* and made the Baroque out of it. Thus the eternal city is crowned not by a symbol of Renaissance worldliness, as Julius II had visualized it, but by an overwhelming synthesis of Mannerism and Baroque, and at the same time of Antiquity and Christianity.

That the final shape Michelangelo wished to give to the dome was less active and violent than the former is a telling sign of his mind during his last years. 'Let there be no more painting, no more carving,' he says in one of his late sonnets, 'to soothe the soul turned towards that Divine Love which opened His arms from the cross to receive us.'

> 'Nè pinger nè scolpir fia più che quieti
> L'anima volta a quell'Amor Divino
> Ch'aperse, a prender noi, 'n croce le braccia.'

He carved after this only three more groups, all three Entombments of Christ. One of them was for his own tomb, one he left unfinished, or rather sublimated to so immaterial a form that it can no longer be regarded as sculpture in the Renaissance sense. His late drawings too are spiritualized to a degree almost unbearable in an artist who had done more than any before him to glorify the beauty and vigour of body and movement. And one of his last architectural plans – a fact not widely enough known – was to design the Roman church of the newly founded, severely counter-reformatory order of the Jesuits. He offered to take charge of the building without any fee, just as he had refused to accept a salary as architect of St Peter's.

The Gesù was not begun until four years after Michelangelo's death. It has perhaps exerted a wider influence than any other church of the last four hundred years. Giacomo Vignola (1507–73), the architect, following probably Michelangelo's ideas, combines in his ground plan the central scheme of the Renaissance with the longitudinal scheme of the Middle Ages – an eminently characteristic fact. The combination as such is not new. It had formed the theme of some of the most beautiful Early Christian and Byzantine churches, including Hagia Sophia. Alberti had created a new combination at S. Andrea in Mantua a hundred years before, and this indeed heralds that of the Gesù. The façade too seems to take up a

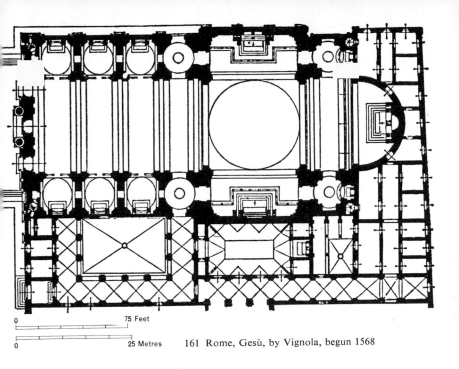

0 75 Feet

0 25 Metres 161 Rome, Gesù, by Vignola, begun 1568

theme that Alberti had conceived. The problem for architects of the
Renaissance, and after the Renaissance, was how to project the
dimensions of tall nave and lower aisles on to the exterior without
abandoning the orders of classical architecture. Alberti's solution
was to have a ground floor on the triumphal arch system and a top
floor the width of the nave only but with volutes, i.e. scrolls, rising
towards it from the entablature in front of the lean-to roofs of the
aisles. This method was adopted by Vignola in his design for the
Gesù façade (though with the fuller and less harmonious orchestration of his age), and then by della Porta, who substituted a new
design for Vignola's. It has been repeated innumerable times and
with many variations in the Baroque churches of Italy and the other
Roman Catholic countries.

As for the interior, Vignola keeps Alberti's interpretation of the
aisles as series of chapels opening into the nave. He does not, however, concede them as much independence as the Renaissance

162 Rome, Gesù, interior by Vignola, begun 1568, façade by della Porta

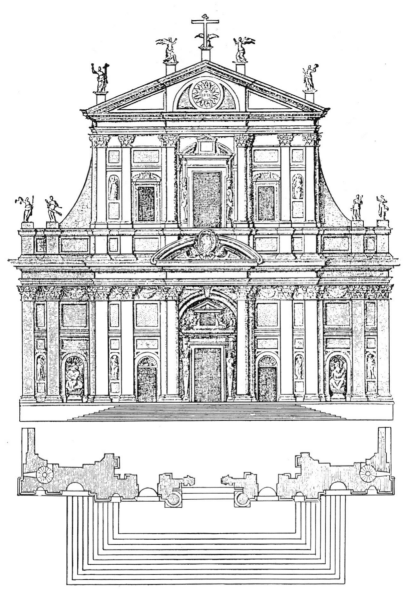

163 Vignola's design for the front of the Gesù

164 Rome, Gesù, interior, by Vignola, begun 1568

architect considered necessary, always anxious as he was to let every part of a building be a whole. The extreme width of the nave under a powerful tunnel-vault degrades the chapels into mere niches accompanying a vast hall, and it has been suggested that the choice of this motif was due to Francesco Borgia, the Spanish General of the Jesuit Order, and thus ultimately to the tradition of the Gothic style in Spain (see p. 147) as already represented in Rome by the Catalan church of S. Maria di Monserrato (1495). If the suggestion is accepted, there is here yet another instance of the post-Renaissance return to medieval ideals – another, after the revival of Catholic faith which showed itself in the new Saints and the new Orders, after the Gothic curve of the dome of St Peter's and the reintroduction of a longitudinal emphasis in the Gesù plan. In the Gesù this emphasis on the eastward drive is obviously deliberate. The tunnel-vault and above all the main cornice, running all the way through without a break, take it up most eloquently in the elevation. There is, however, one element in Vignola's design that it would be impossible to find in the same sense in any medieval church: the light. In the cathedral of the thirteenth century the stained-glass windows glow by means of light penetrating, but light itself is not a positive factor. Later on, in the Decorated style, light begins to model walls with their ogee-arched niches and play over filigree decoration, but it is never a major consideration of architectural design. In the Gesù, on the other hand, certain important features are introduced into the composition exclusively in order to make light-effects possible. The nave is lit from windows above the chapels – an even, subdued light. Then the last bay before the dome is shorter, less open, and darker than the others. This contraction in space and lightness prepares dramatically for the majestic crossing with its mighty cupola. The floods of light streaming down from the windows of the drum create that sensation of fulfilment that Gothic architects achieved in so much less sensuous a way.

The decoration of the Gesù appears sensuous too, luxurious though sombre. However, it is not of Vignola's day. He would have been more moderate, with smaller motifs and shallower relief; this is certain from what we know of late sixteenth-century decoration. Thus the effect of the medieval movement towards the east would have been much stronger, with less to deflect attention from the cornice and the mighty tunnel-vault. The redecoration was done in 1668–73. It belongs to the High Baroque, whereas the building is, to say it again, Mannerist, with neither the equanimity of all High Renaissance, nor the expansive vigour of all Baroque.

6 The Baroque in the Roman Catholic Countries *c.* 1600–*c.* 1760

Mannerism, it has been pointed out, was originally a noun connected with 'mannered' and nothing else. Some forty years ago it changed its meaning and became the term for a specific historic style in art, the post-Renaissance style of the sixteenth century, particularly in Italy. The same process had taken place about forty years earlier with regard to Baroque. Baroque had originally signified odd, especially of odd shape. It was therefore adopted to describe an architectural style which to the classicist appeared to revel in odd, extravagant shapes, that is, the style of Italy during the seventeenth century. Then, chiefly in the eighties of the last century and chiefly in Germany, it lost its derogatory flavour and became a neutral term to designate the works of art of that century in general.

We have seen the Baroque style first heralded in the massive forms and the gigantic *excelsior* of the dome of Michelangelo's St Peter's. We have then seen that these efforts of Michelangelo towards the Baroque remained exceptional and that he himself in other works of architecture gave way to the pressure of Mannerism. It was only after Mannerism had completed its course that a new generation at the beginning of the seventeenth century, especially in Rome, tired of the forced austerity of the late sixteenth, rediscovered Michelangelo as the father of the Baroque. The style thus introduced culminated in Rome between 1630 and 1670, and then left Rome, first for the north of Italy (Guarini and Juvara in Piedmont) and then for Spain and Portugal and Germany and Austria. Rome, after the late seventeenth century, turned back to its classical tradition, partly under the influence of Paris. For the Paris of Richelieu, Colbert, and Louis XIV had become the centre of European art, a position which until then Rome had held unchallenged for well over 150 years.

The popes and cardinals of the seventeenth century were enthusiastic patrons, eager to commemorate their names by magnificent churches, palaces, and tombs. Of the severity of fifty years before, when the Counter-Reformation had been a militant force, nothing was left. The Jesuits became more and more lenient, the most popular saints were of a lovable, gentle, accommodating kind (such as St Francis de Sales), and the new experimental science was promoted under the very eyes of the popes, until in the eighteenth century Benedict XIV could accept books which Voltaire and Montesquieu sent him as presents.

However, a general decline in the religious fervour of the people can hardly be noticed before 1660 or even later. Not the intensity of religious feelings, only their nature, changed. Art and architecture prove that unmistakably. We can here analyse but a few examples, and it is therefore advisable not to choose the most magnificent, say the nave and façade of St Peter's, as Carlo Maderna designed them in 1606, and as they were completed in 1626, but the most significant.

Maderna was the leading architect of his generation in Rome. He died in 1629. His successors in fame were Gianlorenzo Bernini (1598–1680), Francesco Borromini (1599–1667), and Pietro da Cortona (1596–1669). Bernini came from Naples, Maderna and Borromini from the north of Italy, the country round the lakes, and Cortona, as his name shows, from the south of Tuscany. As in the sixteenth century, so there were in the seventeenth only very few Romans amongst the great men of Rome. In architecture the influx from Lombardy had a considerable effect on the appearance of the city. A breadth and freedom were introduced in distinct contrast to Roman gravity. Thus Maderna's ground plan of the Palazzo Barberini – its façade is by Bernini and a good deal of its decorative detail by Borromini – is of a kind wholly new in Rome, but to a certain extent developing what Northern Italian palaces and villas (especially those of Genoa and its surroundings) had done in the later sixteenth century. As against the austere blocks of the Florentine and Roman palaces (cf. the Palazzo Farnese), the Barberini Palace has a front with short wings jutting forward on the right and the left as so far done only in villas near Rome, and a centre opened in wide

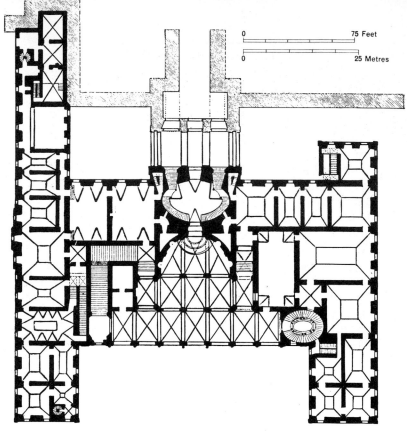

165 Rome, Palazzo Barberini, begun by Maderna, 1628

loggias. Bramante's design of the Damasus Court in the Vatican
with colonnades on all storeys is, one might say, cut into two, and
only one half remains. The colonnades are now part of the façade.
This exposing to the public of what had until then been kept private
is eminently characteristic of the Baroque, as will be seen presently.
The main staircase of the Barberini Palace also is wider and more
open than those of the sixteenth century, the oval second staircase
is a typical Serlio–Palladio motif, and the semicircular niche to the
entrance hall in the centre, as well as the oval saloon to which it
leads, are forms that the architect might have found in Roman

166 Rome, Palazzo Barberini, begun by Maderna, 1628, completed by Bernini and Borromini

churches and in the ruins of Imperial Rome, but that in domestic architecture are also distinctly in the spirit of Palladio (and the Lombards too).

It is important to remember that when Bernini with his South Italian impetuosity won the first place in Roman sculpture and architecture, this infiltration of North Italian elegance had already done its work. His noble colonnades in front of St Peter's have something of the happy openness of Palladian villa architecture, in spite of their Roman weight and their Berninesque sculptural vigour.

167 Rome, St Peter's Square, with the dome by Michelangelo and della Porta, the front and nave by Maderna, 1607–c.1615, and the colonnades by Bernini, begun 1656

For Bernini was the son of a sculptor and himself the greatest sculptor of the Baroque. He incidentally also painted, and as for his reputation as an architect, it was so great that Louis XIV invited him to Paris to design plans' for an enlargement of the Louvre Palace. Bernini was as universal as Michelangelo, and nearly as famous. Borromini, on the other hand, was trained as a mason, and, since he was distantly related to Maderna, found work in a small way at St Peter's when he went to Rome at the age of fifteen. There he worked on, humble and unknown, while Bernini created his first masterpiece of Baroque decoration, the bronze canopy under Michelangelo's dome, in the centre of St Peter's, a huge monument nearly 100 feet high, and with its four gigantic twisted columns the very symbol of the changed age, of a grandeur without restraint, a wild extravagance, and a luxury of detail that would have been distasteful to Michelangelo.

The same vehemence of approach and the same revolutionary disregard of conventions characterize Borromini's first important work, the church of S. Carlo alle Quattro Fontane, begun in 1633. The interior is so small that it would fit into one of the piers which support the dome of St Peter's. But in spite of its miniature size it is one of the most ingenious spatial compositions of the century. It has been said before that the normal plan for longitudinal churches of the Baroque was that of the Gesù: nave with side chapels, short transepts, and dome over the crossing. It was broadened and enriched by the following generations (S. Ignazio, Rome, 1626 seqq.). But the centralized ground plan was not given up either. It was only the predominance of the circle in central churches which the Baroque discarded in Rome. Instead of the circle the oval was introduced, already in Serlio's Book V, i.e. in 1547, and then in Vignola's S. Anna dei Palafrenieri, a less finite form, and a form that endows the centralized plan with longitudinal elements, i.e. elements suggestive of movement in space. An infinite number of variations on the theme of the oval was developed first by the architects of Italy and then by those of other countries. They constitute the most interesting development of Baroque church architecture, a development belonging in Italy chiefly to the second half of the seventeenth century. Serlio and Vignola place the longer axis of the oval at right angles to the façade. This is repeated by most of the others, but S. Agnese in Piazza Navona, begun in 1652 (by Carlo Rainaldi and provided by Borromini with its North Italian two-tower façade), consists of an octagon in a square, with little niches in the corners, and extended by identical entrance and choir chapels at west and east, and by considerably deeper north and south transeptal chapels so as to produce an effect of a broad oval parallel to the façade, with masonry fragments sticking into its outline.

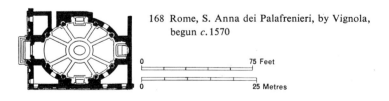

168 Rome, S. Anna dei Palafrenieri, by Vignola, begun *c*.1570

0   75 Feet

0   25 Metres

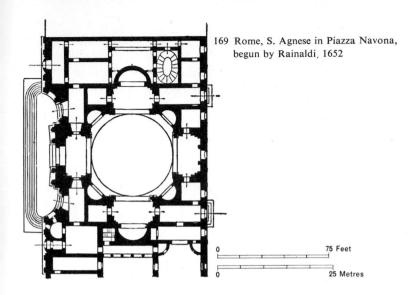

169 Rome, S. Agnese in Piazza Navona, begun by Rainaldi, 1652

0 ⊢——————⊣ 75 Feet

0 ⊢——————⊣ 25 Metres

Bernini had placed a real oval in the same position in his church in the Propaganda Fide (no longer existent) in 1634 and again in his late church of S. Andrea al Quirinale, 1658–78. Vignola's composition was taken up by Maderna at S. Giacomo al Corso, 1594, and by Rainaldi at S. Maria di Monte Santo, 1662. This, incidentally, is one of the two identical churches by the Porta del Popolo, marking the start of three radiating streets towards the centre of Rome.

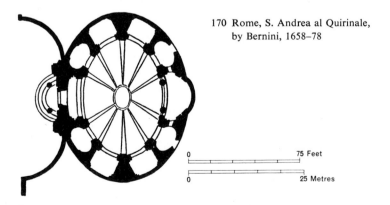

170 Rome, S. Andrea al Quirinale, by Bernini, 1658–78

0 ⊢——————⊣ 75 Feet

0 ⊢——————⊣ 25 Metres

The oval even captured France, especially by the efforts of Louis Levau, as we shall see later. Meanwhile by far the most brilliant paraphrase on the oval theme is Borromini's S. Carlo. The church can serve better than any other to analyse what tremendous advantages the Baroque architect could derive from composing in ovals instead of rectangles or circles. Whereas all through the Renaissance spatial clarity had been the governing idea, and the eye of the spectator had been able to run unimpeded from one part to another and read the meaning of the whole and the parts without effort, nobody, standing in S. Carlo, can at once understand of what elements it is made, and how they are intertwined to produce such a rolling, rocking effect. To analyse the ground plan it will be best not to set out from the oval at right angles to the façade which, broadly speaking, the church seems to be, but from the domed Greek cross of the Renaissance. Borromini has given the dome absolute supremacy over the arms. Their corners are bevelled off so that the walls under the oval dome read like an elongated lozenge opening out into shallow chapels, the dwarfed arms of the original Greek cross. The chapels on the right and the left are fragments of ovals. If completed, they would meet in the centre of the building. The entrance chapel and the apsidal chapel are also fragments of ovals. They just touch the side ovals. Thus five compound spatial shapes merge into

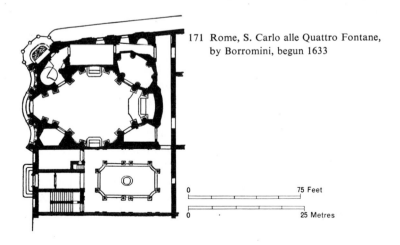

171 Rome, S. Carlo alle Quattro Fontane, by Borromini, begun 1633

0   75 Feet

0   ·   25 Metres

172 Rome, S. Carlo alle Quattro Fontane, by Borromini, begun 1633

each other. We can stand nowhere without taking part in the swaying rhythm of several of them. The Late Gothic churches of Germany had achieved a similar wealth of spatial relations, but by means of forms that seem wiry when compared with the undulating walls of S. Carlo. Michelangelo is responsible for this turn of architecture towards the plastic. Space now seems hollowed out by the hand of a sculptor, walls are moulded as if made of wax or clay.

Borromini's most daring enterprise in setting whole walls into motion is the façade of S. Carlo which was added in 1667, the year of his death. The ground floor and its cornice give the main theme:

173 Rome, S. Carlo alle Quattro Fontane, façade, 16

concave – convex – concave. But the first floor answers by a concave – concave – concave flow, complicated by the insertion of a kind of flattened-out miniature oval temple set into the centre concavity so that this bay seems convex as long as one does not look up to its top part. Such relations in volume and space sound dry when described; when seen, however, there is *brio* and passion in them, and also something distinctly voluptuous, a swaying and swerving as of the naked human form. Watch how the two west towers of S. Agnese stand away from the main front of the church, separated by the convex curves of the two sides of the façade centre, or how in Pietro da Cortona's S. Maria della Pace (1656–7) the front is spread out with straight wings on the ground floor, but a sweeping concave curve on the first floor out of which the centre of the façade reaches forward, ending in a semicircular portico on the ground floor and a

174 Rome, S. Maria della Pace, by Pietro da Cortona, 1656–7

175 Rome, SS. Vincenzo ed Anastasio, by Martino Lunghi the Younger, 1650

slightly set back shallower convex curve on the first floor. Columns and pilasters crowd together on it in a way that makes the composition of Vignola's Gesù front seem restrained in the extreme.

In fact the majority of Roman Baroque façades kept to the basic composition of Vignola and endowed it with a new meaning only by way of an excessive abundance of columns jostling against each other, and the most unconventional use and motives of decoration. One can follow this Baroque development of the Gesù front from Maderna's S. Susanna of *c*. 1596–1603 to the younger Martino Lunghi's SS. Vincenzo ed Anastasio of 1650 and to the excesses of Borromini's S. Carlo façade. Here the curious oval windows on the ground floor should be observed with the palm leaves that surround them, and with a crown above, and some sort of a Roman altar in relief beneath, and so, motif for motif, up the façade until the ogee arch at the top is reached, and the polygons and odd shapes and diminishing sizes that decorate the dome inside. Every one of these details is senseless, unless they are seen together and as parts of a superordinate decorative whole.

To understand the Baroque it is essential to see it in this perspective. We are too much used to looking at decoration as something that may or may not be added to architecture. In fact all architecture is both structure and decoration, decoration for which the architect himself, or the sculptor, the painter, the glass-painter may be responsible. But the relation of decoration to structure varies in different ages and with different nations. In the Gothic style of the cathedrals all decoration served the mason's work. The ornamental sculpture, late in the thirteenth and early in the fourteenth century, seemed to overgrow sculpture. Then, again somewhat later, figure sculpture and painting freed themselves from the supremacy of architecture altogether. A monument like Verrocchio's Colleoni in Venice, standing free in a square without any architectural support, would have been inadmissible in the Middle Ages. Just as novel was the conception of easel painting as such, painting independent of the wall against which it was going to be placed. The Renaissance accepted the independence of the fine arts, but was able to hold them together within a building, because of the principle of relatively independent parts that governed all Renaissance composition. Now, however, in the Baroque, that principle had been abandoned. Again, as in Gothic architecture, parts cannot be isolated. We have seen that at S. Carlo. But the Baroque, although believing in the unity of all art, could not restore the supremacy of structure. Architects of the seventeenth century had to accept the claims of the sculptor and painter, and in fact were sculptors and painters. Instead of the Gothic relation of superordinate and subordinate, there is now a co-operation of all the arts. The result was still that ' *Gesamtkunstwerk*' (total art) which Wagner, in his operas, after it had been wilfully destroyed at the end of the Baroque, endeavoured in vain to recover for the nineteenth century. In the works of Bernini and Borromini, what binds architectural, ornamental, sculptural, and pictorial effects into indivisible unity is the decorative principle common to all.

Now this decorative creed could leave no room in the minds of patrons and artists of the Baroque to be squeamish about honesty in the use of materials. As long as the effect was attained, what could it matter whether you attained it with marble or with stucco, with gold or with tin, with a real bridge or a sham bridge such as we find sometimes in English parks? Optical illusion is in fact (to Ruskin's grave displeasure) amongst the most characteristic devices of Baroque architecture. Bernini's Royal Staircase, the *Scala Regia* in the Vatican Palace, illustrates this at its most suggestive. It was built during the same sixties which saw Borromini's façade of S. Carlo rise from the ground and the colonnades in front of St Peter's. As they are a masterpiece of stage setting, seemingly raising the height and weight of Maderna's façade, and at the same time making the loggia of the Papal benedictions and the *Porta Santa* visible to everybody amongst the tens of thousands who would stand in the forecourt on the occasion of great celebrations, so is the *Scala Regia* designed with a supreme knowledge of scenic effects. It is the main entrance to the palace. Coming from the colonnades, one reaches it along a corridor. The corridor ends in about fifteen or twenty steps, and then there is a slight break just at the point where one enters at right angles from the galilee porch of St Peter's. So here two main directions meet. They had to be joined and connected up. It was a master-stroke of Bernini to place opposite the entrance from the church an equestrian monument to the Emperor Constantine. As

176 Rome, Vatican, *Scala Regia*, by Bernini, 1663–6

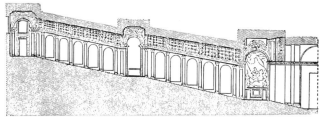

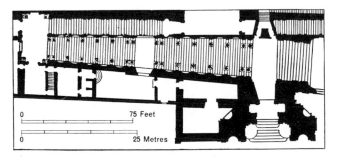

177 Rome, Vatican, *Scala Regia*, by Bernini, 1663–6

we come up from the corridor it appears on the right and forces us to halt, before we enter the Royal Staircase itself. The sudden appearance of the white prancing horse against a storm-swept drapery lit by windows above serves to conceal the otherwise unpleasant change of direction.

The *Scala Regia* had to be fitted into an awkwardly shaped area between church and palace. It is long, comparatively narrow, and has irregularly converging walls. Bernini turned all this to advantage by means of an ingenious tunnel-vaulted colonnade of diminishing size. The principle is that of vistas on the Baroque stage. Streets there were made to appear long by the use of exaggerated perspective. In the same way Borromini treated the niches at S. Carlo and the windows on the top floor of the Palazzo Barberini. Such scenic illusions were not entirely new. They are to be found in Bramante's early works in Milan. Michelangelo too in his design for the Capitol in Rome had placed the palaces on the sides at such an angle as to increase the apparent height of the Senate House. Light is another means for dramatizing the ascent up the Royal Staircase. On the first landing half-way up it falls from the left, on the second in the far distance a window faces the staircase and dissolves the contours of the room. Finally there is the decoration, the splendid angels, for example, with their trumpets holding up the pope's arms, to complete this gorgeous overture to the Vatican Palace. Angels, genii, and suchlike figures, preferably in realistic colouring, are an essential part of Baroque settings. Not only do they serve to cover up structural joints and to hide the contraptions 'behind the scenes' which make these illusions work, but they also act as intermediaries between the real space in which we move and the space created by the artist. The Baroque does not want to keep the border line visible between audience and stage. Such terms from the world of the theatre – or should one rather say the world of the opera, which was an Italian invention of the seventeenth century – come to mind with good reason. However, there is more than a mere theatrical trick in this flow from reality into illusion and from illusion into reality. Bernini's famous chapel of St Teresa in the church of S. Maria della Vittoria in Rome proves that. The chapel, which dates from 1646, is faced with dark marbles, their gleaming surfaces of amber, gold, and pink

178 Rome, S. Maria della Vittoria, Cornaro Chapel, with St Teresa and the
Angel, by Bernini, 1646

reflecting the light in ever-changing patterns. In the middle of the
wall in front of the entrance is the altar of the saint. It is flanked by
heavy coupled columns and pilasters with a broken pediment,
placed on the slant so that they come forward towards us and then
recede to focus our attention on the centre of the altar, where one
would expect to find a painting, but where there is a niche with a

sculptural group, treated like a picture and giving an illusion of reality that is as startling today as it was three hundred years ago. Everything in the chapel contributes to this *peinture vivante* illusion. Along the walls on the right and the left there are also niches opened into the chapel walls, and there Bernini has portrayed in marble, behind balconies, members of the Cornaro family, the donors of the chapel, watching with us the miraculous scene, precisely as though they were in the boxes, and we in the stalls of a theatre.

The boundary line between our world and the world of art is in this most ingeniously effaced. As our own attention and that of the marble figures is directed towards the same goal, we cannot help giving the same degree of reality first to them as to ourselves, and then to the figures on the altar too. And Bernini has used all his mastery in the modelling of St Teresa and the angel to help in that deception. The heavy cloak of the nun, the fluffiness of the clouds, the light drapery of the youthful angel and his soft flesh are all rendered with an exquisite realism. The expression of the saint in the miracle of the union with Christ is of an unforgettable voluptuous ecstasy. She faints as though overwhelmed by a physical penetration. At the same time she is raised into the air, and the diagonal sweep of the group makes us believe the impossible. Beams of gold – they are gilt metal shafts – conceal the back wall of the niche, and an opening high up behind the entablature glazed with a yellow pane models the scene with a magical light.

The chapel of St Teresa is the most daring example of such illusionism in Rome. It is in fact an exception. Rome has never really believed in extremes. Bernini was a Neapolitan; and Naples was Spanish. To experience the thrills of extremes and excesses one must indeed go to Spain, or else to Portugal, or of course to Germany. To these countries the Baroque came late, but it was taken up with tremendous fervour. Italy has no examples of such orgiastic interpenetration of reality and fiction as can be seen in some few Spanish and many more South German churches of the early eighteenth century.

The most outstanding example on Spanish soil is Narciso Tomé's *Trasparente* in Toledo Cathedral. The cathedral is a thirteenth-century building in the style of classic French Gothic. It has a high

179 Toledo Cathedral, *Trasparente*, by Narciso Tomé, completed 1732

180 Toledo Cathedral, *Trasparente*, by Narciso Tomé, completed 1732

altar with a vast Late Gothic reredos. Catholic orthodoxy objected
to people walking along the ambulatory behind the Blessed Sacrament. So an ingenious plan was worked out by which the Sacrament
could be seen and would be respected from the ambulatory as well.
It was placed in a glass-fronted receptacle – hence the name *Trasparente* – and an altar scenery was built up around it of unheard-of
pomp. The work was completed in 1732. Attention was focused on
to the Sacrament by richly decorated columns. They are linked up
with large outer columns by cornices curved upwards. These curves

and the relief scenes in perspective on the panels below give the illusion – in the same way as Bernini's colonnade in the *Scala Regia* – that the distance from front to back of the altar is far deeper than it really is. Moreover, the glass-fronted opening is surrounded by angels to cover all structural props. By the clouds of angels our eyes are led up to where the Last Supper is acted – at a fantastic height – by figures of polychromatic marble. Higher up still is the Virgin soaring up to Heaven. To enhance the effect of a miraculous apparition, the whole scene is floodlit from behind where we stand while we stare at it, lit, that is, in the way special stage lighting is operated today. What the ingenious architect has done is to take out the masonry between the ribs of half a Gothic vault of the ambulatory – the engineering skill of the thirteenth century allowed him to do so without weakening the construction – spread groups of angels around the opening, and then erect above it a dormer with a window, invisible from below, which lets in a flood of golden light past the angels and the bay of the ambulatory in which we stand, on to the altar with its figures and the Sacrament. And when, to discover this source of magic light, we turn round, away from the altar, we see in the dazzling light beyond the angels Christ himself seated on clouds, and prophets and the Heavenly Host surrounding him.

Such spatial extremism, the pulling of a whole room into one vast stupefying ornament, is, it has been said before, exceptional in Spain. What Spain and Portugal excelled in was this same extremism expressing itself in the piling of ornament on to surfaces. This ornamental mania had been a Spanish heritage ever since Mohammedan times, the Alhambra, and the Late Gothic of such works as the front of St Paul's at Valladolid, but never yet had it taken quite such fantastic shapes as it now did in the so-called Churrigueresque style, named after its chief exponent José de Churriguera (1650–1725). The immediate inspiration of the barbaric scrolls and thick mouldings of, for instance, the Sacristy of the Charterhouse at Granada (1727–64 by Luis de Arévalo and F. Manuel Vasquez) must have been native art of Central or South America, as the immediate inspiration of the Manueline style in Portugal has been found in the East Indies. It is in fact in Mexico that the Spanish architects celebrated the wildest of all orgies of over-decoration.

181 Granada, Charterhouse, sacristy, by Luis de Arévalo and
F. Manuel Vasquez, 1727–64

The *Trasparente* stands on a higher aesthetic level no doubt than
the incrustations of the Churrigueresque, though morally, especially
to thc Ruskinian morality of Victorian England, they may both be
equally objectionable. Southern Germany in the eighteenth century
was almost as fond of ornament for ornament's sake as Spain. There
again the tradition leads back to the Middle Ages. But as it has been
shown that German Late Gothic was fonder of spatial complexity
than the Late Gothic of any other country, so the exploitation of
space became now the central problem of German Late Baroque, a
problem occasionally solved with the knock-out technique of the
Trasparente, but more often by purer, strictly architectural means.

The sources of German Late Baroque are Bernini, though he was
imitated chiefly as a sculptor, and Borromini, and, more eagerly
followed than any other, Guarino Guarini, an architect not so far

mentioned at all, because his field of activity was not Rome. He was born in 1624 at Modena, lived mostly at Turin, and died in 1683, which means that he stands just between the generations of Bernini and Borromini and those of the Germans. He was an Oratorian, a professor of philosophy and mathematics, and a designer of buildings. His *Architettura Civile* came out only in 1737, but engravings from it had been known from 1668, and in addition his journeys abroad had acquainted architects with him and his work. Outside Italy he carried out chiefly two churches: Ste Anne in Paris (1662), no longer existent, and the Divina Providência at Lisbon, and he planned a third which was never built, the church of the Virgin of Öttingen on the Kleinseite at Prague (1679). The daring of Guarini's style is apparent for instance in the fact that he alone ventured to transfer to the palace façade the principle of undulation established in Borromini's church fronts. Guarini's Palazzo Carignano at Turin has a centre which undulates in a concave-convex-concave curve. The principal room is oval and two separate staircases run up between the oval and the concave parts of the façade. In his designs for churches, especially S. Lorenzo at Turin of 1666, etc., and the churches for Lisbon and Prague, there is the most fantastic interaction of concave and convex spatial parts, again with a treatment

183 Turin, S. Lorenzo, by Guarini, begun 1666

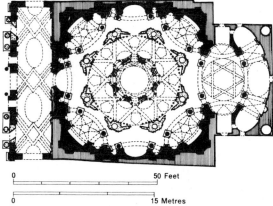

0   50 Feet

0   15 Metres

Granada, Charterhouse, sacristy, detail

in advance of Borromini. It is not easy to understand them solely with the help of one's eyes, and Guarini was probably no less interested in them as a mathematician than as an artist. At S. Lorenzo for instance arches and balconies swing forward into the central space which is crowned by a dome. For the dome Guarini invented (or took over from the Mohammedan mosque of Cordova) an eight-cornered star of ribs flowing forward and backward and crossing on their way. In the longitudinal churches of Lisbon and

184 Turin, S. Lorenzo, by Guarini, begun 1666, view into dome

Prague even the transverse arches across the naves have been pulled into the general undulation and built three-dimensionally (that is, forward as well as upward). This unprecedented effect is due to the composition of the naves out of series of intersecting ovals. Here and in Borromini, as has been said, lie the chief sources of Late German Baroque.

Of the great wealth of ingenious architects working between 1720 and 1760 only two can here be introduced: Cosmas Damian Asam (1686–1739) and Johann Balthasar Neumann (1687–1753).

Cosmas Damian Asam was a painter and decorator, his brother Egid Quirin (1692–1750) a sculptor. The two as a rule worked together, not considered as anything but competent craftsmen and not apparently considering themselves as anything else either. They, and in common with them the majority of the German eighteenth-century architects, were not really architects in the Renaissance or modern sense. They were brought up in villages to know something about building, and that was enough. No big ideas about professional status entered their heads. In fact the sociological position of architecture in Germany before the nineteenth century was still medieval, and most of the patrons were still princes, bishops, abbots, just as they had been three hundred years earlier. Neumann belongs to another category, one that had not existed in the Middle Ages or the Renaissance. Its source is the France of Louis XIV, as will be shown later (see p. 321). He had started in the artillery force of the Prince-Bishop of Würzburg. There he had shown a keen interest in mathematics and fortification. Michelangelo too, it will be remembered, had worked on defence engineering, and some of the other leading sixteenth-century architects in Italy, e.g. Sammicheli, had been distinguished military engineers. The Prince-Bishop singled out young Neumann for architectural work, made him his surveyor of works, and sent him to Paris and Vienna to discuss the plans for his new palace at Würzburg with his opposite numbers there, the French king's and the Emperor's architects, and to learn from them. Thus his most famous work, the palace at Würzburg, is only partly his; but his experience grew, and the Bishop appreciated him more and more. He was made a captain, then a major, then a colonel, but he had no longer any duties of active service and could devote all his

263

time to architecture. He did all the designing and supervising for the Bishop that had to be done, and was soon also asked to design palaces and churches for other clients.

Thus churches of the eighteenth century in Germany may originate from very different milieus: the workshop of the medieval craftsman or the drawing-board of the technically skilled courtier. Differences in architectural character may often be explained in this way. Asam churches are naïve. Neumann's are of an intellectual complexity equal to Bach's. Spatial effects, however, are as important in the Asams' as in Neumann's work. But the Asams stick to the more ostentatious devices of optical illusion (raising them, it is true, to a high emotional pitch), while Neumann composes his configuration of space scorning easy deceptions.

185 Weltenburg, abbey church, by Cosmas Damian and Egid Quirin Asam, 1717–21

At Rohr near Regensburg the Asams placed in the chancel of the church a showpiece, cruder than Bernini's St Teresa, and twice as melodramatic: the Apostles, life-size figures standing round a life-size Baroque sarcophagus, and the Virgin rising to Heaven supported by angels to be received into a glory of clouds and cherubs high above. Wild gesticulation and dark glowing colour all help to inflame the passions of faith. The chancel at Weltenburg, another church near Regensburg, is the stage for a more mysterious apparition: a silver St George on horseback wielding a flame-shaped sword and riding straight towards us out of a background of dazzling light which is let in from concealed windows. The dragon and the princess stand out as dark golden silhouettes against all this glitter. Rohr was built in 1718–25, Weltenburg in 1717–21. They are early works of the Asams.

In their best later work they endeavoured to achieve more than a *Trasparente* effect. Egid Quirin owned a house at Munich; when he approached the age of forty he began to think of a monument that he might proudly leave behind after his death. So he decided in 1731 to build on a site adjoining his house a church as his private offering. The church was built from 1733 to about 1750 and dedicated to St John Nepomuk. It is a tiny church, less than thirty feet wide, relatively tall and narrow with a narrow gallery all the way round, a ground-floor altar, and a gallery altar. The gallery balancing on the fingers of pirouetting termini or caryatid angels sways forward and backward, the top cornice surges up and droops down, the colour scheme is of sombre gold, browns, and dark reds, glistening in sudden flashes where light falls on it, light which comes only from the entrance, that is, from behind our backs, and from concealed windows above the cornice. The top east window is placed in such a way that a group of the Trinity appears against it; God holding the Crucifix, the Holy Ghost above, the whole again surrounded by angels – wildly fantastic, yet of a superb magic reality. What raises St John Nepomuk above the level of Rohr, Weltenburg, and the *Trasparente* is the co-operation of strictly architectural composition with the merely optical deceptions to achieve an intense sensation of surprise which may turn easily into religious fervour.

But sensational it is all the same, sensational in a literal sense: no

186 Munich, St John Nepomuk, by Egid Quirin Asam, 1733–*c.* 50, detail above high altar

artists before Bernini, the Asams, and Tomé had aimed at such violent effects. And are they therefore debauched, unscrupulous, and pagan as our Pugins and Ruskins have made them out? We should not accept their verdicts uncritically, lest we might deprive ourselves of a good deal of legitimate pleasure. We may indeed, up here in the North where we live, find it hard to connect Christ and the Church with this obtruding physical closeness of presentation. To the Southerner, in Bavaria, in Austria, in Italy, in Spain, where people live so much more with all their senses, it is a genuine form of religious experience. While in the North during the lifetime of Bernini, the Asams, and Tomé, Spinoza visualized a pantheism, with God pervading all beings and all things, Rembrandt discovered the infinite for painting in his treatment of light and his merging of action into undefined but live background, and Newton and Leibniz discovered it for mathematics in their conception of the calculus, the South had its more concrete realization of an all-embracing oneness and a presence of the infinite in the architects' and decorators' unification of real and fictitious worlds, in their spatial effects stepping beyond the bounds of what the beholder can rationally explain to himself. And Neumann's work proves conclusively what architectural purity and subtlety can be achieved by such spatial magic, provided the visitor to his buildings is able to follow his guidance. We of the twentieth century do not usually find it easy to concentrate on spatial counterpoint, just as our audiences in church and concert no doubt hear musical counterpoint less distinctly than those for whom Bach wrote. The parallelism is in fact striking, in quality too. The best German eighteenth-century architecture is up to the standard of the best German eighteenth-century music.

Take Neumann's pilgrimage church of Vierzehnheiligen in Franconia, built from 1743 to 1772. The first impression on entering this vast, solitary pilgrimage church is one of bliss and elevation. All is light: white, gold, pink. In this the church testifies to its later date than that of St John Nepomuk. Asam's work is still Baroque in the seventeenth-century sense, Neumann's belongs to that last phase of the Baroque which goes under the name Rococo. For the Rococo is not a separate style. It is part of the Baroque, as Decorated is part of the Gothic style. The difference between Baroque and Rococo is only one of sublimation. The later phase is light, where the earlier was sombre; delicate, where the earlier was forceful; playful, where the earlier was passionate. But it is just as *mouvementé*, as vivacious, as voluptuous as the Baroque. One connects the term Rococo chiefly with France and the age of Casanova on the one hand, Voltaire on the other. In Germany it is not intellectually or sensually sophisticated – it is as direct an expression of the people's aesthetic instinct as Late Gothic architecture and decoration had been, and one can see from the devotion today of the peasants in these German

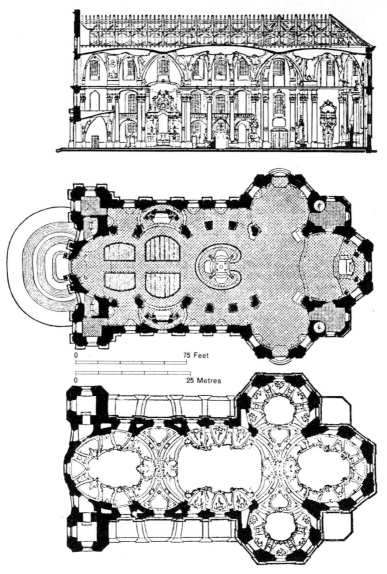

187 Vierzehnheiligen, by Neumann, 1743–72, section, plan on ground-floor level, and plan of vaults

188 Vierzehnheiligen, pilgrimage church, by Balthasar Neumann, 1743–7

Baroque – and the Italian Baroque – churches that their style is not a style of interest only to a privileged set of virtuosi.

Yet the style of Vierzehnheiligen is not an easy style. It is not enough to be overwhelmed by it, as anyone may be in Asam churches; it asks for an exact understanding – which is a job for the expert: architects' architecture, as the fugue is musicians' music. The oval central altar in the middle of the nave may well please the rustic worshippers who kneel round this gorgeous object, half a coral reef and half a fairy sedan chair. Having taken in this glory of confectionery, the layman will then look up and see on all sides glittering decoration, surf and froth and rocket, and like it immensely. But if he starts walking round, he will soon find himself in utter confusion. What he has learned and so often seen of nave and aisle and chancel seems of no value here. This confusion of the lay mind, a keen thrill of the trained, is due to the ground plan, one of the most ingenious pieces of architectural design ever conceived. The church, if one looks at it from outside, has apparently a nave and aisles, and a centrally planned east end with polygonal ends to transepts and choir. In fact the choir is an oval, the transepts are circular, and the nave consists of two ovals following each other so that the first, into which one enters immediately one has passed the Borrominesque undulating front, is of the size of the choir oval and the second considerably larger. It is here that the altar of the fourteen saints stands. Here then is the spiritual centre of the church. So there arises an antagonism of great poignancy between what the exterior promises as the centre and what the interior reveals to be the centre – namely, between the crossing where nave and transepts meet, and the centre of the principal oval. As for the aisles they are nothing but spatial residues. Walking along them, one feels painfully behind the scenes. What matters alone is the interaction of the ovals. At vault height they are separated by transverse arches. These, however, are not simple bands across from one arcade column to the one opposite. They are three-dimensional, bowing to each other, as the nodding arches had done on a small scale in the fourteenth century, one more of the many parallels of Gothic and Baroque.[27] This has the most exciting and baffling effect at the crossing. Here in a church of the Gesù type – and Vierzehnheiligen appears from outside to belong to this type – one would expect a dome, the summit of the composition. Instead of that, there lies, as has been said before, just at the centre of the crossing, the point where choir oval and central oval meet. The two transverse arches struck from the piers of the crossing bend, the western one eastward, the eastern westward, until they touch each other in exactly the same place as the ovals, purposely emphasizing the fact that, where a normal Baroque church would have had the crest of the undulating movement of the vaults, Vierzehnheiligen has a trough – a most effective spatial counterpoint. Yet another spatial complication is incidentally provided by the insertion of a second minor transept farther west than the main one. Side altars are placed in it, just as altars stand against the east end of the church and against the east piers of the crossing. The latter are set diagonally so as to guide the eye towards the splendid high altar – a decidedly theatrical effect.

This is one of the chief objections against such churches. Its validity has already been queried. Besides, why did architects and artists so fervently strive to deceive and create such intense illusion of reality? What reality was the Church concerned with? Surely that of the Divine Presence. It is the zeal of an age in which Roman Catholic dogmas, mysteries, and miracles were no longer, as they had been in the Middle Ages, accepted as truth by all. There were heretics, and there were sceptics. To restore the first to the fold, to convince the others, religious architecture had both to inflame and to mesmerize. But it is brought forward as another argument against Baroque churches that they seem worldly as compared with the churches of the Middle Ages. Now it is true that the character of Baroque decoration in a church and a palace is identical. But is not exactly the same true of the Middle Ages? The idea behind the identity is perfectly sane. By the splendour of the arts we honour a king; is not supreme splendour due to the King of Kings? In our churches today and in those churches of the Middle Ages which the nineteenth century restored, there is nothing of this. They are halls with an atmosphere to concentrate the thoughts of a congregation on worship and prayer. A church of the Baroque was literally the house of the Lord.

Still, there is no denying the fact that we, observers or believers, never feel quite sure where in a church such as Vierzehnheiligen the spiritual ends and the worldly begins. The ecstatic *élan* of the architectural forms at large is irresistible, but it is not necessarily a religious *élan*. There was, it is true, a real mania in Southern Germany and Austria between 1700 and 1760 for building vast churches and monasteries. It is only one expression of the general Baroque mania for building on a colossal scale. 'Bauwurm' is the name given to it by the Schönborns in Germany who were responsible for so much building at Würzburg, in the whole of Franconia, and at Vienna. 'Batissomanie', Catherine the Great called it in a letter to Baron Grimm in Paris. Nor was all the new work in churches and monasteries undertaken entirely *ad majorem Dei gloriam*. Did a monastery like Weingarten near the lake of Constance really need these far-stretched, elegantly curved outbuildings which appear in a rebuilding scheme of 1723? This scheme was never carried out: but others – e.g. at Klosterneuburg, St Florian, and Melk, all three on the Danube – were. Melk was begun in 1702 by Jakob Prandtauer (died 1726); it is in many ways the most remarkable of the three, shooting up out of the rocks, steep above the river. The church with its undulating front, its two many-pinnacled towers, and its bulbous spires is set back. Two pavilions of the monastery buildings, housing the marble hall and the library, jut forward to its right and left, converging as they approach the front bastion. They are here connected

189 Plan for rebuilding the monastery
of Weingarten, 1723

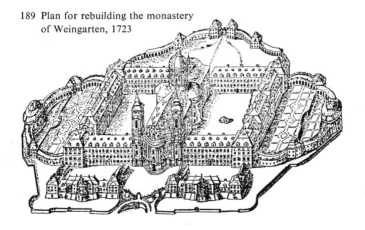

190 Melk, Benedictine abbey, by Jakob Prandtauer, begun 1702

by lower, roughly semicircular wings. Between these, exactly in line with the church, is an oddly Palladian arch to keep the vista open from the west portal towards the river. It is an exquisite piece of visual calculation – a late and subtle development of Palladio's so much simpler connecting of villa and landscape, and evidently the work of the century which discovered landscape gardening (see pp. 345 seqq.).

But, to return to our question, while the towering church on the cliff – a Durham of the Baroque – may rightly be considered a monument of militant Catholicism, the palaces for abbot and monks with their richly ornamented saloons and their terraces are amenities of this world, on exactly the same level, and planned and executed in exactly the same lavish manner, as the contemporary palaces of the secular and clerical rulers of the innumerable states of the Holy Roman Empire, or the country palaces of the English aristocracy, or Caserta, the palace of the King of Naples, or Stupinigi, the palace of the Duke of Savoy and King of Sardinia.

One of the most irresponsible of these schemes is the Zwinger in Dresden, built by Matthäus Daniel Pöppelmann (1662–1736) for the Elector Augustus the Strong, athlete, glutton, and lecher. The Zwinger is a combined orangery and electoral grandstand for tournaments and pageants. It was not supposed to stand on its own, as it does now, attached only to the nineteenth-century picture gallery; it was meant to form part of a palace stretching across to the River Elbe. It consists of one-storeyed galleries with two-storeyed pavilions between. The galleries are comparatively re-strained in design, but the most exuberant decoration is lavished over the pavilions. The gate pavilion especially is a fantasy unchecked by any consideration of use. The ground-floor archway has instead of a proper pediment two bits of a broken pediment swinging away from each other. The first-floor pediment is broken too, but nodding inward instead of outward. The whole first floor is open on all sides – a kiosk or gazebo, as it were – and above its attic, swarming with figures of putti, is a bulbous cupola with the royal and electoral emblems on top.

If those who can admire a Gothic Devon screen feel repelled by the Zwinger, they either do not really look at the object before them,

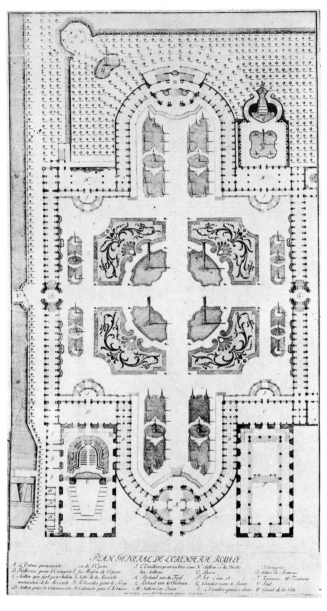

191 Dresden, Zwinger, by Matthaeus Daniel Pöppelmann, 1711–22

192 Dresden, Zwinger, by Matthaeus Daniel Pöppelmann, 1711–22,
gate pavilion

or they look at it with the blinkers of puritanism. What exultation in
these rocking curves, and yet what grace! It is joyful but never
vulgar; vigorous, boisterous perhaps, but never crude. It is of an inexhaustible creative power, with ever new combinations and variations of Italian Baroque forms placed against each other and piled
above each other. The forward and backward motion never stops.
Borromini appears massive against this swiftness of movement
through space.

As in every original style, the same formal intention seems, in the

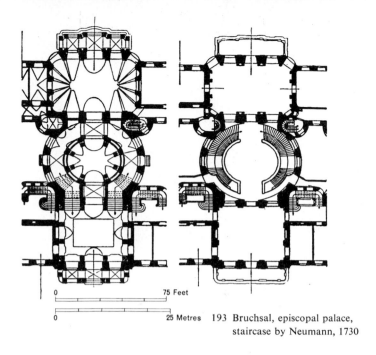

German Rococo, to model space and volume. The three-dimensional curve is the *leitmotif* of the period. It appears at Vierzehnheiligen as it appears in the Zwinger, and it pervades buildings from their main theme of composition down to the smallest ornamental details. Nowhere else perhaps can this be seen as convincingly as in one of Neumann's secular masterpieces, the staircase of the Bishop's Palace at Bruchsal. The palace itself is not by Neumann. It was in quite an advanced state when in 1730 Neumann was called in to redesign the staircase.

The palace consists of a rectangular centre block or *corps de logis* and lower projecting wings, i.e. the Palladian scheme which had spread from Northern Italy to England and also to France, where it has been modified and then, in its revised shape with the space between the wings treated as a formal *cour d'honneur*, taken over by Germany. In the centre of the *corps de logis* is the staircase, an oval room, larger than any other in the palace. This alone is a most significant fact.

277

194 Bruchsal, episcopal palace, staircase, by Johann Balthasar Neumann, designed 1730

In the Middle Ages staircases had mattered little. They were nearly always tucked away – a purely utilitarian part of the building. Newel staircases taking up as little space as possible were the rule. The very latest phase of the Gothic style with its new appreciation of space had sometimes tried to endow them with spatial expression, emphasizing the delights of ever-changing axes. The culmination is such French staircases as those of Blois and Chambord.[28] The Italian Renaissance was on the whole not favourable to developments of the staircase. It is too dynamic a motif to meet with the approval of Renaissance architects. Alberti says this of staircases: 'Scalae, quo erunt numero pauciores . . . quoque occupabunt minus areae . . . eo erunt commodiores' ('The fewer staircases there are in a building and the less space they take up, the better'). Thus the standard Renaissance staircase is one of two flights running up first

195 Bruchsal, episcopal palace, looking down on the staircase from first floor landing

to the intermediate landing between solid walls, then turning by 180 degrees and reaching the upper floor by the second flight also between solid walls. Such staircases, as they occur from Brunelleschi's Foundling Hospital to the Palazzo Farnese and beyond, are really only vaulted corridors running up at an angle. A more imaginative treatment is rare in fifteenth-century Italy. Nothing survives that would be worth mentioning. But Francesco di Giorgio, whose treatise written in the seventies has been mentioned before, apropos the history of central planning, illustrates suggested plans of palaces, and in two of these shows staircases of new types – and, indeed, of types which were to become of the greatest importance for the centuries to come.

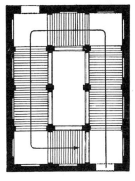

197 Square newel staircase

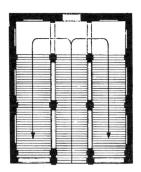

198 Imperial staircase

Their introduction into real architecture, however, or at any rate their popularization, was due to a more restless country than Italy: Spain. The first and most important of these new types is the square newel staircase, with three straight flights of steps around a spacious open well and the landing on the fourth side. This type occurs for the first time after Francesco di Giorgio in Enrique de Egas's part of S. Juan de los Reyes at Toledo (completed 1504), the Hospital of the Holy Cross also at Toledo and also by Egas (1504–14), and in Michele Carlone's castle of Lacalahorra (1508–12). A few years later Diego Siloée erected the magnificent Escalera Dorada inside the cathedral of Burgos, developed essentially on a T-plan, i.e.

281

6 Blois, spiral staircase in the range of Francis I, 1515–c. 1525

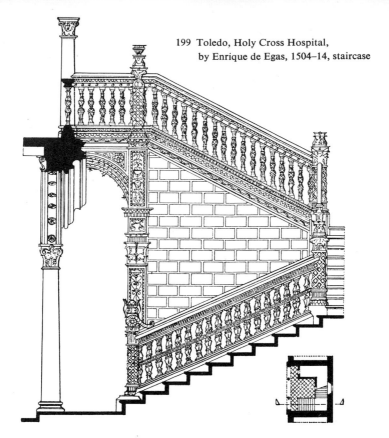

199 Toledo, Holy Cross Hospital,
by Enrique de Egas, 1504–14, staircase

starting with one straight flight and then forking at the landing at an angle of 90 degrees to the left and right. The derivation of this plan from Bramante's outdoor staircase in the vast Belvedere Court of the Vatican has been proved, but again Francesco di Giorgio had come before Bramante (no doubt influencing him). He suggests the same type of staircase for a Palazzo della Repubblica – in exactly the same position, incidentally, in which much later such staircases were popular in Genoese palaces.

Meanwhile, however, Spain had introduced yet another type, the grandest of all, and here also, it seems, on the sole precedent of unexecuted Italian drawings. In the case of this type, known as the Imperial staircase, Leonardo sketches are the pattern. An Imperial

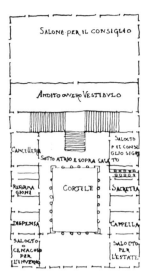

200 Sketch for a staircase
for a Palazzo della Repubblica,
by Francesco di Giorgio

staircase is one which runs in a large oblong cage, starting with one straight arm and then, after the landing, turning by 180 degrees and leading up to the upper floor with two arms to the left and right of, and parallel with, the first arm (or starting with two and finishing with one). This type appears to my knowledge for the first time in Juan Bautista de Toledo's and Juan de Herrera's Escorial (1563–84). It is eminently characteristic that these staircases, in which space is experienced most vividly by those who ascend them or descend them, were developed outside Italy. If we examine the best sixteenth-century staircases in Italy, we find that Bramante's delightful Vatican staircase is of the traditional newel type, though with a wide open well and of gentle rise and generous measurements. Serlio and Palladio followed Bramante in this, although they knew and used the square three-flight type. However, their hearts were not in staircase design. Their only innovations are the newel staircase elongated into an oval shape (Maderna incidentally kept to this in the Barberini Palace) and the flight of stairs corbelled out of the wall without any inner support on the side of the open wall. The Baroque of the seventeenth century, especially in France, only enriched the current types (see page 335). That of the Escorial became in many variations the hall-mark of princely magnificence. Neumann's staircase at Würzburg with its Tiepolo paintings belongs to it.

But the staircase at Bruchsal is unique. Words can hardly re-evoke the enchanting sensation experienced by anybody who has had the good fortune to walk up one of its two arms, when it still existed undamaged by war. The arms started in the rectangular vestibule. After about ten steps one entered the oval. On the ground floor it is a sombre room, painted with rocks in the rustic manner of Italian grotto imitations. The staircase itself then unfolded between two curved walls, the outside wall solid, that on the inside opened in arcades through which one looked down into the semi-darkness of the oval grotto. The height of the arcade openings of course diminished as the staircase ascended. And while you walked up, it grew lighter and lighter around you, until you reached the main floor and a platform the size of the oval room beneath. But the vault above covered the larger oval formed by the outer walls of the staircase. Thus the platform with its balustrade separating it from the two staircase arms seemed to rise in mid-air, connected only by bridges with the two principal saloons. And the vast vault above was lit by many windows, painted with the gayest of frescoes, and decorated with a splendid fireworks of stucco. The spatial rapture of the staircase was in this decoration transformed into ornamental rapture. It culminated in the cartouche over the door leading into the Grand Saloon. The cartouche was not Neumann's design. It was by a Bavarian stuccoist, Johann Michael Feichtmayr. The contract was made in 1752. These Bavarian stuccoists nearly all came from the same village of Wessobrunn, where boys were as a matter of course trained to become proficient in stucco work, just as the decorators of Romanesque churches so often came from certain villages round the North Italian lakes, the makers and vendors of plaster-of-Paris statuettes in the nineteenth century from Savoy, and the onion-men of today from Brittany. Feichtmayr travelled about from job to job, and, when he worked for a monastery, still received wages and board just as the workmen did seven hundred years ago. Neumann must have met him on some job and have recognized his immense wealth of ornamental inventiveness. He appears at Vierzehnheiligen as well as at Bruchsal. In his stucco ornament not

201 Bruchsal, episcopal palace, first-floor landing. The stucco work by Johann Michael Feichtmayr, 1752

one part is symmetrical. The main composition is a zigzag, from the alluring young angel on the right, up to the cupid or cherub higher up on the left, and up again to the cherub at the top. The forms in detail seem to be incessantly changing, splashing up and sinking back. What are they? Do they represent anything? Sometimes they look like shells, sometimes like froth, sometimes like gristle, sometimes like flames. This kind of ornament is called *rocaille* in France, where it was invented in the 1720s by Meissonier, Oppenord, and a few others of provincial or semi-Italian background. It has given the Rococo style its name, and rightly so; for it is a completely original creation, not dependent on anything of the past, as the ornament of the Renaissance had been. It is abstract art of as high an expressional value as any that we are offered today so much more pretentiously.

Bruchsal with its perfect unity of space and decoration was the high-water mark of the Baroque style. It was also its end. For only a few years after it had been completed and Neumann had died, Winckelmann published his first books, initiating the Classical Revival in Germany. Between Neumann's world and that of Goethe there is no link. The men of the new world no longer thought in terms of churches and palaces. No church designed anywhere after 1760 is amongst the historically leading examples of architecture. Napoleon built no palaces.

The English nobility, it must be admitted, did; right into the Victorian age. But they had nothing of the unreflecting attitude of the Baroque. This change from a style binding for all and understood by all to a style for the educated only did not take place in Germany and Italy until 1760. In France and Britain it had come about earlier. But then neither France nor Britain (nor the north of Germany, Holland, Denmark, and Scandinavia) had ever accepted the Baroque with all its implications. Their world – it is in many respects *the* modern world – is that of Protestantism. In Roman Catholic countries medieval traditions lived and flourished down to the eighteenth century. In the North the Reformation had broken that happy unity. But it had also opened the way for independent thinking and feeling. The Protestant countries (and one should include here the France of the Gallicans, Jansenists, and Encyclopedists) had created Puritanism, Enlightenment, the modern predominance of experimental science, and finally the Industrial Revolution in the material and the symphony in the spiritual world. What the cathedral had been to the Middle Ages, the symphony was to the nineteenth century.

7 Britain and France from the Sixteenth to the Eighteenth Century

At the time of Bruchsal and the *Trasparente*, large houses of Palladian or Neo-Classical style appeared all over England, houses such as Prior Park near Bath, Holkham Hall, Stowe, and Kenwood. In France meanwhile the classic grandeur of Versailles had given way to the Neo-Classical delicacy of the Place de la Concorde and the Petit Trianon. Evidently the development of architecture after the end of the Gothic style had been very different in Western Europe from that in Central Europe.

Yet in Britain, France, the Netherlands, Spain, and Germany, the position had been virtually the same early in the sixteenth century. In all these countries artists at the same moment turned their backs on their Gothic past, attracted by the same new style, the Italian Renaissance. Everywhere during the fifteenth century the fascination of Humanism, of Roman literature, and the clarity and suppleness of the classic Latin style had been experienced by scholars. The invention of printing helped to spread the new ideals, and many patrons arose among princes, noblemen, and merchants. A few of these, when for some reason or other they found themselves in Italy, were converted to Italian art as well, as soon as they had understood its humanistic character. How forceful the sensation must have been it is hardly possible for us to appreciate. One keeps forgetting that it was still a time of scanty and slow communications. Perpendicular to the English, Flamboyant to the French, and their national versions of Late Gothic to the Spaniards and Germans were the only architecture they knew. The first French artist to go to Italy himself and be impressed by the Renaissance was Jean Fouquet, who travelled about 1450 and in whose paintings and illuminated manuscripts after his return one finds some Renaissance motifs curiously mixed up with the customary Flamboyant. A little later, in 1461–6, Francesco Laurana, a sculptor and no doubt a relative of the Luciano Laurana we have met at Urbino, worked for King René of Anjou at Aix, and in 1475–81 he built a small chapel in the church of the Major at Marseilles entirely in the Renaissance style. But Aix and Marseilles are close to Italy, and the great change came only when Charles VIII waged war against Italy in 1494, and, as battle followed battle, reached as far south as Naples. He took back with him Guido Mazzoni, called Paganino, who in 1498 carried out the king's funerary monument at St Denis. This monument has been destroyed, but only a year or two later other Renaissance funerary monuments appeared in France: that to the Dukes of Orléans at St Denis in 1502, again the work of an Italian, and that to François II, Duke of Brittany, in the cathedral of Nantes which dates from 1499 and is essentially by the Frenchman Michel Colombe. Also connected with him is the contemporary monument to the children of Charles VIII in the cathedral of Tours. A little later, probably in 1504 or 1505, Antonio and Giovanni Giusti arrived at Tours, settled down, and changed their name to Juste. They also, needless to say, brought the Quattrocento style with them as their sole medium of expression. The transition from decorative sculpture to the sculptural decoration of architecture was made at the château of Gaillon in Normandy. Here in 1508–10 an application of a system of superimposed pilasters to the traditional French body of the building took place which was for a time to become canonical.

It need hardly be said that these are exactly the years in which Dürer went to Italy from Nuremberg and absorbed the Venetian Renaissance. Meanwhile, in Spain also, things moved in the same direction. Here some of the noble families, notably the Mendoza, had been converted to the new style, and Renaissance portals or courtyards appeared here and there already in the eighties (Cogolludo, Vallodolid, etc.), and more often between 1500 and 1510 (e.g. the Hospital of the Holy Cross at Toledo, see p. 281). As for Germany, Dürer in 1506 went to Venice a second time, now to start embellishing his pictures and engravings with Italian ornament. At Augsburg in 1509 a whole large chapel was built at the expense of the Fuggers in a Venetian Renaissance style, even if with a Gothic rib-vault. That is an exception. On the whole in Germany and also in the Netherlands at such an early date it is decoration rather than architecture one must look for. This is true, for example, of Quentin Matsys and the Italian motifs in his paintings of *c.*1508, etc., and it is also true of England. In 1509 Henry VII had an agreement drawn up with Mazzoni, who was, as we have seen, in Paris, to design his tomb. The job did not materialize, but in 1512 Henry VIII found another Italian, Pietro Torrigiani, a fellow-student of Michelangelo in Florence, to design the tomb for his father. As Torrigiani carved it, so it now stands in Henry VII's Chapel in Westminster Abbey, a stranger in the midst of the wonders of Gothic ingenuity that surround it. No more poignant contrast can be imagined than that between Perpendicular panels and these medallions surrounded by wreaths, Perpendicular piers and these daintily ornamental pilasters, Perpendicular mouldings and the Antique mouldings of this base and this cornice, or Perpendicular foliage and the smiling beauty of these roses and acanthus friezes.

So far the conversion to Italian Renaissance motifs has only been discussed for France, Spain, Germany, the Netherlands, and

202 Westminster Abbey, tomb of Henry VII, by Torrigiani, 1512–18

England, but it is a fact well worth a paragraph that the countries of Eastern Europe took more readily to them than the major countries of the West. This applies to Hungary, Russia, Bohemia, Poland, and Austria. In Hungary, houses at Buda were already built 'ad italicorum aedifitiorum symmetriam' before the middle of the fifteenth century. Then King Matthias Corvinus, married to a Neapolitan princess, brought in Italian masons and sculptors and some of their work has been recovered in recent excavations at Buda and Visegrád Castles.[29] One of his Italians, Aristotile Fioravanti of Bologna and Milan, went on from Hungary to Moscow, and there, from 1475 onwards, built the Cathedral of the Dormition. This was followed by the even more convincedly Italian Cathedral of St Michael, begun about 1504, also by an Italian. Both cathedrals retained however the traditional Russo-Byzantine plan. The first purely Italian ecclesiastical building, Italian in plan, elevation, and all decoration, is the Bákocz Chapel at Esztergom Cathedral (Gran) of 1506–7, i.e. of a date sixteen years after the death of Matthias Corvinus. He was succeeded by Vladislav II, King of Bohemia. Under Vladislav the court of Prague also began to take to the new type of decoration. The Vladislav Hall on the Hradshin in Prague, begun in 1493 by Benedict Ried, a German mason, has a brilliant Late Gothic vault with intertwined curved ribs, but windows in a pure Renaissance, the work probably of artists imported from Hungary, and in addition the oddest bastard motifs such as fluted classical pilasters twisted and pilasters placed diagonally – a sign of a confusion, matched for instance on the Vavel, the castle of Cracow (where Vladislav's brother Sigismund resided). Here doorways of *c.* 1502, etc., have fantastic Gothic lintels but outer frames of Renaissance form. Rebuilding continued on the Vavel on a larger scale and in a purer Renaissance from 1507 onwards, and Sigismund's funeral chapel at Cracow Cathedral, built in 1517–33 by a Florentine architect, is of course entirely Italian in style. It is evident from all these data and dates that the East was indeed ahead of the West in the acceptance of the Renaissance. This fact is surprising only at first sight. The national traditions of the Eastern countries were either weaker or so alien to the West, that, once a policy of openness to the West was decided upon, rulers were ready for the most recent, newest, and most novel.

This explanation is confirmed by the situation in Austria, a country a little nearer the German tradition and thus slower in coming to terms with the Renaissance (Portal Salvator Chapel, Vicuna, *c*. 1520–5).[30]

The words recent and novel have just been used. It should however be kept in mind that neither in the Eastern countries nor indeed in the West was the kind of Renaissance taken over with so much delight between 1500 and 1520 the style of the most important work actually going on during the same years in Italy. What the architecture of 1520 was like in Rome has been shown. Bramante, Raphael, and their followers had discarded most of that pretty ornament and turned towards a grave classic ideal. For this, the time was not yet ripe – in France for some twenty years, and in Britain for nearly a hundred. Early Renaissance was in full blossom this side of the Alps, when on the other side art and architecture had already passed the summit of High Renaissance. Michelangelo's Medici Chapel and Laurenziana with their Mannerist discords are earlier than the most exquisite piece of Italian decoration surviving in England, the stalls

203 Cambridge, King's College Chapel, screen, 1532–6

of King's College Chapel, Cambridge, of *c*. 1532–6. Again the contrast between the only slightly older chapel itself and this addition from abroad is striking. And as the one was in the idiom with which everybody had grown up, while the other seemed to speak a foreign language, it is understandable that English patrons wavered between admiration and bewilderment. Very few were prepared to go the whole way (more in fact in France, where there was less of a racial contrast than in England), and those who did had to rely on craftsmen from Italy, because the English or even the French mason could not at once get into a manner so novel both technically and spiritually.

Now of Italians there were more and more who found their way into France and were welcomed by Francis I, but few who travelled on to Britain. Leonardo da Vinci came in 1516, lived near Amboise and died there in 1579. Andrea del Sarto came for a year in 1578–9, and then, after the artists of the High Renaissance, confirmed Mannerists also appear, Rosso Fiorentino, the painter and brilliant decorator, in 1530, Primaticcio, the painter, architect, and decorator, in 1532. They stayed on and helped to establish the new type of architect-designer who was no longer an executant. For the execution of their works they had to rely on the native master masons. Even Geoffrey Tory, a Frenchman who had translated Alberti, calls the Italians only 'souverains en perspective, peinture et imagerie'. So a deep antagonism developed at once between the Italians and the competent traditional craftsmen of France to whom these Italian intruders were mountebanks and jacks-of-all-trades.

However, the antagonism does not often appear in actual buildings. For – again probably thanks to racial affinity – the French master masons very soon adopted the Italian vocabulary and used it to produce an essentially original style neither Gothic nor Renaissance. Three phases must be distinguished, the first that of the Loire school, the second that of Francis I's later years, the third that of Henry II and the final change-over from Italian to French architects. The wing of Francis I at the château of Blois was built between 1515 and 1525. Evey motif used in its decoration is of the North Italian Early Renaissance. The most consistently used motif, and indeed the hall-mark of the Loire School, though first applied at

Gaillon, as we have seen, is the articulation of the whole façade by thin, superimposed pilasters, the motif of the Rucellai Palace, the Cancelleria, and many buildings of a little later date in Northern Italy. The main staircase, however, is of the medieval newel type, and no pretty Renaissance decoration can make it truly Renaissance.

At Chambord, justly the most famous of the Loire châteaux, the newel staircase is inside, the centre of a most interesting plan, Renaissance indeed in its spirit. Yet from outside the château with its mighty round towers and the equally mighty round towers of the corps de logis looks all medieval. As one approaches one does see the Loire pilasters and the gay decoration of the dormers on the roof with colonnettes, typically Venetian pilasters, niches with shell apses, etc. But it is the inside which establishes the significance of

204 Chambord, double-spiral staircase, shortly after 1519

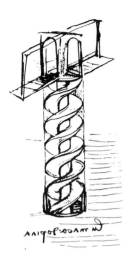

205 Sketch for a staircase, by Leonardo da Vinci

Chambord. The plan is completely symmetrical in all directions. The staircase is in the middle, a double staircase with two corkscrew arms running up one on top of the other so that they never meet. From the staircase emanates a cross of corridors, and they are tunnel-vaulted in a Cinquecento, no longer a Quattrocento way, and on each floor in each corner is a self-contained logis. We do not know who designed Chambord. It was begun in 1519, the year of Leonardo da Vinci's death, and he had certainly played with the intriguing motif of the double spiral staircase. Maybe he advised; the execution for all we know was by Frenchmen.

And Frenchmen also, it seems, designed the two principal châteaux of Francis I's late years, both begun in 1528. Madrid in the Bois de Boulogne is a long oblong, or rather two squares, with corner turrets connected by a hall with open arcades to both sides. Outer arcades indeed characterized the building, a motif of Italian villas rather than palaces. Fontainebleau is Francis I's most ambitious building, vast right from the beginning and with a number of new and influential motifs: the Porte Dorée with its three large arched central recesses one on top of the other and the flanking windows with pediments, the spacious outer staircase towards the Cour du Cheval Blanc with its two curved arms, the former also external staircase inside the Cour Ovale, also in two arms and leading to a

295

frontispiece with detached columns instead of pilasters, a motif heralding the style of the mid-century. Even more up-to-date internationally speaking was the decoration inside Fontainebleau, entrusted to the Italians Rosso and Primaticcio. The rooms painted and stuccoed by them became, as has already once been said, the transalpine school of Mannerism.

The situation in England was characteristically different. Hampton Court had been begun in 1515 for Cardinal Wolsey. In 1529 Wolsey thought it wise to make a present of the palace to his king. Henry added to it, amongst other parts, the Great Hall. Now the palace with its courtyard and gate towers is just as completely in the Gothic tradition as the hall with its hammerbeam roof. Of the Italian Renaissance there is nothing but a limited number of ornamental details, the medallions with the heads of Roman emperors on the gate towers and the putti and foliage in the spandrels of the hall roof. They are competently done, but no attempt is made to bridge the gulf between English construction and Italian decoration.

So while the first stage in the process of assimilation had been identical in Britain and France, their ways separated already at the second. The distance widened at the third. In the thirties two or three of the most talented French architects of the younger generation, Philibert Delorme (c. 1515–70), Jean Bullant (c. 1515–80), and perhaps Pierre Lescot (c. 1510–78), had gone to Rome, where they had devoted their time to the study of Antiquity and the Renaissance. In addition Sebastiano Serlio, a pupil of Peruzzi and an architect,

206 Fontainebleau, Gallery of Francis I, decorated by Rosso, c. 1531–40

207 Hampton Court, great hall, hammerbeam roof, 1533

arrived in France in 1540, and was made *architecteur du roi*. All this we know already, and it will also be remembered that he had in 1537 begun the first of all treatises on architecture. He continued to publish new parts in France, and he designed some few buildings, among them the château of Ancy-le-Franc of about 1546, where the façade still has the pilasters of the Loire School, although Serlio had wanted to use columns in the Bramante way. Inside the courtyard however he succeeded in introducing to France the Bramante *a b a* rhythm in the form of what might be called the triumphal-arch motif, the main bays being flanked by paired pilasters with a niche between each pair. Bramante had used it in the Belvedere Court of

208 Paris, Louvre, façade towards the court, by Pierre Lescot, begun 1546

the Vatican, Serlio used it now, and at the same time two of the three Frenchmen just mentioned also used it. Lescot's façade of the part of the Louvre which he built, a façade towards the inner court, has as its main accents the triumphal-arch motif. Other motifs, however, such as the flat oval shields with garlands hanging down them, the bold crowning segmental pediments, and the extensive use of decorative sculpture, are already French – without losing anything of their Cinquecento classicity. The ensemble which resulted would obviously be impossible in Rome, where at that time Michelangelo placed his mighty cornice on the Farnese palace; impossible also in

209 Anet, by Philibert Delorme, *c.* 1547–*c.* 1552, frontispiece
(now at the École des Beaux-Arts, Paris)

Northern Italy, where Palladio built the first of his serene villas and palaces, and utterly impossible in both Spain and England.

The triumphal-arch motif also appears as the centrepiece of Delorme's façade of Anet, the château of Diane de Poitiers which was begun about 1547 and finished about 1552. This, which is now rather depressingly displayed in the courtyard of the École des Beaux-Arts, has the full orchestration of paired columns in three orders, the top one and the background against which they stand all enriched with carved decoration in the French way. The effect of this showpiece was great. The chapel of Anet on the other hand, the first French religious building in the Renaissance style, was too wilful, with its skew arches between round centre and short cross arms and with the diagonal or lattice coffering of its dome, to inspire others.[31] But the plan of Anet, three ranges and fourth lower entrance range, a plan in fact already worked to at Bury some twenty-five years earlier, became a standard plan in France for several generations and was also occasionally imitated in Elizabethan and Jacobean England.

Bullant's use of the Bramante motif at Écouen about 1555 was

210 Écouen, by Jean Bullant, c. 1555, frontispiece

similar, but he also introduced, in another frontispiece of the same château, a tripartite motif with giant Corinthian columns and a richly carved entablature, and it ought to be remembered that giant orders at the time were still a highly unusual motif to use. Michelangelo introduced giant pilasters on the Capitol a little earlier, Palladio in his Palazzo Valmarana at Vicenza only about ten years later. The motif became indeed for quite a while a French motif.[32]

In Spain the development went the opposite way. After her early

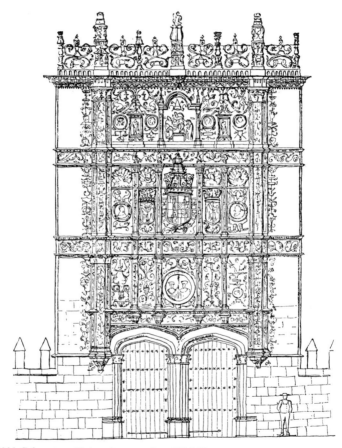

211 Salamanca University, portal, *c.* 1525–30

welcome of the severest Italian sixteenth-century classicism (see p. 215) she had almost at once relapsed into the ornamental vagaries of her past. The austerity of the Escorial, Philip II's vast castle-monastery, with its seventeen courts and its 670 feet of frontage without any decoration, is exceptional. It is also overwhelming, moving no doubt, but frightening. On the other hand, what meets the traveller everywhere is the Plateresque, a wildly mixed style of Gothic, Mohammedan, and Early Renaissance ingredients spread over façades and inner walls as irresponsibly as ever. The Renaissance had evidently not yet been grasped in its meaning.

Almost the same happened in the Netherlands and Germany. An international centre such as Antwerp might put up a town hall (1561–5, by Cornelis Floris), tall, grave, square, of considered proportions, and with a three-bay centre of proud Italian display. The motif of the coupled columns with Ionic correctly placed on top of Tuscan and Corinthian on top of Ionic and the niches between may have been seen by the architect in France rather than Italy, or else it may come from Serlio. The date of the Antwerp Town Hall is too early to make it probable or even possible that another of the popular and soon apparently indispensable Books of Orders or general Books of Architecture served as a model: Hans Blum's *Five*

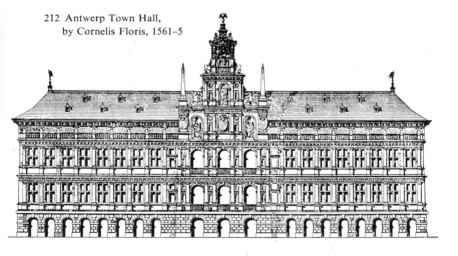

212 Antwerp Town Hall,
   by Cornelis Floris, 1561–5

Orders of 1550, Ducerceau's *Livre d'Architecture* of 1559, Vignola's *Rule of the Five Orders* of 1562, Bullant's *Règle Générale des Cinque Manières* of 1564, Delorme's *Architecture* of 1568, or Palladio's *Architecture* of 1570. How characteristic of the ruling style of Mannerism this sudden outcrop of books on theory is has been pointed out before. It must, however, be emphasized here to what extent France shared in the new zest for publication. Germany, in the person of the humble Blum, made her voice heard, and England took part too, in a somewhat homespun way, with John Shute's *Chief Groundes of Architecture*, published in 1563, and with John Thorpe's drawings at the Soane Museum in London, done no doubt with an eye to publication but never printed. They were worked on late in the sixteenth and even in the first years of the seventeenth century, and Thorpe derived as much inspiration from French and Italian books as he did from the fantastic ornamental pattern books of the Netherlands, especially those by Vredeman de Vries which came out in 1565 and 1568.

These pattern books summed up what is the most remarkable contribution of Flanders and Holland to the style of Mannerism, a novel language of ornament known as bandwork or strapwork. Floris in his town hall handles it with discretion. It hardly appears in the towering gable with its obelisks, scrolls, and caryatid pilasters, the finishing flourish to this ponderous building, and a motif entirely in the Northern medieval tradition. But in the smaller town halls, guild halls, and market halls, and the private houses of the Netherlands these gables, the *leitmotif* of the sixteenth and early seventeenth centuries, are overcrowded with strapwork. The provincial decorator-architects were not prepared to give up any of the exuberance to which the Flamboyant of the fifteenth century had accustomed them. And instead of making up an *olla podrida* of Gothic and Renaissance, such as the Spanish did in their Plateresque, they were headstrong and imaginative enough to invent something for themselves. For invention these forms must be called, even if they can be traced back to such Mannerist detail as that round the top windows of the Palazzo Massimi, and to the work of Rosso Fiorentino at Fontainebleau. They consist chiefly of somewhat stocky thick-set curves of fretwork or leather-strap appearance, sometimes flat, but

213 Leiden, Rhineland County Hall, 1596–8, typical Flemish and Dutch
strapwork ornament

more often three-dimensional and contrasted with naturalistic
garlands and caryatids. The popularity of the strapwork style soon
spread into the adjacent countries – not to France of course, but to
Germany as well as England.

To understand Elizabethan and Jacobean architecture in England
one has to be familiar with the three sources just mentioned: the
Italian Early Renaissance, the Loire style in France, and the strapwork decoration of Flanders. This wide-awake interest in so many
foreign developments is the aesthetic equivalent of England's new
international outlook since Queen Elizabeth, Gresham, and Burghley. However, one has also to remember all the time that a strong
Perpendicular tradition, the tradition of the picturesque, asymmetrical, stone-gabled manor-house, with its mullioned windows
and its extreme ornamental restraint, was still alive. Thus English
architecture between 1530 and 1620 is a composite phenomenon,
with French and Flemish elements prevailing where we are near the
court, and English traditions as soon as we get away from it. Much
of it is derivative, both in the sense of imitation and of conservatism,
but occasionally a new expression is developed as original and as
nationally characteristic as Lescot's Louvre.

Burghley House, near Stamford, is the work of William Cecil,
Lord Burghley, Queen Elizabeth's trusted adviser and friend. It is a
mighty rectangle of about 160 by 200 feet with an inner courtyard.

The central feature of this courtyard is a three-storeyed pavilion, dated 1585. It is again designed on the French triumphal arch motif with the typically French niches between the coupled columns. It has three orders, correctly applied; but on the third floor between the Corinthian columns there sits an utterly incongruous English mullioned and transomed bay window (the English have at no time been happy without bay windows) and above that the pavilion shoots out bits of strapwork and obelisks – a crop of Flemish decoration. The analysis of style is confirmed by documentary evidence. We know that no architect in a modern sense was wholly responsible for the building. Lord Burghley himself must have made a good many of the suggestions embodied in the design. He represents a coming type: the architectural dilettante. In 1568 he wrote to Paris

214 Burghley House, Northamptonshire, central pavilion in the inner courtyard, 1585

for a book on architecture, and some years later he wrote again specifying one particular French book which he desired. On the other hand it is also certain that workmen for Burghley came from the Netherlands and that a certain amount of work was actually done at Antwerp and then shipped to England. Thus Flemish as well as French motifs are easily accounted for. What is harder to understand is why this happy-go-lucky mixing up of foreign phrases with the English vernacular (the chimney stacks are coupled Tuscan Doric columns complete with entablature) does not appear disjointed. The England of Queen Elizabeth – this is all that can be said by way of an explanation – possessed such an overflowing vitality and was so eager to take in all that was sufficiently adventurous and picturesque and in some cases mannered that it could digest what would have caused serious trouble to a weaker age.

However, while Burghley (and Wollaton Hall of 1580 and the entrance side of Hatfield of 1605–12) are spectacular and stimulating enough, the real strength of English building lay in less outlandish

215 Longleat, Wiltshire, begun c. 1568

designs. The earliest in an unmistakable Elizabethan style is Long-leat in Wiltshire, begun in 1568 or earlier. Here you find strapwork only very inconspicuously on the top balustrade. The effect is one of sturdy squareness. The roof is flat, the hundreds of many-mullioned, many-transomed windows are straight-headed, and the bay windows project only slightly and have straight sides. This English squareness and the predominance of large expanses of window create sometimes, for instance at Hardwick Hall and even more in the garden side of Hatfield House, a curiously modern, that is, twentieth-century, effect. More often these large windows, the windows of Perpendicular tradition, are combined with the plain customary English triangular gables. Small houses of this type are still as asymmetrical as of old, larger houses are symmetrical at least in plan, of C or E shape or, if larger, still developed round court-yards. There is a great deal of difference between Longleat and Burghley, but it took a William Cecil and a Raleigh, a Shakespeare and a Spenser, and many clear-minded, hard-headed, and strong-bodied businessmen to make up the England of Elizabeth. Yet it is one England, of one spirit and one style in building, vigorous, prolific, somewhat boastful, of a healthy and hearty soundness which, it is true, is sometimes coarse and sometimes dull – but never effeminate and never hysterical.

Compared with the gulf that separates buildings like Burghley House (or Audley End of 1603–16, or Hatfield) from Inigo Jones's supreme achievements, the Queen's House at Greenwich, designed in 1616, though not completed until immediately before the Civil War, and the Banqueting House in Whitehall of 1619–22, the change in English architecture between 1500 and 1530 seems almost negligible. Only now England experienced what France had experienced before the middle of the sixteenth century, and experienced it far more startlingly, because Inigo Jones transplanted whole buildings of purely Italian character into England, where such men as Lescot, Delorme, and Bullant had only transplanted features and – up to a point – the spirit that stood behind them.

Inigo Jones (1573–1652) began, it seems, as a painter. At the age of thirty-one he appears as a designer of costumes and stage-settings for one of the masques which were a favourite entertainment of the court at that period. He became soon the accepted theatrical designer to the royal family. Plenty of drawings for masques exist. They are brilliantly done, the costumes of that fantastic kind which the Baroque connected with ancient history and mythology, the stage-settings nearly all in the classical Italian style. Jones had, perhaps, been in Italy about 1600, interested probably more in painting and architectural decoration than in architecture proper. Then, however, the Prince of Wales made him his surveyor, i.e. architect, as did a short time later the Queen, and, in 1613, the King. So he went back to Italy, this time, we know from his sketch-books, to study Italian buildings seriously. His ideal was Palladio: an edition of Palladio annotated by Jones is preserved.

Looking back from the Queen's House – a villa in the Italian sense, just outside the rambling Tudor palace of Greenwich – to Palladio's Palazzo Chiericati, the close connexion of style is evident, though nothing is copied. In fact we find nowhere in Jones's work mere imitation. What he had learned from Palladio and the Roman architects of the early sixteenth century is to regard a building as a whole, organized throughout – in plan and elevation – according to rational rules. But the Queen's House has not the weight of the Roman Renaissance or Baroque palace. It was originally even less compact than Palladio's country houses, for it was not a complete block, as it is now, but consisted of two rectangles standing to the right and the left of the main Dover Road and connected with each other only by a bridge (the present centre room on the first floor) across the road – a curious, if not unique, composition of a spatially most effective openness. In contrast to this freedom in general plan, the strictest symmetry governs the grouping of the rooms. Now in Elizabethan country houses we find the decision already taken to tidy up façades into more or less complete symmetry. One may even come across blocked windows and similar contrivances to force into outward symmetry what could not be made to match inside. For wholly symmetrical plans were still rare by 1610, although the trend towards them is unmistakable. In this Inigo Jones is the logical successor to the Jacobeans. But if one takes his elevations, their dignified plainness is in strong contrast to the Jacobean animation by windows of varying sizes, bay windows, rounded and polygonal,

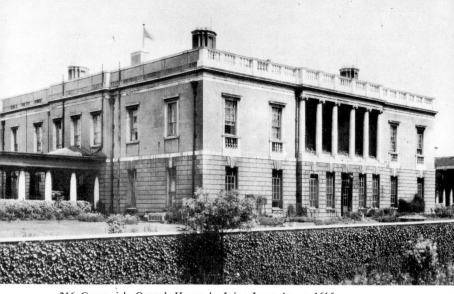

216 Greenwich, Queen's House, by Inigo Jones, begun 1616

dormer windows, gables, and high-pitched roofs. The centre portion of the Queen's House with the loggia projects slightly: that is the only movement of the wall surface. The ground floor is rusticated, the top floor smooth. A balustrade sets the façade off against the sky. The windows are thoughtfully proportioned. There is no ornament anywhere but the delicately moulded cornices above the first-floor windows.

This was a principle with Inigo Jones. He wrote on 20 Jan. 1614: 'Ye outward ornaments oft to be sollid, proporsionable according to the rulles, masculine and unaffected.' The character of the Queen's House could not be better described. And Jones knew that in building thus he was holding up an ideal not only in opposition to contemporary Britain but also to contemporary Rome, i.e. the Baroque. 'All thes composed ornaments,' he added, 'the which Proceed out of ye aboundance of dessigners and wear brought in by Michill Angell and his followers in my oppignion do not well in solid Architecture.' Yet he did not despise ornament altogether. He uses it inside the Queen's House and, with luxurious exuberance, in the so-called double-cube room at Wilton House. Even there, however, there is nothing crowded. The form of his wreaths and garlands of flowers and fruit is compact. They fit into clear-cut panels, and never overgrow the structural divisions of a room. Again, Jones was fully aware of the contrast between his simple exteriors and his rich interiors. He wrote: 'Outwardly every wyse man carrieth a graviti in Publicke Places, yet inwardly hath his imaginacy set on fire, and sumtimes licenciously flying out, as nature hirself doeth often times stravagantly', and demands the same attitude in a good building. And once more the way in which he puts his observation is personal to a degree inconceivable in an architect in England in Elizabethan and Jacobean days. For Inigo Jones is the first English architect in the modern sense. He achieved in this country what the earliest artist-architects had achieved in Italy at the beginning of the Renaissance. And as one is interested in Alberti or Leonardo da Vinci as individuals, so the genius of Inigo Jones makes one deplore over and over again how little is known of his personality.

Of Jones's other works – and those attributed to him with some degree of certainty – only two more can be mentioned. One is Lindsay House in Lincoln's Inn Fields, because with its rusticated ground floor and its giant order of pilasters above, supporting entablature and top balustrade, it is the prototype for a whole series of representational English town houses down to the Royal Crescent at Bath and Nash's Regent's Park terraces. The other is the layout of Covent Garden, with its tall houses, dignified and unadorned, open in galleries on the ground floor, which Jones had taken from a *piazza* at Leghorn (in fact Covent Garden was known in Evelyn's and Pepys's time as the Piazza), because it is the first of the regularly planned London squares. Its west side was centred on the small church of St Paul's with its low, very grave, Antique portico, a design inspired by the Italian sixteenth-century books on architecture, and the earliest classical portico of detached columns erected in the North.

Now here, though only for a moment, a church has to be mentioned. For about a hundred years church architecture had all but stopped in Britain. And in France, although there are a number of interesting sixteenth-century churches with curious mixtures in varying proportion of Gothic conceptions with Southern detail (for instance St Eustache and St Étienne du Mont, both in Paris), they are not amongst the historically leading works. The same might also be said of the seventeenth century, or at least its beginning. Paris now took over the Gesù scheme of façade and interior (see pp. 232 ff.), the scheme which, as has been said before, became more widely popular than any other during the period between 1600 and 1750 (Jesuit Novitiate Church begun 1612, now destroyed; St Gervais façade 1616 by de Brosse (*see* below) or Clément Métézeau; Church of the Feuillants begun 1624 (?) by François Mansart; St Paul et St Louis begun 1634 by Martellange and Derand).

The parallelism between this French development based on Vignola and the English one based on Palladio need not be specially stressed. It was part of the universal tendency of the north of Europe early in the seventeenth century. In Germany at exactly the same time Elias Holl (1573–1646) built his Palladian Augsburg Town Hall (1610–20). And in palace architecture in France Salomon de Brosse (*c.* 1550/60–1626) at the request of Marie de' Medici incorporated into his monumental plan for the Luxembourg Palace, begun in 1615, motifs of the Mannerist parts of the Pitti Palace in Florence. The plan of the Luxembourg on the other hand is traditionally French, the type of Anet with the three ranges round a courtyard and a screen wall on the entrance side instead of a fourth. Even closer is the parallel between the classicism of the Augsburg Town Hall and the striking classicism of de Brosse's last major work, the Palais de Justice at Rennes, which was begun in 1618. Here the ground floor is rusticated, the upper floor articulated with pilasters and coupled pilasters in a generous, relaxed spacing, and the French steep-pitched roof is not broken by raised pavilions. The ensemble is entirely French, and a fit preparation for the classic phase of French seventeenth-century architecture.

But in another even more telling way the period between Delorme and the early seventeenth century also prepared for the classic phase, in the field of sweeping axial planning. A preference for this had already been noticeable at Chambord about 1520, where it resulted from a fusion of the symmetrical discipline of medieval castles and of Italian Renaissance palaces. The key building, Europeanly speaking, of the phase with which we are now dealing was the Tuileries, as designed by Delorme for Catherine de Médicis in 1564. Admittedly the Escorial must have been in Delorme's mind, 670 feet long with four major courts, where the Tuileries were to have 800 and five major courts. A little later, under Charles IX, a yet bigger project was drawn up by Jacques Androuet Ducerceau (*c.* 1510–85), who has so far been mentioned only as a writer on architecture. Charleval in Normandy was intended to be a large square with a square inner courtyard and a *cour d'honneur* in front, possessing on the right and left service wings each again with two courts. The size intended was over 1000 by 1000 feet, far more than that of the Escorial. Very little of it was built.[33] From such schemes Charles I's and Charles II's ideas for a gigantic Whitehall palace were derived, the ideas which were first put on paper by Inigo Jones and then in exactly as Italian a style by John Webb, his pupil.

But before 1650 or 1660 Jones and Webb were almost alone in pursuing such Southern ideas. The popular style in England after the Jacobean and often still side by side with the Jacobean was a homely Dutch style with curved and pedimented gables (Kew Palace, etc.). To this corresponds in France the style of Henri IV still lingering on into the thirties of the seventeenth century, a style of brick buildings with stone quoins and windows, in a gay, a little ruthless but nicely domestic way, best illustrated by the Place des Vosges in Paris (1605–12), by Louis XIII's original little château of Versailles (1624), by such châteaux as Balleroi (*c.* 1626, etc.) and Beaumesnil (1633, etc.), both in Normandy, and by Richelieu's little town of Richelieu, founded in 1631 and designed with his palace by Lemercier (*c.* 1585–1654). The palace, long since destroyed, was modelled on the Luxembourg pattern and thus already a conservative work when it was completed.

For in monumental French architecture Richelieu's period and even more that of Mazarin are characterized by a broad new influx of Italian ideas – and that now meant ideas of the Baroque – and by the way they were developed in the hands of a few leading architects into classic French style which corresponds in terms of building to that of Poussin in painting, Corneille in drama, and Descartes in philosophy. There is no parallel in England to this phase, though from 1660 onwards parallelism, if in very different national idioms, is again patent.

François Mansart (1598–1664) is the first great protagonist, Louis Levau (1612–70) the second. Mansart's two *magna opera* were built between 1635 and 1650: the Orléans wing at Blois and the country house of Maisons Lafitte. The *cour d'honneur* at Blois especially is a masterpiece of civilized reticence, elegant, not very warm-hearted, yet far from pedantically correct with its two-storeyed triumphal arch and the remarkably original little semi-circular third-storey pediment above. The links backward with Lescot's age are as evident as the links forward with the smooth perfection of the Rococo *hôtel*. The curved colonnades especially convey that distinct feeling of Rococo. The way in which they smooth over the angular break at the corners is very French and very accomplished. A similar interior effect is achieved at Maisons Lafitte by the oval rooms in the wings. These were new to France; an Italian motif introduced, it appears, by Mansart and Levau. Of its Italian use in churches and palaces (Palazzo Barberini) enough has been said. Its most prominent occurrence in France is in the mighty, very Italian and very Baroque fancy palaces published in Antoine Lepautre's (1621–91) *Desseins de plusieurs palais* in 1652 –

217 Blois, Orléans wing, by François Mansart, begun 1635

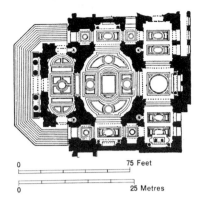

218 Paris, Collège des Quatre Nations,
church, by Louis Levau, 1661

0   75 Feet

0   25 Metres

the parallel to Puget's sculpture – in Louis Levau's church of the
Collège des Quatre Nations (now Institut de France) of 1661 and in
his country house of Vaux-le-Vicomte, begun in 1657. The church
of the Collège des Quatre Nations is, broadly speaking, a Greek
cross, but the arms and the corners between the arms are designed
with considerable freedom and differ widely from each other. The
dominant features of the church are the oval centre with its dome
and an atrium of a similar form. The external composition is one in
which angle pavilions are connected with the church in the centre

219 Paris, Collège des Quatre Nations (Institut de France), begun by
Louis Levau, 1661. After an engraving by Israel Sylvestre

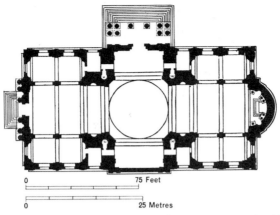

220 Paris, church of the Sorbonne, by Jacques Lemercier, 1635–42

by curved wings. Oval also, at least in effect, is the centre of the church which Lemercier began for Richelieu some twenty-five years earlier, as part of the Sorbonne. Here, in 1635–42, the Greek cross is combined with a circular centre but with a great deal of deliberate stress on one axis of the cross as against the other. There is just as much spatial ingenuity in these plans as in those of contemporary Italy, although their detail appears cold and restrained against the Baroque of Rome. The Sorbonne church is memorable too as by far the most conspicuous of a group of domed churches which, on the Italian pattern, suddenly began to appear in Paris.[34] Mansart's Val de Grâce, even more conspicuous, was begun in 1645. He was soon replaced by Lemercier, and the dome was finally built only about 1660, shortly before that of Levau's Collège des Quatre Nations.

Levau's secular masterpiece, Vaux-le-Vicomte, is in many ways the most important French building of the mid seventeenth century. It was begun by Levau for Colbert's predecessor Fouquet and is surrounded by gardens in which the great Le Nôtre first experimented with ideas later to be developed so spectacularly at Versailles. Lebrun, Louis' *Premier Peintre*, also worked at Vaux before he started at Versailles.

In the house itself (as at Maisons and some others before) the traditional plan of the Luxembourg is given up for that of the

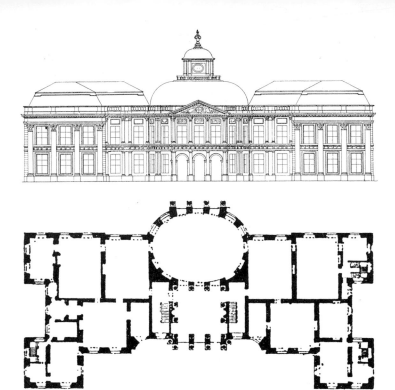

221 Vaux-le-Vicomte, by Louis Levau, begun 1657

Palazzo Barberini, with very much shorter projecting wings, and
the centre pavilion is occupied by a domed oval saloon, again on the
pattern of the Barberini Palace. In the wings the roofs have still
the high pitch characteristic of the French sixteenth and early seventeenth centuries, but slender Corinthian pilasters appear in one giant
order for both storeys. Giant orders were nothing new to the French.
We have seen them at Écouen about 1555, at Charleval in 1573, in
the Hôtel Lamoignon in 1584, and so on. Inigo Jones also used
them, on the precedent of Palladio. But in the manner in which they
appear at Vaux (and also in Levau's Collège des Quatre Nations),
they are slenderer and more elegant and curiously reminiscent of
those which since about 1630 Holland had favoured.

Holland just at that time attained the leadership of Western commerce, and she was much envied and imitated by both Colbert and

the English. She also led in science and could boast more men of artistic genius than at any other period in her national existence. In architecture her development had led her from a gay and jolly style of 1600, parallel to Henri IV's style and the Jacobean, to a new classicism, parallel to Mansart's in France and Inigo Jones's in England. The greatest architect was Jacob van Campen (1595–1657), his first classical house the Coymans House in the Keizersgracht at Amsterdam, datable *c.* 1626. There followed a house for Constantyn Huygens, diplomat, friend of Rubens, and father of the more famous scientist, and the Mauritshuis, built for John Maurice of Nassau-Siegen, both at the Hague, the former of 1634–5, the latter of *c.* 1633–6. Huygens in a letter to Rubens says of his house that he is reviving in it 'l'Architecture ancienne'.[35] We would not call this house or the Mauritshuis antique in style, but without hesitation classical.

The Mauritshuis has a correct pediment or correct giant pilasters, and giant pilasters also along its sides. In this it may well have influenced France and Vaux in particular, but its intimate size for a

222 The Hague, Mauritshuis, by Jacob van Campen, *c.* 1633–6

princely residence, its unpretentious plain brick walls and its all-pervading feeling of solid comfort are very Dutch and quite different from anything French of that period.[36]

England, on the other hand, could sympathize with these North-western qualities of the Dutch. And her architecture after 1660 was indeed greatly influenced by the buildings of van Campen, Post, and Vingboons, and by Vingboons's engraved publications of 1648, 1674, and 1688. However, architects, amateurs, and scholars, and especially the Stuart court, were not blind to either the glamour or the real achievements of the Paris of Colbert and Louis XIV. There was trading success on the one hand, the grandeur of absolute monarchy on the other. Hence representational architecture tended towards the Parisian, domestic architecture towards the Dutch. In Sir Christopher Wren's work inspiration from both sources can be traced. He must have studied engravings of Dutch architecture with great care, and he went to Paris personally, when he had realized that the designing and supervising of buildings was to be his main job in life. For Wren (1632–1723) – this is again characteristic of Renaissance and Baroque – had not been trained as an architect or a mason. Nor was he a painter or sculptor or engineer. He represents yet another type, a type not so far met with in this book.

Wren's father had been Dean of Windsor, his father's brother Bishop of Ely. He was sent to Westminster School. At the age of fifteen, after he had finished school, he was made an assistant demonstrator in anatomy at the College of Surgeons. Then he went up to Oxford. His main interest was science, in that curious mixed and vague sense which science still had in the mid seventeenth century. During those years fifty-three inventions, theories, dis-coveries, and technical improvements are listed as due to 'that miracle of a youth', as John Evelyn called him. Some of them seem trifling now, others aimed right at the central problems of astronomy, physics, and engineering. In 1657 he was made professor of astronomy in London, in 1661 in Oxford. It was the moment when experimental science was just coming to the fore everywhere in Europe. In Paris the Royal Academy of Science was established. The Royal Society in London started its activities even earlier. Wren was one of its founders and most distinguished members.

Newton calls him together with Huygens and Wallis 'huius aetatis geometrarum facile principes'. His most important scientific work is on cycloids, the barometer, and Pascal's problem. In his inaugural lecture in London he revealed a prophetic vision of nebulae as the firmaments of other worlds like ours. In 1664 he illustrated Willis's *Anatomy of the Brain*. Again in 1663 he presented to the Royal Society a model for a building which he had designed at the request of Oxford University, the Sheldonian Theatre, completed in 1669. Its roof is an ingenious piece of timber engineering, but its architecture is awkward, evidently the work of a man with little designing experience. The same can be said of his second work, Pembroke Chapel, Cambridge, of 1663–6. An even earlier connexion with building construction is indicated by Charles II's request to him to fortify Tangier. So architecture, engineering, physics, and mathematics go hand in hand in the development of Wren's mind. The resolution to specialize in architecture may have been brought about by the Fire of London in 1666. Wren found himself a member of the Royal Commission for the rebuilding of the city, and very soon also the elected designer of the many new churches to be built in the city, including St Paul's. In 1669 the King made him Surveyor-General. His only important journey abroad took him not to Italy, but to Paris. That is a very significant fact. At the time of Inigo Jones's *Wanderjahre*, Paris could not have been more than a station on the way to Rome. Now Wren, in a letter, called Paris 'a School of Architecture, the best probably at this Day in Europe'. The most important it certainly was. While Wren was in Paris, Louis XIV, who intended to rebuild the east parts of the Louvre, had invited Bernini to come and contribute designs. He did so, but his plans, a colossal square on the Roman pattern with giant orders of detached columns on the outer and the courtyard fronts, and with a vigorous top cornice crowned by a balustrade, plans which Wren succeeded in examining for only a precious few minutes, were dropped as soon as the great man left. They were replaced by the famous east front with the colonnade which Claude Perrault (1613–88) designed in 1665.

The choice of Perrault was characteristic. He was an amateur and a distinguished doctor. His brother was a lawyer and courtier, had

223 Paris, Louvre, east front, by Claude Perrault, designed 1665

in 1664 been made Inspector-General of the King's buildings, and later wrote a mediocre poem called *Le Siècle de Louis le Grand*. In the history of French literature he is known chiefly as one of the leaders in the *Querelle des Anciens et des Modernes*. Boileau defended Antiquity, Perrault a contemporary style – which of course did not really mean more than a certain amount of freedom in applying the rules of the ancients.

Claude Perrault's Louvre front goes beyond Mansart and Levau in several ways. It represents the change from Mazarin to Colbert, or from early to mature Louis XIV. It has a disciplined formality to which Perrault's knowledge of Bernini's project contributed two important motifs. Bernini as well as Perrault has flat balustraded roofs, and Bernini as well as Perrault models his fronts without any marked projections or recessions of wings. Both these features were new in France. Otherwise, however, Perrault is wholly national. French in feeling, though very original and so unacademic that his less adventurous contemporaries never forgave him, are the slim coupled giant columns of the main storey raised up on the tall, smooth, podium-like ground floor. French are the segment-headed windows, and French (of direct Lescot derivation) the oval shields with garlands hanging down from them.

The whole is of a grandeur and yet a precise elegance that the seventeenth century, in spite of Blois and Maisons, had never before achieved, and that the architects of Louis XIV's later years never surpassed. Perrault has summed up to perfection the various, sometimes seemingly contradictory tendencies of the *siècle de Louis XIV*, the gravity and *raison* of late Poussin, Corneille, and Boileau, the restrained fire of Racine, the lucid grace of Molière, the powerful sense of organization of Colbert.

It is necessary for an appreciation of this style to remember the atmosphere in which it grew, the struggles first between Protestantism and Catholicism in the sixteenth century, Henri IV's decision to return to the Roman Church, because, as he put it, 'Paris is worth a mass', then the spreading of religious indifference, until it became all-powerful in the policy of Richelieu, the cardinal, and Father Joseph, the Capuchin, who fought Protestants in France but favoured them abroad, in both cases purely for reasons of national expediency. For the centre of their thoughts and ambitions was France, and a strong and prosperous France could be created only by first building up a rigorously centralized administration. Now the only visible symbol of the might of the state could be the person of the king. Absolutism was therefore the appropriate form of government for whoever was in favour of a national policy. Thus Richelieu prepared the ground for absolutism. Mazarin followed, and Colbert, the indefatigable, competent, and tenacious bourgeois, made a system of it. He organized France with an unheard-of thoroughness: mercantilism in industry and commerce, royal workshops, royal trading companies, close supervision of roads, of canals, of afforestation – of everything.

Art and architecture were an integral part of the system. A flourishing school of painting, sculpture, and the applied arts stimulated export and at the same time enhanced the glory of the court. Architecture was useful to create work and again to celebrate the greatness of king and state. But there should be no licence; style had to conform to standards set by the prince and his minister. Thus academies were founded, one for painting and sculpture, another for architecture, the earliest of a modern type, both educational and as a means of conveying social status, and the most powerful that have ever existed. And when artists had gone through these schools and gained distinction, they were made royal sculptors or royal architects, drawn nearer and nearer to the court, honoured and paid accordingly, but made more and more dependent on the will of Louis and Colbert. It was in Paris at that time that the principle of architecture as a department of the civil service was established. The French and English kings had had their royal master-masons ever since the thirteenth century. But they were craftsmen, not civil servants. Also the competencies of the various surveyors, inspectors, and whatever they were called later on were never clearly defined. Michelangelo had been Superintendent of the Papal Buildings; but nobody would have considered such an appointment a full-time job. Now the architectural office developed, and a system of training at the drawing board and on the jobs.

Jules Hardouin-Mansart (1646–1708) was the perfect type of the

224 Paris, St Louis des Invalides, by Jules Hardouin-Mansart, 1675–1706

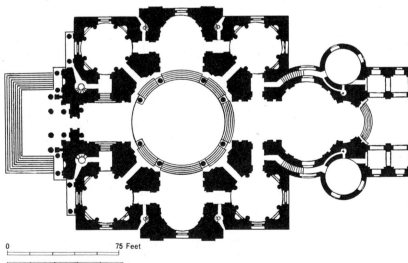

0   75 Feet

0   25 Metres

official French architect, competent, quick, and adaptable. In his church of St Louis des Invalides of 1675–1706 he achieved, just as Perrault did, that specific combination of grandeur and elegance which is not to be found anywhere outside France. The composition, externally and internally, is meant to be taken as an improvement on Lemercier's Sorbonne and Levau's Collège des Quatre Nations. The interior, except for the oval chancel, is more academically balanced, that is, less dynamic in its spatial relations, than the works of Hardouin-Mansart's predecessors. But the dome is constructed so

225 Paris, St Louis des Invalides, by Jules Hardouin-Mansart, 1675–1706

that in looking up one sees through a wide opening in the inner cupola on to the painted surface of a second cupola, lit by concealed windows – a wholly Baroque spatial effect. Examining the façade one will now become aware of its Baroque qualities too, in spite of its seemingly correct portico with Doric and Ionic orders. The free rhythmical spacing of the columns (taken from Perrault) should be noted, and the graded advance in plan towards the centre: first step from the walls to the columns of the wings, second step to the columns on the sides of the portico, and third step to the four middle columns. Not only the Greeks but also Palladio and even Vignola would have deprecated this strongly.

Sir Christopher Wren did not. His St Paul's Cathedral of 1675– 1710, though apparently so much a monument to Classicism, is in fact just as much a blend of the classical and the Baroque as the Dôme des Invalides. The dome of St Paul's, one of the most perfect in the world, is classical indeed. It has a more reposeful outline than Michelangelo's and Hardouin-Mansart's. The decoration, with a colonnade round the drum, is also characteristically different both from the projecting groups of columns and broken entablatures of St Peter's, and from the remarkably domestic-looking segment-headed windows and the slim, graceful shape of the lantern of St Louis. But, looking more closely, even there the alternation of bays where columns flank niches with bays where they stand in front

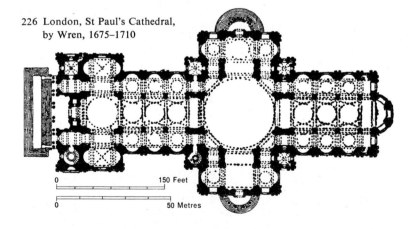

226 London, St Paul's Cathedral,
    by Wren, 1675–1710

0   150 Feet

0   50 Metres

of loggias introduces an element of unclassical variety. The lantern, too, is at least as bizarre as Mansart's. And as for the façade of St Paul's, begun in 1685, it is, with the coupled columns which Wren (just as Hardouin-Mansart) took over from Perrault's Louvre façade, and the two fantastic towers on the sides (designed after 1700), a decidedly Baroque composition. The side elevations are dramatic, though of a secular, palace-like effect. The windows have even a framing of sham-perspective niches of the S. Carlo and Palazzo Barberini type. Inside there is a poignant contrast between the firmness of every part and the spatial dynamics of the whole. The dome is as wide as nave and aisles together – a motif which Wren may have remembered from Ely or from engravings of such

227 London, St Paul's Cathedral, by Sir Christopher Wren, 1675–1710

Italian buildings as the cathedral of Pavia. It adds splendour and surprise to the whole composition. The diagonally placed piers are hollowed out into colossal niches. Niches also set the outer walls of the aisles and choir aisles into an undulating motion. With a similar effect windows are cut into the tunnel-vaults and saucer domes of choir and nave. Wren's style in churches and palaces is classical, no doubt, but it is a Baroque version of classicism. Such city churches as the ingeniously multiform St Stephen's Walbrook (1672–7) show this especially clearly.

To analyse its ground plan is almost as hard as to analyse Vier-zehnheiligen. Yet its expression is of cool clarity. Outside it is a plain rectangle as silent about the interior surprises as Vierzehn-heiligen. Inside its centre is a spacious gently rising saucer-dome (of wood and plaster), resting on eight arches supported by nothing but twelve slender columns. The technical achievement is as remark-able as the effortless lightness of appearance. The twelve columns form a square, and four arches connect the two central columns of each side of the square, while fragmentary vaults curve up from the three columns of each corner of the square to form four more arches in the corners. Now these three corner columns on each side are also tied together by straight entablatures, so that each of the four sides has a rhythm of straight and low – arched and tall – straight and low. Here is a first ingenious interlocking of effects. Looking up to the dome we perceive eight arches of identical height, but looking straight in front of us towards any one side of the square there is differentiation of the bays. However, that is not all. The arched centres of the sides can also be regarded as the entrances to four arms of a cross, a Latin cross, since the tunnel-vaults of the south and north arms are very shallow, whereas the east arm with the altar

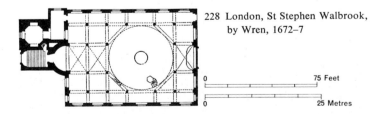

228 London, St Stephen Walbrook,
by Wren, 1672–7

0   75 Feet

0   25 Metres

229 London, St Stephen Walbrook, by Sir Christopher Wren, 16ʼ

has a somewhat longer cross-vault, and the west arm one double the length of the altar arm. To achieve that, the western arm consists of two bays separated by columns in the normal manner of longitudinal churches. As these columns are exactly identical with all the other columns, the first impression one receives on entering the church is one of a short nave with aisles leading towards a dome of unaccountable width. To finish the story, this seeming nave has narrow flat-ceilinged outer aisles as well, and these outer aisles run right through to the east wall. Only we cannot call them aisles all the way through, because at one point they rise into being the north and south arms of the cross and then sink again to become chancel aisles. The inner aisles, of course, one discovers later, run into the wide crossing just as does the nave. The whole rectangle of the church is set out with sixteen columns altogether, noble columns of almost academic neutrality. Yet they are used to create a spatial polyphony which only the Baroque could appreciate – architecture of Purcell's age.

It is in connexion with their spatial qualities that one should consider Wren's other City churches as well. He had to design fifty-one of them after the Fire of London in 1666 and four outside the City, and most of these in the course of a few years. So he treated them as a laboratory for working out a variety of central, longitudinal, and intermediary plans and endowing them with a variety of elevations. The longitudinal churches usually have a nave and aisles. Galleries in the aisles were a Protestant requirement in England. The nave can be divided from the aisles by giant columns (Christ Church, Newgate Street) or piers with attached giant columns (St Mary-le-Bow) or two superimposed orders of columns (St Andrew, Holborn; St James, Piccadilly). There can be a clerestory or no clerestory (St Andrew, Holborn; St Peter, Cornhill); and if there is, clerestory windows can be in the upper wall (St Magnus) or cut into the vault (St Bride; St Mary-le-Bow, etc.). The vault can be of the tunnel (St Mary-le-Bow; St James, Piccadilly; St Bride, etc.) or the groined variety (Christ Church, Newgate Street). This bald enumeration gives no idea of the variety of aesthetic effect achieved by the churches in the flesh.

With the central plans the basic scheme can be the dome on a square (St Mildred) or an octagon (St Mary Abchurch; St Swithin) or the square with a set-in Greek cross, the centre being again a square, with a dome or a groin-vault, and the four corners with lower ceilings or domes (St Anne and St Agnes; St Martin, Ludgate Hill). This quincunx plan has a venerable progeny. It is familiar to us from Mismieh (see p. 31) and then the Venetians of the Renaissance (S. Giovanni Grisostomo). From there the Dutch took it over (Nieuwe Kerk, Harlem, by van Campen). Wren evidently had engravings from Holland, and in his endeavour to introduce ever new plans he was quite ready to accept inspiration from anywhere.

But the planning problem that interested him most was not the longitudinal nor the central type but a synthesis of the two, a longitudinal building with central tendencies or a central building with longitudinal tendencies. In this he was entirely at one with the contemporary Baroque architects of France and Italy. Longitudinal with a centralizing tendency is for instance St James Garlickhythe, with nave and aisles of five bays, but the middle bay to the left and right treated as a transept, that is, without gallery and with end windows as large as that above the altar. Central with a longitudinal tendency were St Antholin and St Benet Fink, with oval domes, the former on columns set as an elongated octagon, the latter an elongated hexagon. The outer walls of St Antholin were basically oblong, those of St Benet an elongated decagon. And so in the end the complexity of St Stephen Walbrook is reached.

Wren's keen scientific interest in church planning was shared by architects in other Protestant countries, notably Holland and the north of Germany. The Silesian Nikolaus Goldmann died at Leiden in Holland in 1665 as Professor of Architecture. He had begun a treatise on architecture, and this was completed by Leonhard Christian Sturm (1669–1719), a mathematician who in his own writings of 1712 and 1718 suggested a number of ingenious and often practical solutions for the planning of Protestant churches.

The fruitfulness of the Dutch influence on the north of Germany is witnessed by such buildings as the so-called Parochial Church at Berlin (1695) by Nering and the parish church of Hehlen in Westphalia (1697–8) by Korb. Both have central plans on the Dutch pattern. At the end of this development stands the powerful

Frauenkirche at Dresden, another of the worst architectural losses of the Second World War. It was built in 1722–43 by Georg Bähr (1666–1738), master carpenter to the City of Dresden. The plan was a square with rounded corners and a chancel projecting in a curve, slightly more than a semicircle. The interior was essentially circular with eight giant piers carrying the steep stone-vaulted dome. Between the piers were galleries in three tiers, a solution aesthetically not wholly satisfactory. On the whole, however, the Frauenkirche was irresistible, thanks to the contrasted curves of its interior and exterior and the delicately balanced relation between the bold sweep of the dome and the daintiness of the four angle turrets. Nothing could illustrate more convincingly the differences between German and West European Baroque.

The principle of central composition which we have found so essential for an understanding of the architecture of Renaissance and Baroque was given its boldest application in town planning. The earliest plans of the type have already been mentioned (p. 185), but whereas at the time of Filarete they were mere plans and remained plans, during Mannerism centrally planned towns were actually built.

The most famous example is Scamozzi's nonagonal town and fortress of Palmanova in the Veneto (1593), of the same year are the long and straight new roads cut through Rome by Sixtus V according to a bold master-plan (see p. 244) – and taken over by the French under Henri IV. The Place de France, planned shortly before the death of the king and never carried out, was a segment, nearly a semicircle, and wide radiating avenues called after the provinces of France.[37] Inspired by Henri, Louis XIV finally adopted the *rond-point* as his chief planning motif, and it became a hall-mark of the Baroque in that country in which the radiating chapels of church chancels had been conceived six hundred years before. From Louis' reign dates the Place de l'Étoile, although it was then in the country and became part of the city of Paris only after 1800.[38] The grandest example of such planning on an enormous scale is, of course, Versailles. Architecturally the château suffers from having been built in three campaigns: Louis XIII's small brick and stone shooting box first, a grand enlargement by Levau second, and

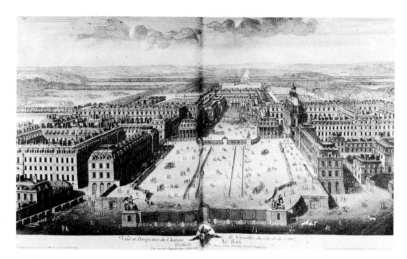

230 Versailles, enlarged by Hardouin-Mansart, 1678, from a core of 1623 with wings by Levau of 1661–5; gardens by Le Nôtre, begun 1667

Hardouin-Mansart's final unprecedented enlargement third. Hardouin-Mansart, when he started in 1678, decided to keep to Levau's system of elevation, and this gave him no lead on motifs splendid enough to dominate a façade in the end made 1,320 feet long. Interiors are more successful than the exterior. The rhetoric of the main *salles* impresses, so does the length of the Galerie des Glaces, and the chapel, added in 1689–1710, though externally not integrated, is one of the noblest rooms of the age, still with a gallery or balcony for the king and his retinue, i.e. still in the tradition of Aachen. So the slender columns rise on a substructure of square pillars and arches, and light streams in through the gallery windows and clerestory windows. But the organ case has whole palm trees as its decoration, a reminder that we are in full Baroque.

The plan of the whole of Versailles, not the palace only, cannot be called anything but Baroque. The palace faces Le Nôtre's magnificent park with its vast parterres of flowers, its cross-shaped sheet of water, fountains, seemingly endless parallel or radiating avenues, and walks between tall, trimmed hedges – Nature subdued by the hand of Man to serve the greatness of the king, whose bedroom was placed right in the centre of the whole composition. On the town side the *cour d'honneur* receives three wide, converging roads coming from the direction of Paris. Town-planning was strongly influenced by these principles everywhere. Of the eighteenth century the most notable examples are perhaps Karlsruhe in South-west Germany, a whole town designed in 1715 as one huge star with the Ducal Palace as its centre, and L'Enfant's plan of 1791 for Washington, D.C.

As for Britain, Wren's plan fell through after having been considered by the king for only a few days. Was it too daring? Could it have been carried out only in an absolute monarchy, where expropriation for schemes of civic grandeur was easier than in the City of London? Or was this logical uncompromising programme to organize the background for future London life simply too un-English ever to be taken seriously? The fact remains that the contribution of London to town-planning of the seventeenth and eighteenth centuries is the square – introduced, as has been said, by Inigo Jones – i.e. an isolated, privately owned area with houses of, as a rule, similar but not identical design, examples of good manners and not of regimentation. It might be worth adding that the sensation in walking through the West End of London from square to square is clearly a modern and secular version of the typically English sensation of the visitor passing from isolated compartment to isolated compartment in a Saxon or Early English church.

Regarding the individual town house, there is the same contrast between London and Paris. In London, but for a few exceptions – though not as few as it seems now – the nobleman and the wealthy merchant lived in terrace houses, in Paris in detached *hôtels*. In London a ground plan had been evolved for these houses that was convenient enough to become standardized before the end of the seventeenth century. With its entrance on one side, leading straight to the staircase, one large front room and one large back room on each floor, and the service rooms in the basement, it remained practically unaltered for the largest and the smallest house until the end of the Victorian era. Of spatially effective elements it has little. In Paris, on the other hand, architects from about 1630 onwards developed house plans with great consistency and ingenuity towards

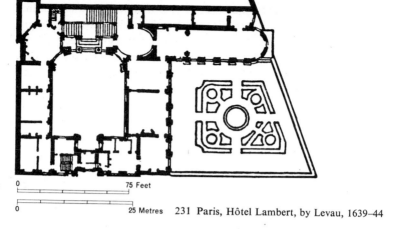

    231 Paris, Hôtel Lambert, by Levau, 1639–44

ever subtler solutions of functional requirements and spatial desires. The standard elements were a *cour d'honneur*, screened off from the street, with offices and stables in wings on the right and the left, and the *corps de logis* at the back. The earliest plans of wholly symmetrical organization are Mansart's Hôtel de la Vrillière begun in 1635 and Jean du Cerceau's Hôtel de Bretonvillers begun about 1637. The first high-water mark is Levau's Hôtel Lambert of 1639–44, with a courtyard with two rounded corners and an oval vestibule, i.e. the very motifs which we have also watched at Blois, Vaux-le-Vicomte, and the Collège des Quatre Nations. A little later Lepautre's Hôtel de Beauvais (1655–60) revels in curves. Then the same reaction took place which we had seen between Vaux and the Louvre. Colbert did not like curves, he called them in 1669 'not in good taste, particularly in exteriors', and the *appartements* of Louis XIV's later years, though grander in scale, motifs, and decoration, are of less spatial interest.

The most important development between 1700 and 1715 is concerned with interior decoration. In the hands of one of Hardouin-Mansart's chief executives, Jean Lepautre, it became more and more delicate and sophisticated. Grandeur was replaced by *finesse*, high relief by an exquisite play on the surface, and a virile deportment by an almost effeminate grace. Thus during the last years of Louis XIV's reign the atmosphere of the Rococo consolidated itself.

The Rococo is indeed of French origin, although we have introduced it in this book first in its German, that is, its extreme and most brilliant, spatial forms. The term Rococo is a pun, it seems, from *barocco*, alluding to the passion for those strange rock-like or shell-like formations which are typical of its ornament and have been analysed apropos Bruchsal and Vierzehnheiligen. They appear there in the thirties, but are a French invention of 1715–30 – or rather an invention made in France. For the leaders of the generation responsible for the step from Lepautre's thin grace to full-blooded Rococo were without exception not properly French: Watteau the painter was a Fleming, Gilles-Marie Oppenord (1672–1742) was the son of a Dutch father, Juste-Aurèle Meissonier (1695–1750) of Provençal stock and born at Turin, Toro has an Italian name and lived in Provence, and Vassé was Provençal too. It is due to these architects and decorators that vigour re-entered French decoration, that curves of Italian Baroque derivation made their appearance once more, that ornament launched out into the third dimension again, and that the fantastic, completely original ornament of the *rocaille* was conceived.

In exterior architecture less can be observed of this development than in interiors. Oppenord's and Meissonier's designs for façades were not carried out. It is in the planning and decoration of houses that the Rococo celebrates its greatest triumphs. The Rococo is a style of the *salon*, the *petit appartement* and of sophisticated living. Decoration is far more graceful and as a rule considerably less vigorous than in Germany, and planning is of an unprecedented subtlety.[39] The development was heralded already in the Grand Trianon in the park of Versailles which Hardouin-Mansart had built in 1687 for royal relaxation and Mme de Maintenon, single-storeyed and on a loose, asymmetrical plan, though of course grand and classical in the details.

One difficulty in the standard Parisian *hôtel* plan which the architects liked to face and overcome was, for instance, the fact that the front towards the *cour d'honneur* and the back towards the garden should both be symmetrical in themselves and even when they did not lie on the same axis. Courtonne's Hôtel de Matignon shows one very neat solution. Here and in any of the other contemporary

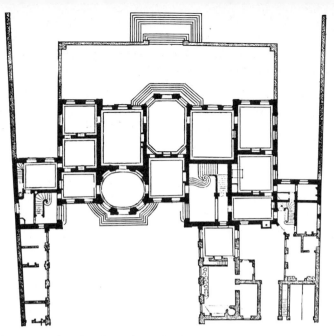

232 Paris, Hôtel de Matignon, by Courtonne, begun 1722

hôtels the ingenious tricks of antechambers and cabinets and *garderobes* and little inner service courts should be studied, all devised to facilitate the running of a house and fill the many odd corners behind curved rooms and alcoves. The form and position of the staircase was another problem. As to its position, it had to communicate easily with vestibule and service rooms, without interfering with the smooth run of room into room and the representational splendour of vistas. The same desire for a smooth run was extended to the interaction between floor and floor, and staircase forms were chosen accordingly. It has been shown that Spain was the most enterprising country in the sixteenth century regarding staircases. Only here the Baroque possibilities of the staircase were sensed as early as that. Her three main new types, the square newel stair with the open well, the staircase on the T-plan, and the so-called Imperial staircase (see pp. 278 ff.), all reached the North in the seventeenth century. The square newel stair became popular in Jacobean England, where it was interpreted in timber, characteristically reduced in size to a somewhat cramped medieval narrowness, but gorgeously decorated by Flemish or English woodcarvers (Hatfield, Audley End, etc.). Only when we come to Inigo Jones at Ashburnham House, Little Dean's Yard, London, is the spaciousness of Spain emulated. However, Ashburnham House and a few other examples of Baroque breadth such as Coleshill, Berks (by Roger Pratt, one of Wren's early competitors), are rare exceptions in England. There were at that time exceptions in Italy too (Longhena: S. Giorgio Maggiore, Venice, 1643–5 – the example from which Coleshill seems to be derived). Only Genoa took a real liking to staircases as wide, light, and airy as those of Spain. France must have got to know of these through several channels. The T-type was taken up by Levau in the Escalier des Ambassadeurs at Versailles, in 1671, the Imperial type by Levau at the Tuileries, the square open newel type earlier still by Mansart at Blois. Mansart took over from Palladio the elegant method of construction by which the flights of stairs, instead of resting on solid walls, are anchored only into the outer walls, and towards the well carried on shallow arches without any other support. This type occurs with countless minor variations, all aiming at yet suppler forms, in most Paris *hôtels* and French country houses.

Externally the Paris *hôtels* are just as elegantly varied, though never anything like as boldly Rococo, as the palaces and houses in Germany and Austria, whereas in London the exterior of the seventeenth- and eighteenth-century brick house was, except for ornamental details, almost standardized. It has no connexion with the classic French style, that much is certain, although it may have had some originally with the less pretentious domestic architecture of Henri IV and later with Holland.

As for country houses, they are – at least after 1660 – of minor importance in France, where the life of the ruling class was centred in the court, while in England most of the noblemen and nearly all the squires still regarded their London houses only as *pied-à-terre*, and looked on their seats in the country as their real homes. Consequently it is here that one can expect variety and, indeed, find it. All the more noteworthy, however, is it that in the second half of the seventeenth century, when the standardized town house had become

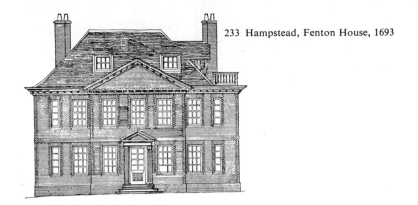

an accepted fact, a type of smaller country house had also been introduced (clearly on the Mauritshuis pattern) that – with many and delightful minor variations – is to be found all over the countryside, in the villages round London, at Hampstead, Roehampton, Ham, Petersham, round the close at Salisbury – everywhere. They are usually built of brick with stone quoins, either completely rectangular or with two short wings on the sides, the entrance with a pediment, hood, or porch, and with a larger pediment to crown the centre of the house. These lovable houses of mellow and undated rightness are too well known to need further description. Their origin and diffusion have, however, not yet been fully elucidated. The earliest example seems to be Eltham Lodge, near London, of 1663. It was designed by Hugh May, with Pratt and Webb, Wren's most important competitor in the sixties. By 1685 or 1690 the type was certainly fully established. It has as a rule a generously spaced three-flight staircase with an open well and rich woodcarving and rooms of simple and straightforward shapes; of that ingenious *commodité* on which all the French eighteenth-century architects insisted in their writings, they have little.

Apparently, to the British, comfort was something quite different from what it was to the French. But while these houses of about 1700 are, whatever French critics might have said against them, as serviceable today as at the time when they were built, there are indeed certain English eighteenth-century country houses on a larger scale which – from our point of view at least – seem to be designed

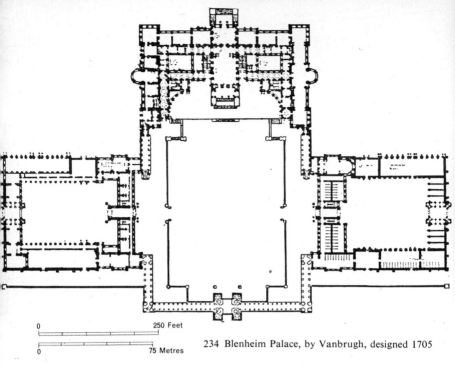

0   250 Feet

0   75 Metres

234 Blenheim Palace, by Vanbrugh, designed 1705

for display and not for comfort. This is an argument heard frequently against Blenheim, near Oxford, the palace which the nation presented to Marlborough. It was designed by Sir John Vanbrugh (1664–1726) in 1705. His style derives from Wren at his grandest and most Baroque – the Wren of Greenwich Hospital – but is always of a distinctly personal character. Wren never seems to forget himself. He is never carried away by forces stronger than his reason. Vanbrugh's designs are of a violence and ruthless directness that could not but offend the rationalists of his age. His family came from Flanders; his expansive temperament seems more of Rubens's country than of Wren's and Reynolds's. He started on a military career, was arrested in France, and imprisoned in the Bastille. After his release he returned to England and began to write plays. They were a huge success. Then suddenly one finds him engaged in architectural work at Castle Howard. In 1702 he was appointed Comptroller of Works – a curious career, very different from Wren's.

338

235 Blenheim Palace, Oxfordshire, by Sir John Vanbrugh, designed 1705

Blenheim is planned on a colossal scale. One does not know whether the Palladian villa with its wings or Versailles with its *cour d'honneur* stands behind its plan. The *corps de logis* has a massive portico with giant columns between giant pillars, and a heavy attic above. The same Baroque weight characterizes the side elevations, especially the square squat corner towers of the wings. If in the case of Wren the term Baroque could be used only with careful qualifications, these towers would be called Baroque by anyone familiar with the work of Bernini, Borromini, and the others in Italy. Here is a struggle, mighty forces opposing overwhelming weights; here are fiercely projecting mouldings and windows crushed by thick-set pilasters placed too close to them; here is the deliberate discordance of the semicircular window placed against a semicircular arch right above, and higher up again a segmental arch. Everything jars, and the top of the daring composition has nothing of a happy end either. Vanbrugh, in the forms which crown the tower, the obelisks and the ball, does not accept any indebtedness to anybody. The pilasters and

236 Blenheim Palace, kitchen wing, 1708–9

the windows are also highly original, but not to the same extreme degree. In some details they appear reminiscent of Michelangelo. However, the mention of Michelangelo makes Blenheim – the whole of the entrance front – at once appear coarse, and certainly theatrical and ostentatious: that is, Flemish as well as Baroque.

But one should be careful not to attribute too much in Vanbrugh to Flemish ancestors. For he was co-operating at Blenheim and in other places with the former principal assistant of Wren, a man with a thorough training in the trade and a long experience, and that man, Nicholas Hawksmoor (1661–1736), was, as far as we can see, entirely English. Yet Hawksmoor's style is as Baroque as Vanbrugh's and as Wren's in the west towers of St Paul's; that is evident in those later works of his where he was fully responsible for design and execution, and especially in his London churches. A building like Christ Church, Spitalfields of 1723–39 – after all no more than a parish church in a growing suburb – is as megalomaniac as anything by Vanbrugh, and as perverse. The composition seems deliberately

237 London, Christ Church Spitalfields, by Nicholas Hawksmoor, 1723–39

disjointed: the portico with its odd arched centre of Late Roman and Wrenian origin, and the next stage, virtually receding and repeating the same motif with pilasters on a surface wider than that of the tower proper. So this middle stage sticks out screenwise to the left and right, and no device is applied on those sides to hide what is done. Finally the composition is crowned by a spire which adds to the Late Roman Baroque of the picture an odd Gothic note. The towers of some of the other Hawksmoor churches are even more frankly gothicizing. For that he had the authority of some of Wren's City churches, and this inclination towards medievalism, far ahead of anything comparable in other countries, is a constituent part of the English Baroque.

For English Baroque is the only reasonable term for the years of Wren's west towers of St Paul's, of Hawksmoor's churches, and of Vanbrugh, in spite of the fact that, in comparison with Bernini, these English early eighteenth-century architects are also classicists. There is very little in them of that plastic treatment of walls which Michelangelo had first conceived and which produced the undulating façades and interiors of Baroque buildings in Italy and Southern Germany. Movement is never in England so insinuating, nor so frantic. Spatial parts never abandon their separate existence, to merge into each other, as they do at S. Carlo or Vierzehnheiligen. The individual members, especially the solid round detached columns, try to keep themselves to themselves. English Baroque is Baroque asserting itself against an inborn leaning towards the static and the sober.

The same conflict will be experienced in interiors of Wren's, Hawksmoor's, and Vanbrugh's time. There again spatial relations bind rooms together which are articulated and decorated according to the principles of classicism – by panelling if they are small, by columns or pilasters if they are larger. At Blenheim there is an enormous entrance hall leading into the saloon which forms the centre of two symmetrical groups of rooms along the whole garden front, with all the doors on one axis, or as it is called, one *enfilade*, as at Versailles. But – this is of the greatest significance – the staircase, the dynamic element *par excellence*, is nothing like as prominent as it would be in a contemporary palace in France or Germany. This lack of interest in spatial dynamics is by no means a sign of meanness in planning. On the contrary, Blenheim is just as vast as the largest new palaces of the minor rulers of Germany, and just as impractical – at least from our point of view.

However, it seems rather cheap to harp on the fact that kitchen and service rooms are far away from the dining-room – in one of the two wings in fact, opposite the other with the stables (an accepted Palladian tradition). Servants may have had to walk a long way, and hot dishes may have got cold long before they reached their destination. To us that may seem a functional error. Vanbrugh and his clients would have called such arguments extremely low. Of servants they had plenty. And what we call comfort mattered less than a self-imposed etiquette more rigid than we can imagine. The function of a building is not only utilitarian. There is also an ideal function, and that Blenheim did fulfil. However, not all Vanbrugh's contemporaries agreed that it did. There is, for example, Pope with his famous, often quoted ' 'tis very fine, But where d'ye sleep, or where d'ye dine?' What did he mean by that? Critics today interpret it as referring to a lack of material comfort. Pope was more philosophical than that. What, in the name of good sense, he asked for, is that a room and a building should look what they are. He disliked Vanbrugh's colossal scale and decorative splendour as unreasonable and unnatural. For 'splendour', he insists, should borrow 'all her rays from sense', and again:

> Something there is more needful than expense,
> And something previous ev'n to taste – 'tis sense.

In this he gave expression to the feelings of his generation, the generation following Vanbrugh's. For Pope was born in 1688, whereas Vanbrugh was almost the same age as Swift and Defoe (and Wren as Dryden).

The architecture that corresponds to Pope's poetry is that of Lord Burlington and his circle. Richard Boyle, Earl of Burlington, was born in 1694, that is he was some years younger than Pope. He was converted to a faith in Palladio's simplicity and serenity by a young Scottish architect Colen Campbell (d. 1729) who had begun in 1715 a large country house near London, Wanstead, in a pure Palladianism.

Probably in this same year he made a start on Lord Burlington's town house in Piccadilly which still exists, though much remodelled. In 1716 a Venetian architect Leoni had started a sumptuous English edition of Palladio's works. In 1717 Burlington himself designed for his gardens at Chiswick near London a Palladian *bagno*. In 1719 he returned to Italy and studied Palladio seriously. In 1730 he paid for the publication of a group of unknown Palladio drawings which he had bought in Italy, and in 1727 for that of Inigo Jones's works by William Kent, painter, landscape gardener, and architect (1727). These publications established the Palladian fashion so firmly in British country houses that it lasted almost unchallenged for fifty years, and with certain modifications for nearly a hundred.

The normal town house, however, was hardly affected. There are very few examples of Palladian influence beyond façade motifs. And where, as in a house designed by Lord Burlington himself, an attempt was made to interfere with the standardized London plan, the outcry against this imposition of the rationalist's new rules was just as pronounced as the rationalist's outcry had been against Vanbrugh's unruliness. Lord Chesterfield suggested to the owner that he should take a house opposite, so as to be able to admire his own at leisure without having to live in it.

It is the country house that became wholly Palladian by Lord Burlington's efforts. In Vanbrugh's work the variety of plans and exterior compositions had been unlimited. Now the *corps de logis* with a centre portico and isolated wings connected to the main body by low galleries became *de rigueur*. Holkham Hall in Norfolk and Prior Park near Bath are typical examples. Holkham was designed in 1734 by William Kent for Thomas Coke, Earl of Leicester, the agricultural reformer. Prior Park was designed for Ralph Allen in 1735 by the elder John Wood (*c.* 1700–54), a local architect, but, by virtue of his talent and the opportunities which he had in the most fashionable spa of England, one of the leading architects of his generation. Compared with Palladio's villas, these British derivations are larger and heavier. They also often incorporate motifs freer than Palladio would have tolerated: more variation in the shapes of rooms, or a boldly curved outer staircase into the garden (the one at Prior Park is of the nineteenth century). But more

238 Bath, Prior Park, by John Wood the Elder, designed 1735

important still is the fact that Palladian country houses in Britain were designed to stand in English parks.

It seems at first contradictory that the same patrons should have wanted the formal Palladian house and the informal English garden, and that the same architect should have provided both. Yet it is a fact that William Kent, Lord Burlington's protégé, was celebrated as one of the creators of the English style in laying out grounds, and that Lord Burlington's own villa at Chiswick (about 1720), a free copy of Palladio's Villa Rotonda, was one of the earliest examples of what was called 'the modern taste' in gardening. How can this have come about? Was the landscape garden just a whim? It was not; it was a conscious part of an anti-French policy in the arts. Le Nôtre's parks express absolutism, the king's absolute rulership over the country, and also Man's rulership over Nature. The active, expansive Baroque force that shapes the house, flows over into nature. Progressive English thinkers recognized this and disliked it. Shaftesbury spoke of 'the mockery of princely gardens', and Pope satirized them in his neat couplet:

> Grove nods at grove, each alley has a brother,
> And half the platform just reflects the other.

Now this enforcing of architectural rule on the garden is certainly something unnatural. And so Addison wrote in *The Spectator* in 1712: 'For my own part I would rather look upon a tree in all its luxuriance and diffusion of boughs and branches than when it is cut and trimmed into a mathematical figure.' That profession of faith in nature not tampered with is evidently a revolt of liberalism and tolerance against tyranny; it is a Whig revolt. But the curious thing about it is that although these attacks were made in the name of nature, nature was still understood by Addison and Pope in Newton's and indeed in Boileau's sense. Boileau's objections in his *Art of Poetry* of 1674 against the Baroque of the South were that it was unreasonable and therefore unnatural. Reason and nature are still synonyms with Addison and Pope, as we have seen in Pope's comments on Blenheim.

Add to this Shaftesbury's 'passion for things of a natural kind' and his idea that 'the conceit or caprice of Man has spoiled their genuine order by breaking in upon (their) primitive state', and you will be near an answer to the puzzling parallelism between classicist architecture and natural gardening. The original state of the universe is harmony and order, as we see it in the ordered courses of the stars which were revealed by the new telescopes, and in the structures of organisms which were revealed by the new microscopes. 'Idea of Sense, Order, Proportion everywhere', to use Shaftesbury's words once more. Now to illustrate the superiority of harmony over chaos Shaftesbury explicitly refers to the superiority of the 'regular and uniform pile of some noble Architect' over 'a Heap of Sand or Stones'. But is not the heap of sand nature in her primitive state? That the early eighteenth century did not want to recognize. So we arrive at this curious ambiguity. Simple nature is order and harmony of proportion. So a natural architecture is an architecture according to Palladio. But simple nature is also, in the common speech of everybody, fields and hedgerows, and of these people were genuinely fond, at least in England. So the garden should be left as close to this simple nature as possible. Addison was the first to reach this conclusion. He exclaimed: 'Why may not a whole estate be thrown into a kind of garden?'; and 'A man might make a pretty landscape of his own possessions.' Pope followed Addison in a contribution to *The Guardian* in 1713 and, more important still, in his own miniature garden at Twickenham. However, when it came to 'improving' Twickenham (to use the eighteenth-century term) in 1719–25 another equally remarkable thing happened. These earliest anti-French gardens were by no means landscape gardens in the later sense. They were not Pope's 'Nature unadorned'. Their plans with elaborately meandering paths and rills are of as artificial an irregularity as Baroque regularity had been before. Or as Horace Walpole put it in 1750: 'There is not a citizen who doesn't take more pains to torture his acre and a half into irregularities than he formerly would have employed to make it as formal as his cravat.' Now all that, this 'twisting and twirling' (to use Walpole's words again), is evidently Rococo, and nearer in spirit to the Bruchsal *rocaille* than to those gardens of the later eighteenth century which really tried to look like untouched nature. It is the English version of Rococo – as characteristically English as Wren's Baroque had been in comparison with Continental Baroque.

So while one remembers the grandeur and elegance of French seventeenth- and eighteenth-century architecture as urban all the way through – for the straight avenues in the park of Versailles are urban in spirit too – one should never forget in looking at the formality of English Palladian houses between 1660 and 1760 that their complement is the English garden. John Wood's Prior Park possesses such informal natural grounds. And even in the most urban developments of Georgian Britain such as New Edinburgh, and above all Bath, nature was close at hand and willingly admitted.

John Wood was the first after Inigo Jones to impose Palladian uniformity on an English square as a whole. All the squares in London and elsewhere laid out since 1660 had left it to each owner of a house to have it designed as he liked, and it was due only to the rule of taste in Georgian society that not one of these houses ever clashed violently with its neighbours. John Wood now made one palace front with central portico and secondary emphasis on the corner blocks out of his Queen Square in Bath. That was in 1728. Twenty-five years later he designed the Circus (1754–c. 1770), again as a uniform theme. His son, the younger John Wood (died 1781), in the Royal Crescent of 1767–c. 1775 broke open the compactness of earlier squares and ventured to provide as the only response to his vast semi-elliptical palace frontage of thirty houses with giant Ionic columns a spacious, gently sloping lawn. Here the extreme opposite of Versailles had been reached. Nature is no longer the servant of architecture. The two are equals. The Romantic Movement is at hand.

In London the principle of the palace façade for a whole row of houses was introduced by Robert Adam in his Adelphi (that magnificent composition of streets with its Thames front known all over Europe, which was destroyed, not by bombs, but by mercenary Londoners just before the war) and then taken up at Fitzroy Square and Finsbury Square. But Adam's work, which won international fame in the sixties and seventies – at the same moment when the English garden also began to influence Europe – should not be discussed so close to the Palladianism of the Burlington group. It is of fundamentally another kind. As a rule this difference is expressed by placing Adam at the beginning of the so-called Classical Revival. But that is not the whole answer, for the Classical Revival is really only a part of a much wider process, the Romantic Movement. So from the renewed direct approach to Greek and Roman antiquities as well as from the English creation of landscape gardening we are led into a consideration of the central European problem of 1760–1830: the Romantic Movement.

239 Bath, Royal Crescent, by John Wood the Younger, 1767–*c*. 1775

8 The Romantic Movement, Historicism, and the Beginning of the Modern Movement

1760–1914

The Romantic Movement originated in England. In literature this fact is well enough known. For the arts and for architecture in particular it has yet to. be established. In literature Romanticism is the reaction of sentiment against reason, of nature against artificiality, of simplicity against pompous display, of faith against scepticism. Romantic poetry expresses a new enthusiasm for nature and a self-abandoning veneration of the whole, elemental, undoubting life of early or distant civilizations. This veneration led to the discovery of the Noble Savage and the Noble Greek, the Virtuous Roman and the Pious Medieval Knight. Whatever its object, the Romantic attitude is one of longing, that is, antagonism to the present, a present which some saw predominantly as Rococo flippancy, others as unimaginative rationalism, and others again as ugly industrialism and commercialism.

The opposition to the present and the immediate past goes through all utterances of the Romantic spirit, although certain tendencies within the new movement grew out of the eighteenth century's Rationalism and Rococo. It has been shown for instance how the conception of the landscape garden – a truly Romantic conception – dates back to Addison and Pope, but appears at first in Rococo dress. Similarly that most popular architectural expression of Romanticism, the revival of medieval forms, started long before the Romantic Movement proper and went through all the phases of eighteenth-century style, before it became wholly Romantic in character.

In fact the Gothic style had never quite died in England. There is unselfconscious Gothic Survival in much provincial work before

1700, and there is selfconscious Gothic Revival as early as the late years of Queen Elizabeth (Wollaton Hall 1580) and the years of King James (Library, St John's College, Cambridge 1624). Wren, as has already been said, also used Gothic forms in some of his London churches, and he argued in their qualified favour in two ways, both heralding the arguments of the eighteenth and nineteenth centuries. He recommended carrying on Gothic where original Gothic work was present because 'to deviate from the old Form, would be to run into a disagreeable Mixture, which no Person of good Taste could relish', but he also wrote that he considered his Gothic churches in London 'not ungraceful but ornamental'. So here Gothicism is advocated for the sake of conformity as well as grace.

Hawksmoor's medievalizing in the towers of his churches was dictated neither by a desire for conformity nor for grace, and his conception of the Middle Ages as a period of primeval virility went beyond Wren's. It is indeed a conception which might be called Baroque Gothicism. Its leader was Vanbrugh, and it was due to him that Baroque Gothicism also entered the field of domestic architecture. His own house at Blackheath of 1717–18 is castellated and has

240 Blackheath, London, Sir John Vanbrugh's house, built for himself in 1717–18

a fortified-looking round tower. He also introduced castellated structures into many of the grounds which he furnished or laid out. We know in his case what were his reasons; for he gave them in his letters. He wished his architecture to be *masculine*; and this crenellations seemed to foster. Hence thick round towers and battlements occur even in his country houses which are otherwise in the current style. However, in addition to their primeval character medieval castles meant something else to him. Not that he actually built sham ruins as the later eighteenth century did, but he defended the preservation of genuine ruins when he found them, because they 'move lively and pleasing reflections . . . on the persons who have inhabited them (and) on the remarkable things which have been transacted in them', and because 'with yews and hollies in a wild thicket' they make 'one of the most agreeable objects that the best of landscape painters can invent'.

Vanbrugh's and Hawksmoor's austere version of medievalism died when they died, but the two passages quoted just now from Vanbrugh's memorandum (on Blenheim) form the foundation of Romantic Revivalism. As will have been noticed Vanbrugh uses two arguments: the associational and the picturesque. Both were developed by theorists of the eighteenth century. A building is clothed in the garb of a special style, because of the meditations which that style will rouse. And a building is conceived in conjunction with the surrounding nature, because the virtuosi had discovered on the Grand Tour amid the ruins of Roman architecture in and around Rome the truth and the picturesqueness of the heroic and idyllic landscapes of Claude Lorraine, Poussin, Dughet, and Salvator Rosa. These were bought freely by English collectors and helped to form the taste of artists and gardeners, amateur and professional.

Lorraine may have been admired by Pope and Kent (who after all was a painter before he became an architect), but the gardens of Twickenham and Chiswick had nothing of the serene calm of a Lorraine landscape. The Rococo had to die before this kind of beauty could be reproduced. The Leasowes, the garden which William Shenstone the poet had laid out for himself about 1745, was apparently amongst the first to replace the 'twisting and twirling' of the earlier style by a gentler flow of curves which, together with the many memorial seats and temples which he erected, helped to create feelings of pleasant melancholy. The great name in the history of mid-eighteenth-century gardening is Lancelot Brown (Capability Brown, 1715–83). His are the wide, softly sweeping lawns, the artfully scattered clumps of trees, and the serpentine lakes which revolutionized garden art all over Europe and America. This is no longer Rococo; it has the gentle simplicity of Goldsmith's *Vicar of Wakefield* and the chaste elegance of Robert Adam's architecture.

But Adam's is a more complex case than Brown's. Robert Adam (1728–92) is internationally known as the father of the Classical Revival in Britain. His revival of Roman stucco decoration and his delicate adaptation of classical motifs have influenced the Continent just as widely as the new English style in gardening. Yet delicacy is hardly what our present knowledge of Greece and Rome would lead us to expect from a true classical revivalist. Where in Adam's work

241 Blenheim Palace from the air. The grounds laid out by Capability Brown

242 Syon House, Middlesex, by Robert Adam, begun 1761 (Copyright *Country Life*)

is the severe nobility of Athens or the sturdy virility of Rome? There is in fact more severity in Lord Burlington's Palladianism and more virility in Vanbrugh than can anywhere be found in Adam. Compare, for example, the walls of Adam's Long Gallery at Syon House with those of any Palladian mansion. Adam covers his walls with dainty and exquisitely executed stucco work in a light and quick rhythm. And he loves to run out a room into a gently rounded niche screened off by two free-standing columns with an entablature above. This veiling of spatial relations, this transparency – air floating from room to apse between the columns and above the entablature – is decidedly anti-Palladian, original, and spirited. It occurs again in exterior architecture in the entrance screen to the grounds of Syon House. Here too Lord Burlington would have spoken of flippancy and frippery. And Vanbrugh's centre pavilions in the wings of Blenheim Palace look, compared with Adam's screen, like boulders piled up by a giant. Adam's gracefully ornamental pilasters and the lion in profile silhouetted against the sky make Vanbrugh

243 Syon House, entrance screen, 1773 (Copyright *Country Life*)

appear a tartar, Burlington a pedant. What Adam admired in a building is, in his own words: 'the rise and fall, the advance and recess, and other diversity of forms', and 'a variety of light mouldings'.

Now this is eminently revealing. It is neither Baroque nor Palladian – although in the exteriors of his country houses Adam did not often depart from Palladian standards – nor is it classical. It is Rococo if anything – yet another passing and concealed appearance in England of the general European style of the mid eighteenth century. All the same, it is not wrong either to see in Robert Adam a representative of the Classical Revival. He did go to Rome as a young man, from there crossed over to Spalato to study and measure the remains of Diocletian's Palace, and after his return home published the results of his research as a sumptuous volume in 1763. Now these engraved folios of the monuments of antiquity are quite rightly regarded as a hall-mark of the Classical Revival. Adam's was preceded by the most important of all, James Stuart and Nicholas Revett's *Antiquities of Athens*, of which the first volume came out in 1762. The two architects had worked at the expense of the recently founded Society of Dilettanti, the London club of archaeologically interested gentlemen. Two years later the temples of Paestum were published by Dumont. In these books the architect and the virtuoso in England could see for the first time the strength and simplicity of the Greek Doric order. For what until then, and ever since the Books of Orders of the sixteenth century, had been known and used as Doric, was the much slenderer variety now known as Roman, if fluted, and Tuscan, if not fluted. The short and thick proportions of the Greek Doric order, and the complete absence of a base, shocked the Palladians. Sir William Chambers, champion of Palladian traditions in the generation after Burlington and one of the founders of the Royal Academy in 1768, called it downright barbaric. Adam did not like it either. Its reappearance in the books of the sixties is memorable. It became the *leitmotif* of the severest phase or variety of the Classical Revival, that known in England as the Greek Revival. Stuart and Revett's work was paralleled in French by Le Roi's skimpier *Ruines de Grèce* of 1758 and in German by Winckelmann's classic *History of Ancient Art* of 1763 – the first book to recognize and analyse the true qualities of Greek art, its 'noble simplicity and tranquil greatness'.

However, Winckelmann's recognition of these qualities was still more literary than visual; for he placed the Apollo Belvedere and the Laocoon, that is, examples of Late Greek Baroque and Rococo, higher than any other antique statuary. Would the figures of Olympia and Aegina and perhaps even those of the Parthenon have shocked him? It is not at all unlikely. His Grecian tastes probably did not go further than, say, Josiah Wedgwood's. Wedgwood copied vases from those Greek examples of the fifth century which were then believed to be Etruscan, and even called his new factory up by Stoke-on-Trent Etruria. But the style of Wedgwood ware is gentle and elegant – an Adam not a Greek style. Still, there is the undeniable desire to be Greek, the marked tendency in archaeological publications to prefer the Greek to the Roman, and there is, if not in Adam, in his contemporary James Stuart, 'Athenian' Stuart (1713–88), the actual copying in earnest of complete Greek structures on Northern soil and the putting up of Doric temples for Northern patrons. If this is not a genuine Greek Revival, what is? But once again, if we forget about associations and intentions and simply use our eyes, we see miniature pavilions in Doric forms placed into landscape gardens – picturesque pieces of garden furnishing. Such a Doric temple of Stuart's, for example, graces the grounds at Hagley, near Birmingham, and close to it the same owner put up at the same time a Gothic ruin as a keeper's lodge and a rustic seat to the memory of Thomson of the *Seasons*. The Doric temple at Hagley was built in 1758 and is the earliest monument of the Doric Revival in Europe.

The only difference between the Doric and the Gothic of Hagley is that the one is correct and the other is not. The owner, owing to his classical education, could watch the one, but could not watch the other. Architects too, and even country builders, knew by 1760 enough of the orders and the details of antiquity to be able to reproduce a Pantheon *en miniature* or a half-broken Roman aqueduct without too many blunders. But in the case of the earliest Gothic Revival antiquarian knowledge was still scanty. Thus while the result in the Greek and Roman copies tends to be somewhat dry,

244 Garden seat from P. Decker's *Gothic Architecture Decorated*, 1759

the innumerable Gothic seats, hermits' cells, 'umbrellos', sham ruins and other follies are charmingly naïve and light-hearted – a Gothic Rococo, as Adam's was a classical Rococo.

To Horace Walpole belongs the credit of having established the Gothic as a style for the English country house. His Strawberry Hill, near London, became famous among connoisseurs and architects of the younger school all over Europe. He gothicized and enlarged the original cottage in 1750. In one respect he was in his Gothic work ahead of others with similar tastes, notably William Kent, whom we have met as a Palladian and a pioneer of picturesque gardening. Walpole insisted that his interiors should have correct details. Fireplaces or wall panelling were copied from engravings after medieval tombs and screens. Yet he evidently admired other qualities in the Gothic style than we do. In letters of 1748 and 1750 he talks of 'the charming venerable Gothic' and the 'whimsical air of novelty' which Gothic motifs give to contemporary buildings. And charming and whimsical Strawberry Hill is indeed with its thin, papery exterior work and the pretty gallery inside whose gilt fan-vaults and tracery have mirrors set in as panels. This playful use of Gothic forms is closer in spirit to Chippendale's Chinese furniture than to Wordsworth's feelings at Tintern Abbey or to Victorian neo-Gothic churches. Walpole himself was against the fashion of the *chinoiserie*; but for a generalizing view of the style of 1750 a Chinese bridge, a miniature Pantheon, and a Gothic ruin all belong together. In fact we find that even Robert Adam enjoyed drawing ruins with all the Rococo sparkle of Piranesi, and occasionally designed

245 Twickenham, Middlesex, Strawberry Hill, enlarged and gothicized, *c*.1750–70, Holbein Chamber (Copyright *Country Life*)

domestic work in a mildly medieval taste. And we also find Sir William Chambers, in spite of his staunch adherence to Palladianism, designing the Pagoda at Kew Gardens.

Kew had originally the most varied set of such Rococo garden extravaganzas: besides the Pagoda (which happily survives) a temple of Pan, a temple of Aeolus, a temple of Solitude, a temple of the Sun, a temple of Bellona, a temple of Victory, a house of Confucius, a Roman theatre, an Alhambra, a mosque, a Gothic cathedral, a ruinous arch, etc. The fun of Turkish, Moorish, Gothic, and Chinese in this *omnium gatherum* of exotic styles is that of Voltaire's *Zadig* and *Babouc* and of Montesquieu's *Lettres Persanes*, that is, one of a sophisticated Rococo double-meaning. Not much of the solemn meditation of the Romantics could in fact be evoked by a Pagoda. When the Romantic Movement somewhat later instilled

359

these sentiments into gardening, a good many of the current garden adornments were eliminated as unsuitable. Yet to Walpole too Strawberry Hill had associational qualities. It was, in some ways, his *Castle of Otranto*. It seems difficult to believe that; but that Beckford's mansion, Fonthill Abbey, with its vast galleries and enormous tower had to him some of the awe-inspiring qualities of the dark Middle Ages can be appreciated from surviving illustrations. Here the eccentricity of a millionaire seems to have created something truly romantic. Fonthill was built by James Wyatt (1746–1813) from 1796 onwards. But already as early as 1772 Goethe in front of Strassburg Cathedral had found words of passionate admiration for the Gothic spirit in architecture. 'It rises like a most sublime, wide-arching Tree of God, who with a thousand boughs, a million of twigs, and leafage like the sands of the sea, tells forth to the neighbourhood the glory of the Lord, his master. . . . All is shape, down to the minutest fibril, all purposes to the whole. How the firm-grounded gigantic building lightly rears itself into the air! How filagreed all of it, yet for eternity. . . . Stop, brother, and discern the deepest sense of truth . . . quickening out of strong, rough, German soul. . . . Be not girled, dear youth, for rough greatness by the soft doctrine of modern beauty-lisping.'[40]

Now here the Gothic style is no longer something in the same category as Rococo, Chinese, and Hindu; it stands for all that is genuine, sincere, elemental – in fact very much for what Winckelmann, and only a little later Goethe himself, saw in the art of Greece. The Greek and the Gothic were both, in the minds of serious aestheticians and artists, the salvation from eighteenth-century flippancy. France had been far more devoted to the Rococo than England, and so the reaction against it was more violent in France. It started as early as the 1750s. The Abbé Laugier, an amateur, published his *Essai sur l'architecture* in 1753 and preached in it: 'Tenons nous au simple et au naturel'. Charles-Nicolas Cochin the Younger (1715–90), a successful young engraver, brought out in the *Mercure de France* in December 1754 his charming 'Supplication aux Orfèvres' imploring the goldsmiths not to go on with their S-curves and other 'formes barroques' and preaching that 'only the right angle can result in good effects'.

The first great French architect to turn to more classical forms was Ange-Jacques Gabriel (1698–1782). He had never been in Italy and must have formed his mature style on the example of the most classical French architects of the seventeenth century – a parallel to the Palladio and Inigo Jones revival in England. Gabriel was Premier Architecte du Roi. His most important works are the École Militaire, begun in 1751, the two buildings along the north side of the Place de la Concorde, begun in 1757, and the Petit Trianon in the gardens of Versailles, begun in 1762. There is nothing revolutionary in any of them. The staircase of the École Militaire for instance is of the type of Mansart's staircase at Blois, but the shallow coffered vaults and the solid bronze hand-rail give a firmness reassuring after the elegancies of the Rococo. The stone masonry, as

246 Paris, École Militaire, by Ange-Jacques Gabriel, begun 1751

in all Gabriel's buildings, is exquisite. The façades of the Place de la Concorde have the loggias on the first floor which Perrault had used in the east front of the Louvre, and the Petit Trianon has no curved projections, nor a curved dome, nor even a pediment. It is an extremely handsome little cube with only a few of the most restrained external enrichments.

It has been said that the Petit Trianon presupposes influences from English Palladianism. But there is little in the general tenor or the details to justify such an assumption. English influence at Versailles arrived a little later, both in the form of Palladianism – the Couvent de la Reine of about 1770 by Richard Mique (1728–94), and in the more eventful form of picturesque garden ornaments: a rotunda or monopteros dedicated to Cupid and built about 1777 also by Mique, and Marie Antoinette's famous Hameau, a mock-Norman farm, built about 1781 again by Mique. The wealthy of Paris were equally keen at the time to have *jardins anglais*. The specialist in these *folies* was François-Joseph Belanger (1744–1818) who laid out the Bagatelle and the Folie St James in the 1770s. Rousseau's Ermenonville is of the same time.[41] In 1775 already a letter was published 'sur la manie des jardins anglais'. Closely connected with Belanger and landscape gardening – and this in itself is a characteristic fact – was a painter: Hubert Robert (1733–1808). He was active at Versailles in 1775 and seems also to have had something to do with the Désert de Retz. Hubert Robert had been sent to Rome in 1754 as a protégé of Mme de Pompadour's younger brother, the Surintendant des Bâtiments. He himself had been sent by his sister four years before. He was accompanied on this memorable tour in search of a more serious and classical style by Cochin of the *Supplication* and by Jacques-Germain Soufflot (1713–80) who was to be the most important French architect of the generation after Gabriel's. Soufflot is principally known for the Panthéon, so-called during the revolution. It had been built as the church of Ste Geneviève in 1755–92. The Panthéon was indeed a revolutionary design for France, even if for England it would have been less so. That Soufflot knew and was in sympathy with English buildings is proved by the evident dependence of the dome of his church on Wren's St Paul's. This splendid dome on its high colonnaded drum rises above

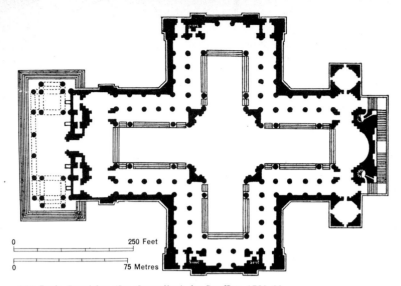

248 Paris, Panthéon (Ste Geneviève), by Soufflot, 1755–92

the crossing of a large building on the plan of a detached Greek cross. Lower domes cover the four arms, much in the same way in which this had been done at Holy Apostles in Byzantium, at Périgueux and at St Mark's in Venice, and in the Sforza Medal of *c*. 1460. But while in these and all similar churches the domes rest on solid walls or piers, Soufflot chose to place his as far as possible on columns carrying straight entablatures. The ambulatories which surround the whole church have nothing but columns, except below the corners of the central dome, where Soufflot introduced slim triangular piers with columns set against them. These were later enlarged and the outer windows filled in. That detracts to a certain extent from the sense of lightness which Soufflot intended to create in his church. The combination of strict regularity and monumental Roman detail with this lightness is his most original contribution. It corresponds convincingly to what Robert Adam was beginning to do in England at the same time. But Adam lightened his models instinctively, Soufflot according to a well-considered theory, a theory so curious and ambiguous that it deserves comment. Laugier and others had denounced pilasters attached to piers as

249 Paris, Panthéon (Ste Geneviève), by Jacques-Germain Soufflot, 1755–92

unnatural – by this they meant as Baroque. The column instead was natural, and also correct according to Greek precedent. At the same time however the column was the slimmer support, and thus, if it could be made to carry its load satisfactorily, it was the more rational solution. Now the model for these considerations of minimum mass to support a maximum load was Gothic churches, and Soufflot said indeed in 1762 that one ought to combine the Greek orders with 'the lightness which one admires in some Gothic buildings'. Perronnet, director of the famous school for bridge- and road-engineers, said the same a few years later: 'Ste Geneviève stands in the middle between the massive architecture of Antiquity and the lighter Gothic architecture.' In that sense then France in the mid eighteenth century also had its Gothic Revival.[42] But whereas the Gothic Revival in England is evocative, in France it is structural, in fact so purely structural that it is scarcely noticed.

Soufflot had given a lecture on Gothic architecture as early as 1741. When he was in Italy in 1750, he went to see the temples of Paestum and indeed drew them in great detail. His drawings were at last published in 1764 by Dumont in the volume already mentioned. But here again Soufflot's appreciation did not lead to imitation. This was different with the young French architects of the next generation who were sent to the Académie de France in Rome in the fifties and sixties. This next generation, architects born in 1725–50, has no real leader in France. Ledoux's is the most familiar name, Boullée's has become more familiar recently, but neither of these was as successful as several of the others; and yet they are hardly known outside a narrow circle: de Wailly and Marie-Joseph Peyre, the two architects of the Odéon, Antoine, Louis, Gondoin, who built the School of Surgery, Brongniart, who worked at the Capuchin house, now Lycée Condorcet, Chalgrin, famous for the Arc de Triomphe and the church of St Philippe du Roule, Desprez who worked in Sweden, Belanger, and others. Their style has much in common and was influenced by Gabriel and Soufflot, by England and Rome. It is characterized by strictly cubic shapes without pavilion roofs or indeed any visible roofs, by hemispherical domes on the pattern of the Pantheon in Rome (as against that of the more Baroque dome of the Panthéon in Paris) and of Bramante, by porticoes with a straight entablature instead of a pediment (Ledoux's Hôtel d' Uzès of 1767 and Château of Bénouville of 1768, Boullée's Hôtel de Brunoy of 1772, Louis's Theatre of Bordeaux of 1772–80, the Odéon of 1779–82, Rousseau's Hôtel de Salm now Légion d'Honneur of 1782–6, Brongniart's Bourse of 1807, etc.), by coffered tunnel-vaults (Chalgrin's St Philippe du Roule 1774–84), and by a preference for Tuscan and Greek Doric over the other more delicate orders. England had of course favoured Tuscan orders ever since the later years of Wren, and introduced the Greek Doric order as early as 1758 at Hagley. In France it appeared in 1778 in Ledoux's Theatre at Besançon and some time between 1778 and 1781 at Antoine's entrance to the chapel of the Hospital of Charity. But the French liked the short stumpy Tuscan column better than the Greek Doric. The absence of fluting made it even more primeval-looking. Brongniart used them in the cloister of the Capuchins (Lycée Condorcet, rue du Havre) in 1780, David, the painter, in his epoch-making Oath of the Horatii in 1784, Poyet along the whole rue des Colonnes in 1798, Thomas de Thomon for his Bourse at St Petersburg in 1801, and so on. Tuscan and Doric columns are the antithesis to the pilasters on curved surfaces which the Rococo had liked. They represent power as against elegance. Similarly, as a

250 St Petersburg, Bourse, by Thomas de Thomon, 1801

counterblast against the delicacy and the *petitesse* of the Rococo, architects began to insist on a grandiose scale. This has often produced architectural dreams on paper totally unconcerned with what might be executed, royal palaces or buildings for more democratic purposes as premises for vaguely defined academies, museums, libraries, or the more than once planned monuments to Isaac Newton, discoverer of order in infinity.

The seducer of all these young men in Rome was Giovanni Battista Piranesi (1720–78), a Venetian architect who lived in Rome, built little, and built disappointingly when he built, but etched innumerable plates of architecture, sometimes fantastic, but more often purporting to be the portraits of Roman Antiquity. They are true in fact in their details, yet in their scale and composition of a visionary sublimity 'beyond', as Horace Walpole wrote, 'what Rome boasted even in the meridian of its splendour'. It is eminently telling that Flaxman confessed that he found 'the ruins of Rome less striking than he had been accustomed to suppose them after seeing the prints of Piranesi'. Piranesi was indeed famous all over Europe for his plates of Roman buildings. He was made an honorary member of the Society of Antiquaries in London in 1757 and dedicated a publication of the Campus Martius to Robert Adam. In his plates all buildings seem the works of giants and man crouches or creeps in and out of them as a puny pigmy (see ill. on p. 24). There is more than a touch of the Rococo *capriccio* in this, as also in Piranesi's spirited handling of the graver and the etcher's needle. But there is also much in it that points forward into the Romantic Age, the fervour with which, to quote Horace Walpole again, he 'scales Heaven with mountains of edifices', and his delight in primeval forms such as the pyramid and – at the very end of his life – the Greek Doric columns of Paestum.

The most spectacular result of the Piranesi cult of the French students of the Académie de France was Peyre's *Œuvres d'architecture* published in 1765. They contain megalomaniac designs for a palace of the French academies, a cathedral, etc. Peyre was in Rome from 1753 to 1757, Chalgrin from 1759 to 1763, Gondoin from 1761 to 1766, and so on. Neither Boullée nor Ledoux knew Italy.[43] But their style cannot be understood without Piranesi and Peyre.

Étienne-Louis Boullée (1728–99) like Piranesi is not of much interest as a practising architect. His glory is a set of large drawings prepared in the 1780s and 90s for lectures or a publication. They are as megalomaniac as any of Peyre's: a cathedral on a Greek-cross plan with porticoes of sixteen giant columns against all four fronts, and a centrally planned museum which is a square block with semi-circular porticoes on all four sides, each with thirty-eight columns repeated fourfold in depth so as to comprise 152 columns for each portico, and a national library with one vast reading room with a tunnel-vault of untold dimensions, and a cemetery with an entrance in the form of a squat pyramid flanked by two obelisks, and a Cenotaph for a Warrior in the form of a sarcophagus apparently about 250 feet high, and a monument to Newton, completely spherical inside and in this case about 500 feet high, if the human figures drawn in can be taken as an accurate measure. But accuracy of proportions is not perhaps what ought to be expected. Piranesi had spoiled the insistence on them. Boullée in the comments to his pictures pleads for a felt not a reasoned architecture, for character, grandeur, magic. Practical needs worried him little.

Claude-Nicolas Ledoux (1736–1806) was more successful. In spite of an eccentric, quarrelsome character he had plenty of commissions for town houses, country houses, and other buildings. Of the richer houses built in Paris during the years 1760 to 1820 only few survive and not the most characteristic. To a visitor perambulating Paris the

251 Design for the entrance to a cemetery, by Étienne-Louis Boullée, c. 1780–90

252 Paris, toll house, by Ledoux, 1784–9

style must have been much more insistent and convincing than it can
be to us now relying almost exclusively on engravings. Of Ledoux's
buildings for other than domestic purposes, the most interesting are,
or were, the following. First the toll houses of Paris, built in 1784–9
with an infinite variety of plans and elevations, but always in a
forceful, massive style, with Tuscan or Doric or heavily rusticated
columns. Then the Theatre at Besançon which was built in 1778–84,
with Greek Doric columns inside, as has already been observed.
They stand, a colonnade, at the top of a semicircular amphitheatre.
The semicircle as a simple geometrical form was bound to please
Ledoux and the others of this group. Gondoin had used it already
in 1769–70 in his designs for the École de Chirurgie, and it was
again used after the Revolution by Gisors and Lecointe for the
Conseil des Cinq-Cents in the Palais Bourbon (1797). But Ledoux's
most exciting work, even in its fragmentary form, is the Salines de
Chaux at Arc-et-Senans on the river Loue near Besançon built
mostly in 1775–9. The gatehouse has a deep portico of sturdy Tuscan
columns and behind it a niche cyclopically rusticated as if it were
rocks left in the raw and with stone-carved urns out of which flows
stone-carved water – the whole a perfect marriage of the classical
and the romantic, attracted to one another by a shared worship of
the elemental and primeval.

These qualities, however, assumed different and seemingly contradictory forms in other designs of Ledoux, designs which for good
reasons were never executed. He wanted to give the house for the
surveyor of the river Loue a barrel-shaped centre through which the
river would flow and come down with 'falling waters' at one end;
or the park-keepers at Maupertuis he suggested houses of com-
tely spheric shape, and for furnaces of a gun-foundry pyramids.

253 Arc-et-Senans, Salines de Chaux, by Claude-Nicolas Ledoux, 1775 -9

Here the longing for those elementary geometric shapes which the Rococo had replaced everywhere by more complex and gentler curves carried an architect away into an architecture for architecture's sake divorced from all consideration of utility. Ledoux also designed an ideal city which he published in a big folio in 1806 with a confused text replete with social reform. The public buildings in this city serve such vague functions as 'Palace dedicated to the Cult of Moral Values'. The vagueness is familiar from the rhetoric of the French Revolution. Ledoux was personally not in favour of the revolution, but the group whose most vociferous representative he was, is yet rightly called the architects of the revolution; for they were in revolt against accepted authority and convention and fought for originality.

The position had characteristically changed against that of 1750–60. Then the enemy had been the Rococo. Now it was the thoughtless acceptance of Antiquity as the law-giver. Ledoux refused to accept either Palladio or the Greeks. He and the others wanted to re-think the problem, and re-feel the character, of every job. They were right to the extent of insisting that no healthy style in architecture is possible as imitation of a past style. The Renaissance had never merely imitated. The Palladians of the eighteenth century, the Grecians of the early nineteenth, did it too often. Goethe in the most classical mood of his *Iphigenia* yet remained essentially original. And in fact what he had praised more than anything at Strassburg was originality in the sense of Young. And so the few architects of Goethe's era who possessed true genius used the forms of Greece and Rome with the greatest freedom.

Two must here be discussed, Sir John Soane in England, and Friedrich Gilly in Prussia. Soane (1753–1837) was, like Ledoux, a difficult character, suspicious and autocratic though generous. He was twelve when Peyre's *Livre d'Architecture* came out and must have been greatly impressed by it, even before he went to Rome in 1776. There he can still have known Piranesi. He certainly knew Paestum and began to use Greek Doric columns – always a telling sign of a longing for severity – in the same year 1778 in which Piranesi's book of engravings of Paestum appeared. In 1788 he was appointed architect to the Bank of England. The exterior, before it

254 London, Bank of England, by Sir John Soane, 1788–1808, design for the Rotunda

was converted by recent governors and directors into a podium for a piece of twentieth-century commercial showiness, indicates this new and, to the majority, shocking austerity. The interiors give an even clearer idea of his sense of surface integrity. Walls flow smoothly into vaults. Mouldings are reduced to a minimum. Arches rise from piers which they seem to touch only in points. No precedent is allowed to cramp the style. The Dulwich Gallery of 1811–14 and Soane's own house in Lincoln's Inn Fields, built in 1812–13 and intended to be carried on to more than double its width, are his most independent designs. The ground floor of the house has severely plain arcading in front of the actual wall; the first floor repeats this

255 London, Sir John Soane's house and museum, Lincoln's Inn Fields, built for himself in 1812–13

unusual motif with the variation of a centre with Ionic columns supporting the thinnest of architraves, and wings where the weight of the piers is lightened by typically Soanian incised ornament. The top pavilions on the left and the right are equally original. Except for the Ionic columns there is not one motif in the whole façade that has a Greek or Roman ancestry. Here more than anywhere in architecture England approached a new style unhampered by the past. But the ingredients of Soane's style are yet more complex, in so far as they are not only Piranesian and French but also English. The façade of Soane's house, as it is now, has only one of the intended external screens, and that, as an additional embellishment, is given four Gothic brackets with nothing on them. These brackets come from Westminster Hall and were incorporated in the front of the house when Soane executed work at the palace of Westminster. This is a most pointed demonstration of what Perronet had called the middle position between Antiquity and the Gothic style, and indeed in the museum which Soane had built and completely equipped at the back of his house, fragments of buildings of Antiquity jostle against Gothic fragments, neo-classical and neo-Gothic details occur, and a genuine Egyptian sarcophagus is the dramatic centre-piece – the centre-piece of a composition of almost unbelievable intricacy, with small rooms stuck into or flowing into each other, with unexpected changes of level, openings appearing over your head and almost below your feet, and mirrors, often distorting mirrors, everywhere to conceal the bounds. In one small room alone there are over ninety of them. This lack of faith in stability and security is utterly un-Grecian and highly romantic. The Classical Revival, as has been remarked before, is only one facet of the Romantic Movement.

The small *œuvre* of Friedrich Gilly (1772–1800) bears this out too. He had his training in Berlin and never saw Italy. However, he had an opportunity of going to Paris and London, and there could see the style of the Ledoux group and possibly of Soane. But their influence ought not to be exaggerated; for before he went, he had designed one of the two masterpieces which are left us to bear witness of his genius – left, however, only in drawings. Neither was ever carried out. The first is the National Monument to Frederick

256 Design for a National Theatre for Berlin, by Friedrich Gilly, 1798

the Great (1797), the second a National Theatre for Berlin – clearly a conception of the Goethe age. The Doric portico without a pediment is a strong and grave opening. The semicircular windows, a favourite motif of the revolutionary architects of Paris, though imported from England, add strength to strength, and the contrast between the semicylinder of the auditorium – Ledoux's semicylinder of the theatre of Besançon – and the cube of the stage is functionally eloquent and aesthetically superb. Here again we are close to a new style of the new century.

Why is it then that a hundred years had to pass before an original 'modern' style was really accepted? How can it be that the nineteenth century forgot about Soane and Gilly and remained smugly satisfied with the imitation of the past? Such a lack of self-confidence is the last thing one would expect from an epoch so independent in commerce, industry, and engineering. It is the things of the spirit in which the Victorian age lacked vigour and courage. Standards in architecture were the first to go; for while a poet and a painter can forget about their age and be great in the solitude of their study and studio, an architect cannot exist in opposition to society. Now those to whom visual sensibility was given saw so much beauty destroyed all around by the sudden immense and uncontrolled growth of cities and factories that they despaired of their century and turned to a more inspiring past. Moreover, the iron-master and mill-owner, as a rule self-made men of no education, felt no longer bound by one particular accepted taste as the gentleman had been who was brought up to believe in the rule of taste. It would have been bad manners to build against it. Hence the only slightly varied uniformity of the English eighteenth-century house. The new manufacturer had no manners, and he was a convinced individualist. If, for whatever reasons, he liked a style in architecture, then there was nothing to prevent him from having his way and getting a house or a factory or an office building or a club built in that style. And unfortunately for the immediate future of architecture he knew of a good many possible styles, because – as we have seen – some sophisticated and leisurely *cognoscenti* of the eighteenth century had explored for fun certain out-of-the-way architectural idioms, and a set of Romantic poets was revelling in nostalgic fantasies of the distant in time and space. The Rococo had reintroduced alien styles, the Romantic Movement had endowed them with sentimental associations. The nineteenth century lost the Rococo's lightness of touch and the Romantic's emotional fervour. But it stuck to variety of style, because associational values were the only values in architecture accessible to the new ruling class.

We have seen Vanbrugh's defence of ruins for associational reasons. Sir Joshua Reynolds in his thirteenth *Discourse* of 1786 made the same point more neatly. He explicitly counts amongst the principles of architecture 'that of affecting the imagination by means of association of ideas. Thus,' he continues, 'we have naturally a veneration for antiquity; whatever building brings to our remembrance ancient customs and manners, such as the castles of the Barons of ancient Chivalry, is sure to give this delight.'

Hence on the authority of the late President of the Royal Academy the manufacturer and merchant could feel justified in placing associational criteria foremost. Visual criteria his eyes were not trained to appreciate. But the eyes of architects were; and it was a grave symptom of a diseased century that architects were satisfied to be storytellers instead of artists. But then painters were no better.

They too, to be successful, had to tell stories or render objects from nature with scientific accuracy.

Thus by 1830 we find a most alarming social and aesthetic situation in architecture. Architects believed that anything created by the pre-industrial centuries must of necessity be better than anything made to express the character of their own era. Architects' clients had lost all aesthetic susceptibilities, and wanted other than aesthutic qualities to approve of a building. Associations they could understand. And one other quality they could also understand and even check : correctness of imitation. The free and fanciful treatment of styles developed into one of archaeological exactitude. That this could happen was due to that general sharpening of the tools of historical knowledge which characterizes the nineteenth century. It is in truth the century of Historicism. After the system-building eighteenth century, the nineteenth appears to an amazing extent satisfied with, say, a historical and comparative study of existing philosophies instead of the study of ethics, aesthetics, etc., themselves. And so it was in theology and philology too. Similarly architectural scholarship abandoned aesthetic theory and concentrated on historical research. Thanks to a subdivision of labour which architecture, like all other fields of art, letters, and science, took over from industry, architects were always able to draw from a well-assorted stock of historical detail. No wonder that little time and desire were left for the development of an original style of the nineteenth century. Even with regard to Soane and Gilly we have to be careful not to over-estimate their originality and 'modernity'. Soane did a great deal that is more conventional than his own house. There are even some Gothic designs by him. And Gilly drew and published in detail the grandest of the medieval castles of the German knights in West Prussia. Exquisite as these drawings are, the attitude that made Gilly spend so much time on them is only partially romantic and patriotic. Antiquarian ambition is at least as conspicuous. The case of Girtin's and Turner's early water colours is very similar. They are the transition (though still a romantic transition full of creative power) between the polite eighteenth-century engravings of Athens and Paestum and the voluminous nineteenth-century books on cathedral antiquities and medieval details.

Amongst such books the transition can also be noted: the earliest are still rather sketchy, while later they become more and more thorough and as a rule rather dull. In actual buildings we find exactly the same development from the elegant and whimsical but sometimes inspired to the learned but sometimes deplorably pedestrian. Strawberry Hill stands for Rococo-Gothic, Robert Adam for a Rococo-Classical Revival. The next generation is characterized by John Nash (1752–1835). Nash had nothing of the intransigent creative fury of Soane. He was light-handed, careless, socially successful, and artistically conservative. His frontages of old Regent Street and most of his palace-like façades round Regent's Park, planned and carried out between 1811 and about 1825, are still of an eighteenth-century suppleness. What makes them memorable is the way in which they form part of a brilliant town-planning scheme, a scheme linking up the Picturesque of the eighteenth century with the Garden City ideas of the twentieth. For these vast terraces face a landscape park, and a number of elegant villas are placed right in the park – the fulfilment of what had been foreshadowed in the juxtaposition of houses and lawn in the Royal Crescent at Bath. While the Regent Street-Regent's Park frontages are almost entirely classical, Nash built Gothic with the same gusto if required. He had a nice sense of associational propriety; as shown in his choice of the neo-Classical for his town house and of the Gothic for his country mansion (complete with Gothic conservatory). Moreover, he built Cronkhill, in Shropshire (1802), as an Italianate villa with a round-arched loggia on slender columns and with the widely projecting eaves of the Southern farmhouse (Roscoe's *Lorenzo Medici* had come out in 1796); he built Blaise Castle, near Bristol (1809), in a rustic Old-English cottage style with barge-boarded gables and thatched roofs (one is reminded of the *Vicar of Wakefield*, Marie Antoinette's dairy in the Park of Versailles, and Gainsborough's and Greuze's sweet peasant children), and he continued the Brighton Pavilion in a 'Hindu' fashion, first introduced just after 1800 at Sezincote, in the Cotswolds, where the owner, because of personal reminiscences, insisted on the style. 'Indian Gothic' was the eminently characteristic contemporary name of the style.

So here, in the early years of the nineteenth century, the fancy-dress ball of architecture is in full swing: Classical, Gothic, Italianate, Old-English. By 1840 pattern-books for builders and clients include many more styles: Tudor, French Renaissance, Venetian Renaissance and others. That does not, however, mean that at all moments during the nineteenth century all these styles were really used. Favourites changed with fashion. Certain styles became associationally branded. A familiar example is the Moorish synagogue. Another is the perseverance of the battlemented castle for prisons. An account of architecture from 1820 to 1890 is bound to be one of the coming and going of period styles.

On the Classical side 1820–40 is characterized by the most correct neo-Greek. Fancy had left the treatment of Antiquity even earlier than that of the Middle Ages. The results are competent and, in the hands of the best architects, of a noble dignity. The British Museum, begun in 1823 by Sir Robert Smirke (1780–1867), is amongst the best examples in Britain, or would be if its front with its grand Ionic order of the Erechtheum in Athens could be seen from a distance;

257 London, British Museum, by Sir Robert Smirke, begun 1823

258 Berlin, Altes Museum, by Schinkel, 1822–30

Carl Friedrich Schinkel (1781–1841), Gilly's pupil, is the greatest, most sensitive, and most original representative on the Continent, William Strickland (1787–1854; cf. p. 443) probably the most vigorous in the United States.

For now, with the Greek Revival, America can no longer be left out of the picture of Western architecture. American building had been colonial to the end of the eighteenth century; colonial as the latest Gothic, Renaissance, and Baroque buildings of the Spanish and the Portuguese in North, Central, and South America. The Greek Revival in the United States is also still closely dependent on European, especially English, examples, but national qualities, such as a remarkable stress on engineering technique, sanitary installation, and equipment in general, now come to the fore. The ideological background of the strict neo-Greek is the liberal humanism of the educated classes in the early nineteenth century, the spirit of Goethe, i.e. the spirit which created our first public museums and art galleries, and our first national theatres, and which is responsible for the reorganization and the broadening of education.

On the Gothic side the corresponding development leads back to the Romantic Movement. Young Goethe's enthusiasm for Strassburg had been a revolutionary genius's worship of genius. To the generation after his, the Middle Ages became the ideal of Christian civilization. Friedrich Schlegel, one of the most brilliant of Romantic writers and one of the most inspired Gothicists, became a convert to the Roman Catholic church. That was in 1808. Chateaubriand had written his *Génie du Christianisme* in 1802. Then, about 1835 in England, Augustus Welby Pugin (1812–52) transferred the equation of Christianity and Gothic into architectural theory and practice. With him, to build in the forms of the Middle Ages was a moral duty. And he went further. He contended that, as the medieval architect was an honest workman and a faithful Christian, and as medieval architecture is good architecture, you must be an honest workman and a good Christian to be a good architect. In this the associational attitude appears fatefully extended. Similarly contemporary Classicists began to brand the architect who favoured Gothic as an obscurantist and, worse still, his work as popery. On the whole the arguments of the Gothicists proved stronger and had, in an unexpected way, a more beneficial effect on art and architecture, but the aesthetic value of the buildings designed by the Classicists was higher. The Houses of Parliament, begun in 1836, are

259 London, Houses of Parliament, by Sir Charles Barry and A. W. N. Pugin, begun 1836

aesthetically more successful than any later large-scale public building in the Gothic style. The competition – a significant symptom – had demanded designs in the Gothic or Tudor style. A monument of national tradition had to be in a national style. The architect, Sir Charles Barry (1795–1860), preferred the Classical and the Italian. But Pugin worked with him and was responsible for nearly all the detail inside and outside. Hence the building possesses an intensity of life not to be found in other architects' endeavours in the Perpendicular style.

Yet even Pugin's Gothic turns out to be only a veneer, as soon as the Houses of Parliament are examined as a whole. They have, it is true, a picturesque asymmetry in their towers and spires, but the river front is, in spite of that, with its emphasized centre and corner pavilions, a composition of Palladian formality. 'All Grecian, Sir,' is what Pugin himself, according to his biographer and pupil Ferrey, said, 'Tudor details on a classic body.' And one can indeed without much effort visualize the façade of the Houses of Parliament with porticoes of a William Kent or John Wood type. And strangely enough the British Museum, perfectly Greek as it appears, reveals to the deeper-searching an equally Palladian structure. Centre portico and projecting wings are familiar features. The Athens of Pericles never conceived anything so loosely spread-out.

So while the battles raged between Goth and Pagan, neither realized how all this application of period detail remained on the surface. Moral arguments and associational tags were freely used, but architecture as a job of designing to fulfil functions remained unheeded – or at least undiscussed. Even today in such cases as the British Museum and the Houses of Parliament people think much too much of aesthetics and too little of function. Yet it should not be forgotten that to build a palace for democratic government and a palace for the instruction of the people was equally new. In fact to erect public buildings, specially designed as such, had been extremely rare before 1800. There were town halls of course, the most splendid of them all that of Amsterdam (now Royal Palace) built by Jacob van Campen in 1648–55, and there were the Exchanges of Antwerp, London, and Amsterdam. Somerset House in London also had been intended from the beginning for Government offices and learned societies. But these were exceptions. If one takes the nineteenth century on the other hand, and tries to pick out the best examples of town architecture of all dates and all countries, a number of churches will have to be included, palaces rarely, private houses of course; but the vast majority of what one would collect are Governmental, municipal, and later private office buildings, museums, galleries, libraries, universities and schools, theatres and concert halls, banks and exchanges, railway stations, department stores, hotels and hospitals, i.e. all buildings erected not for worship nor for luxury, but for the benefit and the daily use of the people, as represented by various groups of citizens. In this a new social function of architecture appears, representative of a new stratification of society. But the work in evolving plan forms for these new uses was more often than not anonymous, or at least appears so to us. The Renaissance library had been a hall of two or three aisles. The Renaissance hospital had been almost exactly identical in plan. Both came without essential modifications from the monastic buildings of the Middle Ages. Now schemes were worked out for special library stores with stacking apparatus. For hospitals, systems were tried of groups of separate wards and separate buildings for each kind of disease. For prisons the star-plan was invented (Pentonville) and accepted. For banks and exchanges the glass-covered centre hall or court proved the most serviceable solution. For museums and galleries a specially good system of lighting was essential, for office buildings the most flexible ground plan. And so every new type of building required its own treatment.

But the successful architects were too busy with new trimmings for façades to notice much of that. Sir George Gilbert Scott (1811–78), more honoured than any other of the High Victorian era, stated that the great principle of architecture is 'to decorate construction', and even Ruskin, who might have known better, said: 'Ornamentation is the principal part of architecture' (*Lectures on Architecture*, 1853, Libr. Ed., vol. XII, p. 83). So when the struggle between Classicists and Gothicists began to subside, other styles took their place. In the medieval field the generations before Pugin had been all for Perpendicular. To Pugin and those who followed him, notably Scott, Perpendicular was anathema. Gothic had now to be of the thirteenth and early fourteenth century to be right, and Scott and his colleagues never minded replacing a genuine Perpendicular window by an imitation earlier one when they had to restore a church. Their archaeological knowledge sharpened and on the whole their imitations grew in sensitivity as the century progressed. The change from Perpendicular to Early English belongs to the thirties, although there was in the fifties and sixties an interlude of Venetian Gothic, brought about by Ruskin's *Stones of Venice*. Of neo-thirteenth-century work the most refined belongs to the Late Victorian decades, Bodley's and especially Pearson's churches (St Augustine's, Kilburn, London; Cathedral, Truro). When it comes to originality, however, these accomplished revivalists were far surpassed by such characters as William Butterfield and James Brooks. Butterfield's detail is original to the extreme of harshness and demonstrative ugliness (All Saints, Margaret Street, London; St Alban's, Holborn, London), and Brooks's plans occasionally abandon all dependence on English Gothic precedent (Ascension, Lavender Hill, London).

No other country took so whole-heartedly to the Gothic revival in all its tendencies and shades as England. France kept away from it for a long time. Picturesque Gothic buildings in the gardens were rare, the romantic Gothic interpretation appears only in the 1820s, the archaeological interpretation gradually in the 1830s and 1840s. An example of the Romantic Gothic is Hittorff's decoration for the christening of the Duc de Bordeaux in 1820, the foremost example of the archaeological Gothic Gau's church of Ste Clotilde begun in 1846; and both Hittorff and Gau were born in Cologne (J. I. Hittorff 1792–1867, F. X. Gau 1790–1853). Cologne in fact became an international centre of Gothic endeavour, ever since the original plans for the cathedral had been found in 1814 and 1816 and the completion of the cathedral according to these plans had been decided on. In 1842 the King of Prussia laid the foundation stone of the new work. After that good Gothic churches and later on public buildings appeared from Hamburg to Vienna. Meanwhile in France Arcisse de Caumont had started the Congrès Archéologiques (1833), founded the Société française d'Archéologie (1834), and started the inventorizing of medieval buildings in a scholarly way (Statistique

Monumentale du Calvados, 1846, etc.) and the Commission des Monuments Historiques had been established (1837).

In the opposite camp of the Southerners the grand style of the Italian High Renaissance *palazzi* replaced the chastity of the neo-Greek. That had already been heralded in Ledoux's and some of his contemporaries' partiality for arcades or loggias with columns, i.e. a Quattrocento motif. But the first truly neo-Renaissance palace in Europe seems to be Klenze's Beauharnais Palace, in Munich, of 1816. Munich after that produced a number of excellent examples in the thirties (National Library by Gärtner, 1831). So did Dresden, thanks to Gottfried Semper (Opera, 1837). In Paris the most interesting early example is the Barracks in the rue Mouffetard of 1827, by Charles Rohault de Fleury (1801–75), with heavy Quattrocento rustication. In London the style makes its appearance with Sir Charles Barry's Travellers' and Reform Clubs (1829 and 1837). What helped to popularize the Renaissance style must have been its high relief as against the flatness of neo-Classical and the thinness

260 London, Travellers' Club, 1829, and Reform Club, 1837,
    by Sir Charles Barry

of neo-Perpendicular form. Also it represented a more substantial prosperity, and this, as is well known, was the ideal of the leading classes during the Victorian age.

Another than the Renaissance way to reintroduce the round arch into architecture was to look to the Northern Romanesque, the Italian Romanesque, the Early Christian, the Byzantine. The Germans were wise in coining a term to cover all these and some of the Italian Renaissance imitation by the one term *Rundbogenstil*. Schinkel began it in Germany in the 1820s with designs for vaguely Early Christian churches. His pupil Ludwig Persius (1803–45) took it up with spectacular success (Heilandskirche, Sacrow 1841; Friedenskirche, Potsdam 1842). In England the leading examples are J. W. Wild's Christ Church, Streatham, London, of 1840–2, clearly influenced by Prussia, and T. H. Wyatt's church at Wilton of 1842–3. In France the neo-Romanesque St Paul at Nîmes by Ch. Aug. Questel (1807–88) dates from 1835–51, the Lombard Romanesque (or Byzantine?) cathedral of Marseilles by Léon Vaudoyer (1803–72) from 1852, etc.

Then, already before 1830, France rediscovered her native Early Renaissance. A genuine Early Renaissance house, the Maison de François I, was re-erected in 1822 as part of a new composition, in 1835 the genuine Early Renaissance town hall was greatly enlarged in the same style by Godde and Lesueur, and in 1839 Vaudoyer began the Conservatoire des Arts et Métiers in the French Renaissance style. To this corresponded in England a revival of Elizabethan and Jacobean forms, especially for country houses. Their associational value was of course national; their aesthetic appeal lay in a still livelier play of ornament on surfaces. Apparently the underground tendency, covered up by changing period costumes, was towards the *mouvementé* and spectacular, the flamboyant style of Disraeli and the pompousness of Gladstone. It can even be said that the French Empire style already is distinguished from the style of Ledoux and his group by a less severe, more rhetorical, more ornate character. The Madeleine of 1816, etc., by Pierre Vignon (1763–1828) is decidedly Imperial Roman in character, no longer Grecian and no longer as original as Ledoux. But only in the 1840s and 1850s did southern forms become more and more undisciplined and vociferous,

261 Paris, Opéra, by Charles Garnier, 1861–74

until a Neo-Baroque was reached. The Opéra in Paris of 1861–74, the master work of Charles Garnier (1825–98), is one of the earliest and best examples. Another is Poelaert's enormous Law Courts at Brussels (1866–83). In England there is little of this *Second Empire* style. A revival of Palladianism in its most Baroque form took its place, and a strong inspiration from the Wren of Greenwich Hospital. Then with a slight sobering of form and a marked influence from a Classical Re-revival in America (McKim, Mead & White) a characteristically prosperous Edwardian Imperial style was arrived at (Selfridge's). In Germany the late nineteenth- and early twentieth-century neo-Baroque goes under the name of Wilhelmian; in Italy it has disgraced Rome with the national monument to King Victor Emmanuel II.

However, by the time these buildings were designed, a reaction

262 Paris, Opéra, staircase

had come and spread against so superficial – truly superficial – a conception of architecture. It did not originate with the architect. It could not; because it concerned problems of social reform and of engineering, and architects were not interested in these. Most of them loathed the industrial development of the age just as heartily as the painters. They did not see that the Industrial Revolution, while destroying an accepted order and an accepted standard of beauty, created opportunities for a new kind of beauty and order. It offered to the imaginative new materials and new manufacturing processes, and opened up a vista towards architectural planning on an undreamt-of scale.

As for new materials, iron, and after 1860 steel, made it possible to achieve spans wider than ever before, to build higher than ever before, and develop ground plans more flexible than ever before. Glass, in conjunction with iron and steel, enabled the engineer to make whole roofs and whole walls transparent. Reinforced concrete, introduced at the end of the century, combines the tensile strength of steel with the crushing strength of stone. Architects knew little of these things. They left them to the engineers. For by about 1800, in connexion with the growing subdivision of competencies, the architect's and the engineer's had become separate jobs for which a separate training was provided. Architects learnt in the offices of older architects and in schools of architecture, until they set up in practice themselves doing what the civil-servant-architect had done in the seventeenth century, but now chiefly for private clients instead of the State. Engineers were trained in special university faculties or (in France and Central Europe) special technical universities. The most perfect examples of early iron architecture, the suspension bridges, such as Brunel's Clifton Bridge, designed in 1829–31 and begun in 1836, are the work of engineers, not of architects.[44] Paxton, who conceived the Crystal Palace of 1851, was a distinguished gardener and horticulturist used to the iron- and glass-work of conservatories. The men who introduced iron stanchions into the construction of American warehouses and occasionally, in the forties and fifties, opened whole fronts by glazing the whole interstices between the stanchions, are mostly unknown or undistinguished as architects. And in France, where a few trained and recognized architects (Bibliothèque Ste Geneviève 1845–50, by Henri Labrouste, 1801–75, externally in a noble and restrained Italian Renaissance, internally with iron columns and vaulting arches) used iron conspicuously – even occasionally for a whole church interior (St Eugène, Paris, begun 1854) – they were attacked and ridiculed by the majority.[45]

In all this a fundamentally unsound conception of architecture as a social service is apparent. This was first recognized by Pugin, who saw only one remedy: the return to the old faith of Rome.

263 London, Crystal Palace, by Joseph Paxton, 1851

Then, shortly after him, John Ruskin preached in *The Seven Lamps of Architecture* (1849) that a building must be truthful first of all. And a little later he began to realize that to achieve this thought had to be given to social as well as aesthetic problems. The step from theory to practice was taken by William Morris (1834–96). He had undergone the influence of Ruskin and the Pre-Raphaelites, had actually been for a time a pupil of Rossetti, and also of one of the most conscientious neo-Gothic architects. But he was not satisfied with either painting or architecture as he saw them practised, i.e. painting as the art of making easel pictures for exhibitions, and architecture as writing-desk and drawing-board work.

And whereas Ruskin kept his social activities apart from his aesthetic theory, Morris was the first to link up the two in the only way they could be successfully linked up. Instead of becoming a painter or an architect, he founded a firm for designing and making furniture, fabrics, wallpaper, carpets, stained glass, etc., and got his Pre-Raphaelite friends to join him. Not until the artist becomes a craftsman again – this was his belief – and the craftsman an artist, can art be saved from annihilation by the machine. Morris was a violent machine-hater. He attributed to mechanization and sub-division of labour all the evils of the age. And from his point of view he was right. The solution he found was aesthetically sound, though socially not in the long run adequate. To build up a new style on design was sound; to try to build it up in opposition to the technical potentialities of the century was just as much escapism as the classicist's disguising of a town hall as a Greek temple. The forms which Morris & Co. chose for their products were inspired by the late Middle Ages, as was Morris's poetry. But Morris did not imitate. He recognized Historicism as the danger it was. What he did was to steep himself in the atmosphere and the aesthetic principles of the Middle Ages, and then create something new with a similar flavour and on similar principles. This is why Morris fabrics and wallpapers will live long after all applied art of the generation before his will have lost its significance.

Morris's social-aesthetic theory as it was embodied in the many lectures and addresses he delivered from 1877 onwards will keep its life in history too. By trying to revive the old faith in service, by indicting the contemporary architect's and artist's arrogant indifference to design for everyday needs, by discrediting any art created by individual genius for a small group of connoisseurs, and by forcing home with untiring zest the principle that art matters only 'if all can share it', he laid the foundation of the Modern Movement.

What Morris did for the philosophy of art and for design, Richardson in the United States and Webb and Norman Shaw in Britain did concurrently for the aesthetics of architecture. Henry Hobson Richardson (1838–86) unquestionably still belongs to the era of period revivals. He studied in Paris and returned to New England deeply impressed by the power of the French Romanesque style. He continued to make use of it for churches, public and office buildings (Marshall Field's Wholesale Store, Chicago), but no longer just for associational reasons. He saw that these plain massive stone surfaces and mighty round arches could convey emotional contents more suited to our own age than any other familiar to him. And he and his followers designed country houses in the eighties freer and bolder than any Europe did at the same time – or should one say Europe with the exception of Philip Webb in England? Webb (1830–1915) liked plain brick walls and introduced into them the plain

264 Bexley Heath, Kent, Red House, built by Philip Webb for William Morris, 1859

slender windows of the William and Mary and Queen Anne period, remaining nevertheless in sympathy with the sturdy honest building traditions of the Gothic and Tudor styles. The Red House at Bexley Heath, near London, his first work, designed for (and with) Morris in 1859, shows already a combination of pointed arches and long segment-headed sash windows.

The picturesque possibilities of a mixture of motifs derived from widely different styles were more readily taken up by Richard Norman Shaw (1831–1912). He had a much lighter touch, a quicker imagination, but a less discriminating taste. In a professional career extending over more than forty years he never ceased to try the contemporary appeal of new period styles. Thus he went in for half-timbered Tudor country houses, then for the many-gabled brick architecture of the Dutch Renaissance, then for a very restrained neo-Queen Anne, or rather neo-William and Mary, and finally joined in the pompous Edwardian Imperial. He enjoyed, however,

265 Bedford Park Garden Suburb, by Norman Shaw, 1878

nothing more than playing with motifs of different centuries. By combining a few Tudor and a few seventeenth-century motifs with others of his own invention, he achieved a lightness and animation that make Morris designs appear gloomy.

Norman Shaw's influence on the architectural profession was immediate and very widespread. A generation of architects came from his studio to whom he left the freedom of following Morris's ideas, while following his own forms. They and some closer disciples of Morris founded the Arts and Crafts Movement. Once one knows what Morris taught, the name becomes self-explanatory. More and more original interpretations of architectural traditions were worked out by the members of this group, almost exclusively in designs for town and country houses. Lethaby, Prior, Stokes, Halsey Ricardo are amongst the most noteworthy names. They are little known nowadays, but the freshness and independence of their approach was unique in Europe at the date of their early activity, say between 1885 and 1895. The most brilliant of them all was connected personally with neither Shaw nor Morris – Charles F. Annesley Voysey (1857–1941). His designs for fabrics, wallpapers, furniture, and metalwork especially, so novel and so graceful, had an effect no less revolutionizing than Morris's. In his buildings he appears just as dainty and lovable. Of period detail little is kept, but no effort is made to eliminate a general period flavour. In fact it is just the effortless, unaffected nature of Voysey's architecture that gives it its charm. Moreover, going more closely into it, one will be struck by the boldness of bare walls and long horizontal bands of windows. In such buildings of the nineties England came nearest to the idiom of the Modern Movement.

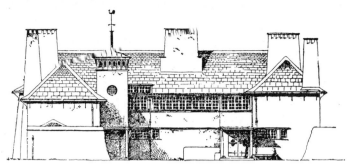

266 Perrycroft, Colwall, Malvern, by Voysey, 1893

For the next forty years, the first forty of our century, no English name need here be mentioned. Britain had led Europe and America in architecture and design for a long time; now her ascendancy had come to an end. From Britain the art of landscape gardening had spread, and Adam's and Wedgwood's style, in Britain the Gothic Revival had been conceived, to Britain the degradation of machine-produced applied art was due, to Britain the constructive reaction against it. The domestic revival of Morris, Norman Shaw, and Voysey was British; British was the new social conception of a unified art under architectural guidance, and British the first achievements of design completely independent of the past. They are to be found in the work of Arthur H. Mackmurdo's Century Guild about 1885.

Art Nouveau, the first novel style on the Continent, and in fact a style, it seems now, desperately set on being novel, drew its inspiration from English design and especially Mackmurdo. It started in Brussels in 1892 (Victor Horta's house in the rue Paul-Émile Janson). By 1895 it had become the 'dernier cri' in France and Germany (Guimard: Castel Béranger, Paris, 1894–8; Endell: Atelier Elvira, Munich, 1897). But it remained almost exclusively a style of decoration. The only exceptions to this rule are two architects working on the periphery of European events: Antoni Gaudí (1852–1926) at Barcelona and Charles Rennie Mackintosh (1868–1928) in Glasgow. Gaudí's style, in spite of certain connexions with Spanish Late Gothic and Spanish Baroque exuberance and fantasy and also of connexions, it seems, with the architecture of Morocco, is essentially

267 Munich, Atelier Elvira, by August Endell, 1897. Destroyed

original – indeed original in the extreme. In the small church of the Colonia Güell (1898–1914), the structures in the Parque Güell (1905–14), the transept front of the church of the Sagrada Familia (1903–26), and two blocks of flats of 1905 forms grow like sugar-loaves and ant-hills, columns are placed out of plumb, roofs bend like waves or snakes, and surfaces display maiolica facings or facings consisting of bits of broken cups and plates set in thick mortar. This may be in bad taste, but it is brimful of vitality and handled with ruthless audacity.

There is none of Gaudí's barbarity in Mackintosh, but he is all the same as original as Gaudí. What the Gothic and Baroque of Spain meant to Gaudí, Scottish castles and manor houses meant to Mackintosh. His work such as the Glasgow School of Art of 1898–9 is distinguished by a combination of the long drawn-out, nostalgic curves and the silvery-grey, lilac and rose shades of Art Nouveau with a straight, erect and resilient, uncompromisingly angular

268 Barcelona, **Sagrada** Familia, by Antoni Gaudí, 1903–26, transept front
    seen from inside

framework. Where this appears in wood, it is lacquered white. In this peculiar combination a possibility of overcoming Art Nouveau appeared, and if Mackintosh was more admired in Austria and Germany than in Britain, the reason was that these countries themselves shortly after 1900 began to search for a way out of the jungle of Art Nouveau. The England of Voysey could be as helpful in this as the Scotland of Mackintosh, and so the Prussian Government in 1896 sent Hermann Muthesius to London to be attached to the Embassy as an observer of matters concerning architecture, planning, and design. He stayed seven years and acquainted Germany thoroughly with the English Domestic Revival. Those responsible for the creation of a new twentieth-century style in Germany have indeed never concealed their indebtedness to England. Here lies the fundamental difference between the situation in Germany and that in France or America. These three countries have the lion's share in the establishment of modern architecture. Britain at this crucial moment gave up. The British character is too much against revolutions, or even logical consistency, drastic steps, and uncompromising action. So progress in Britain stopped for thirty years. Voysey's Tudor traditionalism was followed by a Wren and Georgian traditionalism, equally pleasant in domestic architecture, but feeble if not painfully inflated-looking in large and official buildings.

The first private houses in which the new, original style of the twentieth century can be recognized are Frank Lloyd Wright's (1869–1959), built in the nineties in the neighbourhood of Chicago. They have the freely spreading ground plans, the interweaving of exteriors and interiors by means of terraces and cantilevered roofs, the opening up of one room into another, the predominant horizontals, the long window bands that are familiar in today's houses. Also at Chicago, and as early as the eighties and nineties, the first buildings were erected with steel skeletons (William Le Baron Jenney: Home Insurance Company, 1884–5) and façades not disguising them (Holabird & Roche: Marquette Building, 1894). If a period style was still used for external detail it was usually Richardson's severely plain American Romanesque until Louis Sullivan (1856–1924) in such skyscrapers as the Wainwright Building at St Louis (1890), the Guaranty Building at Buffalo (1895), and the

269 Buffalo, Guaranty Building, by Louis Sullivan, 1895

Carson, Pirie & Scott Store at Chicago (1899–1904) reached complete independence of the past. Sullivan's grid of mullions and sills carried through all floors except the bottom and top ones is the establishment of a system valid to this day.

As against American priority in this field, France was the first country to design houses of a genuine concrete character. They are of the first years of our century and were due to Tony Garnier (1861–1948) and Auguste Perret (1874–1955). Tony Garnier had

270 Administration Building in Tony Garnier's Cité Industrielle, exhibited 1904

gone to Rome as a pensionnaire of the Académie in 1901, and there, instead of obediently studying the remains of Imperial Rome, had worked on an ideal Industrial City, a town as it could be built in his native valley of the Rhône. It was pioneer work from the point of view of planning, as we shall see presently, but also from the point of view of the appearance of the buildings. They were all essentially to be of concrete, private houses severely cubic, public buildings with cantilevering canopies at least as bold as those of Frank Lloyd Wright's houses. The Cité Industrielle was exhibited in 1904 but published only in 1917. That leaves the priority of demonstrating concrete as a more than utilitarian material to Perret. His famous block of flats in the rue Franklin dates from 1902–3, his garage in the rue Ponthieu, where the concrete is exposed without any cladding, from 1905, his Théâtre des Champs Élysées, the first public building constructed of reinforced concrete, from 1911–12.

In exactly the same years Josef Hoffmann (1870–1956) and Adolf Loos (1870–1933) designed buildings and their interiors in a style equally novel and still equally topical. In Germany the most significant date is that of the foundation of the *Deutscher Werkbund*

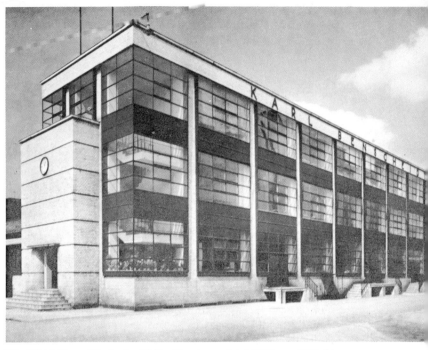

271 Alfeld, Fagus Works, by Walter Gropius and Adolf Meyer, 1911–14

272 Cologne, model factory at the Werkbund Exhibition of 1914,
     by Walter Gropius and Adolf Meyer

(1907). It was intended as a meeting-place of progressive manufacturers, architects, and designers. Indeed, only one year after it had been established the architect Peter Behrens (1868–1938) was asked by the Allgemeine Elektrizitäts-Gesellschaft of Berlin, the AEG, to take charge of the design of their new buildings, their products, their packaging, and even their stationery. Behrens's Turbine Factory of 1909 proclaims a new dignity for industrial architecture. The first work of his most important pupil, Walter Gropius (born 1883), was also a factory, the Fagus Works at Alfeld near Hanover, built in 1911–14. The rhythms of the front of the main block, the glazing continued round the corner without any mullion or post at the angle, the flat roof and the absence of a cornice, the horizontal banding of the porch – all this might be mis-dated by anyone as belonging to the thirties. The same is true of Gropius's next building, the model factory and office block at the Werkbund Exhibition held at Cologne in 1914. Here the most surprising motif was the two staircases entirely encased in curved glass so that the skeleton and the interior workings were proudly exposed. It will at once be recognized that in this motif, as in the floating ground plan of Wright, the eternal passion of the West for spatial movement once more expresses itself.

So by 1914 the leading architects of the younger generation had courageously broken with the past and accepted the machine-age in all its implications: new materials, new processes, new forms, new problems. Of these problems one has not yet been mentioned, although it is perhaps of greater importance to architecture than architecture: town-planning. It has been said before that one of the greatest changes brought about by the Industrial Revolution was the sudden growth of cities. To cope with this, architects should have concentrated on the adequate housing of the vast new working-class populations of these cities and on the planning of adequate routes of traffic for the worker to get to his job and back every day. But they were interested in façades and nothing else; and so in a way were municipalities of the nineteenth century. New public buildings cropped up everywhere. They were as splendid as money could buy. Take Manchester Town Hall, the Royal Holloway College at Egham near London, the Law Courts in Birmingham, London

County Hall. The Opéra in Paris and the Law Courts in Brussels have already been mentioned. There are many more on a similar scale, the Law Courts in Rome, the Rijksmuseum at Amsterdam, the Technische Hochschule at Berlin. The grandest assembly, and the most incongruous, is that along the new Ringstrasse in Vienna : the Gothic Town Hall, the classical Houses of Parliament, the Renaissance museums, etc.; one cannot say that Governments and city councils failed in their undeniable duty to give architecture a generous chance.

Where they failed was in their infinitely greater duty to provide decent living conditions for their citizens. One may say that this was an outcome of the philosophy of liberalism, which had taught them that everybody is happiest if left to look after himself, and that interference with private life is unnatural and always damaging; but while this explanation will satisfy the historian, it could not satisfy the social reformer. He saw that 95 per cent of the new houses in industrial towns were put up by speculative builders as cheaply as the scanty regulations would allow, and acted as best as he could. If he was a man like William Morris, he preached a medievalizing socialism and escaped into the happier world of handicraft. If he was like Prince Albert and Lord Shaftesbury, he founded associations for improving by private generosity the dwellings of the artisan and labourer. If, however, he was an enlightened employer himself, he went one step further and commissioned an estate to be designed and built to a more satisfactory standard for his own workers. Thus Sir Titus Salt founded Saltaire, near Leeds, in 1853. It looks very drab now, but it was pioneer work. Lever Brothers began Port Sunlight in 1888 and Cadbury's Bournville in 1895. These two were the first factory estates planned as garden suburbs. From them – and Bedford Park, near London, which had been designed as early as 1875 by Norman Shaw on the same principle, though for private tenants of a wealthier class – the garden suburb and the garden city movement spread, another British contribution to the pre-history of modern European architecture. It reached its climax in the foundation of the first independent garden city, Letchworth, designed by Barry Parker and Raymond Unwin in 1904, and in the foundation of the aesthetically most accomplished garden suburb, the Hampstead Garden Suburb designed by the same architects in 1907. But all these, in fact the whole conception of the garden city and the garden suburb, are an escape from the city itself. The first architect to grapple with the problem of the city, to recognize the need of considered locations for industries, for housing, for public buildings, was Tony Garnier in his Cité Industrielle of exactly the same years.

9 From the End of the First World War to the Present Day

This last chapter of necessity differs from its predecessors. They were history; how far this can be history may well be called in doubt, considering that it starts more or less accurately where its author 'came in'.

When building activity got going again after the six or seven years' pause of the First World War and its immediate aftermath, the situation was like this: a new style in architecture existed; it had been established by a number of men of great courage and determination and of outstanding imagination and inventiveness. They had achieved a revolution greater than any since the Renaissance had replaced Gothic forms and principles five hundred years before, and their daring appears almost greater than that of Brunelleschi and Alberti; for the masters of the Quattrocento had preached a return to Rome, whereas the new masters preached a venture into the unexplored. Their names and works have been discussed in the previous chapter, and they will appear time and time again in this. That they had all arguments of logic on their side there can be no question. What they had done, had to be done. The style which they had created was patently in accordance with the new social and industrial situation of architecture. The twentieth century – this one can state without undue generalization – is a century of masses and it is a century of science. The new style with its refusal to accept craftsmanship and whims of design is eminently suitable for a large anonymous clientele and with its sheer surfaces and minimum of mouldings for the industrial production of parts. Steel and glass and reinforced concrete did not dictate the new style, but they belong to it. All this being so, one might have expected – and some did expect

– that the new style, once established, would carry on without crisis. But curiously enough the years between 1920 and 1925 were not years of straight progress on the lines laid down by the pioneers of 1900–14.

Instead the troubled mood of 1919, of irretrievably lost confidence in peace and prosperity, of men returning from years spent in violent and primeval conditions, twisted the new architecture and designs into an Expressionism in some ways more akin to Art Nouveau than to the style of 1914. The most famous examples are the Chilehaus in Hamburg (1923) by Fritz Hoeger (1877–1949) with its sensational vertical piers all the way up and its jaggedly cut brickwork, and the interior of the Grosses Schauspielhaus in Berlin (1919) by Hans Poelzig (1869–1936) with its fantastic stalactites. What is less known is that even Gropius in the concrete war memorial at Weimar of 1921 paid a passing compliment to Expressionism and that Mies van der Rohe in 1926 designed a monument to the communists Karl Liebknecht and Rosa Luxemburg in the most massive cubist Expressionism. The design fits uneasily between his perfectly rational blocks of flats of 1925 and 1927. More important for the future than this surprising freak was the Expressionism of Mendelsohn's Einsteinturm at Potsdam of 1920; for side by side with his many drawings of *c.* 1914–24 (which seem to be influenced

273 Potsdam, Einsteinturm, by Erich Mendelsohn, 1920

by Sant'Elia) it established the motif of streamlining which became so fatefully omnipotent in American industrial design. In architecture too Mendelsohn's horizontals sweeping round corners have been imitated more often than can be counted. Even the all-glass walls of the skyscrapers which Mies van der Rohe began to dream up in 1919 have an element of fantasy absent in his earlier work, although their future lay within the rational development of later years. The interest in the skyscraper as such was of course a reflection of a more general fascination with America, and the wonderment at American daring, ruthlessness, and tempo in these years can also be regarded as a sign of a romantic rather than a rational frame of mind. Mendelsohn's picture book of America which came out in 1926 illustrates this attitude convincingly. Le Corbusier also (born 1888) came forward in 1922 with a fantastic project for a city of three million inhabitants to be housed according to a rigid grid plan and to work in a city centre of twenty-four cross-shaped skyscrapers.

This Expressionist tendency was – no doubt for political reasons, notably the inflation – strongest in Germany. But it is not entirely absent in some other countries, as is witnessed by the façade of P. V. J. Klint's Grundtvig Church at Copenhagen (competition 1913, foundation stone 1921) with its tiny portals, its sheer brick wall above, and its organ-pipe-like climbing gables at the top. Internationally the best known contribution to Expressionism in architecture is the Dutch, its craziest early monument J. M. van der Mey's Scheepvaarthuis in Amsterdam of 1911–16. The source was the much soberer work of Hendrik Petrus Berlage (1856–1934), notably the Exchange at Amsterdam (1897–1903), which is a parallel to the moderate and judicious contemporary innovations of a man like Voysey in domestic architecture. Berlage, in spite of all his sanity and honesty, liked to play with brick and to work out odd angular patterns. The large-scale Amsterdam housing designed by Michel de Klerk (1884–1923), Piet Kramer (born 1881) and others from 1917 onwards has the oddest angular or curved sudden projections and the oddest roofs and skylines. Willem Marinus Dudok (born 1884) started in a similar vein when he had been made town architect of Hilversum, but soon cast off the Art Nouveau atavisms and turned to a more crisply cubic grouping of brick blocks which became

276 Amsterdam, Eigen Haard housing estate, by Michel de Klerk, 1921

widely influential outside Holland. His masterpiece is the Hilversum
Town Hall, of 1928–32, and at that time the Expressionist episode
was definitely over.

In fact it had exhausted itself by 1924 or 1925. The years between
1925 and the outbreak of the Second World War were years of a
different character. The new style of 1914, temporarily doped by the
fumes of Expressionism, re-established itself and developed in some
countries into the accepted, leading style for all kinds of jobs. In
others it was turned into a semi-classical monumentality more
acceptable to those who were too weak to absorb the exacting new
or too eager to please the as yet unconvinced masses. The degree of
acceptance of the twentieth-century style can be mapped like this.
In Central Europe, i.e. Germany, Austria, Holland, Switzerland, it
was universal; in France it never reached beyond the small clientele
of a few enterprising architects, led from 1923 onwards by Le
Corbusier. Sweden made the change in 1930, in Italy there was

275 Copenhagen, Grundtvig Church, by P. V. J. Klint, begun 1921

nothing before Terragni's Casa del Fascio at Como of 1932, in England nothing before Peter Behrens built a house at Northampton for an English manufacturer in 1926, and then extremely little for another five years, after which the arrival of refugees from Germany helped to speed things up (Gropius, Mendelsohn, Breuer, etc.). In the United States the beginning is some skyscrapers by Raymond Hood in New York (1928, and especially the Daily News of 1930 and McGraw-Hill Building of 1931) and Howe & Lescaze's Philadelphia Savings Fund Society of 1931, and little before the Second World War. In Brazil the first appearance of the new style was due to a Russian, Gregori Warchavchik, and some houses he built at São Paulo in 1928, but nothing much followed for nearly ten years after that. In Russia bold if rare beginnings were firmly checked in 1931 and the clock put back to a conventional naïvely rhetorical classicism. In Germany Hitler put the clock back in 1933, and the country, after years of leadership, disappeared from the stage of modern architecture.

But Germany had absorbed too much already to be in danger of a return to giant columns and fat mouldings. The country joined those, such as France, which believed in the possibility of a revival, or indeed a survival, of classical principles and proportions by shaving off bases and capitals from piers and making them unrelievedly square, by shaving off mouldings round doors and windows, and by shaving off cornices. This style, handled more or less successfully, existed in France (where it still exists), in Italy, and in Germany. In France it was the outcome of a personal development of Perret, who after his bold beginnings had turned to the problem of classical measure in reinforced concrete. His church at Raincy near Paris (1922–3), with its glass walls patterned by a grid of close geometrical motifs in concrete, had still much of the courage of his early work, and in its jerkily stepped-up tower more than a little of the then current Expressionism, his Museum of Furniture and Office Building for the French Navy, both in Paris and both of 1930, are safely within the negative virtues of concrete classicism. Perret never ceased to handle this style with conviction, especially in his post-war composition of office blocks, etc., on the sea front of Le Havre (1948–50). The most elegant and perhaps most French expression of this classicism (whose so much more timid and un-original version in England goes under the name neo-Georgian) is the work of Michel Roux-Spitz (born 1888; blocks of flats Paris, 1925, etc.). Of the German buildings for the National Socialist party in Munich and for the Government in Berlin the less said the better.[46] The Fascists in Italy certainly were more successful in handling this style, whose terms of reference were to be imposing and easily under-stood. Their classical tradition was stronger and the revival came more naturally to them. They had also had less of the new style and could turn to the Fascist idiom more easily and naturally. Moreover, for a noble, unvulgar display, no one can compete with the Italians. Hence such buildings as those in the new Bergamo and Brescia, in the new towns of Littoria and Sabaudia, as the Paris Exhibition pavilion of 1937 (by Marcello Piacentini and Pagano), as the Foro Mussolini in Rome of 1937, etc., and much that went up of com-mercial buildings and blocks of flats in the city centres will one day once again come into their own. They all combine a convincing rectangularity with fine shows of shining marbles inside and out. But Mussolini never turned away entirely from the style of the twentieth century and much was tolerated (even the excellent, entirely uncompromising new station in Florence of 1936 by Giovanni Michelucci (born 1891), which lies right opposite Alberti's apse of S. Maria Novella) that would have been impossible in Germany or Russia.

The classicism of Denmark and Sweden was of a different kind, much less pretentious, in fact without imperial claims, and much less rigid. Examples in Denmark are the Police Headquarters by H. Kampmann, Aage Rafn and others (1925) and Kay Fisker's Hornbækhus (1923), both at Copenhagen, and the Øregaard School at Hællerup by E. Thomson (1923). In Sweden the treatment was more original and more playful, with delicately attenuated columns (Ivar Tengbom's Concert Hall of 1926, and Asplund's eary Library of 1921 and Scandia Cinema of 1922, all three in Stockholm). But what made Swedish architecture all of a sudden famous in the whole of Europe was not the classicist contribution but the delightfully free and subtle eclecticism of the Stockholm Town Hall by Ragnar Östberg (1866–1945). This building was begun in 1911 but completed only in 1923. Here was a bold plan for a superb site, with a strong tall angle tower crowned by a pretty little open lantern. Here was a touch of the Doge's Palace, a touch of the Romanesque, and details of sturdy Swedish sixteenth-century derivation set against others of a playful Expressionism. The design was honest and original, but it gave a dangerous sanction to the continuation of the old play with period motifs which had been natural to Östberg's youth.

All this has been described before the return to the main stream of development, the stream whose source was the work of the pioneers of 1900–14, because it is essential to bear in mind that the new style was by no means in sole possession of the field between 1924 and 1939. The degree of acceptance has already been listed. Examples in the following pages will be taken chiefly from the countries of most convinced adherence. Yet, in spite of French recalcitrance, the first architect to be introduced must be Le Corbusier (born 1888) who, though Swiss by birth, settled in Paris after a training under Perret in Paris and Peter Behrens in Berlin, and has lived in Paris ever since. He is the Picasso of architecture, brilliant, of inexhaustible inventiveness, incalculable and irrespon-

277 Garches, villa by Le Corbusier and Pierre Jeanneret, 1927

sible. He is the extreme contrast to Gropius, whose sanity, whose social conscience, whose pedagogic faith have helped to establish him as firmly in international esteem as Le Corbusier's glittering penmanship and draughtsmanship have established him. Yet there is a common ground on which both stand, the language of style developed before 1914 and indeed largely created by Gropius. Buildings of 1925–30 were white (though they did not keep white) and cubic. That applies to Le Corbusier's villas at Vaucresson (1922), Auteuil (1923), Boulogne-sur-Seine (1926), Garches (1927) as much as to the excellent J. J. P. Oud's working-class housing at and near Rotterdam (1924–30) and to Gropius's Bauhaus buildings at Dessau on which more will be said later. The parallelism to the problems of the cubists in painting is clear, especially in Le Corbusier, who is a painter himself and among those architects who allowed fantasy more play than Gropius and Oud (Rietveld in Holland, *c.* 1924, Mendelsohn in a pair of semi-detached houses at Berlin already in 1922, Robert Mallet Stevens in Paris *c.* 1927, etc.). Fantasy of a higher architectural order kept Le Corbusier safely from making a manner out of the cubism of his villas. Already in the

278 Utrecht, villa by Gerrit Rietveld, 1924

Pavillon de l'Esprit Nouveau at the Paris Exhibition of 1925 he allowed a tree to stand inside the house and rise through the roof, and already in his Swiss Students' Hostel in the Cité Universitaire in Paris of 1930 random rubble – a natural, only roughly treated material – appears side by side with glass and the white concrete and plaster. Nature in the sense of the irrational claimed a re-entry. But for this the time was not yet ripe – and on the whole there is reason to be thankful for that.

Le Corbusier's was here and always is individual work, inimitable work, however much it tended to be imitated and establish clichés. The work that was the best standard of 1925–30 was less personal, often almost anonymous in its absence of self-consciously demonstrated individuality. Among the best examples Gropius's Bauhaus at Dessau will be singled out on the one hand, a number of blocks of flats on the other. The Bauhaus was built in 1925–6. It consists of a central range with attachments of varying height and volume, the whole roughly like two Ls overlapping. The centre is the two-storeyed office block on stilts. Attached to it on the north is the four-storeyed block of the trade school, on the south a cross wing

279 Dessau, Bauhaus, by Walter Gropius, 1925–6, workshop block

with auditorium, canteen, etc., and stretching out from the ends of this the six-storeyed tower-like dormitory block with its many small balconies and the all-glass workshop block. The composition is both logical and visually satisfying. Of blocks of flats those by Mies van der Rohe at Berlin (1925) and Stuttgart (Weissenhof, see below; 1927) deserve mention, of large estates of flats those by Bruno Taut (1880–1938) in Berlin and Ernst May (born 1886) in Frankfurt, both begun about 1926, the one public utility, the other municipal housing. A summing up of the best so far achieved was the experimental estate of the Deutscher Werkbund at the Weissenhof near Stuttgart (1927) in which architects from Gropius and Mies van der Rohe to Oud and Le Corbusier co-operated. The white cubes and groups of diversely composed cubic blocks are unmistakably 1925–30 in style.

The liberation from the dictatorship of cubes began about 1930, though Le Corbusier had never fully accepted it. The principal event was the Stockholm Exhibition in the summer of 1930, where Gunnar Asplund (1885–1940), until then essentially a sensitive classicist, turned modern and demonstrated the possibilities of lightness and transparency which convinced many of the architect visitors. The intimate interconnexion between inner and outer spaces, already exploited for many years by Frank Lloyd Wright in America, and the faith in the delicacy of exposed steel members rather than solid concrete surfaces characterizes the best work of the years following 1930. If one were compelled to choose one work as the most perfect,

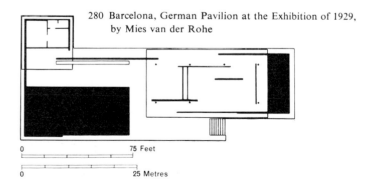

280 Barcelona, German Pavilion at the Exhibition of 1929, by Mies van der Rohe

0   75 Feet

0   25 Metres

281 Barcelona, German Pavilion at the Exhibition of 1929,
by Ludwig Mies van der Rohe

it ought probably to be the German Pavilion at the Barcelona
Exhibition of 1929 by Ludwig Mies van der Rohe (born 1886 at
Aachen), low, with a completely unmoulded travertine base, walls
of glass and dark green Tinian marble, and a flat white roof. The
interior was entirely open, with shiny steel shafts of cross section
and divided only by screen walls of onyx, bottle-green glass, etc. In
this pavilion, unfortunately long since demolished, Mies van der
Rohe proved, what the enemies of the new style had always denied,
that monumentality was accessible to it by means not of columnar
shams but of splendid materials and a noble spatial rhythm.
Religious architecture had naturally suffered most from this hostility.
It is true that in Switzerland uncompromisingly modern churches
had appeared as early as 1925–7 (St Antonius Basel, by Karl
Moser),[47] but the problem was obviously less complex for the

282 Stockholm, Crematorium, by Gunnar Asplund, 1935–40

reformed church of Switzerland than for any other. Asplund, however, in his last work, the Crematorium for Stockholm of 1935–40, succeeded in achieving awe as well as comfort. The approach to the portico with its unrelieved uprights and horizontals – not too distant in character from the best Italian work of the moment – and with the large plain cross standing as a beacon isolated from the building is truly monumental, the chapels inside and the small waiting rooms are intricate and soothing. The austerity of the exterior finally is wonderfully relieved by the most sensitive siting on the rising ground, with lawns, a pool, and the trees in the background. Never before in the twentieth century had architecture and landscape been blended so perfectly. It was to be one of the most beneficial lessons for the future. Under more workaday conditions the same blend had been demonstrated earlier in the design of a flour-mill with the housing belonging to it which Eskil Sundahl (born 1890) built on Kvarnholm near Stockholm in 1927–8. Grain elevators, factory, flats and small houses are arranged ingeniously between the rocks and pine trees of the island.

The work was commissioned by the Co-operative Society, one of the most enlightened patrons in the world during those years, carrying on what had been pioneered by the AEG in Berlin. The other patron to be singled out was London Transport, guided in its design policy by Frank Pick. The fact that in the twentieth century such large bodies have taken the place of the Sugers, the Medicis, the Louis XIVs of the past is of great significance. If they act as bodies represented by committees, as in the majority of cases they do, the aesthetic result will as a rule drop at once to the lowest common denominator of the committee, and even where that is not so it will lack individuality. An individual patron is more likely to have courage and faith in an architect than a committee. Cases where a committee is headed by a man who is a born patron and in addition has the ability to convince and carry away a stodgy committee are extremely rare. Frank Pick's was such a case. He had already before the First World War begun to reform the lettering used, had one of the best modern type-faces designed especially for his purpose and impressed it so deeply on the minds of millions that a revolution in British lettering ensued. Concurrently he started a campaign for better posters, and again succeeded in establishing Britain in the front rank of modern poster art. And when in the twenties and thirties many new stations had to be built, he realized that the Continent had evolved a style infinitely more suitable for the job than the genteel neo-Georgian or the pompous neo-Palladian Baroque that were current in England. So he travelled with his architect Dr Charles Holden (1875–1960), and the result was suburban station buildings as good as any on the Continent, functional in plan and restrained in elevation – in fact not at all in contrast to the English Georgian traditions if they are understood sufficiently deeply. They date from 1932, etc., and helped more than anything to pave the way for the twentieth-century style in England. Le Corbusier's most brilliant performances could not have done that.

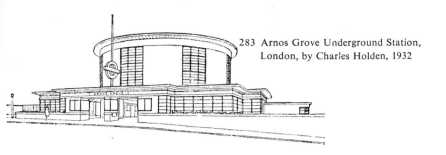

283 Arnos Grove Underground Station, London, by Charles Holden, 1932

The same is true of Le Corbusier's (and Mies van der Rohe's) dreams of skyscrapers. Their very daring confined them to an existence on the printed page. It was different with the Hochhaus rather than the skyscraper. Its occasional acceptance into Continental cities (Antwerp is another, 1924–30) has already been mentioned. They now also began to appear for residential purposes, the first to deserve and gain notice being that by J. F. Staal at Amsterdam of 1931.[48] But they became a feature of domestic planning only fifteen years later, when the Swedes took them up and built estates consisting entirely or partly of groups of them. The first of these is Danviksklippan at Stockholm of 1945–8 (by Backström & Reinius).

With this the barrier of the Second World War is passed. The war meant to many countries – though not to all – another break of five years and more. Brazil had built what she liked, the United States had built large factories and much emergency housing and in the process convinced herself of the twentieth-century style which from about 1947 onwards began a spectacular conquest right through the Continent. Italy proclaimed her conversion at the same time and exceedingly enthusiastically. England did the same, though more hesitantly and more moderately. Germany, rid of National Socialism and benefiting from the *Währungsreform*, made a new start where she had left off in 1933 and reached the front rank in a few years with ease. Only Russia and Spain remained unconvinced. But is the style of the century, which is now so widely recognized, still the style created by the giants of the early years and advocated by the leaders of 1925–35? In many ways it is, in others – alarmingly so – no longer.

We must here follow both what is changing and what has remained unchanged. Changing first of all are the conditions under which architecture is operating. One major change has already been referred to, because it was heralded at the beginning of the century though it is gathering more and more strength now. It is the change from the personal to the impersonal client. That an impersonal style such as the rationalism and functionalism of 1930 largely was suits these conditions better than any style derived from the past goes without saying. That the anonymity of the committee, whether municipal or commercial, tends to discourage individual enterprise, and indeed genius, is equally patent. Long and exasperated were the tussles between Le Corbusier and the authorities for Pessac near Bordeaux first, for the Unité d'Habitation at Marseilles second, for Interbau at Berlin third. That a large commissioning body can successfully maintain high architectural quality was shown between the wars by the Gehag in Berlin and the municipal housing department of Frankfurt (see above) and is being shown now by the Ina Casa in Italy. That finally the personal client can still exist, even if only as a manufacturer or manager, was proved between the wars by Frank Pick in England and after the war by the late Adriano Olivetti in Italy. As the client ceases to be a man and becomes a committee, so the architect is on the way from being a man to being a partnership or firm. The Architects Department of the County of London employs 3,000 (of which 1,500 are trained architects). Skidmore, Owings & Merrill in the United States, a firm not producing anything that is not of the highest standard, had in 1953 ten Directors, seven Associate Partners, eleven Participating Associates, and a staff of 1,000. Other successful firms in America and England have staffs of a hundred and more. On the Continent this development is as yet less marked, but it is bound to come – a parallel to the decline of the small shopkeeper – as part of the process of the universal Americanization of Europe. In connexion with this development one should also understand those cases where a group of individual architects are supposed to have designed one building. Such was the case of the United Nations Secretariat, built by W. K. Harrison in consultation with Le Corbusier, Markelius, Niemeyer, Sir Howard Robertson, N. D. Bassov, Ssu-Cheng-Liang, and four others. Such is also the case of Unesco in Paris by Breuer, Zehrfuss, and Nervi. The Interbau rebuilding of the Hansaviertel in Berlin in 1956–8 can also be seen in this light. Over a dozen German architects collaborated, and nine from abroad, including Oscar Niemeyer from Brazil. Nothing could be more telling of the most spectacular change between 1930 and 1950, the change from a style of pioneers and pioneer countries to a style producing outstanding work all over the world. The Gothic style had been created in the Île de France; it took one full generation to introduce it to England, two or three to introduce it to Germany, Italy, and Spain. The Renaissance style had been created in Florence. It took one generation to acclimatize it in Rome and Venice and eighty years and more to introduce it to Spain, France, Germany, and England. The style of the twentieth century, thanks to easier travelling, the spread of cheap printing, and the well illustrated technical press, has been faster. Fifty years after its creation it has its outposts nearly everywhere, and nothing short of a journey round the world can acquaint the critic or the enthusiast with its outstanding or its most sensational achievements. He has to visit Brazil without any doubt, and Venezuela, and Chandigarh in the Punjab, and Japan, and certain educational buildings by English architects in West Africa as well as Burma. He can sample Le Corbusier at Chandigarh and Berlin, Niemeyer, as we saw, also at Berlin, Skidmore, Owings & Merrill at Istanbul, Breuer in Paris, Eero Saarinen in London, Alvar Aalto at Cambridge, Massachusetts, and so on.

This increased internationalism – for the new style was of course, like any healthy style, essentially international at its beginning – has been welcomed by some, abused by others. The arguments in favour are that in an age of such rapid communication as ours and of such international achievements as those of modern science national styles in architecture and design would be an atavism, and that furthermore everyone can see what dangers increased nationalism has brought to peace and prosperity. The argument against is that, though all healthy styles of the past have begun essentially internationally, they have all assumed decided national characteristics in the end, the Perpendicular in England as against the *Sondergotik* in Germany, the style of Delorme in France as against that of Burghley House in England. Now should this be discouraged? for national characters exist as undeniably as languages exist, and they enrich the international scene and need not endanger it. In any case, even now, the critic can as a rule distinguish a recent major building at Essen from one at Rio or one in Milan. In that sense the Interbau venture in Berlin, with all respect for the boldness of its conception and its execution, may well turn out to have done more harm than good to Germany.

The change of scale between the Weissenhof Estate of 1927 and the Hansaviertel of 1957 is eminently characteristic. Scale of building is growing everywhere. Half a dozen New Towns near London are planned for 60–80,000 inhabitants each, the suburban spread of London covers about 32 miles from West to East and 16 from North to South, the horrifying idea of a linear town without end from Portland, Maine, to Norfolk, Virginia, was recently conjured up by Professor Tunnard in America, where Los Angeles already stretches out for 70 miles in either direction. The corollary to this growth of cities and their dormitory suburbs is the growth of roads and the unbelievable degree of ingeniousness that goes into their layout. The clover-leaf crossings, the under- and overpasses, the two-storeyed roads of America, especially in and near New York, will puzzle the excavators of the year A.D. 7000 as much as Karnak and Stonehenge puzzle us.

284 New York, Henry Hudson Parkway at 79th Street

The dividing line between engineering and architecture in such works of planning does not exist any longer. It had for the first time been called in question when the early suspension bridges rose. The Werkbund and Le Corbusier extolled grain elevators, Le Corbusier also the ocean liner and the aeroplane. Today in major architectural jobs the engineer must be named side by side with the architect, and his contribution sometimes is architecturally more stimulating than the architect's. Pier Luigi Nervi (born 1891), the concrete engineer, is in fact one of the greatest living architects. He came to the fore with his Stadium of 1930–2 in Florence, with its scissor structure, its pair of intertwined cantilevered spiral stairs at the back, and its curved cantilevered roof reaching effortlessly forward some 50 feet. He followed this by the hangar of Orbetello (1938), 300 feet long with a 120-foot span and a concrete lamella construction, by the fabulous exhibition hall of 1948–50 in Turin, with a span of nearly 300 feet, and then one after another by designs of equal boldness, inventiveness and, it must be added firmly, soundness.

The spiral stairs of the Florence Stadium curve forward without any supports because they are curved concrete slabs in tension. The discovery that reinforced concrete need not be treated on the old

285 Orbetello, aircraft hangar, by Pier Luigi Nervi, 1938

principle of post and lintel, as Perret did, but can be treated mono-lithically in terms of the curved slab, or the complete unity of support and weight, goes back to the year 1905 when Maillart built his first concrete bridge in Switzerland with arches that were curved slabs in tension and 1908 when he built the first mushroom ceiling, that is, a ceiling consisting of the joining curves of a mushroom on umbrella-like spreading posts.

Full use of this new principle has up to date been made only by few and only in the last few years. The result is aesthetically a revolution as great as that of 1900–14, if not greater. The out-standing works are – which is in itself very telling – all American. Pride of place belongs to the Arena Buildings at Raleigh, North Carolina, designed by the brilliant young Polish-American Martin Nowitzki who died at the early age of forty-one in 1951. He had designed the Arena in that year, in collaboration with the engineer W. H. Dietrick, and it was completed in 1953. It consists of two interlocked arches leaning outward excessively as they rise and supported on vertical posts (set more densely than the architect had intended). From these arches is suspended a membrane-thin roof, sagging rather than rising over the middle. The space is 300 feet. The same principle has been exported to Europe even more recently in the American Hugh Stubbings's Congress Hall for Berlin. The arches here do not interlock but stretch away from two joint foundations. The space is again about 300 feet in each direction. The hall itself seats 1,250.

Forms such as these had never before been seen in architecture or engineering. The same is true of the very different forms on which Felix Candela is working in Mexico. Candela (born 1910) is a Spaniard, and the jagged, cliff-like peaks and spikes of his church of the Miraculous Virgin at Mexico City (1955–7) are, if anything, reminiscent of Gaudí. Structurally Candela is as novel as Nervi and Nowitzki. His use of hyperbolic paraboloids in the handkerchief-like membranes of his roofs which rise in sudden sharp angles is as interesting as Nowitzki's arches. Candela's first building of inter-national importance was the Cosmic Ray Institution in the Univer-sity City of Mexico (1954), still closer in structural thought to the designs of these other pioneers. But the church as well as the Market

Hall at Mexico City prove conclusively that extreme individual expression is possible within these innovations in the use of concrete. Their effect on architecture as an art has indeed been a revival of radical individualism.

That may be to the good. It certainly was an answer to the layman's arguments against the style of 1900–14 or in its maturity of 1930. What were these arguments? The style was called on formal grounds a style of cigar boxes, on human grounds it was called hard, intellectual, mechanized, lacking in grace, lacking in fullness – in short inhuman. And as no-one could deny its functional merits, it was said to be all right for factories but for nothing else. The validity or otherwise of these arguments can today be judged with greater impartiality than twenty-five years ago. First of all, cigar-boxes was certainly true in essence in so far as the cube and the group of cubes were as characteristic of 1930 as was the pointed arch of the thirteenth century. To the transparent style of the thirties it hardly applies. Lack of grace was equally true, and even inhumanity sometimes – although it remains a disturbing fault that the most inhuman regimes, those of the National Socialists and of the Communists, were the greatest enemies of the inhuman style and most anxious to clothe their inhumanity in giant columns or giant square piers. Mechanization is a true characteristic of the style also, but there a cloak of giant columns or giant square piers would not make any difference. 'Mechanization takes Command' is the title of one of Dr Giedion's searching books, and the title formulates one of the basic facts of the nineteenth and twentieth centuries. The new style admits it, the imitation-old disguises it – that is all. Hence there is even a grain of truth in the indictment that the new style is a style for factories. That it can be an ideal style for factories was shown early by the van Nelle factory outside Rotterdam (by Brinkman & van der Vlucht, 1929). It also has among its remote ancestors the undisguised utilitarianism of late eighteenth- and early nineteenth-century factories and the metallic boldness of early bridges made of factory-produced parts, and among its more immediate ancestors the grain elevators and ocean liners. It is in addition of course also true that a style which emphasizes the frank display of function so much would be specially suitable for buildings whose function is

425

plain to everybody because it is practical, and less for buildings whose function is spiritual rather than practical. That is why religious and major civic architecture lagged behind.

Nervi's Turin Exhibition Hall or Nowitzki's Raleigh Arena can surely not be called, to go to the layman's arguments once more, cigar-boxes, nor hard-looking, nor mechanized-looking, nor lacking in fullness, nor graceless. They may look industrial rather than individual, but only in so far as all designed rather than hand-made objects look industrial. But they look organic and not crystalline, and personal and not anonymous. So they should meet many of the objections of between the two wars. And they meet them with admirable daring and the boldest inventiveness. These unprecedented formal solutions were found by men whose first concern was with the age-old Western desire to span space. But coupled with this there went a new desire, a desire which had been absurd in 1900–50, the direct desire for novelty of form. This desire has returned only in the last ten years, and one ought to appreciate its reappearance as a positive value. Once again, just as in Abbot Suger's time, the spiritual urge for a new expression has created new forms and found the technical means to express them.

The urge was great, and it has only rarely taken the arduous road of mathematical calculation and the endeavour towards a synthesis of form with structure. Far more often it has appeared purely and simply as a revolt against reason. Not all roofs of the last years which curve up and down, which snake along like the Loch Ness Monster, which curve forward as they surge upward, which sag over the middle, were the result of a serious consideration of needs and cost. They are indeed what Nervi privately calls structural acrobatics, motifs hard to calculate and to construct, introduced for the fun of them. And for the fun of them means of course, more seriously speaking, for the sake of a relish for such bizarre forms which had not existed twenty years before, even if it had existed fifty years before, when Art Nouveau held sway.

Brazil is the country in which the fascination and the dangers of the mid-century irresponsibility appear most concentratedly. No wonder perhaps, because Brazil was still unconverted about 1930–5 and it has, moreover, a tradition of the boldest, most irresponsible

286 Pampulha, San Francisco, by Oscar Niemeyer, 1943

eighteenth-century Baroque. So in Brazil one finds the most fabulous structures of today but also the most frivolous. Niemeyer's church at Pampulha of 1943, with its parabolic section to the nave, its little transeptal parabolas, and its square tower starting slender and widening as it rises, and Affonso Reidy's Pedregulho Estate of 1950–2 at Rio, with its double-curved long block of flats, lone blocks, a school and gymnasium, a swimming pool, shops, etc., are the most daring examples. The school as well as the shop has walls centred backwards. Such mannerisms as these or Niemeyer's tapering-down towers or a porch of his with the curving band of a roof which gives no protection (Casino Pampulha, Minas Gerais, 1942), or plans which contract and expand in the freest curves quite independent of function, occur far too often. Nor is Brazil unique in this revolt from reason. Le Corbusier was consulted on the new building for the Ministry of Education at Rio in 1937 and visited Brazil, and it is conceivable that the country had the effect on him

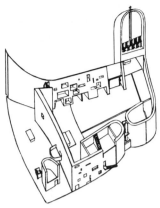

287 Ronchamp, Notre Dame du Haut,
by Le Corbusier, 1950–5

288 Ronchamp, Notre Dame du Haut, by Le Corbusier, 1950–5

of forcing into the open the irrational traits of his character and that he then passed on his impulsive enthusiasm to his young admirers. However that may be, Le Corbusier has since changed the style of his own buildings completely, and the pilgrimage chapel of Ronchamp (1950–5) not far from Besançon is the most discussed monument of a new irrationalism. Here once again is the roof moulded as if it were the cap of a mushroom, and here in addition is lighting by innumerable very small and completely arbitrarily shaped and placed windows. The chapel is quite small, only for a congregation of 200, and built entirely of rough concrete. Some visitors say that the effect is movingly mysterious, but woe to him who succumbs to the temptation of reproducing the same effect in another building, a building less isolated, less remote, less unexpectedly placed, and less exceptional in function.[49]

The revolt from reason is not confined to Le Corbusier and the Brazilians. It has made its appearance in most countries. In England the form it takes is, needless to say, less drastic. Architects like to apply geometrical surface patterning to walls, balconies, etc. A façade with uniform access balconies to flats may place the vertical supports of the balconies so as to create a kind of chequer-board effect, or the balconies themselves may alternate between solid concrete and an iron grid for such an effect. Some Italian architects go further, e.g. Luigi Moretti (born 1909) who cantilevers the narrow end of the upper eight or ten storeys of a tall block forward above a ground floor placed at an angle to it, and in addition cants the walls vertically so that unexpected angles of the walls recur both to each other and to the ground floor. In other buildings a sudden narrow cleft opens between two halves of a block. Germany kept away from this new trend, protected no doubt by the initial thrill of her return to reason after the ten years of enforced bogus classicity. Now however it has reached her too, more in monumental buildings than in offices and flats, and some of her new concert halls and opera houses are as bizarre as any. But might this criticism not be answered by a plea for the bizarre? Why should architecture and design be debarred from it? And why should Reidy and Moretti be criticized and Nowitzki and Candela not? Is the argument that their forms are structural, those of the others decorative, an aesthetically valid argument? Surely, it would be contended, in aesthetic matters the eye must be the judge, and to the eye it must be the same whether an unexpected, perhaps unprecedented form is used for structural or for decorative reasons. However, this argument is highly artificial. It is true that everyone likes one curve better than another or no curve better than some curves, but man is endowed with reason and cannot without a conscious effort exclude it. This effort, it is true, is to a certain degree that specifically aesthetic effort, but only to a certain degree. Just as an appreciation of a painting under no other than aesthetic criteria impoverishes the experience of painting, so the exclusion of the intellect impoverishes the experience of architecture and design. If a garden seat built of rough branches and a garden seat cast in iron to produce exactly the same surfaces can for argument's sake be called the same to the eye, our reason accepts the one as perfectly sound and rejects the other as silly, even if we are ready to be amused by it. In the same way the sham streamlining of the motor-cars of yesteryear cannot be acceptable to reason. It can in addition hardly amuse, because on an Autobahn or in the thick of the traffic of a city one does not want to be amused by the machine one is operating.

All this is true of architecture too. If a normal wall carries Art Nouveau decoration, we can appreciate this as a pattern, aesthetically; but if a wall has its windows disposed arbitrarily and without a visually convincing relation to the plan, or if a whole wall cants forward without a visually convincing structural reason, we are inclined to reject it as silly. And architecture can rarely afford to be silly; it is as a rule too permanent and too big merely to amuse. It is all very well to plead for the survival of small pavilions in exhibitions to be as frivolous as they can be made, but other building must be acceptable in all moods, that means, must have a certain seriousness. Seriousness does not exclude a challenge to reason, but it must be a serious challenge, as many visitors feel Ronchamp to be. What it cannot be is irresponsible, and most of today's structural acrobatics, let alone purely formal acrobatics imitating structural acrobatics, are irresponsible. That is one argument against them.

The other is that they are not in conformity with the basic social conditions of architecture. These conditions have not changed between 1925 and 1955. The architect still has to build predominantly for anonymous clients and large numbers of clients – see the factories, office buildings, hospitals, schools, hotels, blocks of flats he is asked to design – and he has still to build with industrially produced materials. The latter combination excludes decoration, since machine-made decoration, i.e. decoration not made by the individual, lacks sense; the former also excludes it, since decoration acceptable by all, i.e. decoration not made for the individual, also lacks sense.

Yet the craving for relief seems to us so understandable when we now examine a perfectly good estate of the thirties, such as the Dammerstock Estate at Karlsruhe (1927–8) or the Siemensstadt Estate near Berlin (1929), both by Gropius and others, with their lines of exactly parallel, exactly orientated ranges. However excellent the design of the elevation, however well functioning the plan, there is indeed something lacking here, and one finds oneself longing for the organic instead of the mechanic, the imaginative instead of the intellectual, the free instead of the rigidly organized.

Here lies the explanation of why Ronchamp and Pampulha had to come, and the structural acrobatics and the veneers of chequerboard patterns. But explanation is not justification. Such a statement might be considered entirely outside the province of the historian. Yet the historian cannot help being drawn into this topical controversy; for to him the question is whether the style created between 1900 and 1914 is still the style of today or whether 1950 has to be defined in completely different, largely opposite terms.

This historian denies such a necessity, and does so on the strength of the fact that Neo Art Nouveau is not the whole answer of today to the charges of mechanization and inhumanity. There are other recent buildings in which the challenge is accepted and met fully without jettisoning the conquests of 1930. They are what in a future history of twentieth-century architecture will represent evolution as against the revolution of Ronchamp. The discovery of these evolutionaries is threefold, though discovery is perhaps too strong a word, as the three innovations are anticipated here and there in earlier twentieth-century work. The first of these new theses is that relief need not rely on decoration, but can be achieved by variety of

grouping and surfaces; the second is that the principle of variety of grouping can be extended to a whole estate or indeed a whole city centre; the third is that variety can be accomplished in the relation of buildings to nature even more effectively than of buildings to each other. By these three means uniformity is avoided, fantasy is let in, and a sense of human satisfaction created without recourse to wilfulness. As examples of the first I would cite the United Nations Headquarters in New York and even more the Lever Building (by Skidmore, Owings & Merrill) with its brilliantly handled contrast of the twenty-four-storeyed glass slabs and the two-storeyed block beneath with its enclosed garden piazza inside. The best example of the second is Vällingby near Stockholm with its market place, surrounded by point-blocks. This was designed by Sven Markelius and others and built in the mid fifties.[50] It is the centre of a group of new suburbs to house about 60,000, the number more or less of the New Towns started in England during the war. Of these the best is Harlow, 40 miles north of London (by Frederick Gibberd), but this is far less urban in character than Vällingby. That is no doubt due to the universal tradition in England of living in small houses, not in flats, and of tending one's own garden. It is a healthy tradition, even if it makes aesthetically convincing planning difficult. But there is another allied English tradition which is proving of renewed significance today: that of the Picturesque. It had, as we have seen, found its original expression in parks and gardens, and the relation of buildings to them. The principles of the Lever Building and Vällingby are in architectural terms clearly the same as those of the eighteenth-century improvers: irregularity, informality, surprise, intricacy. But they are expressed in buildings. To express them in a synthesis of buildings and nature was bound to become an English task. It was taken up brilliantly by the then architect to the County of London, J. Leslie Martin, and his Roehampton Estate near London (1952–9) is aesthetically the best housing estate to date. It consists of about two dozen point-blocks in three groups, a number of parallel high slabs, many blocks of flats of five storeys and many small houses in terraces, and in addition schools and some shops. The whole is to house nearly 10,000. Yet there is nowhere a feeling of a mere provision for masses. This is avoided not by inventing

289 New York, Lever House, by Skidmore, Owings & Merrill
    (Gordon Bunshaft), 1950–1

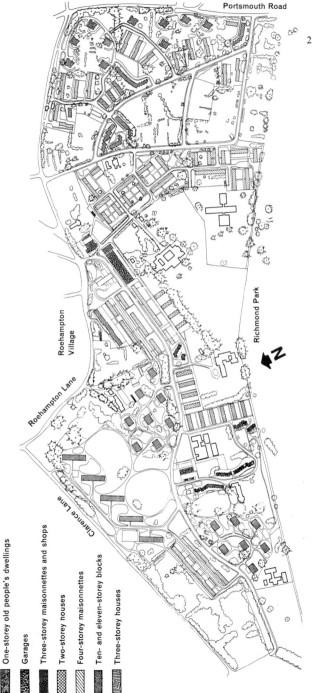

290 Roehampton,
housing estate, by
Sir Leslie Martin
and others,
1952–9

Portsmouth Road

Richmond Park

Roehampton
Village

Roehampton Lane

Clarence Lane

N

K E Y

One-storey old people's dwellings

Garages

Three-storey maisonnettes and shops

Two-storey houses

Four-storey maisonnettes

Ten- and eleven-storey blocks

Three-storey houses

patterns for façades but by siting and landscaping. The whole area was one of large obsolete Victorian villas in their gardens. So there are plenty of old trees and lawn. All this has been kept and reinstated, and consequently nature creates the relief and the branches and leaves of the trees for which architects are now craving. The combination of modern blocks with trees is Swedish, as is the use of groups of point-blocks. If the total effect is superior to any in Sweden, the reason is scale. The area is greater than those of privately built estates there, and scale helps to create the satisfactory unity-in-variety.

The Roehampton Estate is as complete a proof of the assertion that architecture has developed between 1925 and 1956 as are the structures of Nervi. Both are also complete proof of the other assertion that evolution leads from 1925 to 1955 and that revolution can be neither necessary nor welcome. Let us be grateful by all means if the individual genius is given a chance, as Le Corbusier was at Ronchamp, or if he grasps an exceptional possibility, as L. Calini, E. Montuori, and their partners did in the Rome railway station, when they sloped the roof in a double curve to echo the outline of the top of the picturesque fragment of the Servian wall behind a sheet of glass, but let us beware of little geniuses trying to provide for our daily needs.

'Let us' sounds like a sermon rather than a history book. And it can indeed not be avoided that the historian turns advocate if he chooses to lead his history up to current events. Yet there is a great temptation to do so. History writing is a process of selection and of valuing. To avoid its being done arbitrarily the historian must never forget Ranke's ambition to write of events 'as they really were' ('wie es wirklich gewesen ist'). This ambition, taken seriously enough, includes selection and valuation upon criteria of the age one deals with rather than one's own age. Should not a lifetime spent in adhering to these criteria equip a historian safely to cope with the case in which the age he deals with is also his own? It must be left to the reader of this book to decide whether the last few pages are a fair treatment of architectural problems and solutions 'as they really are'.

American Postscript

The most obvious difference between the history of architecture in the United States and in Western Europe is that American architecture, as part of Western architecture, is less than five hundred years old, whereas in England, in France, in Italy, in Germany, in the Netherlands, in Spain, one coherent and unbroken development runs through the last thousand years and more. During these ten or eleven centuries every new step of importance was taken within the compass of no more than fifteen hundred miles across from the German Sea to Sicily and from Ireland and Galicia to West Prussia and Bohemia. In this territory, much less in extent than the United States, Charlemagne restored a Roman Empire and, against his will, helped to raise the first monuments of a youthful Western spirit, the Cluniacs in France and the Saxon Emperors in Germany evolved the Romanesque style, in the Île de France ingenious masons devised the Gothic system, English, Spanish, German, Italian masons somewhat later modified it to suit their growing national consciousness, Italy revolted against it for a new purity, scientific order, and grace, then for a newer gravity and solemnity, and then for a forced, self-tormenting artificiality, in her Early Renaissance, High Renaissance, and Mannerism.

All this – this mighty drama of the birth, adolescence, virile maturity, and first symptoms of ageing of the West – had taken place before any buildings of Western character existed in the United States. And even if we take the whole of the Americas there is only a faint echo here and there – say in the belated rib-vaults of some Friars' churches in Mexico – of posthumous Western Gothic. Otherwise Mannerism is the first European style reflected on American soil.

Prehistory, on the other hand – in the sense in which we use the term in Europe for the Mediterranean before the advent of historic styles first in Egypt and Asia Minor, then in Greece and the Hellenistic States, and then in Rome and the Roman Empire, and for the North roughly up to the coming of Roman and in some parts Carolingian civilization – applies in the Americas to everything before Columbus, before Cortez, before Pizarro, before Raleigh, the Pilgrim Fathers, and Penn.

Thus not even the shortest outline of prehistoric art and architecture could afford to omit Mexican, Maya, and Inca temples and the artefacts of North American Indians; but an outline of Western architecture can, it is my contention, do without any mention of buildings in America prior to the eighteenth, or indeed the nineteenth century. In a book in which the severe Mannerism of Herrera and his followers in Spain appears only in a few lines, it would be as perverse to devote space to the ruin of Tecali – the 'purest' Franciscan church in Mexico, dated 1569 – as it would be to choose Dalmatian examples to discuss Venetian architecture or Nicosia in Cyprus to discuss French Gothic church buildings.

Again, the *incunabula* of New England's domestic architecture, while they are rightly treasured by New Englanders and treated with all the affectionate respect and care with which the English should treat (and often don't) their heritage of farm- and manor-house all up and down a country altogether not so much bigger than New England, can have no place in a brief textbook. What America did during the seventeenth century in the way of house-building has all 'the charm of sincere effort, naïve ignorance, and unskilful execution', as Talbot Hamlin says, but it is not one of the essential tributary forces to the main stream of architectural development.

However, with the eighteenth century emphasis changes. American architecture is still Colonial, that is, primarily dependent on colonizing countries – England, Spain, and Portugal, and up to a point France – but dependence is no longer complete and aesthetic quality certainly no longer necessarily provincial. The cathedral of Zacatecas, in Mexico, or the church of the Third Order of St Francis at Bahia, in Brazil, may be somewhat barbaric and sensational, but so is much of the Churrigueresque in Spain. And as this riotous

superabundance, this overcrowding with clamorous detail, is part and parcel of less Pyrenean Baroque, it would have been no less legitimate to illustrate it from Mexican or Brazilian examples than from the Cartuja of Granada, as I have done. It is true that certain features in America may be due less to Spanish and Portuguese precedent than to Indian workmen, for whom the wildly distorted and elaborately intertwined decoration of Aztec and Inca temples was still alive and valid. Indian influence as early as about 1500 has been assumed (page 169) to explain Portuguese Manueline ornament. But there it was European artists impressed by the achievements of the natives; now it is the natives themselves transforming European patterns. In North America during the same decades a similar change of balance can be observed, but with eminently significant modifications. Prosperity was just as firmly established in North as in Central and South America, but instead of the Roman Catholic social pattern of mission and skilled native labour, there grew in the North a system of secular land ownership and Protestant town civilization. The style of architecture was as English as it was Pyrenean in the South. Local variation on the home themes was as conspicuous. But as in the future United States both patrons and builders were Western by origin and traditions, and often even by birth, these variations were the outcome of climatic rather than racial conditions. Red Indian ingenuity was, alas, expelled and by degrees eradicated. Thus the colonial style of North America, the Colonial Style *par excellence*, is wholly English Georgian. The most notable American modifications are due to the prevalent use of timber as a building material. Wood accounts for the slimness of the columns, and wood also for the cheerful colour schemes. A warmer climate permitted terraces, porches, and loggias, and the wide spaces, only gradually to be populated, a more generous siting, the preservation of many trees, and, in the little towns, the planting of those venerable avenues and greens which now give to Salem, Nantucket, Charleston, and so on, and even to what is left of the oldest manufacturing towns of New England, their delightful garden-city character.

Still, while a short general history of architecture could illustrate Christ Church, Philadelphia, or one of the churches of Charleston

292 Nantucket, a street

instead of an English church, or Salem or Nantucket as particularly carefully preserved specimens of the Georgian country town, there is certainly no necessity that it should. What there is of differences between American and English Georgian does not go beyond the differences, say, between Bavarian and Dresden Rococo. And as far as quality goes, while the Mexican Baroque may be regarded in some ways as the climax of Spanish Baroque, even the best examples of American Colonial can hardly be placed upon the same level as Vanbrugh's or Adam's works.

This last remark and all else I have so far ventured to say about America is, I think, borne out by the published views of American scholars. When it comes to the early nineteenth century, however, I am a little at variance with at least some of the most distinguished architectural historians in the United States. Talbot Hamlin has as Chapters 2 and 3 of his immensely knowledgeable *Greek Revival Architecture in America* 'The Birth of American Architecture', dealing chiefly with Latrobe, and 'American Architecture comes of age', dealing with Mills, Strickland, and the other Greek Revivalists. So the contention is that the Greek Revival is the first national American style. I fail to see that. There is to my mind no more that separates Latrobe from Soane, or Mills and Strickland from Smirke and Hamilton, than there is between the eighteenth-century country houses of Virginia and Louisiana and those by Robert Adam or Henry Holland. So the relation between Europe and America cannot, I think, be regarded as changed between 1770 and 1820. America developed away from delicacy towards a new grandeur and severity during these fifty years; but so did England, France, and Germany.

Thomas Jefferson was enthusiastic about the Roman remains of Nîmes when he saw them in the 1780s, and the result was a style ranging from the imitation of that sober Palladianism which Paris at that moment was evolving from English precedent (Monticello, Capitol Richmond – cf. Clérisseau, and especially Ledoux and his group of French architects) to a much more naïve imitation of Roman detail (University of Virginia). Latrobe, Ramée, Mangin were themselves of French origin. Latrobe had passed through English training, Ramée had worked in Germany (and his son edited the second volume of Ledoux's *Architecture*). When Latrobe left England to settle in America in 1796, he could just have seen designs and perhaps more of Soane's revolutionary work at the Bank of England and at Tyringham. They would account for the most striking innovations in Latrobe – for instance, his determined change from Tuscan to Greek Doric – and also for some of the details inside North America's most beautiful church, Latrobe's Baltimore Cathedral of 1805–18. Here for once is true spatial composition, bold and imaginative, if dependent on Wren's St Paul's as much as on Soane.

England also is the background of Latrobe's Gothic Revival. He seems to have introduced the fashion to America ('Sedgeley'; Gothic designs for Baltimore Cathedral) in its romantic, not in its

293 Baltimore Cathedral, by Benjamin Latrobe, 1805–18

Rococo, form. The Gothic Rococo of Strawberry Hill is missing in the United States. The development of neo-Gothic forms into antiquarian correctness, however, is again exactly parallel in England and the United States (Upjohn, Renwick), with English inspiration maintained by journeys as well as pattern-books and archaeological publications.

So by 1850, while American architecture was throughout no longer colonial and in the work of the leading architects no longer provincial, it was not yet essentially original. It possessed a full share of Greek Revival on the largest and the smallest scale, and a fair dose of Gothic, Egyptian, and Old English Cottage Revival (complete with Downing's picturesque gardens – see Llewellyn Park), but all this had been introduced on the strength of European and chiefly English precedent.

When original features and original points of view are looked for, they will be found, I think, in such things as the adolescent vigour and crudity with which State Capitols and other public buildings went on trying to combine the Greek temple shape with a central dome (Davis and others). The Madeleine in Paris had domes behind its colonnades, but wisely refrained from showing them outside. Americans were not so squeamish. But more important for the future role of America in Western architecture than such lusty monstrosities is a marked interest amongst architects in engineering and in up-to-date equipment. Latrobe, we are told, studied under Smeaton, the great engineer, as well as under S. P. Cockerell; Strickland 'was almost better known as an engineer than as an architect' (Hamlin). Town, of Town & Davis, was the inventor of a successful type of truss for wooden bridges, McComb designed lighthouses and fortifications besides the old New York City Hall, Willard invented quarrying machinery, and so on. As for the American advance over Europe in matters of mechanical equipment, domestic comforts, sanitation, etc., it is enough to follow the reactions of older nations to the American exhibits at Philadelphia in 1876, or to compare the history of the hotel between 1825 and 1875 in America and in England and France.

Special emphasis has lately been laid (Giedion) on the American introduction of the balloon frame about 1825 or so – a primitive system of timber building with prefabricated parts and exclusively unskilled labour on the site – and on the American development of iron construction for office buildings, warehouses, and the like. How far the United States in either of these fields were really inventors, and how far only eager and intelligent promoters, is not yet clear. Regarding iron, England had certainly done more on the engineering side between 1800 and 1850 than has yet been acknowledged, while Labrouste's outstandingly sympathetic handling of the new material is known. In France also the idea of a complete iron frame for buildings seems to have been conceived (by Viollet-le-Duc about 1870) and the iron skeleton with outer walls bearing no weight and serving only as screens carried out (Meunier's Chocolate Factory 1871–2, according to Giedion).[51]

While in America as in Europe iron developments took place

essentially behind the architectural scene, and the new material was as a rule allowed to show only in utilitarian and temporary structures, architecture as a profession stopped within the framework of historicism as firmly on the west as on the east of the Atlantic.

However, one new development must now be listed. The United States freed themselves at last from English tutelage – a war of independence some eighty years late. And as after the political struggle the young nation first looked to France for inspiration (and Thomas Jefferson did in architecture too, although to a France under English influence), so now the young profession did the same. Richard M. Hunt (1828–95) studied under Lefuel in Paris, while the Louvre was finally completed in the revived florid style of Lescot and Delorme, and brought back the glamour of the Third Empire, ready for millionaires and proud municipal bodies to imitate.

But more significant than the neo-French Renaissance is the other slightly later Franco-American relation, that between Henry Hobson Richardson (1838–86) and the Romanesque style of southern France.

294 Chicago, Marshall Field's wholesale store, by H. H. Richardson, 1885–7

For here for the first time do we find an American architect acting independently, and here for the first time therefore an American architect appears in the text of this book. So it is to the text that the reader of this postscript has to refer (p. 391) for Richardson's faith in the French Romanesque style and its possibilities for the nineteenth century. A Romanesque Revival was not a completely new idea. There existed already in various countries round-arched buildings called Early Christian, or Byzantine, or Norman, as the case might be. But at that moment – Richardson returned to America from France in 1865 and started on his consistent neo-Romanesque campaign about 1870 – neither England nor France nor Germany specialized in the Romanesque. Richardson's determination to build Romanesque and Romanesque only was a personal decision dictated by a strong feeling for the modern qualities which could be brought out by the use of such plain, elementary forms. Into his historic detail he instilled an uncouth, primeval directness, all American of his age. His sense of texture and rich surface pattern underlining the massive compactness of his buildings, on the other hand, was entirely his own.

Richardson's influence was great. Somehow he must have been felt, if subconsciously, to be more American, that is, more direct, than any of the other architects of his generation. Sullivan (see p. 397) cannot be understood without Richardson, nor can the forms in which skyscrapers first presented themselves to an amazed Europe. With Sullivan the United States reached the front of architectural creativeness. Up to the end of the eighteenth century America had been Colonial; between 1800 and 1880 it was one of the many provinces of the West. Now it had become one of the few centres of progress – unnoticed, it must be said, by the most successful American or European architects and critics of the day. Official, generally accepted architecture in America was, it must not be forgotten, still as imitative in 1890 and 1920 as it was in England. Sullivan was no more widely acknowledged than Voysey or Mackintosh. Growing American importance was, however, reflected in the fact that academic architecture of the United States now influenced England, and no longer English academic architecture America. The Edwardian Imperial style of Britain and the Dominions (p. 387) derived a considerable amount of encouragement, if not more, from the Classical Re-Revival which in the United States had followed the Chicago Exhibition of 1893, and indeed had sometimes taken forms grander, vaster, and simpler than in England. Of the Chicago Exhibition Sullivan said that the damage wrought by it would last for half a century. The prognostication has proved accurate, if we accept the Modern Movement as the only truthful expression of the spirit of our age. It had won a great victory in the Middle West just before 1893, and Chicago might have become the international centre of early modern architecture, if it had not been for the 'World's Fair'. For Chicago was not only the home of the steel-skeleton skyscraper, and the peculiar, wholly original idiom worked out by Sullivan, but also of Sullivan's great pupil Frank Lloyd Wright. No European country had at the time of Wright's early houses done any to compare with his. Their first publication in Germany in 1910 and 1911 helped towards the elaboration of the Continental modern style quite as much as the more familiar houses of Voysey, Baillie Scott, and Mackintosh. France and Austria, on the other hand, in their contribution of 1900–5 (Garnier, Perret, Loos, Hoffmann) seem to have been independent of America.

I have found it necessary in the foregoing pages to mention European architects left out of the chapters dealing with European architecture. This applies, for instance, to Holland and Lefuel. My reason is that with the known history of architecture in the United States being virtually compressed into two hundred years, each trend assumes a greater importance than a corresponding trend in the longer history of buildings in Europe. All the interest we spend over here on Greek and Roman, Romanesque and Gothic, Renaissance and Baroque, goes in the United States into the achievement of these two centuries.

This has another consequence, and one I want to point out in conclusion. With intensity of interest goes intensity of research. In Britain architectural research has not been very intensive during the last thirty years or so. After Prior and Lethaby medieval research of an international outlook all but stopped, and it is only catching up now. Renaissance research is as scarce as everywhere. So it is in the English sixteenth to nineteenth centuries chiefly that consistent

295 Chicago, Carson, Pirie & Scott store, by Louis Sullivan, 1899–1904

intelligent work is done. In the United States, thanks to a much more firmly and widely established system of teaching the history of art and architecture in the universities and colleges, and thanks to a national penchant towards doing things thoroughly and with international documentation, once they are being done at all, architectural research is infinitely more active and successful.

This is especially noticeable if we compare books brought out between the two wars on matters referring to American architecture of the eighteenth and nineteenth centuries in America with books on English architecture of the same period in England. I can enumerate only a few. First of all the State guides of the Federal Writers' Project (1937), etc., uneven in quality, but on the whole far more alive and architecturally comprehensive than English guidebooks. Then there is the work of such scholars as Mr Fiske Kimball and Mr Talbot Hamlin. On British Georgian and Greek Revival architecture no such detailed handbooks and papers as theirs are yet in existence. Again books dealing with the interaction of social and architectural matters as soundly and attractively as Mr John Coolidge's *Mill and Mansion* are absent in England. Finally there are the monographs on the architects of 1760 to 1900. We have books (of varying standard) on Adam, Soane, Wyatt, Nash, and Pugin, and on Webb, Norman Shaw, and Mackintosh. But where are modern biographies of Barry, Scott, Burges, Street, Brooks, Pearson, Sedding, and so forth? In America not every one of the leaders has his book yet either, but between the wars, and particularly in the last fifteen years, monographs have come out on McIntire, Jefferson, Bulfinch, Latrobe, Strickland, Mills, Town and Davis, Upjohn, Richardson, Burnham, McKim, Goodhue, to say nothing of additional papers in the magazines.

Readers may well ask why America should be singled out at the end of this English book with a list of publications referring to architects and works hardly appearing in the text? The answer is that there is a lesson in it for the British as well as the Americans. One reason not yet sufficiently stressed for the more coherent progress of architectural research in the United States is that America is prouder of her achievements than Britain, or at least more attached to them. This leads to a most laudable seriousness in research even on such initially unpromising-looking topics as the development of architecture in Victorian Detroit (B. Pickens), whereas in England what attention is paid to Victorian buildings and design still tends, with the glorious exception of the American, Professor Hitchcock, and a few others, to the whimsical variety.

On the other hand, there is in the American concentration on local, regional, and national architecture the danger of parochialism. Things are regarded as peculiarly American, because all their antecedents, phases, and particulars are by now far better known in America than in Europe. Thus English or Continental precedent is often disregarded because not familiar. Even Hamlin's exemplary integrity and thoroughness have not always protected him from this unevenness of judgement.

If that is so with the scholars, may there not be quite an acceptable reason for offering to the layman in America this outline of architectural events on our side of the Atlantic?

Notes

1 Transepts also had the two major early fourth-century churches of Trier excavated after the Second World War, and transepts with aisles all round St Demetrius at Saloniki *c*. 410 (or after a fire of *c*. 630?), and St Menas in Egypt of the early fifth century.

2 The alternation of piers with groups of columns at St Demetrius Saloniki is unique.

3 In one of the Mausolea of the Roman cemetery found recently underneath St Peter's in Rome are Christian third-century glass mosaics, the earliest so far known.

4 Trefoils were also in use and must be mentioned here, although they are, of course, not strictly central. They occur in the catacomb of S. Calixtus in Rome, and on a large scale in the two great early Egyptian monasteries of Sohag, known as the White and the Red Monastery (fifth century).

5 Similar must have been the cathedral at Trier as altered about 370.

6 There are plenty of other fifth- and sixth-century examples of the penetration of longitudinal and central, none more monumental than the ruins of St John at Ephesus (*c*. 550) which was domed throughout and derived from Holy Apostles, but with the addition of one more nave bay to create longitudinal predominance.

7 Excavations in Germany after the Second World War have proved that such buildings were also erected there. Examples of long, aisleless churches with square-ended chancels are Echternach *c*. 700, St Salvator (Abdinghof) Paderborn mentioned in 770, the first cathedral at Minden, etc., examples of *porticus* St German at Speier of the fifth century and the well-known first buildings at Romainmôtier in Switzerland of *c*. 630 and *c*. 750.

8 The plan may have suggested itself on the strength of St Denis near Paris which seems to have had it at the time of a consecration in 775 –

a very early example of Carolingian innovations. There may, however, have existed a yet earlier Northumbrian precedent, if the published plans of excavations at Hexham (apparently badly handled and recorded) are at all reliable. They show a large church of the same type of plan, and there is no reason not to assume that it is Wilfrid's, that is, a building of the seventh century.

9 A later example is S. Stefano at Bologna.

10 But some French archaeologists attribute the same plan to the rebuilding of the cathedral of Clermont-Ferrand in 946, and some American archaeologists even wish to take it back to an earlier rebuilding at Tours which took place in 903–18. The case is uncertain and would require further investigations on the spot. What is certain, however, is that in Carolingian architecture already, especially at St Philibert de Grandlieu (Déas) in 836–53, at St Germain Auxerre in 841–59, and at Flavigny before 878, the form of an ambulatory behind the apse with chapels of some sort attached to its end wall had been experimented with, even if only at crypt level. Parallel German developments are marked by Corvey, consecrated in 844, Verden of *c*. 840, and perhaps the cathedral of Hildesheim. The step from such solutions to the final Romanesque ones seems short, but it was the step from a vague to a spatially firmly determined and standardized form. On this see above.

11 The west end had an outer ambulatory around the apse as had been designed for Carolingian St Gall, had existed at Carolingian Cologne, and still exists at Brixworth. At Hildesheim it was open to the crypt below apse and chancel by heavy arcades and was – a very curious fact – much higher than the crypt. It had a west doorway.

12 French oratories and crypts such as St Irénée at Lyons of the fifth century, Glanfeuil of the sixth century, St Germain at Auxerre of *c*. 850, and outside France the east parts of S. Maria della Valle at Cividale of the eighth or ninth century, the chapel of St Zeno at S. Prassede in Rome of *c*. 820, St Wipert at Quedlinburg in Saxony of *c*. 930, and St Martin du Canigou in French Catalonia of 1009, a latecomer, not a pioneer, and vastly overrated in its historical importance by Puig y Cadafalch.

13 *Archaeological Journal* 1922, reporting the results of investigations carried out in 1915. I am explicitly referring to this paper, because it contradicts a theory held erroneously by me and others (E. Gall) in the past and still expounded in earlier editions of this book.

14 I am greatly indebted to the Mediaeval Academy of America and Professor Conant for allowing me to illustrate his reconstruction.

15 The term *classic* is used throughout in this book with a meaning different from *classical*. *Classical* applies to anything inspired by, or copied from, the style of Antiquity, *classic* to the short moments of perfect balance achieved by many styles. When we say of a work of literature or art that it is *a classic*, we mean something similar, namely, that it is perfect of its kind, and universally accepted as such.

16 No more than three heads are preserved, which are now in the museums of Harvard and Baltimore.

17 The quotations are from Mr Charles Cotton's edition (*Canterbury Papers* No. 3. Published by the Friends of Canterbury Cathedral, 1930).

18 It ought to be remembered, however, that such steepness was not alien to all schools of Romanesque architecture. At Arles in Provence the ratio is 1 : 3·5, at Ely 1 : 3·2.

19 Though not as exaggeratedly depressed as they are at Salisbury a little later.

20 The dates are as follows: Clermont-Ferrand begun 1248, Narbonne and Toulouse 1272, Limoges 1273, Rodez 1277. Regional schools lost proportionately in importance, but Poitou and Anjou remained faithful to the hall-type which had culminated in the Early Gothic cathedrals of Angers begun before 1148 and Poitiers begun in 1162. A specially elegant smaller hall-church of *c.* 1200 is St Serge at Angers. Normandy also kept a regional character, internally, with its galleries and tracery details close to the Early English of England, but externally characterized by specially fine steeples, the finest of all being those of Coutances. There is also Burgundy, where, after a long resistance against the Île de France Gothic, the cathedral of Auxerre of *c.* 1215, etc., Notre Dame at Dijon of *c.* 1220, etc., and others developed a very personal style of detached, very slim internal shafts of metallic thinness. Tall triforia were kept, as Normandy (and England) also kept their tall galleries or triforia. On the south-west, and especially Albi, see the next chapter.

21 The first of these chapels between buttresses in France are, incidentally, to be found at Notre Dame in Paris after 1235 (see plan on p. 102).

22 The motif, curiously enough, recurs also in the work of Bramante in Milan (Canonica of S. Ambrogio).

23 In one spectacular case the new delight in the single tower was applied even to a cathedral front designed to carry two. At Strassburg, the designs referred to earlier on were abandoned and a tower with spire 565 feet high was built on the lower structure of one of them, leaving

the rest of the top of the façade like a terrace stretching out in only one direction at the foot of the tower. It is a most baffling sight, but has grown on all visitors through the ages until it became unquestioningly accepted and indeed beloved. At Beauvais Cathedral incidentally the flèche over the crossing was raised early in the sixteenth century to the height of 502 feet. It collapsed in 1573.

24 The Warburg Institute kindly arranged for me to have the plan of the Zagalia church and some others specially photographed from Filarete's *Codice Magliabecchiano* (Biblioteca Nazionale, Florence, II, 1, 140; già XVII, 30). The Zagalia plan is not illustrated in Lazzaroni and Muñoz's book on Filarete and has never been published before. Redrawing was necessary for reasons of clarity and has been done by Miss Margaret Tallet.

25 Brunelleschi had already thought along the same lines, see his never-completed Palazzo di Parte Guelfa.

26 But to Jacob Burckhardt, the Swiss historian of the nineteenth century and the discoverer of the Renaissance in the sense in which we understand the style today, the anteroom of the Laurenziana is but 'an incomprehensible joke of the great master' (*Geschichte der Renaissance in Italien*, 7th edition, 1924, p. 208; written in 1867).

27 These three-dimensional arches are not an invention of Neumann. He took them over from Bohemian buildings of slightly earlier date (Brevnov) and their Franconian counterparts (Banz). They in their turn had derived them from Guarini (cf. p. 262), but their original conception was probably stimulated by their automatic appearance where tunnel-vaults have penetrations from clerestory windows. The arched penetrations, if the diameter of the arches is smaller than that of the tunnel vault, meet the vault in such three-dimensional arches, for instance, inside St Paul's Cathedral in London, but also much earlier. One of the earliest cases is the church of the Carmine at Padua, before the year 1500. Philibert Delorme in France in the middle of the sixteenth century was the first to be fascinated by them and use them for positive aesthetic effects.

28 Their origin was the famous late-fourteenth-century *Vis du Louvre* in Paris.

29 It is known that he also possessed a copy of Filarete's Treatise.

30 Funeral monuments and other church furnishings had started earlier – about 1500.

31 In Italian classicity it was soon to be superseded by the Valois Chapel added to St Denis Abbey about 1560 and probably designed by Prima-

ticcio. This was purely Cinquecento: a round domed structure – the first dome in France – with six radiating trefoil chapels and internal columns in two orders on the Bramante motif. Its place is in the evolution of the centrally planned church in Italy rather than in France.

32 It even invaded the design of the hôtels of Paris – with the Hôtel Lamoignon of 1584, by one of the Ducerceau.

33 Ducerceau designed also the only other major château of the years of Charles IX: Verneuil, begun in 1565, simpler in plan, with the typically French three ranges and the fourth serving as an entrance screen, and in detail of a barbaric multiplicity of forms. On the whole the years between Henri II and Henri IV were meagre years for France. Her energies went into the murderous religious struggles.

34 The others are St Paul-St Louis, 1627–41; St Joseph des Carmes, contract for the dome 1628; Ste Marie des Visitandines, 1632–4, the latter by Mansart.

35 Karel van Mander, the Vasari of Holland, in his *Schilderboek* of 1600 had already referred to the 'frenzy of ornament' of that Dutch style which corresponds to English Jacobean – *see* illustration on p. 304.

36 It should even be noted in this context that the oval, though an Italian motif of Mannerism and Baroque, also appeared early in Holland: at the country palace of Honselaardyck built in 1634–7. On the other hand Honselaardyck was built by the Frenchman Simon de la Vallée.

37 Henri IV to the architectural historian is altogether more important as a town-planner of Paris than as a patron of palaces. The first of his schemes was the Place Royale, now Place des Vosges, designed in 1603, an oblong of well-to-do houses with all entries masked, the second the Place Dauphine begun in 1607, a triangle of ranges of houses with at its apex the statue of the king on the Pont Neuf. The architecture is that of the comfortable brick and stone type which we have met in buildings up to the twenties and thirties. Henri IV's inspiration for the planned square was the Piazza at Leghorn, begun by Cosimo I, grand duke of Tuscany, in 1571.

38 In the town the chief planning schemes were the Place des Victoires of 1685 and the Place Vendôme of 1698.

39 The same subtlety makes the group of the Place Royale at Nancy by Emmanuel Héré (1705–63) an unmatched achievement of eighteenth-century planning. The way in which the square in front of the Hôtel de Ville is followed by a triumphal arch, then the longitudinal Carrière with its four rows of pleached trees, then the transverse hemicycle with its colonnades, and finally the square in front of the

Palais de l'Intendance has the variety and unexpectedness of the Rococo and yet the French axiality. The work was done in 1752–5.

40 Geoffrey Grigson's translation, published in *The Architectural Review*, vol. 98, 1945.

41 But Montesquieu's English garden at La Brède goes back to about 1750.

42 I am here anticipating what is to be demonstrated in much more detail in a study which Dr Robin Middleton is preparing.

43 In the case of Boullée it has recently been assumed, but the evidence is not convincing.

44 The earliest suspension bridges are Chinese. The earliest in Europe was built very primitively in England about 1740. The earliest iron bridge – not on the suspension principle – is the Coalbrookdale Bridge in England of 1777–81. The possibilities of the suspension bridge were first seen in America by James Finley, who built a number of them from 1801 onwards, the longest with a span of 306 feet. In England Thomas Telford's Menai Bridge of 1815 is the first major example.

45 Iron was first used in architecture purely as a structural expedient, tie-rods already in the Middle Ages, and then posts, beams, etc., to make the roof of a theatre fireproof (Louis, Theatre, Bordeaux, 1772–80) or a whole factory fireproof (English factories of the 1790s). The iron and glass dome was a French innovation. It appeared first in the Halle au Blé in 1805–11 (by Belanger).

46 By P. L. Troost (1878–1934) the Haus der Deutschen Kunst, the temples, etc., on the Königsplatz, the Führerbau, and the building for the party administration, all designed in 1932–4; by A. Speer (born 1905) the Nuremberg Stadium of *c.* 1936 and the Reichskanzlei in Berlin, by E. Sagebiel the vast Air Ministry in Berlin, by the older and better Werner March Olympia Stadium, etc., in Berlin.

47 The dependence on Perret is here still patent. The step to the airier and more metallic style of 1930 was taken in E. F. Burckhardt & Egender's Johanneskirche at Basel of 1936.

48 Side by side with this an early case of a 'high-slab', another form with a great future, occurs in Holland: the Bergpolder Flats at Rotterdam of 1934, by W. van Tijen, H. A. Maaskant, J. A. Brinkman, and L. C. van der Vlucht.

49 The unavoidable is already happening everywhere, including Britain.

50 Even more urban and architecturally the finest of its kind yet designed is Sir William Holford's Precinct of St Paul's for the City of London, the proof that a consistently modern and entirely unrhetorical treat-

ment of a central area round a major historical monument is possible, that the richer forms of the monument can act as the desired relief to the rectangularity of the new buildings, and that these in their turn can enhance the effect of the monument. But the Holford Plan is not fully accepted yet, and building has not started.

51 From *The Builder*, vol. 23, 1865, pp. 296–7, it sounds as if Préfontaine and Fontaine's St Ouen Docks were constructed already on the same principle.

Bibliography

GENERAL

Encyclopaedia of World Art, 14 vols. New York, 1959–67.
PIERRE LAVEDAN: *Histoire de l'art*, 2. *Moyen âge et temps modernes*, 2nd ed. Paris, 1950.
E. LUNDBERG: *Arkitekturen's Kunstspräk*, 10 vols. Stockholm, 1945–61.
Wasmuths Lexikon der Baukunst, 5 vols. Berlin, 1929–37.
U. THIEME and F. BECKER: *Allgemeines Lexikon der bildenden Künstler*, 37 vols. Leipzig, 1907–50.
M. S. BRIGGS: *The Architect in History*. Oxford, 1927.
G. DEHIO and F. VON BEZOLD: *Die kirchliche Baukunst des Abendlandes*, 10 vols. Stuttgart, 1884–1901.

Britain

P. KIDSON, P. MURRAY and P. THOMPSON: *A History of English Architecture*. Harmondsworth, 1966 (Penguin Books).
N. LLOYD: *A History of the English House*. London, 1931.
H. AVRAY TIPPING: *English Homes*, 9 vols. London, 1920–37.
N. PEVSNER (and others): *The Buildings of England*. London, 1951 *seqq.* So far 43 volumes published. Only three are still missing.

France

C. ENLART: *Manuel d'archéologie française*, 2nd ed., 4 vols. Paris, 1919–32.
P. LAVEDAN: *L'architecture française*, Paris, 1944; English edition (Penguin Books), London, 1956.
A. BOINET: *Les églises parisiennes*, 3 vols. 1958–64.

Germany

G. DEHIO: *Geschichte der deutschen Kunst*, 2nd ed., 6 vols. Berlin, 1921–31.
E. HEMPEL: *Geschichte der deutschen Baukunst*. Munich, 1949.

Holland

F. VERMEULEN: *Handboek tot de Geschiedenis der nederlandsche Bouwkunst*, 3 vols. The Hague, 1928 *seqq.*
S. J. FOCKEMA ANDREAE, E. H. TER KUILE, and M. D. OZINGA: *Duizend Jaar Bouwen in Nederland*. 2 vols. Amsterdam, 1957–8.
H. E. VAN GELDER (and others): *Kunstgeschiedenis der Nederlanden*, 1936; 2nd ed. Utrecht, 1946.

Italy

A. VENTURI: *Storia dell'arte italiana*. 21 vols. Milan, 1901 *seqq.*
Storia dell'arte classica e italiana, 5 vols. Turin, 1920–61:
    Vol. 1. P. DUCATI: *L'Arte classica*, 1920; revised reissue 1952.
    Vol. 2. E. LAVAGNINO: *Storia dell'arte medioevale italiana*, 1936; 2nd ed. *L'arte medioevale*, 1960.
    Vol. 3. M. L. GENGARO: *Umanesimo e Rinascimento*, 1940; revised ed. by P. d'Ancona, 1948.
    Vol. 4. V. GOLZIO: *Il Seicento e il Settecento*, 1950; 2nd ed., 2 vols., 1960.

Vol. 5. E. LAVAGNINO: *L'Arte moderna dei neoclassici ai contemporanei*, 2 vols., 1956; revised reissue 1961.

M. SALMI: *L'arte italiana*, 3 vols. Florence, 1943–4.

A. CHASTEL: *L'art italien*. Paris, n.d. [1956].

W. BUCHOWIECKI: *Handbuch der Kirchen Roms*, 2 vols. so far published. Vienna, 1967, 1970.

Spain

Ars Hispaniae. Madrid, 1947–65 (published so far to the end of the eighteenth century, 19 vols.).

B. BEVAN: *A History of Spanish Architecture*. London, 1938.

MARQUÉS DE LOZOYA: *Historia del arte hispanico*, 5 vols. Barcelona, 1931–49.

LATE ROMAN

A. BOËTHIUS and J. B. WARD-PERKINS: *Etruscan and Roman Architecture* (Pelican History of Art). London, 1970.

D. S. ROBERTSON: *A Handbook of Greek and Roman Architecture*, 1929; 2nd ed. Cambridge, 1943.

L. CREMA: *L'Architettura Romana*. Turin etc., 1959.

W. ZSCHIETZSCHMANN: *Die hellenistische und römishe Kunst* (Handbuch der Kunstwissenschaft). Neubabelsberg, 1939.

W. L. MACDONALD: *The Architecture of the Roman Empire*, I. New Haven, 1965.

EARLY CHRISTIAN AND BYZANTINE

R. KRAUTHEIMER: *Early Christian and Byzantine Architecture* (Pelican History of Art). London, 1965.

O. WULFF: *Altchristliche und Byzantinische Kunst* (Handbuch der Kunstwissenschaft), 2 vols. Neubabelsberg, 1914–18; Supplement 1935.

J. G. DAVIS: *The Origin and Development of Early Christian Church Architecture*. London, 1952.

O. M. DALTON: *East Christian Art*. Oxford, 1925.

J. B. WARD-PERKINS: 'Constantine and the Origin of the Christian Basilica', *Papers of the British School at Rome*, vol. 22, 1954.

J. B. WARD-PERKINS: 'The Italian Element in Late Roman and Early Medieval Architecture', *Proc. Brit. Academy*, vol. 33, 1948.

E. MÂLE: *The Early Churches of Rome*. London, 1960.

R. KRAUTHEIMER: *Corpus Basilicarum Christianarum Romae*, 4 vols. so far published. Rome, 1937–70.

M. DE VOGÜÉ: *Syrie Centrale*, 2 vols. Paris, 1865–77.

H. C. BUTLER: *Early Churches in Syria*. Princeton, 1929.

J. LASSUS: *Sanctuaires chrétiens de Syrie*. Paris, 1944.

W. RAMSAY and G. L. BELL: *The Thousand-and-one Churches*. London, 1909.

U. MONNERET DE VILLARD: *Les couvents près de Sohag*. Milan, 1925–6.

U. MONNERET DE VILLARD: *Le chiese della Mesopotamia*. Rome, 1940.

G. A. SOTIRIOU: Χριστιανικὴ καὶ Βυζαντινὴ Ἀρχαιολογία vol. 1. Athens, 1942.

D. TALBOT RICE: *Byzantine Art*, 1935; 3rd ed. Penguin Books, 1968.

C. DIEHL: *Manuel d'art byzantin*, 2nd ed. Paris, 1925–6.

L. BRÉHIER: *L'art byzantin*, 1910; Paris, 1924.

J. EBERSOLT: *Manuel d'architecture byzantine*. Paris, 1934.

J. EBERSOLT: *Les églises de Constantinople*. Paris, 1913.

W. F. VOLBACH and J. LAFONTAINE-DOSOGNE (ed.): *Byzanz und der christliche Osten* (Propyläen-Kunstgeschichte, vol. 3). Berlin, 1968.

K. WESSEL (ed.): *Real-Lexikon der byzantinischen Kunst*. Stuttgart, 1963 *seqq*. So far one volume and seven parts of the second have been published.

W. R. LETHABY and H. SWANSON: *The Church of St Sophia*. London, 1894.

W. R. ZALOZIECKY: *Die Sophienkirche in Konstantinopel*. Freiburg i. B., 1936.

H. JANTZEN: *Die Hagia Sophia*. Cologne, 1967.

H. KÄHLER: *Die Hagia Sophia*. Berlin, 1967.

MIDDLE AGES

General

P. FRANKL: *Die Frühmittelalterliche und Romanische Baukunst* (Handbuch der Kunstwissenschaft). Neubabelsberg, 1926.

K. J. CONANT: *Carolingian and Romanesque Architecture: 800–1200* (Pelican History of Art). London, 1959; 2nd ed., 1966.

A. W. CLAPHAM: *Romanesque Architecture in Western Europe*. Oxford, 1936.

P. FRANKL: *Gothic Architecture* (Pelican History of Art). London, 1963.

H. R. HAHNLOSER: *Villard de Honnecourt*. Vienna, 1935.

W. GROSS: *Abendländishe Architektur um 1300*. Stuttgart, 1948.

J. FITCHEN: *The Construction of Gothic Cathedrals*. Oxford, 1961.

Early Middle Ages

V. H. ELBERN: *Das erste Jahrtausend*, 2 vols. Munich, 1962–4.

K. BÖHMER: *Die Kunst der Merowingerzeit*, 2 vols. 1958.

F. OSWALD, L. SCHAEFER and H. R. SENNHAUSER: *Vorromanische Kirchenbauten* (so far published A–Q). Munich, 1966–8.

P. VERZONE: *The Dark Ages from Theodoric to Charlemagne*. London, 1968.

S. DEGANI: *L'architettura religiosa dell'alto medioevo* (da lezioni di Luigi Crema). Milan, 1956.

J. HUBERT: *L'art pré-roman en France*. Paris, 1938.

J. HUBERT: *L'architecture religieuse du haut moyen-âge en France*. Paris, 1952.

P. VERZONE: *L'architettura religiosa dell'alto medioevo nell'Italia settentrionale*. Milan, 1942.

E. LEHMANN: *Der frühe deutsche Kirchenbau*. Berlin, 1938; 2nd ed. 1949.

W. BRAUNFELS and H. SCHNITZLER: *Karolingische Kunst*. Düsseldorf, 1965.

H. E. KUBACH: 'Übersicht über die wichtigsten Grabungen in . . . Deutschland', *Kunstchronik*, vol. 8, 1955.

H. E. KUBACH and A. VERBEEK: 'Die vorromanische und romanische Baukunst in Mitteleuropa', *Zeitschrift für Kunstgeschichte*, vol. 16, 1951, and H. E. KUBACH *ibidem*, vol. 18, 1955.

L. GRODECKI: *L'architecture ottonienne*. Paris, 1958.

Centula: W. EFFMANN, Münster, 1912.

Aachen: H. SCHNITZLER, *Der Dom zu Aachen*. Düsseldorf, 1950.

Lorsch: F. BEHN, *Die karolingische Klosterkirche von Lorsch a. d. Bergstrasse, nach den Ausgrabungen von 1927–28 und 1932–33*. Berlin, 1934.

Corvey: W. RAVE, Münster, 1958.

F. KREUSCH: *Bonner Jahrbücher*, Beiheft 10. 1963.

Ingelheim: *Rheinhessen in seiner Vergangenheit*, vol. 9, 1949.

Britain

J. HARVEY: *English Medieval Architects, a Biographical Dictionary*. London, 1954.

G. WEBB: *Architecture in Britain: The Middle Ages* (Pelican History of Art). London, 1956.

F. BOND: *Gothic Architecture in England*. London, 1906.

F. BOND: *An Introduction to English Church Architecture*, 2 vols. London, 1913.

E. S. PRIOR: *A History of Gothic Art in England*. London, 1900.

E. S. PRIOR: *The Cathedral Builders in England*. London, 1905.

J. HARVEY: *The English Cathedral*. London, 1950.

M. HÜRLIMANN and P. MEYER: *English Cathedrals*. London, 1950.

A. CLIFTON-TAYLOR: *The Cathedrals of England*. London, 1967.

A. HAMILTON THOMPSON: *The Ground Plan of the English Parish Church*. Cambridge, 1911.

A. HAMILTON THOMPSON: *The Historical Growth of the English Parish Church*. Cambridge, 1913.

J. C. COX: *The English Parish Church*. London, 1914.

F. E. HOWARD: *The Medieval Styles of the English Parish Church*. London, 1936.

G. H. COOK: *The English Medieval Parish Church*. London, 1954.

G. HUTTON and E. SMITH: *English Parish Churches*. London, 1952.

A. HAMILTON THOMPSON: *Military Architecture in England during the Middle Ages*. London, 1912.

D. RENN: *Norman Castles in Britain*. London, 1968.

H. BRAUN: *The English Castle*, 1936; 3rd ed. London, 1948.

M. WOOD: *The English Medieval House*. London, 1965.

G. BALDWIN BROWN: *The Arts in Early England. Vol. 2: Anglo-Saxon Architecture*. 2nd ed. London, 1925.

H. M. and J. TAYLOR: *Anglo-Saxon Architecture*, 2 vols. London, 1965.

A. W. CLAPHAM: *English Romanesque Architecture*, 2 vols. Oxford, 1930–4.

T. S. R. BOASE: *English Art 1100–1216* (Oxford History of English Art). Oxford, 1953.

P. BRIEGER: *English Art 1216–1307* (Oxford History of English Art). Oxford, 1957.

J. BILSON: papers on the earliest rib-vaults in *Journal Royal Institute of British Architects*, vol. 6, 1899; *Archaeological Journal*, vol. 74, 1917; and *Archaeological Journal*, vol. 79, 1922.

C. ENLART: *Du rôle de l'Angleterre dans l'évolution de l'art gothique*. Paris, 1908.

J. BONY: Articles of great importance on Norman and Early English architecture in *Bulletin Monumental*, vol. 96, 1937 and vol. 98, 1939, in *Journal of the Warburg and Courtauld Institutes*, vol. 12, 1949 and in *Gedenkschrift Ernst Gall*, 1965.

N. PEVSNER: 'Bristol, Troyes, Gloucester', *The Architectural Review*, vol. 113, 1953.

M. HASTINGS: *St Stephen's Chapel*. Cambridge, 1955.

JOAN EVANS: *English Art 1307–1461* (Oxford History of English Art). Oxford, 1949.

H. BOCK: *Der Decorated Style*. Heidelberg, 1962.

D. ETHERTON: 'The Morphology of Flowing Tracery', *The Architectural Review*, vol. 138, 1965.

France

H. FOCILLON: *Art d'Occident; le moyen âge roman et gothique*. Paris, 1938.

R. DE LASTEYRIE: *L'architecture religieuse en France à l'époque romane*, 1912; 2nd ed. Paris, 1929.

M. AUBERT and S. GOUBERT: *Romanesque Cathedrals and Abbeys of France*. London, 1966 (in French, Paris, 1965).

J. BAUM: *Romanesque Architecture in France*, 2nd ed. London, 1928.

ZODIAQUE, Paris (name of publisher). Series on Romanesque architecture of French regions by various authors. Each volume is called by the region with 'roman' behind, e.g. *Poitou roman*. So far 36 vols, but not all of them on French regions.

J. EVANS: *The Romanesque Architecture of the Order of Cluny*. Cambridge, 1938.

R. CROZET: *L'art roman en Poitou*. Paris, 1948.

E. PANOFSKY: *Abbot Suger*. Princeton, 1946.

E. GALL: *Die gotische Baukunst in Frankreich und Deutschland*, vol. 1. 1925; 2nd ed. Leipzig, 1957.

R. DE LASTEYRIE: *L'architecture religieuse en France à l'époque gothique*, 2 vols. Paris, 1926–7.

H. JANTZEN: *High Gothic*. London, 1962.

M. AUBERT: *Gothic Cathedrals of France*. London, 1959.

R. BRANNER: Recent papers in the *Journal of the American Society of Architectural Historians*, vol. 18, 1958 and vol. 21, 1962, the *Bulletin Monumental*, vol. 118, 1960, *Art de France*, vol. 2, 1962, and the *Art Bulletin*, vol. 44, 1962 and vol. 45, 1963.

J. BONY: 'The Resistance to Chartres', *Journal of the British Archaeological Association*, 3rd series, vols. 20–21, 1957–8.

R. BRANNER: *St Louis and the Court Style*. London, 1965.

P. ABRAHAM: *Viollet-le-Duc et le rationalisme médiéval*. Paris, 1934.

R. REY: *L'art gothique du midi de la France*. Paris, 1934.

L. SCHÜRENBERG: *Die kirchliche Baukunst in Frankreich zwischen 1270 und 1380*. Berlin, 1934.

É. MÂLE: *L'art religieux du XIIᵉ siècle en France*. Paris, 1922.

É. MÂLE: *L'art religieux du XIIIᵉ siècle en France*. Paris, 1902 (English translation: *The Gothic Image*, London, 1961).

St Denis: S. McK. CROSBY. Paris, 1953.

  J. FORMIGÉ. Paris, 1960.

Noyon: C. SEYMOUR. New Haven, 1939.

Laon: H. ADENAUER. Düsseldorf, 1934.

Notre Dame, Paris: M. AUBERT. Paris, 1928.

Bourges: R. BRANNER. Paris, 1960.

Reims: H. REINHARDT. Paris, 1963.

Amiens: G. DURAND. Paris, 1901–3.

Troyes: F. SALET, *Congrès Archéologique*, vol. 113, 1955.

Italy

P. TOESCA: *Storia dell'arte italiana*, vols. 1 and 2. Turin, 1927 and 1951.

A. KINGSLEY PORTER: *Lombard Architecture*, 4 vols. New Haven, 1915–17.

C. RIC∈I: *Romanesque Architecture in Italy*. London, 1925.

M. SALMI: *L'architettura romanica in Toscana*. Milan, 1927.

J. WHITE: *Art and Architecture in Italy: 1250–1400* (Pelican History of Art). London, 1966.

G. C. ARGAN: *L'architettura del Duecento e Trecento*. Florence, 1937.

C. ENLART: *Les origines de l'architecture gothique française en Italie*. Paris, 1894.

R. WAGNER-RIEGER: *Die italienische Baukunst zu Beginn der Gotik*, 2 vols. Vienna, 1956–7.

W. PAATZ: *Werden und Wesen der Trecento-Architektur in der Toskana*. Burg bei Magdeburg, 1937.

W. PAATZ: *Die Kirchen von Florenz*. 6 vols. Frankfurt, 1940–55.

Spain and Portugal

V. LAMPÉREZ Y ROMEA: *Historia de la arquitectura cristiana española en la edad media*, 1908; 2nd ed. Madrid, 1930.

ZODIAQUE, Paris (*see* France, above). Spanish vols. are Castille (2), Aragon, León.

G. G. KING: *Pre-Romanesque Churches of Spain*. Bryn Mawr, 1924.

M. GOMEZ-MORENO: *El arte románico español*. Madrid, 1934.

É. LAMBERT: *L'art gothique en Espagne*. Paris, 1931.

P. LAVEDAN: *L'architecture religieuse gothique en Catalogne*. Paris, 1935.

R. C. SMITH: *The Art of Portugal*. London, 1968.

R. DOS SANTOS: *O estilo manuelino*. Lisbon, 1952.

Germany and Austria

H. SCHMIDT-GLASSNER and J. BAUM: *German Cathedrals*. London, 1956.

E. LEHMANN: *Der frühe deutsche Kirchenbau*, 1938; 2nd ed., Leipzig, 1949.

Hildesheim: H. BESELER and H. ROGGENKAMP, *Die Michaeliskirche in Hildesheim*. Berlin, 1954.

Speier: R. KAUTZSCH, 'Der Dom zu Speier', *Staedel Jahrbuch*, vol. 1, 1921.
    F. KLIMM, *Der Kaiserdom zu Speyer*. 2nd ed. Speier, 1953.

Worms: R. KAUTZSCH, *Der Wormser Dom*. Berlin, 1938.

Middle Rhine: H. WEIGERT, *Kaiserdome am Mittelrhein*. Berlin, 1933.

Cologne: W. MEYER-BARKHAUSEN, *Das grosse Jahrhundert Kölnischer Kirchenbaukunst*. Cologne, 1952.

K. M. SWOBODA: *Peter Parler, der Baukünstler und Bildhauer*. Vienna. 1939.

E. HANFSTAENGL: *Hans Stetthaimer*. Leipzig, 1916.

K. GERSTENBERG: *Deutsche Sondergotik*. Munich, 1913.

RENAISSANCE, MANNERISM, AND BAROQUE IN ITALY

J. BURCKHARDT: *Geschichte der Renaissance in Italien*, 1867; 7th ed. Esslingen, 1924.

P. MURRAY: *The Architecture of the Italian Renaissance*. London, 1963.

C. von Stegmann and H. von Geymüller: *Die Architektur der Renaissance in Toskana*, 12 vols. Munich, 1909.

A. Haupt: *Renaissance Palaces of Northern Italy and Tuscany*, 3 vols. London, c. 1931.

D. Frey: *Architettura della Rinascenza*. Rome, 1924.

P. d'Ancona: *Umanesimo e Rinascimento*, 1940; 3rd ed. Turin, 1948.

R. de Fusco: *Il Codice dell'Architettura; Antologia di Trattatisti*. Naples, 1968.

J. Baum: *Baukunst und dekorative Plastik der Frührenaissance in Italien*. Stuttgart, 1920.

C. Ricci: *Baukunst der Hoch- und Spätrenaissance in Italien*. Stuttgart, 1923.

G. Giovannoni: *Saggi sull'architettura del Rinascimento*, Milan, 1931.

N. Pevsner: 'The Counter-Reformation and Mannerism' in *Studies in Art, Architecture and Design*, I, London, 1968 (in German, 1925).

N. Pevsner: 'The Architecture of Mannerism', *The Mint*, 1946.

R. Wittkower: *Architectural Principles in the Age of Humanism*. London, 1948, 2nd ed. 1952, paperback, New York, 1965.

R. Wittkower: *Art and Architecture in Italy: 1600–1750* (Pelican History of Art). London, 3rd ed. 1972.

V. Golzio: *Seicento e Settecento*, 1950; 2nd ed., 2 vols. Turin, 1960.

A. E. Brinckmann: *Die Baukunst des 17. and 18. Jahrhunderts in den Romanischen Ländern* (Handbuch der Kunstwissenschaft). Neubabelsberg, 1919 *seqq.*

C. Ricci: *Baroque Architecture and Sculpture in Italy*. London, 1912.

D. Frey: *Architettura barocca*. Rome and Milan, 1926.

A. Muñoz: *Roma barocca*. Milan, 1919.

T. H. Fokker: *Roman Baroque Art*, 2 vols. Oxford, 1938.

P. Portoghesi: *Roma barocca*. Rome, 1966.

Brunelleschi: H. Folnesics. Vienna, 1915.

    L. H. Heydenreich, *Jahrbuch der preussischen Kunstsammlungen*, vol. 52, 1931.

P. Sanpaolesi: *La Cupola di S. Maria del Fiore*. Rome, 1941.

E. Carli, Florence, 1950.

G. C. Argan, Mondadori, 1955.

P. Sanpaolesi. Milan, 1962.

E. Luporini. Milan, 1964.

Michelozzo: L. H. Heydenreich, *Mitteilungen des Kunsthistorischen Instituts in Florenz*, vol. 5, 1932, and *Festschrift für Wilhelm Pinder*, Leipzig, 1938.

O. Morosini, Turin, 1951.

Alberti: M. L. Gengaro. Milan, 1939.

    R. Wittkower, *Journal of the Warburg and Courtauld Institutes*, vol. 4, 1941.

    (ed. G. Orlandi and P. Portoghesi) *L. B. Alberti, L'Architettura*. Milan, 1966.

Filarete: P. Tigler. Berlin, 1963.

    J. R. Spencer: *Filarete:Treatise on Architecture*. New Haven, 1965.

Francesco di Giorgio: R. Papini, 3 vols. Florence, 1946.

    (ed. C. Maltese) *Francesco di Giorgio, Trattati*. Milan, 1967.

Ducal Palace, Urbino: P. Rotondi, 2 vols. Urbino, 1950.

Bramante: C. BARONI. Bergamo, 1941.

O. H. FOERSTER. Vienna, 1956.

Leonardo da Vinci: L. H. HEYDENREICH. London, 1954.

The Literary Works of Leonardo da Vinci: ed. J. P. RICHTER. London, 1883.

Leonardo as an Architect: G. CHIERICI and C. BARONI in *Leonardo da Vinci,* commemorative volume of the Exhibition of 1939. Novara and Berlin, *s. d.*

A Chronology of Leonardo da Vinci's Architectural Drawings: C. PEDRETTI. Geneva, 1962.

Raphael: T. HOFMANN, 4 vols. Zittau, 1900–14.

Michelangelo as an architect: J. S. ACKERMAN, 2 vols. London, 1961.

Giulio Romano: E. GOMBRICH, *Jahrbuch der Kunsthistorischen Sammlungen in Wien,* N.F., vols. 8 and 9, 1935–6.

F. HARTT. 2 vols. New Haven, 1958.

Serlio: G. C. ARGAN, *L'Arte,* New Series, vol. 10, 1932.

W. B. DINSMOOR, *The Art Bulletin,* vol. 24, 1942.

Palladio: J. S. ACKERMAN (Penguin Books), London, 1966.

R. PANE. Turin, 1961.

J. S. ACKERMAN: *Palladio's Villas.* New York, 1967.

E. FORSSMANN: *Palladios Lehrgebände.* Stockholm, 1965.

G. ZORZI: *Le opere pubbliche e i palazzi privati di Andrea Palladio.* Vicenza, 1965.

Corpus Palladianum. Vicenza, 1968–71. So far 6 vols. have been published.

Vignola: M. WALCHER-CASOTTI, 2 vols. Trieste, 1960.

Maderna: H. HIBBARD. London, 1971.

Bernini: S. FRASCHETTI. Milan, 1900.

R. PANE: *Bernini architetto.* Venice, 1953.

V. MARTINELLI: Mondadori, 1953.

Borromini: E. HEMPEL, Vienna, 1924.

H. SEDLMAYR. Munich, 1939.

P. PORTOGHESI. London, 1968 (Milan, 1967).

G. C. ARGAN. Mondadori, 1952.

Quaderni dell'Instituto di Storia d'Arte, ser. IV, 1955, 1957, 1959, 1961.

Guarini. P. PORTOGHESI. Milan, 1956.

Architettura Civile, ed. N. CARBONERI and B. TAVASSI LA GRECA. Milan, 1968.

SIXTEENTH TO EIGHTEENTH CENTURY IN BRITAIN, FRANCE, GERMANY, AND SPAIN

General

Palladianism: N. PEVSNER in *Venezia e l'Europa,* Atti del xviii Congresso Internazionale di Storia dell'Arte. Venice, 1957.

E. KAUFMANN: *Architecture in the Age of Reason.* Harvard U.P., 1955.

Britain

J. SUMMERSON: *Architecture in Britain: 1530–1830* (Pelican History of Art), 1953; 5th ed. London, 1969; paperback, 1970.

H. M. COLVIN: *A Biographical Dictionary of English Architects 1660–1840.* London, 1954.

T. GARNER and A. STRATTON: *Domestic Architecture of England during the Tudor Period*, 2nd ed., 2 vols. London, 1929.

J. A. GOTCH: *Early Renaissance Architecture in England*. London, 1914.

J. LEES MILNE: *Tudor Renaissance*. London, 1951.

M. WHIFFEN: *An Introduction to Elizabethan and Jacobean Architecture*. London, 1952.

M. GIROUARD: *Robert Smythson and the Architecture of the Elizabethan Era*. London, 1966.

M. D. WHINNEY and O. MILLAR: *English Art, 1625–1714* (Oxford History of English Art). Oxford, 1957.

O. HILL and J. CORNFORTH: *English Country Houses, 1625–85*.

K. DOWNES: *English Baroque*. London, 1966.

C. HUSSEY: *English Country Houses, 1715–1840*, 3 vols. 1955–8.

J. SUMMERSON: *Georgian London*. London, 1946. (Penguin Books, 1962.)

S. E. RASMUSSEN: *London, the Unique City*. London, 1937. (Penguin Books, 1960.)

Inigo Jones: J. SUMMERSON. London, 1966 (Penguin Books).

J. A. GOTCH. London, 1928.

J. LEES MILNE. London, 1953.

Thorpe: JOHN SUMMERSON, Walpole Society, Vol. 40, 1966.

Wren: E. SEKLER. London, 1956.

G. WEBB. London, 1937.

J. SUMMERSON. London, 1953.

K. DOWNES. London, 1971.

M. WHINNEY. London, 1971.

WREN SOCIETY, 20 vols. London, 1923–43.

Vanbrugh: H. A. TIPPING and C. HUSSEY (English Homes, vol. 4, part 2) London, 1928.

L. WHISTLER. London, 1938.

L. WHISTLER. London, 1954.

Hawksmoor: K. DOWNES. London, 1959.

S. LANG: 'Vanbrugh's Theory and Hawksmoor's Buildings', *Journal of the Society of Architectural Historians*, vol. 24, 1965.

Lord Burlington: R. WITTKOWER, *Archaeological Journal*, vol. 102, 1945.

Wood: W. ISON: *The Georgian Buildings of Bath*. London, 1948.

J. SUMMERSON: *Heavenly Mansions*. London, 1949.

Adam: A. T. BOLTON, 2 vols. London, 1922.

J. LEES MILNE. London, 1947.

J. FLEMING (to 1758). London, 1962.

France

L. HAUTECOEUR: *Histoire de l'architecture classique en France*, 4 vols. in 6 parts (to the end of the eighteenth century). Paris, 1943–52. Second edition of vol. 1 in four parts, Paris, 1963–7.

ANTHONY BLUNT: *Art and Architecture in France: 1500–1700* (Pelican History of Art). London, 1953; 3rd ed. 1970.

A. HAUPT: *Baukunst der Renaissance in Frankreich und Deutschland* (Handbuch der Kunstwissenschaft). Neubabelsberg, 1923.

A. E. BRINCKMANN: *Die Baukunst des 17. und 18. Jahrhunderts in den Romanischen Ländern* (Handbuch der Kunstwissenschaft). Neubabelsberg, 1919 *seqq.*

M. Roy: *Architectes et monuments de la Renaissance en France*, vol. 1. Paris, 1929.

H. Rose: *Spätbarock*. Munich, 1922.

F. Kimball: *The Creation of the Rococo*. Philadelphia, 1943.

F. Kimball: *Le Style Louis XV* (mostly a translation of the previous volume). Paris, 1950.

E. de Ganay: *Châteaux de France*. Paris, 1949.

E. de Ganay: *Châteaux et manoirs de France*, 11 vols. Paris, 1934–8.

J. Vacquier and others: *Les anciens châteaux de France*, 14 vols. *s. d.*

F. Gébelin: *Les châteaux de la Renaissance*. Paris, 1927.

L. Hautecoeur: *L'histoire des châteaux du Louvre et des Tuileries* . . . Paris and Brussels, 1927. (English: London, 1964.)

G. Brière: *Le château de Versailles*, 2 vols. Paris, *c.* 1910.

P. de Nolhac: *Versailles et la Cour de France*, 10 portfolios. Paris, 1925–30.

P. Verlet: *Versailles*. Paris, 1961.

J. Vacquier and P. Jarry: *Les vieux hôtels de Paris*, 22 portfolios. Paris, 1910–34.

G. Pillement: *Les hôtels de Paris*, 2 vols. Paris, 1941–5.

J. P. Babelon: *Demeures parisiennes sous Henri IV et Louis XIII*. Paris, 1965.

M. Gallet: *Demeures parisiennes, époque de Louis XVI*. Paris, 1964 (English: London, 1972).

P. Delorme: A. Blunt. London, 1958.

S. de Brosse: R. Coope. London, 1972.

François Mansart: A. Blunt. London, 1941.

A. Le Nôtre: E. de Ganay. Paris, 1962.

J. Hardouin-Mansart: P. Bourget and G. Cattani. Paris, 1960.

Gabriel: Comte de Fels. Paris, 1912.

G. Gromort. Paris, 1933.

Soufflot: J. Mondain-Monval. Paris, 1918.

Germany and Austria

E. Hempel: *Baroque Art and Architecture in Central Europe* (Pelican History of Art). London, 1965.

W. Pinder: *Deutscher Barock*, 2nd ed. Königstein, 1924.

W. Hager: *Die Bauten des deutschen Barock*. Jena, 1942.

M. Hauttmann: *Geschichte der kirchlichen Baukunst in Bayern, Schwaben und Franken*. Munich, 1924.

H. R. Hitchcock: *Rococo Architecture in Southern Germany*. London, 1968.

A. Feulner: *Bayrisches Rokoko*. Munich, 1923.

N. Lieb: *Barockkirchen zwischen Donau und Alpen*. Munich, 1953.

G. Barthel and W. Hege: *Barockkirchen in Altbayern und Schwaben*. Munich, 1953.

M. Riesenhuber: *Die kirchliche Barockkunst Österreichs*. Linz, 1924.

Pöppelmann: B. Döring, Dresden, 1930.

Asam: E. Hanfstaengl. Munich, 1955.

H. R. Hitchcock: *Journal of the American Society of Architectural Historians*, vols. 24–25, 1965–6.

Neumann: M. H. von Freeden. Munich and Berlin, 1953.

Vierzehnheiligen: R. Teufel. Berlin, 1936.

H. Eckstein. Berlin, 1939.

Zimmermann: H.-R. HITCHCOCK: *German Rococo; the Zimmermann Brothers.* London, 1969.

Spain

G. KUBLER and M. SORIA: *Art and Architecture in Spain and Portugal and their American Dominions: 1500–1800* (Pelican History of Art). London, 1959.

F. CHUECA GOITIA: *Arquitectura del siglo xvi* (Ars Hispaniae, vol. 11). Madrid, 1953.

G. KUBLER: *Arquitectura dos siglos xvii e xviii* (Ars Hispaniae, vol. 14). Madrid, 1957.

Netherlands

H. GERSON and E. H. TER KUILE: *Art and Architecture in Belgium 1600–1800* (Pelican History of Art). London, 1960.

J. ROSENBERG, S. SLIVE and E. H. TER KUILE: *Dutch Art and Architecture 1600–1800* (Pelican History of Art). London, 1966; paperback, 1972.

van Campen: P. T. A. SWILLENS. Assen, 1961.

FROM 1800 TO 1920

H.-R. HITCHCOCK: *Architecture: Nineteenth and Twentieth Centuries* (Pelican History of Art). London, 1958; 2nd ed., 1963.

N. PEVSNER: *Some Architectural Writers of the Nineteenth Century.* Oxford, 1972.

S. GIEDION: *Spätbarocker und Romantischer Klassizismus.* Munich, 1922.

N. PEVSNER and S. LANG: 'The Doric Revival' in *Studies in Art, Architecture and Design*, I. London, 1968.

N. PEVSNER: 'The Genesis of the Picturesque' in *Studies in Art, Architecture and Design*, I. London, 1968.

KENNETH CLARK: *The Gothic Revival.* London, 1928; 2nd ed., 1950.

C. L. EASTLAKE: *A History of the Gothic Revival in England.* London, 1872. (Paperback: Leicester, 1970, ed. J. M. Crook.)

T. S. R. BOASE: *English Art 1800–1870* (Oxford History of English Art). Oxford, 1959.

M. GIROUARD: *The Victorian Country House.* Oxford, 1971.

H. R. HITCHCOCK: *Early Victorian Architecture in Britain*, 2 vols. New Haven and London, 1954.

S. MUTHESIUS: *The High Victorian Movement in Architecture.* London, 1972.

P. FERRIDAY (ed.): *Victorian Architecture*, London, 1963.

R. FURNEAUX JORDAN: *Victorian Architecture.* Penguin Books, 1966.

N. PEVSNER: *Pioneers of Modern Design, from William Morris to Walter Gropius*, 1936; 3rd ed. (Penguin Books). London, 1960.

S. GIEDION: *Space, Time and Architecture*, 1941; 3rd ed. Harvard, 1954.

L. HAUTECOEUR: *Histoire de l'architecture classique en France*, vols. 5, 6, and 7 (1792–1900), 1953, 1955, and 1957.

Laugier: W. HERRMANN. London, 1962.

Boullée: E. KAUFMANN: 'Three Revolutionary Architects: Boullée, Ledoux and Lequeu', *Transactions of the American Philosophical Society*, New Series, vol. 42, 1952.

H. ROSENAU (ed.): *Boullée's Treatise on Architecture.* London, 1953.

J. M. PÉROUSE DE MONTCLOS. Paris, 1968.

Ledoux: E. KAUFMANN: 'Three Revolutionary Architects: Boullée, Ledoux and Lequeu', *Transactions of the American Philosophical Society*, New Series, vol. 42, 1952.

    G. LEVALLET-HAUG. Paris, 1934.

    M. RAVAL and J.-C. MOREUX. Paris, 1946.

Soane: D. STROUD. London, 1961.

    J. SUMMERSON. London, 1952.

    J. SUMMERSON. *Journal of the Royal Institute of British Architects*, vol. 58, 1951.

    A. T. BOLTON. London, 1927.

Nash: J. SUMMERSON. London, 1935.

    T. DAVIS. London, 1960.

Gilly: A. ONCKEN. Berlin, 1935.

Schinkel: A. GRISEBACH. Leipzig, 1924.

    Lebenswerk (ed. P. O. Rave). Berlin, 1939–62. So far 11 vols.

    N. PEVSNER in *Studies in Art, Architecture and Design*, I. London, 1968.

Pugin: B. FERREY. London, 1861.

    P. STANTON. London, 1971.

Butterfield: P. THOMPSON. London, 1971.

William Morris: J. W. MACKAIL. 2nd ed. London, 1922.

    P. THOMPSON. London, 1967.

    P. HENDERSON. London, 1967.

P. Webb: W. R. LETHABY. London, 1935.

Norman Shaw: SIR REGINALD BLOMFIELD. London, 1940.

    N. PEVSNER. In *Victorian Architecture* (ed. P. Ferriday), London, 1963.

Mackintosh: T. HOWARTH. London, 1952.

    N. PEVSNER in *Studies in Art, Architecture and Design*, II. London, 1968.

    R. MCLEOD. London, 1968.

Gaudí: G. COLLINS. New York, 1960.

    J. J. SWEENEY and J. L. SERT. London, 1960.

    C. MARTINELL. Barcelona, 1967.

    R. PANE. Milan, 1964.

Perret: P. COLLINS: *Concrete*. London, 1959.

    E. N. ROGERS. Milan, 1955.

Garnier: G. VERONESI. Milan, 1958.

    C. PAWLOWSKI. Paris, 1967.

Otto Wagner: H. GERETSEGGER and M. PEINTNER. Salzburg, 1964. (English: London, 1970.)

Hoffmann: L. W. ROCHOWALSKI. Vienna, 1950.

    G. VERONESI. Milan, 1956.

Loos: H. KULKA. Vienna, 1931.

    L. MÜNZ. Milan, 1956.

    L. MÜNZ and G. KÜNSTLER. London, 1966.

Gropius: G. C. ARGAN. Einaudi, 1951.

    H. M. WINGLER. *Das Bauhaus*, Bramsche, 1962 (English: London, 1970).

Frank Pick: N. PEVSNER. *Studies in Art, Architecture and Design*, II. London 1968.

F. L. Wright: H.-R. HITCHCOCK. *In the Nature of Materials*. New York, 1942.

America

D. ANGULO INíGUEZ: *Historia del arte hispano-americano*. Madrid, 1945.

M. J. BUSCHIAZZO: *Estudios de arquitectura colonial en Hispano-América*. Buenos Aires, 1944.

P. KELEMEN: *Baroque and Rococo in Latin America*. New York, 1951.

J. ARMSTRONG BAIRD Jr: *The Churches of Mexico, 1530–1810*. University of California Press, 1963.

G. BAZIN: *L'architecture religieuse baroque au Brésil*, 2 vols. Paris, 1956–9.

J. M. FITCH: *American Building*, 2 vols. New York, 1966–72.

W. ANDREWS: *Architecture in America. a photographic history*. London, 1960.

W. JORDY: *American Buildings and their Architects*. Garden City, 1972.

HUGH MORRISON: *Early American Architecture*. New York, 1952.

F. KIMBALL: *Domestic Architecture of the American Colonies and of the early Republic*. New York, 1922.

T. HAMLIN: *Greek Revival Architecture in America*. New York, 1944.

C. W. CONDIT: *American Building Art: The Nineteenth Century*. New York, 1960.

C. W. CONDIT: *The Chicago School of Architecture*. Chicago, London, 1964.

H. ALLEN BROOKS: *The Prairie School*. Toronto, 1972.

Jefferson: F. KIMBALL. Boston, 1916.

Latrobe: T. HAMLIN. New York, 1956.

Mills: H. M. P. GALLAGHER. New York, 1935.

Strickland: A. ADDISON GILCHRIST. Philadelphia, 1950; enlarged ed., New York, 1969.

Davis: R. HALE NEWTON. New York, 1942.

Richardson: H.-R. HITCHCOCK. 3rd ed., New York, 1969; paperback, 1971.

Sullivan: H. MORRISON. New York, 1935.

F. L. Wright: see above.

G. MANSON. New York, [1958].

FROM 1920 TO 1970

J. M. RICHARDS: *An Introduction to Modern Architecture,* Penguin Books, 4th ed., 1963.

J. JOEDICKE: *A History of Modern Architecture*. London and New York, 1959.

H.-R. HITCHCOCK: *Architecture: Nineteenth and Twentieth Centuries* (Pelican History of Art). 2nd ed. London, 1963.

L. BENEVOLO: *Storia dell'Architettura Moderna*. Bari, 1960. (English: London, 1971.)

B. ZEVI: *Storia dell'Architettura Moderna*. Turin, 1950; 3rd ed., 1955.

G. E. KIDDER SMITH: *The New Architecture of Europe*. Penguin Books, 1962.

Brazil

P. L. GOODWIN and G. E. KIDDER SMITH. New York, 1943.

H. E. MINDLIN: *Modern Architecture in Brazil*. London, 1956.

Great Britain

J. SUMMERSON: *Ten Years of British Architecture*. London, 1956.

T. DANNATT: *Modern Architecture in Britain*. London, 1959.

G.L.C. Roehampton Estate: N. PEVSNER, *The Architectural Review*, vol. 126, 1959.

469

Sweden

G. E. KIDDER SMITH: *Sweden builds.* 1950; 2nd ed., London, 1957.

United States

E. B. MOCK: *Built in US.* New York, 1944.

H. R. HITCHCOCK and A. DREXLER: *Built in US.* New York, 1952.

IAN McCALLUM: *Architecture USA.* London, 1959.

Monographs on Architects

Aalto: F. GUTHEIM. London, 1960.

H. GINSBERGER (ed.) London, 1963.

Asplund: G. HOLMDAHL, S. I. LIND, and K. ODEN. Stockholm, 1950.

B. ZEVI. Milan, 1948.

Candela: C. FABER. London, 1963.

Gropius: see above.

Le Corbusier: L'Oeuvre complète, vols. 1–8. Zürich, 1930–61.

P. BLAKE, Penguin Books, 1963.

Mies van der Rohe: P. JOHNSON. New York, 1947; 2nd ed., 1953.

A. DREXLER. New York, 1960.

Nervi: E. N. ROGERS. London, 1957.

G. C. ARGAN. Milan, 1955.

A. L. HUXTABLE. New York, 1960.

Skidmore, Owings and Merrill: H.-R. HITCHCOCK and E. DAUZ. London, 1963.

Sources of Illustrations

Aerofilms and Aero Pictorial Ltd, London 241. Alinari, Florence 7, 15, 16, 59, 115, 123, 152, 154, 155, 166, 172, 177, 184. Alterocca, Terni 167. American Embassy, Bad Godesberg 269, 284, 289. Anderson, Rome 126, 136, 137, 144, 146, 148, 149, 173, 178. Andrews, Wayne 292. *Architectural Review*, London 290. Archives Photographiques, Paris 62, 84, 91, 208, 209, 261. Aufsberg, Lala, Sonthofen 185, 186. Baerend, Hans, Munich 160. Baldwin Smith, E., *The Dome* 13. Batsford, Messrs B. T., London 104, 105, 116, 199. Bertotti Scamozzi, *Le fabbriche e i disegni di Palladio e le terme* (redrawn by Sheila Gibson) 157. Biblioteca Nazionale, Florence 130. Bibliothèque Nationale, Paris 143. Blauel-Bavaria, Munich 151. Brogi, Florence 124, 156. *Builder, The* (1892) 100. Busch, Harald, Frankfurt on Main 24. Chicago Architectural Photographing Co. 294, 295. Combier, Macon 57. *Country Life*, London 242, 243, 245. Crossley, F. H. (Courtauld Institute of Art, London) 93, 98, (National Buildings Record) 101. Dehio and von Bezold, *Die kirchliche Baukunst des Abendlandes* 4, 48, 72, 88. Deutsche Fotothek, Dresden 192. Esparcieux, Claude, Fontainebleau 206. Foto Marburg, 79, 114, 219, 225, 246, 247, 262, 267. Gabinetto Fotografico Nazionale, Rome 133, 135, 150. Gemeentelijke Woningdienst, Amsterdam 276. Grimm, Kurt, Feucht bei Nürnberg 103. Guarini, *Architettura civile* (redrawn by Sheila Gibson) 183. Gudiol, Barcelona 31. Gundermann, Leo, Würzburg 194, 201. Haverbeck, Anneliese, Hanover 60. Hervé, Lucien, Paris 277, 288. Hewicker, Friedrich, Kaltenkirchen 1. Hildebrandt, Lily, Munich 274. Hitchcock, H.-R. (courtesy of) 250. Johnson, Philip, *Mies van der Rohe* 280. Jonals Co., Copenhagen 275. Judges Ltd, Hastings 117. Kersting, A. F., London 33, 41, 86, 89, 94, 99, 109, 111, 112, 215, 223, 236, 239, 240, 249, 255, 259. Kidder Smith, G. E., New York 282. Kusch, Eugen, Nürnberg 291. Mas, Barcelona 32, 106, 120, 180, 181, 182. Matt, Leonard von, Buochs 174. Medieval Academy of America 49. National Buildings Record, London 38, 95, 107, 108, 118, 214, 227, 260, 264. Papini, R., *Francesco di Giorgio, architetto* 200. Photo Service d'Architecture de l'Œuvre

Notre Dame, Strasbourg 121. Piranesi, G. B., *Antichità romane* (Rome, 1756) 5. Popper, Paul, London 286. Powell, Josephine, Rome 18. Prestel Verlag, Munich 263. Ravaisson-Mollien, *Les manuscrits de Leonardo da Vinci* (photographer W. J. Toomey, Chobham) 143. Renger-Patzsch, A., Wamel-Dorf über Soest i. W. 195. Retzlaff, Hans, Tann 26. Richter, E., Rome 10. Rietdorf, Alfred, *Gilly* (Berlin, 1940) 256. Rijksdienst v. d. Monumentenzorg, The Hague 222. Roubier, Jean, Paris 45, 46, 47, 50, 51, 52, 53, 54, 56, 68, 70, 73, 80, 81, 210. Royal Commission on Historical Monuments (England), Crown Copyright 113, 203, 216. Sandrart, Joachim von, *Teutsche Akademie* (Nürnberg, 1768) 162. Sartoris, Alberto, *Gli elementi dell'architettura funzionale* (Milan, 1941) 279. Schaefer & Son, J. F., Baltimore 293. Schmidt-Glassner, Helga, Stuttgart 78, 122, 188, 190, 196, 204, 217. Scott, Walter, Bradford 39. Smith, Edwin, London 37, 90, 92, 229, 235, 237, 257. Staatliche Graphische Sammlung, Munich 85. Stoedtner–Heinz Klemm, Düsseldorf 272, 278, 281. Trustees of Sir John Soane's Museum, London 254. Vasari, Rome 285. Weigert, *Geschichte der europ. Kunst* 55. Winstone, Reece, Bristol 238. Wolgensinger, Michael, Zürich 268. Zentralinstitut für Kunstgeschichte, Munich 164, 273.

The publishers would also like to make grateful acknowledgement to Prestel Verlag, Munich, for their friendly and helpful co-operation in matters connected with illustration.

Some Technical Terms Explained

Only unfamiliar architectural terms are included, and only those which have not already been explained in the places where they first occurred in the text. Bracketed references refer to drawings illustrating technical terms.

Ambulatory: Aisle round an apse or a circular building.

Arcade: Group of arches on columns or pillars.

Architrave: Bottom member of an entablature (c3).

Attic: Low storey above main cornice.

Basilica: Church with aisles and a nave higher than the aisles.

Bay: Vertical unit of a wall or façade; also compartments into which a nave is divided.

Caryatid: Sculptured figure used as a support.

Clerestory: Upper part of church nave with windows above the roofs of the aisles.

Cornice: Projecting top portion of an entablature or any projecting top course of a building (a3 and c4).

Cross: Cf. Greek cross.

Cross Rib: (e1).

Drum: Circular or polygonal structure on which a dome is raised (b2).

Entablature: The horizontal top part of an order of classical architecture. It is supported by columns and consists of architrave, frieze, and cornice (c5).

Greek Cross: Cross with all four arms of equal length.

Jamb: Vertical part of the masonry of a door or window (d1).

Lantern: Small open or glazed structure crowning a dome or a roof (b1).

Lierne: A decorative rib in a Gothic vault which does not spring from the wall and does not touch the central boss (e5).

Metope: Panel filling the space between triglyphs (c1). *See* Triglyph.

Mullion: Vertical division of a window.

Narthex: Porch in front of the nave and aisles of a medieval church.

Ogee Arch: Cf. p. 475 (d).

Pediment: Triangular or segmental upright front end of a roof of moderate pitch (a1).

Plinth: Projecting base of a building or a column.

Quoins: Corner stones at the angle of a building (A2).

Ridge Rib: (E2).

Rustication: Wall treatment with large freestone blocks, either smooth with recessed joints, or with a rough, rock-like surface and recessed joints.

Solar: Chamber on an upper floor.

Spandrel: Space between the curve of an arch; the vertical drawn from its springing and the horizontal drawn from its apex (c6).

String course: Projecting horizontal band along the wall of a building (A4).

Tierceron: Rib inserted in a Gothic vault between the transverse and diagonal ribs (E4).

Transom: Horizontal division of a window.

Transverse Arch: (E3).

Triforium: Wall passage between the arcade of a church nave and the clerestory, or between the gallery and the clerestory. It opens in arcades towards the nave. The arcading can also be blind, with no wall passage behind. Some writers call the gallery a triforium.

Triglyph: Vertical grooved member of the Doric frieze (c2).

Voussoir: A wedge-shaped block forming part of the arch of a door or window (D2).

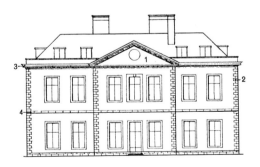

A. – Queen Anne house

1. Pediment
2. Quoins
3. Cornice
4. String course

B. – Dome

1. Lantern
2. Drum

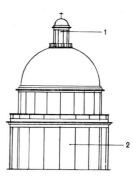

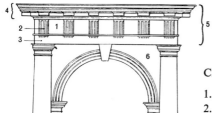

C. – Classical Details

1. Metope
2. Triglyph
3. Architrave
4. Cornice
5. Entablature
6. Spandrel

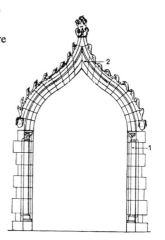

D. – Ogee arch

1. Jamb
2. Voussoirs

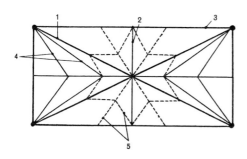

E. – Gothic vault

1. Diagonal rib
2. Ridge rib
3. Transverse arch
4. Tiercerons
5. Liernes

Index

Numbers in italics refer to illustrations

Héré, Emmanuel, n. 39
Herland, Hugh, 163
Herle, William, 139
Herrera, Francisco de, 283
Hexham, priory church, 42–3, n. 8
Hildesheim, Cathedral, 69, n. 10
  St Michael, 58–9, 60, 68–9, n. 11;
  36, 42, 44
Hilversum, Town Hall, 409
Hitler, Adolf, 410
Hittorff, J.-I., 384
Hoeger, Fritz, 405
Hoffmann, Josef, 399, 446
Holabird & Roche, 397
Holden, Charles, 418; *283*
Holford, Sir William, n. 50
Holkham Hall, 288, 344
Holl, Elias, 215, 311
Holland, Henry, 441, 446
Hollar, Wenzel, *85*
Honselaardyck, n. 36
Hontañon, Juan Gil de, *104*
Hood, Raymond, 410
Horta, Victor, 394
Howe & Lescaze, 410
Hull, Holy Trinity, 163
Humbertus de Romanis, 142
Hunt, Richard M., 444
Huygens, Christian, 317, 319
Huygens, Constantin, 317

Ignatius Loyola, St, 227
Ina Casa, 420
Incas, 437, 439
Ingelheim, Charlemagne's palace, *23*
Iona, 40
Isidore of Miletus, 34

Jaca Cathedral, 67
Jarrow, church, 42
Jeanneret, Pierre, *277*
Jefferson, Thomas, 441, 444
Jenney, William Le Baron, 397
Jerome, St, 21

Jerusalem, church of the Holy
  Sepulchre, 25, 34
John of Gaunt, 154
John of Salisbury, 118
John Maurice of Nassau-Siegen, 317
Jones, Inigo, 215, 307–10, 312, 316,
  317, 332, 336, 344, 347; *216*
Joseph, Father, 321
Juan Bautista de Toledo, 283
Julius II, pope, 198, 204, 220, 232
Julius III, pope, 225
Jumièges, Notre Dame, 60, 70, 79,
  103; *52*
Juste, A. and G., 289
Justinian, emperor, 31, 34, 38, 83
Juvara, Filippo, 238

Kalat Seman, church, 26
Kampmann, Hack, 411
Karlsruhe, 332
  Dammerstock estate, 431
Kenilworth Castle, 154
Kent, early churches, 42
Kent, William, 344, 345, 352, 358
Kenwood, *see* London
Kew, Gardens, 359
  Palace, 312
Kilburn, *see* London: St Augustine
Kilian, St, 40
King's Lynn, St Nicholas, 162–3; *116*
Klenze, Wilhelm von, 385
Klerk, Michel de, 407; *276*
Klint, P. V. J., 407; *275*
Klosterneuburg, monastery, 272
Koja Kalessi, church, 34
Korb, Hermann, 329
Kramer, Piet, 407
Kvarnholm, flour-mill, 418

Laach, *see* Maria Laach
La Brède, Montesquieu's garden, n.
  41
Labrouste, Henri, 389, 443
Lacalahorra, Castle, 281

Luxeuil, 40
Lyons, St Irénée, 39, n. 12

Maaskant, H. A., n. 48
McComb, 443
Macchiavelli, 183
Machuca, Pedro, 215; *151*
McKim, Mead & White, 387
Mackintosh, Charles Rennie, 394, 395-7, 445, 446
Mackmurdo, Arthur H., 394
Maderna, Carlo, 230, 239, 242, 244, 249, 283; *165, 166, 167*
Maillart, Robert, 424
Maintenon, Madame de, 334
Mainz Cathedral, 85
Maisons Lafitte, 313, 315
Majeul, abbot, 56, 57
Malatesta, Sigismondo, 189
Malines, 160
Mallet Stevens, Robert, 413
Manchester, Town Hall, 401
Mander, Karel van, n. 35
Mangin, 441
Mansart, François, 311, 313, 315, 317, 333, 336, 361, n. 34; *217*
Mansart, Jules Hardouin-, 322-4, 331, 334; *224, 225, 230*
Mantua, Cathedral, 223
    Giulio Romano's house, 213-14; *150*
    Palazzo del Tè, 214
    S. Andrea, 196-7, 201, 232; *138*
    S. Sebastiano, 196-7, 201; *139*
Manuel I, king of Portugal, 169
March, Werner, n. 46
Maria Laach Abbey, 85
Marie Antoinette, queen of France, 363, 378
Marie de' Medici, queen of France, 311
Markelius, Sven, 420, 433
Marlborough, 1st duke of, 338
Marseilles, baptistery, 39
    Cathedral, 386

church of the Major, 289
    Unité d'Habitation, 420
Martel, Charles, 39
Martellange, Étienne, 311
Martin, Sir Leslie, 433; *290*
Mateo, Maestre, 85
Matsys, Quentin, 290
Matthias Corvinus, king of Hungary, 291
Maupertuis, projected lodges for, 370
Maxentius, emperor, 24
May, Ernst, 415
May, Hugh, 337
Maya, 437
Mazarin, Cardinal, 312, 320, 321
Mazzoni, Guido, 289, 290
Medici family, 156, 174, 175, 185, 220
Medici, Cosimo, 174, 176
Medici, Lorenzo, the Magnificent, 174, 183, 184, 220
Medici, Marie de', queen of France, 311
Meissonier, Juste-Aurèle, 286, 334
Meledo, Villa Trissino, 219; *153*
Melk, monastery, 272-4; *190*
Menai Bridge, n. 44
Mendelsohn, Erich, 405-7, 410, 413; *273*
Mendoza family, 289
Métézeau, Clément, 311
Metz, St Peter, 39
Mexico, 258, 437
    friars' churches, 436
Mexico City, church of the Miraculous Virgin, 424
    Cosmic Ray Institution, 424
    Market Hall, 424-5
Mey, J. M. van der, 407
Meyer, Adolf, *271, 272*
Michelangelo Buonarroti, 176, 188, 198, 209, 220-3, 226-32, 238, 242, 246, 253, 263, 292, 298, 301, 309, 322, 324, 340, 342; *148, 155, 159, 160, 167*